MENTAL DISORDER AND CRIME

MENTAL DISORDER AND CRIME

Sheilagh Hodgins
editor

SAGE Publications
International Educational and Professional Publisher
Newbury Park   London   New Delhi

For information address:

SAGE Publications, Inc.
2455 Teller Road
Newbury Park, California 91320

SAGE Publications Ltd.
6 Bonhill Street
London EC2A 4PU
United Kingdom

SAGE Publications India Pvt. Ltd.
M-32 Market
Greater Kailash I
New Delhi 110 048 India

Printed in the United States of America

Library of Congress Cataloging-in-Publication Data

Main entry under title:

Mental disorder and crime / edited by Sheilagh Hodgins.
      p.   cm.
   Includes bibliographical references and index.
   ISBN 0-8039-5022-5.—ISBN 0-8039-5023-3 (pbk.)
   1. Insane, Criminal and dangerous.   2. Violent crimes—
Psychological aspects.   3. Violent crimes—Forecasting.
I. Hodgins, Sheilagh.
RC569.5.V55C75   1993
616.85'82—dc20   92-33063

93 94 95 96 97 10 9 8 7 6 5 4 3 2 1

Sage Production Editor: Astrid Virding

Contents

Acknowledgments

This book emerged from an Advanced Study Institute on Crime and Mental Disorder that was sponsored by the scientific affairs division of NATO. The grant allowed scholars from around the world, knowledgeable in the field of mental disorder and crime, to meet together for 10 days. During the meeting, lectures (of an hour's duration) were presented, followed by a prepared response, and then lengthy discussion among all the 50 or so participants. This format allowed active researchers in the field to interact and exchange ideas in a way that is not possible at the usual scientific meeting. We gratefully acknowledge the grant from NATO and hope this book demonstrates that it was money well spent.

Introduction:
Mental Disorder and Crime

In recent years much evidence has suggested that major mental disorder (schizophrenia, major affective disorders, and other psychotic disorders) and violence are associated. Even such an eminent scholar as John Monahan, who previously argued against such a relation, has now concluded that "there is a relationship between mental disorder and violent behavior, one that cannot be fobbed off as chance or explained away by third factors that cause them both" (Monahan, in press). People have always feared the violence of the mentally disordered. Both criminal and civil law include specific provisions for restraining the mentally disordered when they present a threat to the security of others. Until now, the scientific community was not convinced that mental disorder increased the risk of violence. Data from methodologically sound investigations of the issue were simply unavailable.

This volume presents new findings and conclusions about the violence of the mentally disordered. Reporting such data is discomforting, for it could contribute to reinforcing the stigma of mental illness and the community's rejection and fear of the mentally disordered. However, describing a problem is the necessary first step to solving it. We know that families of mentally disordered persons, while often victims of their aggressive behavior, fail to report acts of violence. Shame and guilt inhibit them from mentioning these behaviors to mental health professionals and also from taking appropriate measures to protect themselves. In some instances this lack of action has had tragic consequences. Staff of psychiatric wards also report only a fraction of the aggressive behavior of their patients. Hiding the problem, even in an effort to protect the mentally disordered persons from possible negative consequences, only perpetuates the violence. To develop violence prevention programs that are effective with these populations it is first necessary to describe the problem and to identify its causes. In this volume the leading investigators in the field provide recent descriptive and explanatory findings relevant to developing humane prevention strategies.

This book is divided into three sections. Part I reviews recent investigations on the criminality and violence of those who suffer from major mental disorders. This section provides the reader with the most up-to-date knowledge on the subject. Part II presents investigations of the determinants of antisocial, aggressive, and violent behavior. The first three chapters in this section employ a developmental framework and review findings from prospective studies that follow children through to adulthood. Four subsequent chapters examine biological factors associated with aggressive behavior. The final chapter in this section critically reviews current knowledge of alcohol and drug consumption as triggers of violent behavior. Part III presents a reassessment of knowledge about crime and mental disorder and proposals for future research programs and policies concerning violent, mentally disordered persons. The volume ends with a description of an early intervention program that has successfully reduced aggressive behavior among school boys, and thereby reduced the likelihood of the development of more violent men.

It is important for the reader to note that the term *mental disorder* is used differently by the authors. In some chapters it refers only to the major disorders, while in other chapters it includes anxiety disorders, dysthymia, and personality disorders. At the beginning of each chapter the use of the term is clarified by the author. The term *aggressive behavior* refers to responses that deliver noxious stimuli to another person. The term *violence* refers to the more extreme forms of aggressive behavior that cause significant injuries to the victim.

Part I: The Criminality of Mentally Disordered Persons

In my chapter, I present the findings on the prevalence of major mental disorder and criminality in an unselected birth cohort. I was privileged to work with Professor Carl Gunnar Janson of Sweden, who has followed a cohort of 15,117 people born in Stockholm during one 12-month period from prebirth to age 30. Although the subjects had not passed through the risk periods for criminality or mental disorder, by age 30, convictions for criminal offenses and for violent crimes were statistically more likely among those who developed a major mental disorder as adults than among those with no mental disorder or intellectual disability. These mentally disordered offenders generally began their criminal careers early in life and had many convictions. Childhood substance abuse, even more than substance abuse in adulthood, appears to be an important factor associated with crime among subjects with a major mental disorder. However, slightly more than half of the men and women with major mental disorders who were convicted of crimes had no history of substance abuse.

Christopher D. Webster, a clinical psychologist and Director of the Impulse Disorder Clinic at the Clarke Institute of Psychiatry in Toronto, has teamed up with his former colleague, Robert J. Menzies, a professor of criminology. They assess their own and other well-known attempts to identify the factors that predict violent behavior among mentally disordered persons. In so doing, these researchers provide a vivid picture of the dismal lives of mentally disordered men who shuffle from hospital to jail and back again in a large North American city. The authors' frustration is evident and it mirrors that of many clinicians in the field. Despite much goodwill, much scientific and clinical expertise, and much money, little progress has been made in improving decision-making procedures so that the violent patients are kept in custody and the nonviolent ones are allowed to live in the community. The cycling from the health system to the criminal justice system and back again continues without interruption.

Henry J. Steadman, the leading researcher in the area of crime and mental disorder for many years, writes here in collaboration with a number of other members of the MacArthur Foundation's Research Network on Mental Health and Law. Steadman and his coworkers have taken up the challenges of determining which factors predict violent behavior in mentally disordered persons and identifying the most effective strategies for managing patients who present a risk of violence. After detailed examination of current knowledge about violence and mental disorder and consultations with experts from around the world, these scientists and clinicians drew up a list of the factors to be studied. Practical, feasible measures of each factor were then developed. A study, conducted in three hospitals, involved assessing and then following patients discharged to the community. The results of this study are reported here. Across all three sites within 3 months of discharge, 26.7% of the patients reported behaving violently at least once. A higher proportion of the female (32.8%) than of the male patients (22.4%) reported behaving violently. A large-scale investigation based on these findings is now under way. The design and measures being used are described.

Pamela J. Taylor, a clinical psychiatrist, is Head of Medical Services for the Special Hospitals Authority in Great Britain. Taylor reports here on a study of violent offenders referred for psychiatric evaluation. She interviewed five groups of male inmates: violent, nonmentally disordered; violent schizophrenics; nonviolent schizophrenics; violent affective disordereds; and nonviolent affective disordereds. As a result of these in-depth interviews and reviews of subjects' files, Taylor concludes that the violent behavior of schizophrenic men is a direct consequence of their illness and thus always occurs during acute episodes. Taylor's findings are similar to those of Link, Cullen, and Andrews (1990) and suggest that individuals who develop schizophrenia do not show more aggressive behavior before the onset of their illness than other people. Further, this hypothesis presumes that the aggressive or antisocial behavior of persons suffering from schizophrenia is not a stable trait, as it is in nonmentally disordered persons. An alternative explanation of the violent behavior of men with schizophrenia emerges from investigations that have used a developmental frame of reference. Several of the other authors' work leads to the hypothesis that the aggressive behavior of schizophrenics is observable before the onset of the disorder and, as in nonmentally disordered persons, is a relatively stable behavioral trait. Currently no adequate data exist to verify either of these hypotheses. Longitudinal investigations of the behavior of children at risk for schizophrenia are needed.

Linda A. Teplin, Director of Psycho-Legal Studies at Northwestern University Medical School, and her coworkers present a study of jail inmates. The violence of the mentally disordered inmates is found to be similar in frequency and severity to that of the nondisordered inmates. These findings correspond to those presented in previous chapters showing that mentally disordered persons repeatedly commit crimes.

Robert D. Hare, world renowned for his work on psychopathy, and his collaborator, Stephen D. Hart, review 25 years of research and provide convincing evidence of the importance and usefulness of the diagnosis of psychopathy. The authors describe the development and factor structure of the Psychopathy Checklist. Not only is this diagnostic instrument reliable and psychometrically adequate, its validity is far greater than that of many other, more frequently used, diagnostic instruments. Male psychopaths, as diagnosed by this instrument, have distinctive biological characteristics. Both male and female psychopaths are responsible for a disproportionate amount of criminal violence even as compared to non-psychopathic offenders. They are very likely to have a long history of alcohol and/or drug abuse. They usually refuse to participate in criminal rehabilitation programs, and even if they do join a program, they quickly abandon it. If they do complete a program, new evidence reveals that not only do they fail to improve, they may get worse. An understanding of psychopathy is of vital importance for developing violence prevention programs directed at this specific type of individual. It may be that some people with major mental disorders also present symptoms of psychopathy or antisocial behavior. This combination is difficult to diagnose, for the moment impossible to treat effectively, and time consuming, frustrating, and unrewarding for the mental health professionals who have to manage it.

Part II: Risk Factors for Violent Behavior

The section on risk factors for violent behavior begins with three chapters by authors who use a developmental perspective. Models of the complex interactions between stable individual characteristics of the child and parenting practices are proposed. Barbara Maughan is a researcher with many years of experience conducting longitudinal research projects with children out of the Institute of Psychiatry in London. Maughan explains how and why this methodology is so valuable for our understanding of the development of both criminal behavior and mental disorder, but also points out the major pitfalls that characterize these types of investigations. Recent findings concerning the developmental factors important for determining delinquency and various types of mental disorders are clearly distilled from a huge, dispersed literature. She concludes that the patterns of childhood difficulty most likely to persist to adulthood begin early and involve a wide range of antisocial behaviors. Further, she proposes that hyperactivity, impulsivity, and inattentiveness in early childhood lead to aggressive conduct symptoms in some children. If this hypothesis is correct, deficits in social learning are among the central factors predisposing to adult criminality. In addition to adverse family circumstances and poor parenting practices, Maughan reports that both genetic factors and minor neurological damage contribute to the development of adult antisocial behavior.

Gerald R. Patterson has studied families with antisocial children for more than 30 years. He and coauthor Karen Yoerger describe recent findings demonstrating that there are two types of delinquents and two different pathways to adult criminality. The first type of delinquent, the early starter, begins his or her criminal career before age 15 and from a very early age is characterized by a distinctive interpersonal style. This type of child is highly aversive to those around him; he is generally noncompliant, he whines, yells, throws temper tantrums, threatens, and hits. These behaviors are not curbed by the parents, who fail to use punishment effectively. They also fail to use positive reinforcers to teach the child prosocial skills. By the time the child reaches school age, his or her aversive style and lack of prosocial behavior lead to rejection by teachers and peers. Consequently, a series of other problems develop, and eventually the child begins offending. The second type of delinquent, the late starter, does not have an interpersonal style that is aversive to others. Rather, it appears that a disruption of parenting pushes him or her toward deviant peers.

Lee N. Robins, a researcher in the fields of psychiatric epidemiology, and antisocial personality and conduct disorder, has combined her two areas of expertise to explore the links between childhood conduct disorder, adult mental disorder, and crime. Robins analyzes data from three sites of the Epidemiologic Catchment Area study. This investigation was designed to establish prevalence rates of mental disorders among a representative sample of the general U.S. population. Examining responses from 10,711 persons, Robins discovers that, as would be expected, childhood conduct disorder is highly significantly associated with adult antisocial symptoms (other than criminal behavior) and substance abuse, but also with psychosis, depression, and anxiety. These relations all hold for both men and women. Psychosis, depression, and anxiety are found to be associated with criminality. Further analyses reveal that these associations are mediated by substance abuse and antisocial personality. These findings confirm the relation between the major mental disorders and crime. They suggest that the mentally disordered at risk for crime are abusing alcohol and/or drugs and have a history of conduct problems in childhood.

Burr Eichelman is a forensic psychiatrist and animal researcher. He uses his extensive knowledge of violent mentally disordered patients to identify animal research that may be relevant for exploring the determinants of his patients' violent behavior. Eichelman reviews many types of research with animals that are largely unknown to clinicians and researchers in the field of crime and mental disorder. He examines the role of biological factors, such as genes, abnormal electrical and neurochemical activity in the brain, and peripheral hormones, in determining violent behavior. He suggests that an understanding of the neurochemical bases of social dominance hierarchies, social coping strategies, and stress in animals may provide potentially fruitful hypotheses for investigations with humans. Eichelman notes that this strategy of identifying the determinants of violent behavior among animals and then verifying if these models apply to human violent behavior has successfully been employed in work with the brain serotonergic and catecholaminergic transmitter systems.

Daisy Schalling has made a substantial contribution to the understanding of the biological basis of personality over the past 30 years. Here, she reviews recent work on the neurochemical correlates of personality traits. She focuses principally on the trait of impulsivity because it is so often associated with alcohol abuse, suicidal behavior, hyperactivity, and psychopathy. Impulsivity in adults is predicted by motor restlessness and attention difficulties in childhood. It has distinctive psychophysiological and neurochemical correlates. Schalling reviews new findings that have revealed that individuals who commit suicide using violent methods and those who violently attack others are characterized by low brain serotonin levels. She suggests that both the human and animal studies indicate that impulsivity mediates the relation between low brain serotonin levels and violent behavior.

Matti Virkkunen, a forensic psychiatrist, has evaluated hundreds of persons accused of violent crimes. His chapter is coauthored by Markku Linnoila, a Finnish psychiatrist who is now Director of the Laboratory of Clinical Studies at the National Institute of Alcohol Abuse and Alcoholism. These two clinicians present a detailed review of the work on the relation of brain serotonin to violent behavior. While Schalling reviews the neurochemical bases of personality traits, both clinical psychiatrists focus on one neurotransmitter system and its relation to violent behavior among men with specific mental disorders.

The role of minor brain damage, caused by perinatal complications, in determining the violent behavior of mentally disordered persons is explored in the chapter by Patricia A. Brennan, Birgitte R. Mednick, and Sarnoff A. Mednick. The authors have examined three different samples of men who have been followed prospectively from birth to adulthood. They demonstrate that pregnancy and delivery complications are associated with violent criminal offenses only in the presence of a genetic predisposition for major mental disorder. Further, they suggest that this combination of pregnancy and delivery complications and a genetic loading for a major mental disorder damage the child's brain. They hypothesize that the damage leads to the motor restlessness, impulsivity, and attention difficulties, so often the precursors to adult criminality. These startling new findings, if replicated, suggest a relatively simple, cost-effective strategy to prevent violent behavior among the mentally disordered. Good prenatal care for mothers of babies at genetic risk for mental disorder could eliminate most, if not all, of the pregnancy and delivery complications shown to be associated with violence.

Robert O. Pihl is renowned for his research on the effect of alcohol on aggressive behavior. With a postdoctoral student, Jordan B. Peterson, he synthesizes a wealth of animal research and laboratory studies of humans in an attempt to explain why violent crime is so often committed by individuals who are intoxicated by alcohol and/or drugs. While noting the overwhelming evidence showing that alcohol causes aggressive behavior, these authors carefully present evidence demonstrating how other factors modify this effect via neurochemical and neurological circuits. A model of these complex interactions of the pharmacological, cognitive, and social factors in determining aggressive behavior is proposed. The authors conclude by reminding readers that this multifactorial relationship between alcohol and violence is even more difficult to unravel when it occurs in the presence of a major mental disorder or personality disorder.

Part III: Conclusions

John Monahan has a worldwide reputation for his scholarly work on the prediction of violence. Here, Monahan reassesses what is known about mental disorder and violence and concludes that "mental disorder may be a robust and significant risk factor for the occurrence of violence, as an increasing number of clinical researchers in recent years have averred." Monahan notes that his former position that there was no relation between mental disorder and violence was "premature" and "may well be wrong." This about-face results from a critical, thorough assessment of the relevant scientific literature, which Monahan documents and interprets for the reader.

Saleem A. Shah reviews the wide range of research findings presented in the volume, and focuses on their practical application to policies and programs for mentally disordered offenders. Drawing extensively on his knowledge of both criminal and civil law and practices of mental health professionals, Shah identifies the findings most relevant to improving programs and policies concerning mentally disordered offenders. He describes how they could be implemented and applied. Shah also has extensive knowledge of the research community, as a result of his years as director of the program on violence and antisocial behavior at the National Institute of Mental Health. He is thus well placed to make recommendations on research priorities in this area.

Dan Olweus in 1979 published a literature review of great importance. Pulling together a mass of data, he demonstrated that human aggressive behavior is stable over the life span. In fact, it is probably the most stable human trait we know about. Several longitudinal investigations conducted in a number of different countries have shown that aggressive behavior in childhood is highly predictive of repeated adult offending. These findings convinced Olweus of the importance and necessity of early intervention programs to prevent crime. He designed, managed, and evaluated a school-based program for aggressive children. Here he presents results documenting the success of this program, which is now being used in a number of different countries. Olweus's work clearly shows that science can contribute in significant ways to solving social problems. While findings presented in other chapters may appear discouraging as they document the increased risk of violence associated with mental disorder, and the difficulty of identifying the determinants of this violence, Olweus provides hope. His work is a model of how to use research findings to develop effective, yet feasible, prevention programs.

This volume presents the work of leading scholars from around the world on the violent and criminal behaviors of persons who suffer from major mental disorders. These antisocial behaviors are described and examined. Investigations of the complex chain of factors that determine these behaviors are presented. While these data could be used to further stigmatize the mentally disordered, they can also be used to treat and manage more adequately persons who suffer from these debilitating disorders and to design humane, effective violence prevention programs. Only by openly discussing this social problem and investigating its causes can a solution be found.

—Sheilagh Hodgins

References

Link, B., Cullen, F., & Andrews, H. (1990). *Violent and illegal behavior of current and former mental patients compared to community controls.* Paper presented at the meeting of the Society for the Study of Social Problems, San Francisco.

Monahan, J. (in press). "A terror to their neighbors": Mental disorder and violence in historical and cultural context. *Bulletin of the American Academy of Psychiatry and the Law.*

I

The Criminality
of Mentally Disordered Persons

1

The Criminality of
Mentally Disordered Persons

SHEILAGH HODGINS

The association between mental disorder and crime has long been debated. Literature and art have historically reflected the view that the mentally disordered are violent. Both civil and criminal law around the world recognize that some mentally disordered persons must be restrained because they pose threats to themselves and/or to others. Yet it is only in recent years that methodologically sound data have been collected in order to examine this association.

This chapter will first briefly and critically review the scientific literature on crime and mental disorder. An effort is made to synthesize results of investigations in this area, noting the methodological weaknesses that limit the knowledge base. A study is presented that overcomes some of these methodological weaknesses and documents the relations between crime and mental disorders in an unselected birth cohort followed to age 30. Finally, conclusions are drawn about the association between major mental disorder and crime.

Before briefly reviewing current knowledge, two conceptual issues require clarification. The first is the concept of mental disorder per se. The various mental disorders differ considerably in symptomatology, course, response to treatment, and etiology. It is reasonable to presume, unless it is proven otherwise, that the associations with criminality also differ. In fact, if, as has been suggested (Hodgins, 1988), some disorders lessen the risk of criminal behavior while others increase it, grouping together various disorders could mask any associations that do exist. Therefore, one objective of research may be to identify the associations, or lack of associations, between the various mental disorders and crime. A very different set of

3

questions related to mental health and criminal justice policies and programs may be addressed by examining the criminality of persons who have
received different kinds of services, for example, psychiatric care, drug
treatment, and social welfare. In these investigations, the samples studied
are defined by the service received, not by the presence of a specific
disorder. Generally, conclusions from these policy-oriented investigations
cannot be used to address the issue of the associations between the various
psychopathologies and crime.

The second conceptual issue relates to the major mental disorders—
schizophrenia, major depression, and bipolar disorder. Researchers from
the psychopathology tradition view individuals who develop these disorders as being different, from a very early age, from people who do not
develop these disorders. Therefore, they would ask if these people (for
example, those who develop schizophrenia) are more often convicted of
crimes than people who do not develop schizophrenia. A second question
might be the relation between the criminal behavior and various phases of
the disorder. In the literature on crime and mental disorder a very different
understanding of the major disorders has been reflected. For example, in
Rabkin's (1979) well-known literature review on the criminal behavior of
discharged mental patients, she suggested that "the causal direction between mental illness and crime" would become evident if arrests were
classified as preceding or succeeding psychiatric hospitalization (p. 17).
Further, she suggested that less criminal activity after hospitalization than
before "would provide support for the notion of a causal association
between mental status and crime" (p. 24). Rabkin suggests, then, that if an
acute episode precedes arrest, the mental disorder caused the criminal
behavior. She thus fails to separate two questions. She confuses the issue
of the temporal relation between the acute episodes of a disorder and
conviction with the more basic question of whether or not persons with
these disorders, or persons who will eventually manifest these disorders,
are at increased risk for criminality. This conceptualization of the major
mental disorders is inconsistent with current knowledge about their etiology and development. Throughout this chapter the view that individuals
who develop major mental disorders do differ from others from an early
age will be reflected.

Psychiatric Patients Compared to Community Controls

In a carefully designed investigation, Link, Andrews, and Cullen (in press)
examined the criminality of psychiatric patients compared to subjects who
lived in the same neighborhood of New York but who had never received

any mental health treatment. Subjects were divided into four groups: (1) patients who received psychiatric treatment for the first time in the year preceding the study; (2) patients who were in treatment during the previous year and once before; (3) former patients who received no treatment in the previous year; and (4) a community sample with no history of psychiatric treatment. Among the patients, 34% had received a diagnosis of major depression, 19% schizophrenia, 10% another psychotic disorder, and 37% another mental disorder. Of the community cohorts, 6.7% had been arrested; 6.0% of the first contact patients, 12.1% of the repeat treatment patients, and 11.7% of the former patients had been arrested. The arrests of the patients were more likely to be for felonies and for violent behavior than the arrests of the subjects in the community sample. According to the authors, there was no evidence that patients were arrested for trivial matters.

Follow-Up Studies of Discharged Psychiatric Patients

A number of follow-up studies of patients discharged from psychiatric wards (Durbin, Pasewark, & Albers, 1977; Giovannoni & Gurel, 1967; Lindqvist & Allebeck, 1990; Rappeport & Lassen, 1965, 1966; Sosowsky, 1974, 1978, 1980; Steadman, Cocozza, & Melick, 1978; Zitrin, Hardesty, Burdock, & Drossman, 1976) have suggested that more of these persons, as compared to the nondisordered population of the community where they are released, commit crimes. These studies have consistently shown that discharged male patients are at greater risk for criminality than males from the general population, or than females. The differences between the rates of conviction for the ex-patients and the general population are generally found to be greater for violent than nonviolent crimes (Giovannoni & Gurel, 1967; Sosowsky, 1974, 1978; Zitrin et al., 1976). Only a few investigations presented conviction rates for different diagnostic groups (see, e.g., Rappeport & Lassen, 1966; Zitrin et al., 1976). There is a suggestion that men with substance abuse problems and those with schizophrenia are at increased risk for criminality, as well as men with both of these disorders (Cohen, 1980; Giovannoni & Gurel, 1967; Mesnikoff & Lauterbach, 1975; Rappeport & Lassen, 1966).

The validity of these results remains in doubt, however, for these studies are characterized by numerous methodological weaknesses. Follow-up periods were short, and samples of ex-patients rarely remained intact throughout. Consequently, patients who committed crimes would be more likely to be counted at the end of the follow-up period than patients who left treatment and had no contacts with the police. Data on criminal convictions were in many studies limited to one state or jurisdiction. Diagnoses were taken from hospital files and not validated in any way. As well, it is difficult to compare the results from these various studies as there is no way of knowing if the distributions of diagnoses in the samples are similar.

A recent investigation that has none of these methodological flaws was conducted by Lindqvist and Allebeck (1990). The sample included all inpatients in Stockholm county with a diagnosis of schizophrenia who were born between 1920 and 1959 and discharged in 1971. Patients were rediagnosed by an independent clinician, using DSM-III criteria, and 85% (644) met the criteria for schizophrenia. These 644 patients were followed for 14 years. Excluded from the study were 142 subjects deceased at the end of the follow-up period. The effect of excluding these subjects on the results is unknown. The relative risk of a criminal offense among schizophrenics as compared to the general Swedish population was 1.2 for the men and 2.2 for the women. However, the schizophrenics "committed four times as many violent offenses as the general population" (pp. 346-347). Fifty-five percent of the schizophrenic subjects with a criminal record also had a history of substance abuse (Lindqvist & Allebeck, 1989). These findings are consistent with a number of other studies showing that schizophrenics and their biological relatives are at increased risk for crime (for a review see Hodgins, 1992).

Studies of Psychiatric Inpatients

Results of several investigations demonstrate that many patients behave aggressively in the days preceding admission to hospital and while in hospital (Convit, Isay, Gadioma, & Volavka, 1988; Lagos, Perlmutter, & Saexinger, 1977; Lion, Snyder, & Merrill, 1981; Macmillan & Johnson, 1987; Psychiatric News, 1984 ; Skodol & Karasu, 1978; Tardiff & Sweillam, 1982). However, none of these investigations examine the aggressive behavior of persons who are not admitted or of nondisordered persons obliged to live on a psychiatric ward. These investigations of newly admitted patients do not verify the validity of the reports of aggressive behavior. Consequently, conclusions cannot be drawn about the associations between the various disorders and criminality, or even aggressive behavior. However, these investigations do provide important clues about the factors associated with aggressive and violent behavior (Kay, Wolkenfeld, & Murrill, 1988a, 1988b; Krakowski, Convit, Jaeger, Lin, & Volavka, 1989).

Studies of Persons Excused From
Criminal Responsibility Because of a Mental Disorder

Numerous investigations (Häfner & Böker, 1982; Hodgins, 1987a, 1987b; Hodgins, Webster, Paquet, & Zellerer, 1989; Hodgins, Webster, & Paquet, 1990, 1991; Pasewark, Bieber, Bosten, Kiser, & Steadman, 1982; Rogers & Bloom, 1982; Soothill, Way, & Gibbens, 1980) from around the world have described subjects excused from criminal responsibility because of a mental disorder. While these investigations have great importance for jurists and policymakers, and they do provide hypotheses about correlates of crime within in each diagnostic group, they do not address the associations between the various mental disorders and crime.

Studies of the Mental Health of Offenders

Recent investigations of representative samples of U.S. prison inmates (Collins & Schlenger, 1983; Daniel, Robins, Reid, & Wilfley, 1988; Hyde & Seiter, 1987; Neighbors et al., 1987) and Canadian penitentiary[1] inmates (Hodgins & Côté, 1990; Motvik & Porporino, 1991) have shown that the prevalence of major mental disorders (schizophrenia, major depression, bipolar disorder) within these populations exceeds that in the general population. Two other studies demonstrate that large numbers of the male inmates with major disorders are also substance abusers (Abram, 1990; Côté & Hodgins, 1990). While it has long been hypothesized that the prevalence of the major disorders is higher among convicted offenders than in the general population, until these five studies no methodologically sound investigation had tested this hypothesis (for reviews see Wormith & Borzecki, 1985; Monahan & Steadman, 1983).

These investigations have corrected the weaknesses that characterized the previous studies. All employed the same diagnostic criteria (DSM-III; American Psychiatric Association, 1980), thus making the results comparable. All used standardized, reliable, and valid instruments to measure mental disorder. These same instruments have been used to examine the prevalence of mental disorders in the general population (see, e.g., Robins et al., 1984). Consequently, comparisons between the prevalence of disorders in the general population and inmate populations can be made with some confidence. Finally, these recent studies, unlike the earlier ones, examined random samples of inmates.

While these recent investigations have many strengths, the conditions under which they were conducted lead to questions about the results. There are important differences in the published results of lifetime prevalence rates of major mental disorders found among incarcerated offenders. These may reflect real differences in the criminality of mentally disordered persons or in the way they are treated by the criminal justice systems in various jurisdictions. However, the differences in the prevalence rates may be due to the conditions under which the studies were conducted. These conditions need to be closely evaluated in order to make a judgment about the validity of the results. Inmates may fail to report symptoms of a mental disorder or pretend to have (or to have had) symptoms in an attempt to influence decisions regarding their legal status or their status within the correctional facility. In the studies of jail populations it is important to know whether or not subjects were intoxicated at the time of the assessment interview.

A second problem is that the samples of inmates assessed in the studies reviewed here were probably biased in that they did not include subjects with paranoid symptomatology. It is reasonable to hypothesize that paranoia may be associated with certain types of criminality, and therefore may be more prevalent within a correctional facility than in the general population. Excluding subjects with paranoid symptomatology would lead to an underestimation of the association between crime and mental disorder. This problem is not particular to incarcerated offenders, but it could be more exaggerated in this population.

A third problem with these investigations (and others) is the assessment of the history of alcohol and drug abuse. While nondisordered persons appear to be able to document their histories of consumption with great detail (see, e.g., McLellan, Luborsky, Woody, & O'Brien, 1980), persons with thought disorders and memory distortions, particularly schizophrenics, have great difficulty with this task. This problem is exacerbated if the subject is not appropriately medicated at the time of the interview, as is the case with many mentally disordered inmates (see, e.g., Drake et al., 1990; Hodgins & Côté, 1990).

Investigations of the Mental Health of Homicide Offenders

An exhaustive critical review of investigations of homicide offenders (Côté, 1990) noted the paucity of valid data on the mental health of these offenders. Most of these investigations were conducted in common law countries and involved simply a compilation of the assessments conducted at the request of the court. These samples of subjects are biased and represent only a small proportion of homicide offenders.

In Scandinavia, all persons accused of homicide are evaluated by at least one psychiatrist and these assessments are reviewed by panels composed of a number of other psychiatrists. Gottlieb, Gabrielsen, and Kramp (1987) studied all homicide offenders in Copenhagen over a 25-year period. They found that 20% of the men and 44% of the women were diagnosed psychotic. Their results indicate that when psychosis is present, the risk of homicide for men increases by a factor of 6 and for women by a factor of 16. Among the psychotics, 13% of the women and 41% of the men were found to be substance abusers. At the time of the homicide, 89% of the psychotic men and 21% of the psychotic women were intoxicated.

Lindqvist (1986) studied all persons who committed a homicide in Northern Sweden between 1970 and 1981. Thirty-four of 64 (53%) were found to suffer from a major mental disorder. Ten other cases were not included in the study because the perpetrator was not prosecuted. Inclusion of these cases may have increased the proportion of homicide offenders who suffered from a major mental disorder. Among those with a major mental disorder, 38% were also substance abusers, of whom 85% were intoxicated at the time of the homicide. Among those with a major disorder who were not substance abusers, 33% were intoxicated when they killed.

Côté and Hodgins (1992) have examined a representative sample of 495 male penitentiary inmates in Canada, using the Diagnostic Interview Schedule (Robins, Helzer, Croughan, & Ratcliff, 1981). Significantly more (35%) of those who had been convicted of at least one homicide received a lifetime diagnosis for a major mental disorder as compared to those (21%) who had never been convicted of a homicide [χ^2 (1, $N = 460$) = 6.19, $p = .01$]. Among the mentally disordered homicide offenders, 83% had a history of alcohol abuse/dependence and 64% of drug abuse/dependence.

Birth Cohort Studies

In order to examine the criminality of persons with various mental disorders, as compared to those with no disorders, the research design with the least weaknesses is that of a longitudinal prospective study of an unselected birth cohort. This design limits any sampling bias, particularly if the cohort remains intact throughout the study. The use of central registers ensures that all convictions are compiled. Two such studies have now been carried out. Both however, are limited by the use of hospitalization as an indicator of mental disorder.

The Danish Metropolitan Project

Ortmann (1981) examined the criminal records of an entire birth cohort composed of 11,540 men born in Copenhagen in 1953 and still alive in

Denmark in 1975. Data on convictions were collected from the central police register in 1976 when the subjects were 23. Data on admissions to psychiatric wards were collected from the central Danish psychiatric register in 1978 when the subjects were 25. While 34.8% of all the men with no disorder had been convicted of at least one offense, 43.5% of those admitted with a major disorder, 83.2% of those admitted with abuse and/or dependence, and 50.9% of those with other diagnoses had been convicted of an offense. In fact, significantly more of those with psychiatric admissions, as compared to the others, had been convicted for every category of offense. While there were not many subjects within each diagnostic group, Ortmann's results suggested that rates of convictions varied considerably by diagnosis.

The Swedish Metropolitan Project

The Swedish Metropolitan Project examined all 15,117 persons born in Stockholm in 1953 and residing there in 1963. In 1983, criminal records were collected from the National Police Register and mental health records were collected from the Stockholm county register. I have used these data to examine the criminality of subjects with various mental disorders.[2] Only subjects living in Sweden at the end of the follow-up period were included in the analyses. Another 203 subjects placed in institutions or special classes for the intellectually disabled were excluded from these analyses.

Subjects who had been admitted to a psychiatric ward were divided into three groups based on the most serious discharge diagnosis: major mental disorder (psychoses, schizophrenia, affective psychoses, paranoid states); alcohol and/or drug abuse and/or dependence; and all other mental disorders. Among the 7,362 men, 1.1% (82) were classified as having a major mental disorder, 2.1% (156) as being alcohol and/or drug abusive or dependent, and 0.9% (64) as suffering from other mental disorders. Of the 7,039 women, 1.1% (79) were classified as having a major mental disorder, 1.4% (98) alcohol and/or drug abuse or dependence, and 1.8% (124) another mental disorder. Studies of the schizophrenia diagnoses in this register (Kristjansson, Allebeck, & Wistedt, 1987), and in other Swedish registers (Wetteberg & Farmer, 1990), have suggested that these diagnoses are valid and closely resemble the DSM-III diagnosis.

The Criminality of the Mentally Disordered. Among the men with no disorder or disability, 29.4% were registered for a crime. In comparison, 34.4% of those with other mental disorders [χ^2 (1, $N = 7,011$) = 0.74, $p = .390$], 47.6% of those with a major mental disorder [χ^2 (1, $N = 7,020$) =

TABLE 1.1 Percentage Subjects in Each Group First Registered at Different Ages (Men)

	No Mental Disorder	*Major Mental Disorders*	*Other Mental Disorders*	*Substance Abuse*
Less than 15 years	9.5%	12.2%[a]	9.4%[e]	36.4%[i]
15 to 17 years	8.4%	18.3%[b]	9.4%[f]	33.8%[j]
18 to 20 years	6.6%	7.3%[c]	12.5%[g]	12.3%[k]
21 to 30 years	4.9%	9.8%[d]	3.1%[h]	7.1%[l]

NOTES: a. NOMD × MMD χ^2 (1, N = 7,029) = 0.71
b. NOMD × MMD χ^2 (1, N = 7,029) = 10.12*
c. NOMD × MMD χ^2 (1, N = 7,029) = 0.06
d. NOMD × MMD χ^2 (1, N = 7,029) = 3.97
e. NOMD × OMD χ^2 (1, N = 7,011) = 0.00
f. NOMD × OMD χ^2 (1, N = 7,011) = 0.07
g. NOMD × OMD χ^2 (1, N = 7,011) = 3.49
h. NOMD × OMD χ^2 (1, N = 7,011) = 0.45
i. NOMD × SA χ^2 (1, N = 7,101) = 120.75*
j. NOMD × SA χ^2 (1, N = 7,101) = 115.44*
k. NOMD × SA χ^2 (1, N = 7,101) = 7.77*
l. NOMD × SA χ^2 (1, N = 7,101) = 1.55
*p = .05 corrected for Type I error by the Bonferonni formula = .006

12.74, p = .000], and 89.7% of those with a diagnosis of substance abuse/dependence [χ^2 (1, N = 7,103) = 260.34, p = .000] were registered for at least one crime. The pattern is similar among the women. While 5% with no disorder were registered for at least one crime, 9.7% of those with other mental disorders [χ^2 (1, N = 6,783) = 5.57, p = .020], 17.7% of those with a major mental disorder [χ^2 (1, N = 6,738) = 26.00, p = .000], and 64.3% of those with diagnoses of substance abuse/dependence [χ^2 (1, N = 6,757) = 617.03, p = .000] were registered for at least one crime.

As can be observed in Table 1.1, while more than half of the men with major disorders were first registered for a crime before the age of 18, another 10% of them were first registered after the age of 21. This is double the percentage of men with no disorder who were first registered after age 21. It suggests that there are two groups of offenders with major mental disorders; one group begins offending early before the symptoms of the disorder would be present, while the second begins offending only later when the disorder is likely to be evident. This hypothesis applies equally well to the women with major mental disorders, as can be observed in Table 1.2. The men with diagnoses of substance abuse/dependence and those with other mental disorders resemble the nondisordered men in that the proportions who begin offending diminish with age.

Among the male offenders with no disorders, the mean number of convictions was 7.3 (SD = 19.6); among the offenders with other mental

TABLE 1.2 Percentage Subjects in Each Group First Registered at Different Ages (Women)

	No Mental Disorder	Major Mental Disorders	Other Mental Disorders	Substance Abuse
Less than 15 years	1.5%	3.8%[a]	2.4%[e]	8.7%[i]
15 to 17 years	1.2%	3.8%[b]	1.6%[f]	17.4%[j]
18 to 20 years	1.0%	3.8%[c]	1.6%[g]	19.6%[k]
21 to 30 years	1.2%	6.3%[d]	4.0%[h]	19.6%[l]

NOTES: a. NOMD × MMD χ^2 (1, N = 6,738) = 2.80
b. NOMD × MMD χ^2 (1, N = 6,738) = 4.22
c. NOMD × MMD χ^2 (1, N = 6,738) = 5.63
d. NOMD × MMD χ^2 (1, N = 6,738) = 15.65*
e. NOMD × OMD χ^2 (1, N = 6,783) = 0.71
f. NOMD × OMD χ^2 (1, N = 6,783) = 0.16
g. NOMD × OMD χ^2 (1, N = 6,783) = 0.39
h. NOMD × OMD χ^2 (1, N = 6,783) = 7.39
i. NOMD × SA χ^2 (1, N = 6,751) = 30.23*
j. NOMD × SA χ^2 (1, N = 6,751) = 167.65*
k. NOMD × SA χ^2 (1, N = 6,751) = 244.92*
l. NOMD × SA χ^2 (1, N = 6,751) = 244.92*
*p = 0.05; corrected for Type I error by the Bonferonni formula = .006

disorders, it was 12.0 (SD = 16.4) [t(2,066) = 1.13, p = .261]; among offenders with a major mental disorder, it was 13.2 (SD = 16.4) [t(2,083) = 1.87, p = .062]; and among substance abusers, it was 29.5 (SD = 39.3) [t(143.78) = 6.64, p = .000]. Similarly, among the female offenders, those with no disorder and no disability had a mean number of convictions of 3.3 (SD = 7.0); those with other mental disorders, 3.8 (SD = 3.6) [t(14.09) = 0.41, p = .691]; those with a major disorder, 3.8 (SD = 4.8) [t(344) = 0.26, p = .795]; and those with substance abuse, 10.8 (SD = 19.3) [t(65.11) = 3.06, p = .003]. While the within-group variances are large, it appears that male and female offenders with a major disorder commit as many, or more, offenses than nondisordered offenders.

The category "violent crimes" includes all offenses involving physical violence or threat thereof (e.g., assault, rape, robbery, unlawful threat, molestation) (Wikström, 1989). Less than 6% of the men with no disorder were registered for a violent offense. In contrast, 6.3% of those with other disorders [χ^2 (1, N = 7,011) = 0.042, p = .838], 14.6% of those with a major mental disorder [χ^2 (1, N = 7,029) = 12.03, p = .001], and 49.4% of those with a diagnosis of substance abuse/dependence [χ^2 (1, N = 7,103) = 471.58, p = .000] were registered for a violent offense. Less than 0.5% of the nondisordered women were registered for a violent offense by age 30. However, 1.6% of those with other mental disorders [χ^2 (1, N = 7,039) = 0.66, p = .418] and 6.3% of the women with major mental disorders [χ^2

TABLE 1.3 Risk of Crime and Violence by Men With Major Mental Disorders

	Odds Ratios for Crime	*95% Confidence Bounds*	*Odds Ratios for Violent Crime*	*95% Confidence Bounds*
Major mental disorder (*n* = 82)	2.56	(1.66-3.97)	4.16	(2.23-7.78)
Major mental disorder, no substance abuse in childhood or adulthood (*n* = 47)	1.33	(0.72-2.45)	1.66	(0.51-5.37)
Major mental disorder plus childhood substance abuse (*n* = 18)	14.13	(4.09-48.88)	15.45	(5.94-40.20)
Major mental disorder plus adult substance abuse (*n* = 27)	6.71	(2.93-15.36)	8.50	(3.56-20.28)
Major mental disorder plus substance abuse in childhood and/or adulthood	6.17	(3.01-12.62)	8.40	(3.90-18.13)

(1, N = 6,738) = 50.51, p = .000] were registered for violence, as well as 24.5% of those with a diagnosis of substance abuse/dependence [χ^2 (1, N = 7,039) = 603.29, p = .000].

Summary. Among both men and women, the proportions of subjects with at least one criminal conviction by age 30 vary significantly by adult mental status. The subjects with a major mental disorder are at increased risk for crime as compared to subjects with no disorders. There is no increased risk of criminality among the men with other mental disorders, whereas with the women there is. While criminality among the men with no disorder decreases with age, this is not the case for those with major mental disorders. Significant numbers of these subjects begin their criminal careers at all ages. The offenders with major mental disorders commit multiple offenses of all types. Among both men and women, more of those with a major mental disorder, as compared to those with no disorder, commit violent offenses.

Correlates of Crime. The relationships of substance abuse in both childhood and adulthood to criminality were examined within each group. The child welfare committee records were used to index childhood substance abuse.

As can be seen in Table 1.3, substance abuse in childhood increases the risk of crime and violent crime among the men with major mental disorders

TABLE 1.4 Crime and Violence by Women With Major Mental Disorders

	Crime	Violent Crime
Major mental disorder	14/79	5/79
Major mental disorder, no substance abuse in childhood or adulthood	6/66	2/66
Major mental disorder plus childhood substance abuse	4/7	1/7
Major mental disorder plus adult substance abuse	6/8	3/8
Major mental disorder plus substance plus substance abuse in adulthood or childhood	8/13	3/13

more than substance abuse/dependence in adulthood. However, it is important to note that not all of the offenders with major mental disorders were substance abusers. Of those men with major disorders who offended before the age of 18, only 48.0% were identified as abusing alcohol and/or drugs as children, and 56.0% as adults. Of those who began offending after age 18, 21.4% were identified as abusers before the age of 18 and 35.7% after.

As there are even fewer female than male subjects with these various combinations of disorders, no statistics were calculated for the women. The raw data are presented in Table 1.4. Six of the eight women with adult diagnoses of major mental disorders and substance abuse/dependence were registered for a crime, and three of eight for violence. In contrast, only 8 of the 71 disordered women without substance abuse were registered for a crime and 2 of them for violence. These results correspond closely to those from follow-up studies of discharged patients and of homicide offenders in showing that substance abuse in adulthood is not always associated with criminality among offenders with major mental disorders. In fact, it may be that substance abuse is less important among mentally disordered offenders than among nondisordered criminals, as Lindqvist has suggested (1986). However, the accuracy of the history of substance abuse among subjects with major mental disorders is, as was noted previously, problematic.

Strengths and Weaknesses of the Present Investigation

These results are surprising given that the subjects were young when convictions were verified. Both investigations of persons responsible for violent crimes and judged mentally abnormal (Häfner & Böker, 1982; Hodgins, Webster, & Paquet, 1990, 1991; Hodgins, Webster, Paquet, & Zellerer, 1989; Walker & McCabe, 1973) and of inmates who suffer from major mental disorders (Hodgins & Côté, 1990) suggest that the mentally disordered commit crimes later in life than the non-mentally disordered. As well as not having passed through the risk period for criminal behavior, the subjects in both the Danish and Swedish cohorts had not passed through the risk periods for the major mental disorders (see, e.g., Robins et al., 1984). Thus, the age of the subjects in these two cohorts would be expected to lessen the possibility of finding a difference in the proportions of the mentally disordered and the non-mentally disordered convicted of crimes. Yet in both the present investigation and Ortmann's (1981) study such a difference was observed.

The observed association between major mental disorder and crime was weakened by excluding all subjects who were deceased before the end of the follow-up period. A group of Swedish investigators (Lidberg, Wiklund, & Jakobsson, 1989) have shown increased mortality rates among mentally disordered offenders under age 30.

Janson (1989) has noted other factors that mitigated against finding such a difference in the Stockholm study. Persons sent to hospital by the court were not counted. All had a diagnosis of psychosis and "they would increase that male category's total offender rate by some six percent and the specific rates accordingly" (p. 49). As well, men with psychoses had less opportunity than other subjects to commit crimes as they were hospitalized, on average, 552 days. Another factor, which would also lessen the likelihood of finding higher rates of crime registration for those suffering from major mental disorders, is the way in which admissions were documented. Patients still in hospital at the time the data were collected were not included in the mentally disordered category.

Do the results of this study generalize? The specific crime rates are not generalizable to other jurisdictions. The between-group comparisons are probably only generalizable to other countries with mental health systems, criminal justice systems, and social welfare systems similar to those in Sweden. To illustrate, the present results are similar to those of Ortmann working in Denmark. But consider extrapolating these results to the United States. Presume that in the United States there is more crime and substance abuse than in Sweden, but similar prevalence rates for the major mental disorders. A sample of U.S. offenders then would have very few subjects with major mental disorders. Generally, that is precisely what is reported. In other words, given the large amount of crime and crime by substance abusers, the crimes of those with major disorders seem insignificant in comparison.

The within-group rates from the present investigation may be generalizable. The external validity of these findings may depend on the similarity of the ratio of crimes leading to prosecution compared to crimes committed and the similarity of the attitudes of the police and prosecutors toward the mentally disordered and intellectually disabled.

Conclusion

These studies suggest that certain major mental disorders increase the risk of criminal offending and of violence among both men and women. Some significant proportion of the offenders with major mental disorders, but not nearly all, also abuse alcohol and/or drugs. There is evidence to suggest that some of these individuals begin offending in childhood, before the major disorder would be manifest, while others offend for the first time as adults. It is important always to be cognizant of a possible bias present in all of these investigations. Teplin (1984) has found that the Chicago police are more likely to arrest mentally disordered persons than nondisordered persons. If these results generalize to other jurisdictions, all of the studies referred to simply document a bias in the criminal justice systems of jurisdictions around the world. If, on the other hand, mentally disordered persons are often excused for behavior that would lead to criminal charges for nondisordered persons (Hodgins, 1988; Steadman & Felson, 1984), the results of these investigations underestimate the criminal behavior of the mentally disordered. Either way, the comparability of official crime rates for those with major mental disorders to those without remains unknown.

This problem is compounded by a lack of knowledge of the prevalence of illegal behaviors among the disordered as compared to the nondisordered. Consider, for example, the self-report studies of aggressive behavior. In the United States, investigations generally find that between 30% and 40% of adults report physically aggressive behavior toward another person (Elliot, Huizinga, & Morse, 1986; O'Leary, Barling, Arias, & Rosenbaum, 1989). These self-reports are corroborated by victim reports. This prevalence is slightly higher than what is found in longitudinal studies of children. In these investigations, depending on definitions and measurement procedures, 20% to 30% of children are judged by peers, teachers, and parents as behaving aggressively during the past year (Olweus, 1979). A recent U.S. publication (Swanson, Holzer, Ganju, & Jono, 1990) compared reports of aggressive behavior among subjects with and without mental disorders. However, only 2.7% of the nondisordered men and 1.1% of the nondisordered women reported behaving aggressively. These results are very different from all the other published findings. It would appear as if the nondisordered subjects in this investigation failed to report their aggressive behavior. Among the subjects with major mental disorders, about 13% of the men and 10% of the women reported interpersonal aggressive behavior during the year preceding the interview.

In the Link, Andrews, and Cullen (in press) study described previously, self-reports of aggressive behavior were also examined. More of the patients than subjects in the community sample reported hitting someone during the past month, being in a fight during the past 5 years, having hurt someone badly, and using a weapon during the past 5 years. Link and his colleagues argue that the consistent findings of higher arrest rates among former patients are a reflection of the high rates of aggressive behavior and weapon use in this population. Consequently, these authors reject the hypothesis that the mentally disordered are subject to discriminatory arrest practices. This conclusion is consistent with an older study (Steadman & Felson, 1984), also carried out in New York City, in which more patients reported behaving violently and reported incidents involving weapons than did subjects in a matched community sample. In this investigation, it was found that police were no more likely to arrest a former patient than a subject with no history of mental disorder. Taken together, the investigations reviewed here provide good evidence that persons with, or persons who will develop, major mental disorders are at increased risk for committing a crime and for committing a violent crime.

Notes

1. In Canada, a penitentiary houses offenders sentenced to be incarcerated for 2 years or longer.
2. This work is being conducted with the collaboration of C.-G. Janson. Financial support has been provided by the Enskilden Banken of Sweden to S. Hodgins and L. Öjesjö.

References

Abram, R. M. (1990). The problem of co-occurring disorders among jail detainees: Antisocial disorder, alcoholism, drug abuse and depression. *Law and Human Behavior, 14,* 333-345.

American Psychiatric Association. (1980). *Diagnostic and statistical manual of mental disorders* (3rd ed.). Washington, DC: Author.

Cohen, C. I. (1980). Crime among mental patients: A critical analysis. *Psychiatric Quarterly, 52,* 100-107.

Collins, J. J., & Schlenger, W. E. (1983, November). *The prevalence of psychiatric disorder among admissions to prison.* Paper presented at the 35th Annual Meeting of the American Society of Criminology, Denver, CO.

Convit, A., Isay, D., Gadioma, R., & Volavka, J. (1988). Underreporting of physical assaults in schizophrenic inpatients. *Journal of Nervous and Mental Disease, 176,* 507-509.

Côté, G. (1990). L'homicide et la recherche quantitative: Aspects méthodologiques. *Revue Internationale de Criminologie et de Police Technique, 4,* 499-520.

Côté, G., & Hodgins, S. (1990). Co-occurring mental disorder among criminal offenders. *Bulletin of the American Academy of Psychiatry and the Law, 18*(3), 271-281.

Côté, G., & Hodgins, S. (1992). The prevalence of major mental disorders among homicide offenders. *International Journal of Law and Psychiatry, 15,* 89-99.

Daniel, A. E., Robins, A. J., Reid, J. C., & Wilfley, D. E. (1988). Lifetime and six-month prevalence of psychiatric disorders among sentenced female offenders. *Bulletin of the American Academy of Psychiatry and the Law, 16*(4), 333-342.

Drake, R. E., Osher, F. C., Noordsy, D. L., Hurlbut, S. C., Teague, G. B., & Beaudett, M. S. (1990). Diagnosis of alcohol use disorders in schizophrenia. *Schizophrenia Bulletin, 16,* 57-68.

Durbin, J. R., Pasewark, R. A., & Albers, D. (1977). Criminality and mental illness: A study of current arrest rates in a rural state. *American Journal of Psychiatry, 134,* 80-83.

Elliot, D. S., Huizinga, D., & Morse, B. J. (1986). Self-reported violent offending: Descriptive analysis of juvenile violence offenders and their offending careers. *Journal of Interpersonal Violence, 4,* 472-514.

Giovannoni, J. M., & Gurel, L. (1967). Socially disruptive behavior of ex-mental patients. *Archives of General Psychiatry, 17,* 146-153.

Gottlieb, P., Gabrielsen, G., & Kramp, P. (1987). Psychotic homicides in Copenhagen from 1959 to 1988. *Acta Psychiatrica Scandinavica, 76,* 285-292.

Häfner, H., & Böker, W. (1982). *Crimes of violence by mentally abnormal offenders* (H. Marshall, Trans.). Cambridge: Cambridge University Press. (Original work published in 1973)

Hodgins, S. (1987a). Étude des rechutes constatées dans une cohorte de personnes jugées inaptes à subir leur procès ou acquittées pour cause d'aliénation mentale. *Revue Canadienne des Sciences du Comportement, 19,* 441-453.

Hodgins, S. (1987b). Men found unfit to stand trial and/or not guilty by reason of insanity: Recidivism. *Canadian Journal of Criminology, 29,* 51-70.

Hodgins, S. (1988). Antisocial behavior of persons suffering from mental disorders. In W. Buikhuisen & S. A. Mednick (Eds.), *Explaining criminal behavior: Interdisciplinary approaches* (pp. 143-159). New York: E. J. Brill.

Hodgins, S. (1992). Mental disorder, intellectual deficiency and crime: Evidence from a birth cohort. *Archives of General Psychiatry, 49,* 476-483.

Hodgins, S., & Côté, G. (1990). The prevalence of mental disorders among penitentiary inmates. *Canada's Mental Health, 38,* 1-5.

Hodgins, S., Webster, C., & Paquet, J. (1990). *Annual report year-2 Canadian database: Patients held on Lieutenant-Governor's warrant.* Ottawa: Department of Justice.

Hodgins, S., Webster, C., & Paquet, J. (1991). *Annual report year-3 Canadian database: Patients held on Lieutenant-Governor's warrant.* Ottawa: Department of Justice.

Hodgins, S., Webster, C., Paquet, J., & Zellerer, E. (1989). *Annual report year-1 Canadian database: Patients held on Lieutenant Governor's warrants.* Ottawa: Department of Justice.

Hyde, P. S., & Seiter, R. P. (1987). *The prevalence of mental illness among inmates in the Ohio prison system.* Springfield: The Department of Mental Health and the Ohio Department of Rehabilitation and Correction Interdepartmental Planning and Oversight Committee for Psychiatric Services to Corrections.

Janson, C.-G. (1989). Psychiatric diagnoses and recorded crimes. In C.-G. Janson & A.-M. Janson (Eds.), *Crime and delinquency in a metropolitan cohort* (pp. 31-55). Stockholm: University of Stockholm.

Kay, S. R., Wolkenfeld, F., & Murrill, L. M. (1988a). Profiles of aggression among psychiatric patients: I. Nature and prevalence. *The Journal of Nervous and Mental Disease, 176,* 539-546.

Kay, S. R., Wolkenfeld, F., & Murrill, L. M. (1988b). Profiles of aggression among psychiatric patients: II. Covariates and predictors. *The Journal of Nervous and Mental Disease, 176,* 547-557.

Krakowski, M. I., Convit, A., Jaeger, J., Lin, S., & Volavka, J. (1989). Neurological impairment in violent schizophrenic inpatients. *American Journal of Psychiatry, 146,* 849-853.

Kristjansson, E., Allebeck, P., & Wistedt, B. (1987). Validity of the diagnosis schizophrenia in a psychiatric inpatient register. *Nordisk Psykiatrisk Tidsskrift, 41,* 229-234.

Lagos, J. M., Perlmutter, K., & Saexinger, H. (1977). Fear of the mentally ill: Empirical support for the common man's response. *American Journal of Psychiatry, 134,* 1134-1137.

Lidberg, L., Wiklund, N., & Jakobsson, S. W. (1989). Mortality among criminals with suspected mental disturbance. *Scandinavian Journal of Social Psychiatry and Medicine, 17,* 59-65.

Lindqvist, P. (1986). Criminal homicide in Northern Sweden 1970-1981: Alcohol intoxication, alcohol abuse and mental disease. *International Journal of Law and Psychiatry, 8,* 19-37.

Lindqvist, P., & Allebeck, P. (1989). Schizophrenia and assaultive behaviour: The role of alcohol and drug abuse. *Acta Psychiatrica Scandinavica, 82,* 191-195.

Lindqvist, P., & Allebeck, P. (1990). Schizophrenia and crime: A longitudinal follow-up of 644 schizophrenics in Stockholm. *British Journal of Psychiatry, 157,* 345-350.

Link, B. G., Andrews, H., & Cullen, F. T. (in press). *Reconsidering the dangerousness of mental patients: Violent and illegal behavior of current and former patients compared to controls.*

Lion, J. R., Snyder, W., & Merrill, G. L. (1981). Under reporting of assaults on staff in a state hospital. *Hospital and Community Psychiatry, 32,* 497-498.

Macmillan, J. F., & Johnson, A. L. (1987). Contact with the police in early schizophrenia: Its nature, frequency and relevance to the outcome of treatment. *Medicine, Science and the Law, 27,* 191-200.

McLellan, A. T., Luborsky, L., Woody, G. E., & O'Brien, C. P. (1980). An improved diagnostic evaluation instrument for substance abuse patients, the Addiction Severity Index. *The Journal of Nervous and Mental Disease, 168,* 26-33.

Mesnikoff, A. M., & Lauterbach, C. G. (1975). The association of violent dangerous behavior with psychiatric disorders: A review of the research literature. *The Journal of Psychiatry & Law, 3,* 415-445.

Monahan, J., & Steadman, H. J. (1983). Crime and mental disorder: An epidemiological approach. In M. Tonry & N. Morris (Eds.), *Crime and justice: An annual review of research* (Vol. 4, pp. 145-189). Chicago: University of Chicago Press.

Motvik, L., & Porporino, F. J. (1991). *The nature and severity of mental health problems among federal inmates in Canadian penitentiaries.* Research Report R4. Ottawa: Correctional Services in Canada.

Neighbors, H. W., Williams, D. H., Gunnings, T. S., Lipscomb, W. D., Broman, C., & Lepkowski, J. (1987). *The prevalence of mental disorder in Michigan prisons* (Final report). Lansing: Michigan Department of Corrections.

O'Leary, K. D., Barling, J., Arias, I., & Rosenbaum, A. (1989). Prevalence and stability of physical aggression between spouses: A longitudinal analysis. *Journal of Consulting and Clinical Psychology, 57,* 263-268.

Olweus, D. (1979). Stability of aggressive reaction patterns in males: A review. *Psychological Bulletin, 86,* 852-875.

Ortmann, J. (1981). Psykisk afvigelse og kriminel adfaerd: En undersøgelse af 11533 mænd født i 1953 i det metropolitanske område København. *Forksningsrapport* (Vol. 17).

Pasewark, R. A., Bieber, S., Bosten, K. J., Riser, M., & Steadman, H. J. (1982). Criminal recidivism among insanity acquittees. *International Journal of Law and Psychiatry, 5,* 365-374.

Psychiatric News. (1984, June 15). Incidence of violent patient admissions apparently stabilized at 37 percent. Washington, DC.

Rabkin, J. G. (1979). Criminal behavior of discharged mental patients. A critical appraisal of the research. *Psychological Bulletin, 86,* 1-29.

Rappeport, J. R., & Lassen, G. (1965). Dangerousness arrest rate comparisons of discharged patients and the general population. *American Journal of Psychiatry, 121,* 776-783.

Rappeport, J. R., & Lassen, G. (1966). The dangerousness of female patients. A comparison of the arrest rate of discharged psychiatric patients and the general population. *American Journal of Psychiatry, 123,* 413-419.

Robins, L. N., Helzer, J. E., Croughan, J., & Ratcliff, K. S. (1981). National Institute of Mental Health Diagnostic Interview Schedule: Its history, characteristics, and validity. *Archives of General Psychiatry, 38,* 381-389.

Robins, L. N., Helzer, J. E., Weissman, M. M., Orvaschel, H., Gruenberg, E., Burke, J. D., & Regier, D. A., Jr. (1984). Lifetime prevalence of specific psychiatric disorders in three sites. *Archives of General Psychiatry, 41,* 949-958.

Rogers, J. L., & Bloom, J. D. (1982). Characteristics of persons committed to Oregon's psychiatric security review board. *Bulletin of the American Academy of Psychiatry and the Law, 10,* 155-164.

Skodol, A. E., & Karasu, T. B. (1978). Emergency psychiatry and the assaultive patient. *American Journal of Psychiatry, 135,* 202-205.

Soothill, K. L., Way, C. K., & Gibbens, T. C. N. (1980). Subsequent dangerousness among compulsory hospital patients. *British Journal of Criminology, 20,* 289-295.

Sosowsky, L. (1974). Violence and the mentally ill. In *Putting state mental hospitals out of business—The community approach to treating mental illness in San Mateo County* (pp. 17-33 processed). Berkeley: University of California Graduate School of Public Policy.

Sosowsky, L. (1978). Crime and violence among mental patients reconsidered in view of the new legal relationship between the state and the mentally ill. *American Journal of Psychiatry, 135,* 33-42.

Sosowsky, L. (1980). Explaining the increased arrest rate among mental patients: A cautionary note. *American Journal of Psychiatry, 137,* 1602-1605.

Steadman, H. J., Cocozza, J. J., & Melick, M. E. (1978). Explaining the increased arrest rate among mental patients: The changing clientele of state hospitals. *American Journal of Psychiatry, 135,* 816-820.

Steadman, H. J., & Felson, R. B. (1984). Self-reports of violence. Ex-mental patients, ex-offenders, and the general population. *Criminology, 22,* 321-342.

Swanson, J. W., Holzer, C. E., Ganju, V. R., & Jono, R. T. (1990). Violence and psychiatric disorder in the community: Evidence from the Epidemiologic Catchment Area surveys. *Hospital and Community Psychiatry, 41,* 761-770.

Tardiff, R., & Sweillam, A. (1982). Assaultive behavior among chronic inpatients. *American Journal of Psychiatry, 139,* 212-215.

Teplin, L. A. (1984). Criminalizing mental disorder: The comparative arrest rate of the mentally ill. *American Psychologist, 39,* 794-803.

Walker, N., & McCabe, S. (1973). *Crime and insanity in England, II.* Edinburgh: Edinburgh University Press.

Wetteberg, L., & Farmer, A. E. (1990). Clinical polydiagnostic studies in a large Swedish pedigree with schizophrenia. *European Archives of Psychiatry and Clinical Neuroscience, 240,* 188-190.

Wikström, P.-O. H. (1989). Age and crime in a Stockholm cohort. In C.-G. Janson & A.-M. Janson (Eds.), *Crime and delinquency in a metropolitan cohort* (pp. 85-115). Stockholm: University of Stockholm.

Zitrin, A., Hardesty, A. S., Burdock, E. T., & Drossman, A. K. (1976). Crime and violence among mental patients. *American Journal of Psychiatry, 133,* 142-149.

2

Supervision in the Deinstitutionalized Community

CHRISTOPHER D. WEBSTER

ROBERT J. MENZIES

> The same point needs to be made . . . about the individuals who are regarded as dangers because of what they have done, and who are in mental hospitals, in prisons, or under what is optimistically called "supervision" in what is euphemistically called the "community."
>
> Walker, "Dangerous Mistakes," 1991, p. 752

> The current term for these misfortunates was "street people" an expression that had taken over from bag ladies, winos, and bums. . . . The term was too easy by half. It casually lumped together the criminal and the innocent, the dangerous and the safe. It included long-term mental patients discharged from hospitals under what was called, in a sublime euphemism, the "deinstitutionalization program," along with crack addicts, thieves, alcoholics, hobos, the temporarily jobless, the alimony defaulters, rent-hike victims and everyone else who'd fallen short of the appallingly high standards that Manhattan set for staying properly housed and fed.
>
> Raban, *Hunting Mister Heartbreak: A Discovery of America*, 1991, p. 64

AUTHORS' NOTE: This research has been supported by a number of institutions, most notably the Social Sciences and Humanities Research Council (Grant 410-85-1429); the Ministry of Health, Ontario; the Ministry of the Solicitor General, Canada; the Canadian Psychiatric Research Foundation; the LaMarsh Institute for Research on Violence and Conflict Resolution; the Impulsivity Programme of the Clarke Institute of Psychiatry, the Clarke Institute of Psychiatry Research Fund; and the Sustaining Grant provided to the Centre of Criminology, University of Toronto, by the Solicitor General, Canada.

Our interest in the fate of persons remanded by courts for psychiatric assessment began in the late 1970s. As researchers attached to the Metropolitan Toronto Forensic Service (METFORS), a subunit of the Clarke Institute of Psychiatry, we were expected to amass and analyze information about the 600 or so persons each year given brief, one-day assessments. These prisoners were brought to METFORS daily from one of three detention centers in the city. Most were at a pretrial stage and the forensic psychiatric major issue was fitness to stand trial. After an interview with a group of forensic psychiatric clinicians and the administration of psychological tests, the prisoners were returned to detention. Reports were sent to court. Some prisoners were subsequently remanded to METFORS again on the same charge for further detailed inpatient assessment. This practice continues to the present time with only minor changes.[1] The general procedures in use at METFORS have been described elsewhere (Turner, 1979, 1981; Webster, Menzies, & Jackson, 1982).

The clinical prediction of future dangerous behavior appeared early in our experience as a topic of great importance. Steadman and Cocozza (1974) had published *Careers of the Criminally Insane,* showing beyond doubt that violent behavior is largely overpredicted, and Thornberry and Jacoby (1979) had confirmed their findings in *The Criminally Insane: A Community Follow-Up of Mentally Ill Offenders.* Monahan's (1981) influential book on the conceptual problems associated with the making and validating of clinical predictions had not appeared, but Pfohl (1978) had published his ideas on the manner in which "dangerousness" may, in some instances be "constructed" in the clinic.

It occurred to us that what was needed was an instrument or scale that clinicians could use in the assessment of dangerousness potential and that would have proven psychometric properties. The best starting point at that time seemed to be Megargee's (1976) paper, which is helpful in showing that the dangerousness concept is an amalgam of anger, hostility, habit strength, availability of weapons, and the like. Armed with Megargee's basic ideas, we endeavored to construct from it a scale to measure the various items.

That done, we persuaded our clinical colleagues to learn the scheme and to use it provisionally in pretrial brief assessments. But after a few weeks it became clear from our discussions that the psychiatrists, psychologists, social workers, nurses, and correctional officers were not using the terms as we understood them or as Megargee had intended them. So it seemed that, despite our best efforts, our colleagues had different understandings of phrases like *instrumental aggression* than had we or Megargee. Then began a long series of meetings in which together we hammered out a new set of definitions. These actually produced a solution very similar to that of Megargee's (1976), but at least we now stood on common ground with the clinicians. Implementation of this system, called the Dangerous Behavior Rating Scheme (DBRS), began in early 1979. The DBRS was used by all clinicians present at the brief assessment and also by three uninvolved raters, one who sat with the clinicians and two who observed the proceedings from behind a one-way mirror.

From the outset we planned to do thorough searches of the criminal justice and mental health records at 2 years post assessment. We had contemplated trying to interview former patient-prisoners but discarded the idea on a variety of practical and ethical grounds. We knew that it would be difficult to retrieve the file information we wanted. For one thing, mental health records are not coordinated provincially, let alone nationally. This means searching files in individual hospitals, which is not only a daunting and expensive task but is also without the desired effect, since information is inevitably lost. While Canadian police data can be obtained nationally, given the appropriate cooperation, the eventual information is usually rather cryptic and can underestimate actual offending. The same problems of data access and underreporting afflict the search for correctional information at a federal and provincial level. Our work on this project, which continues, needs to be seen in the light of these practical considerations.

Tracking, as readers will know, is deficient in establishing reliable, clinically pertinent predictor variables and accurate, comprehensive outcome variables (see Monahan, 1988), and also has some fundamental and seemingly intractable problems. There is general acknowledgment that clinical measures are almost bound to accentuate trait qualities at the expense of situational variables, that of necessity clinicians form impressions under highly restricted, artificial, and at times misleading circumstances (Monahan, 1981). Another difficulty is that clinical opinions are not only sought by the courts but even accepted by them (Jackson, 1982). So when, for example, clinicians imply that a correctional solution through incarceration might be best, they restrict to some extent the opportunity for future violence against other persons. Their predictions influence outcome in complicated ways that largely defy later statistical disentanglement. Another difficulty is that with the passage of time, more and more of the sample drift out of orbit; some move to distant parts of the country or are deported; some die. Yet another problem, one we have encountered, is that almost no matter how long the follow-up interval is, some patients will commit highly violent offenses right after the close of the period. This is all by way of saying that it is unwise to expect high prediction-outcome correlations in studies of this kind.

In what follows we shall: (a) review our already-published findings on the DBRS regarding dangerous behavior to others at 2 years post assessment (Menzies, Webster, & Sepejak, 1985); (b) report on as yet unpublished

TABLE 2.1 Results of DBRS Factor Analysis (15 Items)

Factor	Variable Included	Percentage of Variance Explained	Eigenvalue
1. Potential for violence	Anger	33.5	5.03
	Rage		
	Tolerance		
	Dangerous to others in present		
	Dangerous to others in future		
2. Interpersonal responsibility	Guilt	18.5	2.77
	Capacity for empathy		
	Capacity for change		
	Environmental support		
	Accurate information		
	Sufficient information		
3. Dangerousness to self	Dangerousness to self in present	11.7	1.75
	Dangerousness to self in future		
4. Controlled aggression	Passive aggressive	8.7	1.28
	Hostility		

preliminary data at 6 years following initial evaluation; (c) show how the prediction issue shades almost imperceptibly into the broader matter of how some individuals alternate their roles of prisoner and patient (Toch, 1982); and (d) comment generally on what sorts of administrative and clinical responses are seemingly necessary to prevent wasting expensive clinical services to no noticeably good end so far as mentally disordered offenders are concerned.

The DBRS: Outcome at 2 Years

The use of two thoroughly trained coders independent of clinical work and scores on some 200 consecutive assessments enabled us to determine interrater reliability for the DBRS. Most items (each scored on a scale of 1 to 7 [lowest to highest]) yielded satisfactory interrater reliability, though some had to be dropped either because they failed to achieve .50 correspondence, they were bimodally distributed, or they yielded nonresponses from coders in more than 20% of cases (control over actions, emotionality, self-perception as dangerous, environmental stress, dangerousness increased under alcohol, dangerousness increased under drugs, manipulative).[2] The surviving 15 items were factor analyzed, yielding four factors accounting for 72% of the variance (see Table 2.1).

As already mentioned, our first follow-up took place at 2 years. We searched records in six major psychiatric hospitals in Ontario, examined the Province of Ontario Ministry of Correctional Services' files, obtained case-by-case information from the Royal Canadian Mounted Police, and examined the Ontario death registry. We ended up with information in four categories: criminal charges, reasons for contact with psychiatric hospitals, misconducts while in prison, and incidents during incarceration. All this information was integrated into case profiles for each subject, typed onto sheets, and rated for dangerousness by nine independent M.A.-level students in criminology. The ratings yielded a Dangerousness Outcome Score (DOS) on an 11-point scale. Correlations among these raters on the DOS was generally in the .7 to .8 range. It became clear from early inspection of the data that there was considerable movement of prisoner-patients back and forth between the criminal justice and mental health systems. Deleting 7 individuals who died or moved out of the area during the follow-up period left us with 203 subjects. Only one of these spent the subsequent entire 2 years in prison. It was of interest to establish the mean number of months spent in various institutions. The group averaged about 4.7 months in prison and about 2.0 months in psychiatric hospitals. The balance of more than 17 months was spent in what Walker (1991) euphemistically calls "the community." Also following Walker we can say that for 9 of those months, the subjects were "supervised" via parole.

The data allowed us to determine the amount of violence that was reported during the 2-year follow-up period. We split it up according to victim (self or others) and degree of completion (whether accomplished or threatened). Robbery, arson, and indecent assault were coded as violent. A total of 158 patients had at least one subsequent recorded contact. These were involved in 1,555 incidents, almost 10 per person. Separate charges were included as incidents in the case of criminal arrests (i.e., there will have been some slight inflation due to "overcharging"). The total number of violent acts was 178 (i.e., about one per person). A further 84 entailed threats of violence. There were 33 suicide attempts and 32 suicide threats.

Our DOS scores correlated, as would be expected, with length of time spent in institutions. We split amount of time spent "in the community" and in institutions, prisons, or hospitals, and correlated it with DOS scores. In this way we obtained a +.43 correlation between DOS scores and numbers of months in institutions. And there was a −.43 correlation between DOS and time in the community. In Table 2.2 we show the prediction-outcome correlations based on the mean scores of the two independent coders against DOS scores. The table shows the 15 surviving items from the DBRS, the four scores from the factor analysis, and an aggregate DBRS rating based on an addition of the four factor scores for

TABLE 2.2 Pearson Correlation Between DBRS Predictions and Dangerousness
Outcome Scores

	DBRS Items
Accurate information	.06
Sufficient information	.08
Passive aggressive	.12
Environmental support	.14
Anger	.17
Rage	.18
Guilt	.18
Dangerous others, present	.19
Dangerous others, future	.19
Dangerous self, present	.20
Dangerous self, future	.20
Hostility	.22
Capacity for change	.22
Capacity for empathy	.27
Tolerance	.32
Factor items	
1	.09
2	.20
3	.21
4	.22
Aggregate DBRS Factor score	.34

each case. It is evident from these correlations that, as might be expected, individual items tend to correlate only weakly with outcome. It is also worth noting that, again according to expectation, the strongest correlation is achieved when all four overall factors are brought into play. But even here only 12% of the variance in DOS scores is accounted for.

The present data set also enabled us to examine the types of errors made by the coders. We restricted the analysis to clear examples by setting up advantageous cutoff scores (see Menzies et al., 1985, p. 61). The coders obtained 28 true positives (high prediction, high outcome) and 25 true negatives (low prediction, low outcome). But they also predicted 18 patients to be dangerous when they (apparently) were not (false positives) and 6 to be nondangerous when they (definitely) were (false negatives). The point is that the ratio of hits (even when defined to advantage through exclusion of cases where predictions are relatively indefinite) to false positives is only 1.6 to 1.0. When all the data are included, the ratio drops to 1.2 to 1.0. So we can at least conclude that projections of dangerousness or nondangerousness will be relatively more accurate in cases where the perceived dangerousness is high or the nondangerousness low.

Were the coders' predictions more accurate in some contexts than others? To answer this question we divided the sample of 203 into four groups. A first group spent 20 or more months "in the community." A second spent 12 or more months in prison. A third spent 12 or more months in hospital. A fourth group contained a mixture of institutional conditions. The data showed that DBRS predictions were most accurate when the individuals ($n = 35$) were confined to prison post assessment (.41). That the hospital sample achieved a low correlation (.10) may have been mainly due to the small sample size ($n = 13$). When we grouped the hospital sample with the prison sample ($n = 48$), the correlation rose to .44. It is perhaps not surprising that correlations were higher when based on institutional rather than community subjects (.27 with $n = 110$). The mixed group ($n = 45$) yielded an intermediate correlation (.31). This presumably has to do with the relatively greater "supervision" in hospitals and prisons, leading to probable higher rate of detected violence.

The DBRS: Preliminary Outcome at 6 Years

When we published the outcome of the DBRS study we were very careful to limit the results and to make no claims about the validity of the instrument. We talked about the "modest correlations" and concluded that "the prediction of dangerous behavior can be justified only under the most rigorous qualifications" (Menzies et al., 1985, p. 66). Based on our experience with the DBRS, we suggested that "incorporation of psychometric instruments into the resolution of such a complex forensic problem must await further testing and higher standards" (p. 66). Despite these caveats, we received a flood of requests for the manual on which the DBRS was based. These came in the form of sometimes cheerful notes from independent clinicians, who seemed to think that the DBRS could beef up their ability to predict in custody disputes and the like, and from big organizations like the United States Secret Service, which did not disclose what it had in mind for DBRS application. Certainly we ourselves wondered if our future efforts would not better be applied to short-run predictions in controlled environments (cf. Monahan, 1984) and to studies investigating how clinicians perceive "dangerousness" (cf. Esses & Webster, 1988).

Although our interest in the DBRS was diminished by our study of the results, we nonetheless decided to persist through a 6-year follow-up. The main reason for this was that it had become clear that the "careers," institutional and community, of our cohort would yield important information for the planning of new services. As well, there remained a subsidiary but persistent reminder from Shah (1981): "To say that something is difficult to do (namely, to achieve high levels of accuracy in predicting events with very low base rates) is *not* the same as asserting that the task is impossible and simply cannot be done" (p. 161, original emphasis).

One objection to the DBRS study was that the predictions were based on two coders who were not clinically trained. It could well be that psychiatrists, psychologists, social workers, nurses, and correctional officers could yield appreciably more reliable and valid predictions than intelligent, trained, but clinically unschooled raters. Another possible problem was that the follow-up interval at 2 years was too short to be ideal. Yet another was the hope that we could retrieve slightly more information than was previously obtained from follow-up records. For these and other reasons we resurveyed the same outcome sources with some additions. These data are just now in the process of being analyzed.

At this time, with outcome data still incomplete in a few instances, we are not in a position to establish DOS scores at 6 years. It has proven extremely time consuming and difficult to obtain follow-up information from provincial correctional ministries and the like. This much said, there are some correspondences between basic descriptive variables and outcome so far at 6 years. Although the sizes of the correlations are not high by usual standards, we nonetheless find it encouraging that there are some agreements in this data set, which, like others, and despite our best efforts, necessarily has much incomplete information. Of some interest, though without much power, is the relation between age and total number of violent incidents over 6 years. As expected, the relation is negative ($-.14, p < .05$) as is that with days in prisons ($-.22, p < .01$). A little less obvious was the observation that number of suicide attempts during the 6 years correlated significantly with days in prison over that period ($.23, p < .01$) and also that total self-harm during follow-up correlated negatively with the extent to which the patient deemed the assessment as helpful ($-.20, p = .02$).

Using as outcome measure, not the DOS score as outlined above, but the balder measure of total number of violent incidents over 6 years, we found that the two coders mentioned earlier did achieve significant correlations with two DBRS items, "guilt" and "capacity for empathy." Again, the averaged correlations are low ("guilt," .16; "capacity for empathy," .14). These same items and "capacity for change" also correlated with time spent in institutions over 6 years (.16, .15, and .14, respectively). Days spent in prison correlated with "dangerousness increased under alcohol" (.16), as well as with "dangerousness to self at present" (.12) and "dangerousness to self in the future" (.18). Of some note was the observation that days in prison correlated for these two coders negatively with "accurate information" ($-.23$) and "sufficient information" ($-.18$). The former item

TABLE 2.3 Correlations for Coders Between Total Number of Self-Injurious Incidents Over 6 Years and Selected DBRS Items

Anger	.13
Control over actions	−.13
Dangerousness increased under drugs	.21
Dangerousness increased under alcohol	.13
Dangerousness to self, present	.22
Dangerousness to others, future	.19
Global predictors	.12

deals with the extent to which the clinician or rater considers that information given by the prisoner-patient is correct; the latter, the extent to which it was sufficient to form proper judgments. The fifth outcome variable, total number of self-injurious incidents over the 6 years, yielded several reliable correlations ("anger," .13; "control over actions," −.13; "dangerousness increased under alcohol," .13; "dangerousness increased under drugs," .21; "dangerousness to others in the future," .19). The correlations of the fifth outcome variable are stated in Table 2.3.

Of the various items in the scale as used by the coders, it seems that "dangerousness increased under alcohol," "dangerousness increased under drugs," "accurate information," "sufficient information," and "dangerousness to self" are relatively strong predictors. One of the psychiatrists assessed 154 cases. His significant DBRS scores center on these same items. Charges over 6 years correlated positively with "dangerousness increased under alcohol" (.15) and "dangerousness increased under drugs" (.25), and negatively with "accurate information" (−.21) and "sufficient information" (−.29). Similarly, "dangerousness increased under alcohol" and "dangerousness increased under drugs" correlated with days in prison (.18 and .29, respectively). Again, there were negative correlations with "accurate information" (−.22) and "sufficient information" (−.15).

Although our data are not complete it does not seem as though the eventual outcome will be much different from that already published. Likely we shall show that the clinicians are in rough agreement with the coders and, as before in other studies, that some clinicians are more able predictors than others (cf. Shah, 1981; Webster et al., 1984). But we continue to question whether an instrument like the DBRS, at least as applied to such a heterogeneous group under such unfavorable clinical circumstances,[3] could ever yield much by way of high prediction-outcome correlations. This "prediction" does, of course, seem more obvious in 1991 than it did in 1981. But as Brizer and Crowner (1989) have recently pointed out, "awareness of the methodological problems of past prediction studies points the way to future efforts" (p. xxii). We shall in the future do well to identify specific populations at high risk for violence and also to combine clinical and actuarial data (Webster & Menzies, 1987). Our guess is that the greatest interest in our project from the prediction perspective will be that which centers on a relatively small group of repeatedly violent offenders.

"Careers" of the Cohort Over Time

As well as the sample assessed via the DBRS described above, we have been following over the same 2- and 6-year periods a cohort of 571 persons assessed consecutively at METFORS during 1978 (Menzies & Webster, 1987). Aside from the fact that this group was not evaluated for dangerousness using the previously described scale, the clinical and research procedures were identical. From these data we learned that 61% (349 persons) received a total of 663 terms of imprisonment (averaging 1.6) over 2 years. During that period one individual received nine imprisonments, and five individuals were incarcerated seven times. The 571 persons remanded received 2,204 months of confinement, which averages close to 4 months per individual. One sixth of the 2-year period was spent in prison on average. It would be fascinating to know the extent to which brief forensic psychiatric assessments reduced or extended those periods and if particular kinds of offenders were affected in particular ways.

As would be expected in a sample of this sort, the members of the cohort also received extensive hospitalizations. Forty-nine percent (281 persons) received 592 inpatient admissions (i.e., an average of one per individual). Some of the hospitalizations were voluntary, some were coerced; some were for treatment, some for assessment; some were dealt with by mental health acts, some by Canada's Criminal Code. In all, 1,145 patient-months were spent in hospital (i.e., an average of 2 months per person). A quarter of the sample (141 patients) was confined both in prison and in hospital during the 2 years post assessment. Only 82 persons escaped, so far as we know, confinement of one sort or the other. On average, the prisoner-patients spent 6 months of the 2-year period confined one way or the other. We also discovered that, of the total number of months available to be spent "in the community," a little more than half (54%) were spent by the individuals under conditions of probation. In addition, 28% received outpatient or day-care referrals to psychiatric hospitals. That figure accounts for only the initial contact. Many prisoner-patients were in more or less continuous contact with hospitals over the 2-year period.

TABLE 2.4 Analysis of Incidents Over 2 Years

Community—New criminal charges	1,332	51.0%
Community—Contact with psychiatric facilities	326	12.5%
Institution—Misconducts in prisons	535	20.5%
Institution—Hospital	423	16.0%
Total	2,616	

A particularly surprising finding to us was that 138 of the 571 patients received one or more subsequent forensic psychiatric assessments over the 2-year period. A total of 229 brief or inpatient assessments were conducted. These were carried out at METFORS or elsewhere. These 229 assessments do *not* include inpatient remands following the original brief assessment (i.e., they were new remands). Two individuals received six subsequent remands; another two received five. The important point is that almost a quarter (24%) of the cohort was reassessed within the 2-year follow-up. Repeat remands have gradually increased over years at METFORS from 10% in 1978 to 34% in 1988. Menzies (1987) has treated the subject of repeat remands in considerable detail. The present numbers of repeat remands at METFORS are very much higher than those given by Soothill (1974), who reported 5% repeat remands in a British forensic psychiatric population. His view was that most of these repeat remands were unnecessary and that they did not add much information from one assessment to the next. Certainly the METFORS figures are very much higher than those reported in Thailand, where only 22 cases resurfaced out of 2,112 cases over 15 years (Dasananjali & Soothill, 1991). However, it is not clear in this study whether or not this happy outcome is "one of good management or good fortune or, quite simply, that no news is bad news in so far as Thailand's lack of record-linkage fails to provide the necessary information" (pp. 63, 64).

Most major writers on the prediction of dangerousness point out that it is a challenge to predict behaviors with low base-rate frequency (e.g., Monahan, 1981; but see Quinsey, 1980). Perhaps that is why our raters in the studies sketched above did not achieve higher prediction-outcome correspondences. Yet a review of what actually occurred during the 2-year interval deems that a little unlikely. We coded a total of 2,616 "incidents." These incidents included incarceration misconducts in prisons, entries in progress notes in hospital charts, and the like. Almost three-quarters of the sample had at least one incident to their credit. The bulk of these incidents occurred "in the community" (63%). Table 2.4 shows where the incidents took place.

TABLE 2.5 New Charges Over 2 Years

Common assault	51
Assault causing bodily harm	48
Dangerous weapons	28
Robberies	20
Assault police	14
Indecent assault	14
Assaults while resisting arrest	12
Arson	10
Rapes	3
Woundings	2
Kidnapping	1
Choking	1
Murder	1

One third of the cohort exhibited overt violent behavior during the follow-up period. Of the 258 assaultive acts occurring in the community, 213 led to criminal charges with the balance (45) to psychiatric interventions. There were 106 assaults in prison and 138 acts in hospitals. As well, there were 100 incidents, involving 60 persons, of attempted or threatened suicide or self-injury. Of those, 54 occurred in hospitals, 43 in the community, and 3 in prison. The distribution of these acts over time was more or less linear (i.e., it was stable from month to month and did not drop off over the follow-up interval). New charges for the cohort are shown in Table 2.5. Ours is clearly a heavily criminalized population, with 56% of those who spent at least some time "in the community" being charged with at least one criminal offense. At the end of the 2-year period, only 35% were under no form of supervision, confinement, or constraint. About one fifth of the group was still in prison or hospital.

We have some preliminary data on the 6-year fate of our 1979 cohort, the one assessed for dangerousness via the DBRS (McMain, Webster, & Menzies, 1989). Almost all (98%) of the 195 persons followed had some additional contact with the mental health system or the criminal justice system. That figure does, however, include inpatient assessments that followed brief assessments on the same charge in some cases. The majority, 92%, were hospitalized or imprisoned. A total of 158 persons incurred 702 terms of imprisonment (i.e., 4.4 terms per individual). One man received 24 terms, another received 29, and yet another received 48. Of the group imprisoned, the members averaged 11.4 months per person. A little more than half of the sample (51%) had at least one admission to a psychiatric hospital. That group averaged close to three inpatient admissions (2.9).

TABLE 2.6 Experiences of the 1979 Cohort Over 6 Years

	n	%
No prison, no hospital	15	8
Prison only	81	42
Hospital only	22	11
Prison and hospital	77	39
Total	195	100

Altogether the admitted group spent 624 months in hospitals (i.e., 6.3 months on average). Fifteen percent of that time was due directly to legal complications. Only 15 people (8%) stayed out of hospital and/or prison during the 6 years. Eighty-one (42%) were in prison only, 22 (11%) were in hospital only, and 77 (39%) were both in prison and hospital (see Table 2.6).

As would be expected, members of this group, once outside the hospitals and prisons, spent a good deal of time under "supervision." They averaged 21.7 months on probation and 2.6 months as hospital outpatients. So far as we could tell, about three quarters of the sample (74%) were not under any form of supervision or constraint at the end of 6 years. This means that, over time, there was a general decrement in this group's mental health and correctional involvement. We noted above that this did not seem to be the case within a 2-year follow-up. Although there was certainly a decline in use of institutionalizations over the longer span, it is still to be noted that 59% of the cohort continued to be imprisoned and confined beyond the second year. Also, half of those people with continued connections had a history of being held in both mental health and correctional systems.

Implications for Policy Development

The statistical figures sketched above give some help in trying to understand the lives of mentally disordered offenders. Most readers will recognize the phenomenon and will be able to flesh it out with case histories. Our files too are eloquent testimonies to the way in which the present "service systems" fail. METFORS in Toronto is now an entrenched part of our local pattern of forensic psychiatric "agencies." Never designed to be more than an assessment unit for the courts, it has been appreciated by the judiciary. One of its main values is that it has actively fostered research into many areas and it has not shied away from work that has been critical of its basic functions (cf. Menzies, 1989). With results in hand, however, the organization itself and government ministries have been unable to create a "second generation" of services (a problem not peculiar to METFORS). Adding a high-intensity assessment service to a system otherwise deficient in ability to deliver actual treatment and rehabilitation programs may in fact do more harm than good. Judges remand some prisoners over and over again for evaluations that, it would seem, do not yield the kind of advice and help they think their accused persons actually need. It is almost as though the judges cannot believe that forensic clinicians are unable to be of greater assistance. "Recycling" becomes a way of life for the prisoner-patients, the courts, the correctional staff, the mental health staff, the welfare agencies, and so on. As Toch and Adams (1989) have pointed out, "a problem person can become a correctional client for life on the installment plan" (p. 153).

Of course, it is easy in a spirit of reform to underplay the inherent difficulty of assisting even "ordinary" mentally ill persons, those who have been fortunate enough to avoid legal entailment. These people also spend a large part of their lives being readmitted to hospitals. But there would appear now to be ways of being maximally, if not ideally, helpful (Linn, Caffey, Klett, Hogarty, & Lamb, 1979). Case management principles to date have not been well applied to forensic psychiatric patients. Some programs specifically debar persons with criminal records. Many hospitals, having achieved "deinstitutionalization," understandably shudder at the thought of erecting new secure forensic psychiatric facilities on their premises. Although it may not actually make sense to establish separate specific forensic psychiatric services, this may well be the only realistic course. Integration of forensic psychiatric patients into the ordinary remedial and support stream may be more easily possible once they have been given the chance to establish something of a crime-free record.

Recently, Quinsey, Cyr, and Lavalle (1988) (see also Rice, Harris, Quinsey, & Cyr, 1990) and Toch and Adams (1989) have tried to create out-of-the-ordinary typologies from statistical analyses. Quinsey et al., working from the perspective of the secure hospital, talk of institutional management problems, depressives, good citizens, personality disorders, institutionalized psychotics, and nonpsychotic social isolates. Toch and Adams, approaching the issue from the prison side, center on offenders with histories of mental health problems and offenders with substance abuse histories. They produce categories for mentally disordered impulsive burglars, impulsive robbers, long-term explosive robbers, young explosive robbers, mature muggers, acute disturbed exploders, chronic disturbed exploders, disturbed sex offenders, and composite career offenders. Categories for the abusers include dependent burglars, skid row robbers, skid row exploders, multiproblem robbers, addicted burglars, addicted robbers, alcohol exploders, and drug exploders.

It seems clear that once our data are finally in and consolidated, we must recognize and transcend the limitations of such categorization. We must discern workable typologies that may incorporate psychiatric diagnoses, but that must also go beyond clinical classification as the exclusive or main focus of attention. The point is that categorization with patients, whether by clinicians or by researchers, must always take into account the wider systems and ideas that both inform and restrict our typologies. And in order to enhance policy reform, we need to acknowledge that the task is not only to treat damaged people and contain their "dangerousness," but also to foster the institutional and social conditions that will lessen the burden for patients, professionals, and policymakers alike. The challenge must be one of sitting with administrators and planners from various government ministries, including housing authorities, in the hope that we can create a "hybrid" scheme that will reduce the imposition of actually unnecessary sentences (cf. Cooke, 1991), lower criminal recidivism, and at the same time improve the mental, physical, and social well-being of such unfortunate people so evidently in need.

Notes

1. Originally, all persons remanded for brief assessment were seen by a group of clinicians who jointly conducted the interview, which was normally led by a psychiatrist or resident psychiatrist. Later, the social worker and psychologist were withdrawn and currently the interview is usually conducted by a psychiatrist aided by a nurse and a correctional officer.

2. We are currently in the process of analyzing DBRS ratings from the third coder, the BAU psychiatrists, and other clinicians, with a view to comparing the method and success of instrument use by both clinical and nonclinical predictors.

3. The pretrial detainees often come to METFORS under duress. Occasionally they are even advised by their lawyers not to cooperate with the assessment. The evaluations are of necessity short and there is little opportunity to seek corroborative evidence from relatives, other hospitals, and the like.

References

Brizer, D. A., & Crowner, M. (Eds.). (1989). *Current approaches to the prediction of violence.* Washington, DC: American Psychiatric Press.

Cooke, D. J. (1991). Treatment as an alternative to prosecution: Offenders diverted for treatment. *British Journal of Psychiatry, 158,* 785-791.

Dasananjali, T., & Soothill, K. (1991). Readmission of mentally ill offenders: A descriptive study from Thailand. *Criminal Behavior and Mental Health, 1,* 55-68.

Esses, V. M., & Webster, C. D. (1988). Physical attractiveness, dangerousness, and the Canadian Criminal Code. *Journal of Applied Social Psychology, 18,* 1017-1031.

Jackson, M. A. (1982). The outcome of brief forensic psychiatric assessment: A study of 188 cases over an eight-month period. In C. D. Webster, R. J. Menzies, & M. A. Jackson (Eds.), *Clinical assessment before trial* (pp. 239-248). Toronto: Butterworths.

Linn, M. W., Caffey, E. M., Klett, J., Hogarty, G. E., & Lamb, R. (1979). Day treatment and psychotropic drugs in the aftercare of schizophrenic patients. *Archives of General Psychiatry, 36,* 1055-1066.

McMain, S., Webster, C. D., & Menzies, R. J. (1989). The postassessment careers of mentally disordered offenders. *International Journal of Law and Psychiatry, 12,* 189-201.

Megargee, E. I. (1976). The prediction of dangerous behavior. *Criminal Justice and Behavior, 3,* 3-22.

Menzies, R. J. (1987). Cycles of control: The transcarceral careers of forensic patients. *International Journal of Law and Psychiatry, 10,* 233-249.

Menzies, R. J. (1989). *Survival of the sanest: Order and disorder in a pre-trial psychiatric clinic.* Toronto: University of Toronto Press.

Menzies, R. J., & Webster, C. D. (1987). Where they go and what they do: The longitudinal careers of forensic patients in the medico-legal complex. *Canadian Journal of Criminology, 29,* 275-293.

Menzies, R. J., Webster, C. D., & Sepejak, D. S. (1985). The dimensions of dangerousness: Evaluating the accuracy of psychometric predictions of violence among forensic patients. *Law and Human Behavior, 9,* 35-56.

Monahan, J. (1981). *Predicting violent behavior: An assessment of clinical techniques.* Beverly Hills, CA: Sage.

Monahan, J. (1984). The prediction of violent behavior: Toward a second generation of theory and policy. *American Journal of Psychiatry, 141,* 10-15.

Monahan, J. (1988). Risk assessment of violence among the mentally disordered: Generating useful knowledge. *International Journal of Law and Psychiatry, 11,* 249-257.

Pfohl, S. (1978). *Predicting dangerousness: The social construction of psychiatric reality.* Lexington, MA: D. C. Heath.

Quinsey, V. L. (1980). The baserate problem and the prediction of dangerousness: A reappraisal. *Journal of Psychiatry and Law, 8,* 329-340.

Quinsey, V. L., Cyr, M., & Lavalle, Y. J. (1988). Treatment opportunities in a maximum security psychiatric hospital: A problem survey. *International Journal of Law and Psychiatry, 11,* 179-194.

Raban, J. (1991). *Hunting Mister Heartbreak: A discovery of America.* New York: HarperCollins.

Rice, M. E., Harris, G. T., Quinsey, V. L., & Cyr, M. (1990). Planning treatment programs in secure psychiatric facilities. In D. N. Weisstub (Ed.), *Law and mental health: International perspectives.* (Vol. 5, pp. 162-230). Elmsford, NY: Pergamon.

Shah, S. A. (1981). Dangerousness: Conceptual, prediction and public policy issues. In J. R. Hays, T. K. Roberts, & K. S. Solway (Eds.), *Violence and the violent individual* (pp. 151-178). New York: SP Medical & Scientific Books.

Soothill, K. L. (1974). Repeated medical remands. *Medicine, Science and the Law, 14,* 189-199.

Steadman, H. J., & Cocozza, J. J. (1974). *Careers of the criminally insane.* Lexington, MA: Lexington Books.

Thornberry, T. P., & Jacoby, J. E. (1979). *The criminally insane: A community follow-up of mentally ill offenders.* Chicago: University of Chicago Press.

Toch, H. (1982). The disturbed disruptive inmate: Where does the bus stop? *Journal of Psychiatry and Law, 10,* 327-349.

Toch, H., & Adams, K. (1989). *The disturbed violent offender*. New Haven, CT: Yale University Press.

Turner, R. E. (1979). The development of forensic services in Toronto. *Canadian Journal of Criminology, 21,* 200-209.

Turner, R. E. (1981). The delivery of mental health services to the criminal justice system and the Metropolitan Toronto Forensic Service. *Law Society Gazette, 15,* 69-97.

Walker, N. (1991). Dangerous mistakes. *British Journal of Psychiatry, 158,* 752-757.

Webster, C. D., & Menzies, R. J. (1987). The clinical prediction of dangerousness. In D. N. Weisstub (Ed.), *International yearbook on law and mental health, 3* (pp. 158-208). Elmsford, NY: Pergamon.

Webster, C. D., Menzies, R. J., & Jackson, M. S. (1982). *Clinical assessment before trial: Legal issues and mental disorder*. Toronto: Butterworths.

Webster, C. D., Sepejak, D. S., Menzies, R. J., Slomen, D. J., Butler, B. T., & Jensen, F. A. A. (1984). The reliability and validity of dangerous behavior predictions. *American Academy of Psychiatry and the Law, 12,* 41-50.

3

From Dangerousness to Risk Assessment: Implications for Appropriate Research Strategies

HENRY J. STEADMAN

JOHN MONAHAN

PAMELA CLARK ROBBINS

PAUL APPELBAUM

THOMAS GRISSO

DEIDRE KLASSEN

EDWARD P. MULVEY

LOREN ROTH

Throughout the world, dangerousness is a major criterion by which the police power of the state is exercised to deprive persons of their liberty who are believed to be mentally ill. Dangerousness is a well-accepted legal concept (Curran, 1978; Shah, 1978; Steadman & Cocozza, 1979). In fact, the February 5, 1991, report of the United Nations Commission on Human Rights, "Report of the Working Group on the Principles for the Protection of Persons with Mental Illness and for the Improvement of Mental Health Care," offered two rationales for involuntary mental health inpatient treatment. The first is a dangerousness criterion, "that, because of the mental illness, there is a serious likelihood of immediate or imminent harm to that person or to other persons." The second criterion relates to the prospect of "serious deterioration" as a result of mental disorder.

Dangerousness can be legally employed to detain involuntarily only one group that has *not* been arrested for a criminal offense—the mentally ill.

Because the mentally disordered are seen as violent-prone and nonresponsi-
ble as a result of their disorders (Link & Cullen, 1986), it has been widely
accepted by the public that their preventative detention is appropriate, if
certain criteria are met. For the most part, the criteria to be met rely on
assessments and recommendations to a court by a psychiatrist, a physician
of some other type, or a clinical psychologist. The criteria generally focus
on the imminence, seriousness, and probability of harming another person
as a result of mental disease or defect. While clinicians make recommendations, it is usually a court that ultimately makes the decision to commit
or to leave the person in the community.

As Monahan and Shah (1989) have recently discussed, the use of dangerousness that involves the largest number of persons is involuntary civil
commitment. In the United States in 1980, the most recent year for which
national data are available, this amounted to 306,468 persons. Comparable
cross-national data are not available. Soothill et al. (1981) have examined
some of the issues of compulsory admissions in Brazil, Denmark, Egypt,
Swaziland, Switzerland, and Thailand, but their data were limited to statutes
and 10 consecutive admissions and 10 consecutive discharges in each country. Likewise, Basaglia (1980) analyzed the changing Italian system, but
focused on the politics and processes of mental health system change without
reporting admission statistics. What is clear from both of these articles,
however, is that in almost every jurisdiction where compulsory admissions
occur, dangerousness is the primary rationale.

The Emergent Risk Assessment Paradigm

While dangerousness is a widely employed rationale for involuntary
detention, there is a substantial body of research that suggests there are
several limits to the ability of clinicians to assess it accurately. Among the
major problems that have been identified are that the criteria clinicians say
they are using to predict dangerousness do not appear to be the ones they
use in practice (Steadman, 1973), the accuracy of clinical predictions is
poor (Cocozza & Steadman, 1978), and the types of errors made are
consistently ones of overpredicting dangerousness (Steadman & Morrissey,
1981).

Some recent research in the area of predicting dangerousness has suggested that better accuracy may be possible using statistical approaches
(Klassen & O'Connor, 1988), and other work has demonstrated that clinical
decision making about dangerousness is more complex than previously
thought, that is, clinicians think in terms of contingent conditions in their

assessments, rather than making outright behavior predictions of future violence (Mulvey & Lidz, 1988).

While these recent research efforts have moved the field of dangerousness research forward, what appears to be an even more important development is a reconceptualization that may hold substantial prospects for a more effective balancing of individual and societal rights with regard to dangerousness. This movement is a shift toward considering these research and policy issues in terms of risk assessment, rather than in terms of dangerousness. A major stimulus for this shift has been the recent introduction of the public health perspective into the area of violence. As Mercy and O'Carroll (1988) note, "the enormous public health implications of violence have only recently gained attention" (p. 287). Further, they observe that a core component of a public health perspective is that "interventions are focused whenever possible towards those at greater risk" (p. 289). Thus risk becomes the nexus of all other issues. Two excellent examples of this approach are the June 1986 issue of the *Bulletin of the New York Academy of Medicine* on "Homicide: The Public Health Perspective" and the U.S. Public Health Service's recent report, *Healthy People 2000: National Health Promotion and Disease Prevention Objectives*, in which violent and abusive behavior is approached from a traditional public health perspective (U.S. Department of Health and Human Services, 1991).

The main points of this emergent reconceptualization are:

- moving away from a focus on the *legal* concept of dangerousness to the *decision making* concept of risk;
- leading decision makers and researchers to consider prediction issues as being on a continuum rather than simply being a dichotomy (i.e., Yes/No);
- shifting from a focus on one-time predictions about dangerousness for the court to ongoing, day-to-day decisions about the management and treatment of mentally disordered persons; and
- balancing the seriousness of possible outcomes with the probabilities of their occurrence based on specific risk factors.

This approach attempts to create a more empirical framework whereby decisions about the deprivation of liberty focus on what needs to be known in order to decide where and under what level of restriction a mentally ill person should be treated. It is attentive to the legal principle of treatment in the least restrictive alternative. It highlights how these detention decisions should relate to the treatment and management of mentally disordered persons.

MacArthur Risk Assessment Study

One research effort in the mental health arena that has espoused this "risk assessment" approach, promising an exacting test of its utility, was undertaken in 1989 by the John D. and Catherine T. MacArthur Foundation's Research Network on Mental Health and the Law, consisting of 12 people from the disciplines of law, psychiatry, psychology, and sociology.[1] Some of the core ideas being developed by our group were first discussed in Monahan's (1988) application of risk assessment ideas to mental health law.

Monahan's review of prior research on dangerousness concluded that four major problems had limited the ability of existing research to provide useful information on violence by the mentally disordered: (a) the range of predictor variables studied has been very narrow, often no more than diagnosis or demographic information; (b) the measures of the criterion variable—violence—have been very weak, typically arrest for a new violent crime or rehospitalization; (c) the patient samples have been highly restricted, usually to institutionalized males with a prior history of violence; and (d) research efforts have been fragmented and have lacked coordination.

The early efforts of the MacArthur Research Network have focused on two primary initiatives: (a) to develop a series of valid and robust "markers" of risk that would allow testing of an expanded set of predictor variables; and (b) to link these markers together in a coordinated, multisite clinical field study using a broad array of acute psychiatric inpatients whose outcomes in the community would be rigorously measured.

Risk Markers

After thoroughly reviewing the empirical and clinical literature on the assessment of risk and conferring with a large number of leading researchers and clinicians, the Network concluded that there were five factors that were thought to hold promise, but that were not yet thoroughly tested as markers of increased risk of violence among the mentally disordered, and perhaps among other groups as well. Those factors are: (a) the amount and type of *social support* available to the person; (b) *impulsiveness;* (c) reactions to provocation (*anger*); (d) an ability to empathize with others (*"psychopathy"*); and (e) the nature of the *delusions and hallucinations* that sometimes accompany mental disorder. Robust measures of these five risk markers, however, were either unavailable or had not been validated in mentally disordered populations. Our initial task was to develop state-of-the-art instruments for use in our research.

Sue Estroff of the University of North Carolina developed for us a streamlined version of her extensive assessment instrument to measure the emotional and behavioral support received by mentally disordered persons and how these indicators of *social support* may relate to violent behavior.

Recent studies demonstrated that treating clinicians perceive that approximately one third of hospitalized mental patients have significant problems with the expression of *anger,* and that these patients may be disproportionately involved in violent behavior. An instrument for measuring an individual's typical anger level and changes in those levels as a result of certain provocations was developed specifically for mentally disordered persons by Raymond Novaco at the University of California, Irvine.

The Psychopathy Checklist (PCL) by Robert D. Hare of the University of British Columbia appeared to be very promising, but a clinical version of the PCL that could be administered by a structured interview in less than half an hour and that was valid for disordered populations was required for our research. Therefore, Hare developed a reduced form version of his PCL and pilot tested that instrument for us.

The Barratt Impulsiveness Scale (BIS), developed by Ernest Barratt of the University of Texas Medical Branch in Galveston, is the most reliable and valid instrument available for measuring impulsivity. This instrument, however, has been developed exclusively in nondisordered populations. Because many of the items were inappropriate for mentally disordered people, Barratt developed a version of his instrument for use with mentally disordered persons.

The precise characteristics of delusions that relate to violence (e.g., the type of delusion, the intensity of the delusion) and how those characteristics are best measured are really quite unclear. Pamela J. Taylor and her colleagues of the Institute of Psychiatry at the University of London developed for this research a new and more clinically sensitive instrument to measure delusions, the Maudsley Assessment of Delusions Schedule (MADS), than had previously been available.

Framework for MacArthur Risk Assessment Study

The design of the pilot study described below was contingent on a number of key assumptions that will also underlie the full-scale study we are about to undertake. These reflect our reading of the literature on mental disorder and violence and the approach that we feel offers the greatest possibility of payoff.

(1) We are interested in studying the relationship between violent behavior against others and mental disorder. We have chosen to study violence to

others by released mental patients for two reasons. It is a fundamental issue in mental health law and policy, and it is an important clinical and social issue, independent of its pivotal nature in formal mental health law.

We have chosen not to focus on violence to self (although we do gather limited information on this) and not to focus on samples of disordered people who have not been hospitalized (such as was done in the National Institute of Mental Health Epidemiological Catchment Area study). Further, we concluded that violence to others by mental patients was likely to be an enduring issue in mental health law. As Monahan (Chapter 15, this volume) so clearly points out, compulsory admission under the aegis of dangerousness has been part of written law since Roman times. There is certainly no indication that history will be controverted in these regards in the foreseeable future. It should be clear that to single out violence to others as a fundamental issue in mental health law is not to reduce the significance of other core issues (e.g., danger to self or grave disability) or to claim that dangerousness to others is the paramount issue in the field. It is, however, one very significant issue and the one with which we will grapple in this research.

(2) There are two aspects of violent behavior to others by mental patients that we have chosen to address: risk assessment and risk management.

While a study of either risk assessment or risk management would be very valuable, we have decided to balance two foci in our research. Risk assessment without risk management leads only to dichotomous "in/out" judgments for institutionalization, without much relevance for clinical practice. Risk management without risk assessment, on the other hand, is not directly responsive to the concerns of mental health law, which often does call for "in/out" decisions. The main implication of including a risk management approach is that we plan to study how risk levels *change* over time.

Even to focus on both of these issues, of course, removes the potential focus of the research from many other important aspects of the relationship between violence and mental disorder that are worthy of study. For example, it removes the focus from studying the "basic" or "fundamental" nature of any relationship between violence and mental disorder (we are not comparing the violence rates of disordered and nondisordered groups to estimate whether mental disorder, per se, is a risk factor for violence). And it removes the focus from studying the treatment ("risk reduction") of violence by the mentally disordered. The former would require laboratory or epidemiological methods. The latter would require randomized clinical trials of various treatment modalities. We have chosen not to do these, at least at this point in the Network.

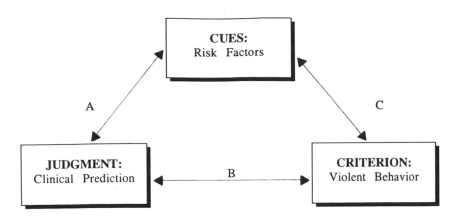

Figure 3.1. Three Approaches to the Study of Risk

(3) We have chosen to focus on one component of risk assessment and risk management: the association between certain kinds of anticipatory "cues" and the "criterion" of violent behavior.

We have found the overarching framework for the study of risk that Network member Thomas Grisso (Grisso, Tomkins, & Casey, 1988) developed from Egon Brunswick's (1956) "lens theory" to be a valuable heuristic. It is presented in Figure 3.1. As this figure makes clear, there are three possible approaches to the study of risk.

(1) We could study the relationship between cues or risk factors (anger, diagnosis, age, etc.) and judgment or clinical prediction ("A" in Figure 3.1);

(2) We could study the relationship between judgment or clinical prediction and the criterion of violent behavior ("B" in Figure 3.1); or

(3) We could study the relationship between cues or risk factors and the criterion of violent behavior ("C" in Figure 3.1).

Since excellent research on the relationship between cues and judgments (A) is already ongoing in the form of an NIMH-funded project directed by Network member Edward P. Mulvey, with Charles Lidz, and a great deal of research on the relationship between judgments and the criterion (B) already exists, we have chosen to focus our efforts on the understudied relationship between cues and the criterion (C). We believe that this type of research has the largest potential payoff for mental health law.

The Brunswick/Grisso framework relates most directly to risk assessment—but it can drive risk management as well. Some of the cues that will be uncovered will be static, unchangeable ones (e.g., gender, age, past history). But other cues may "naturally" vary (e.g., over the course of a disorder) and a clinician may be able to take advantage of these changes in managing risk. Still other cues may be directly manipulated (e.g., via anger treatment programs or compliance enhancement programs, if anger and compliance turn out to be cues predictive of violence).

(4) The ultimate goals of our research on the association between cues or risk factors and the criterion of violent behavior are: improving the validity of clinical risk assessment, improving the effectiveness of clinical risk management, and providing information useful to reforming mental health law and policy.

If our efforts in establishing robust relationships between cue or predictor variables and the criterion variable of violent behavior (C) were successful, future research could address methods for training clinicians in the use of these cues (A), with the result that the validity of clinical risk assessments and the effectiveness of risk management (B) would be improved. If we found that some cues currently used to predict violent behavior were not, in fact, associated with violence, or were associated with only a certain type of violence, or that other cues not now used to predict violence were actually quite predictive, this might have implications for changes in mental health policy. For example, statutes could be written to provide extra treatment resources to "high-risk" groups (as California has done for some released mentally disordered groups). Or perhaps outpatient commitment, if it were to be imposed on the basis of dangerousness to others, might be limited to groups for whom lack of compliance with medication was a key predictor of violence.

(5) The cues whose association with violence we plan to investigate are intended to be both a reasonably comprehensive set of the cues that we believe actually anticipate violence among mental patients and a reasonably feasible set to measure in actual clinical practice.

One of the central problems we identified with existing risk research was that the research used what we called "impoverished predictor variables." Each investigation tended to study only one of a few things (e.g., diagnosis, or symptom severity scores, or past history). We wanted to combine these various risk factors, and others, in a single comprehensive study, both to compare predictive value and to investigate interactions. We also wanted the ultimate set of predictors that emerged from the research to be easily "transported" into actual clinical practice. For example, we had Robert Hare develop a brief clinical version of his 3-hour Psychopathy Checklist (PCL), knowing that clinicians in practice would be unlikely to use the full PCL. Our goal is that the set of predictors we ultimately arrive at—hopefully a small subset of the cues we are investigating—will be useful in actual clinical practice. Also, we wished to employ factors that clinicians seemed to hold in high regard for determining risk of violence. Were these to be shown to have little relationship to subsequent violence, another set of implications for clinical practice would be clear.

It should be evident that we have made trade-offs between "breadth" and "depth." If we did not care about being reasonably comprehensive, we could focus more in depth on a much more limited set of predictors. If we just wanted to study delusions and violence, for example, we could ask about even very rare delusions, and use several complementary measurement instruments. But we have opted for reasonable comprehensiveness—touching a number of bases—rather than exhaustive attention to any one predictor.

(6) We have selected the cues we will investigate based upon three criteria: (a) associations with violence uncovered in prior research, (b) associations with violence commonly held by experienced clinicians, and (c) associations with violence hypothesized by "minitheories" of violence or of mental disorder.

We are aware of the way that textbooks say variable selection is supposed to be done: by deductions from a fully articulated and validated (big "T") Theory. We are also aware that no such Theory of violence or of mental disorder exists. Nor is it plausible to hope that we will produce a grand Theory in the near future. Therefore, we took a more eclectic and heuristic approach to variable selection. We looked at cues that had been validated as predictors in the existing research literature (e.g., work variables). We looked at factors mentioned in the clinical literature or that emerged from our own clinical experiences as predictive of violence (e.g., delusions). And we looked at those "minitheories" of aggression and violence that exist, and sought cues there (e.g., anger, psychopathy). Adequate measures seemed to exist for some of these cues (e.g., stress). For other cues, we developed our own measures (e.g., Network member Thomas Grisso developed a measure of violent fantasies). And for still other cues we contracted and collaborated with leading figures in several fields to develop new measures, or to adapt existing measures, for the purposes of our research (see above).

(7) Our chosen set of cues fall into four generic "domains": (a) dispositional cues, (b) historical cues, (c) contextual cues, and (d) clinical cues.

A listing of our current set of cues is contained in Table 3.1. One domain of our variables can be thought of as "dispositional." This would refer, for

TABLE 3.1 Cue Domains in the MacArthur Risk Assessment Study

I. Dispositional cues	C. History of crime and violence
A. Demographic	1. Arrests
1. Age	2. Incarcerations
2. Gender	3. Self-reported violence
3. Race	4. Violence toward self
4. Social class	III. Contextual cues
B. Personality	A. Perceived stress
1. Personality style	B. Social support
2. Anger	1. Living arrangements
3. Impulsiveness	2. Activities of daily living
4. Psychopathy	3. Perceived support
C. Cognitive	4. Social networks
1. IQ	C. Means for violence (e.g., guns)
2. Neurological impairment	IV. Clinical cues
II. Historical cues	A. Axis I diagnosis
A. Social history	B. Symptoms
1. Family history	1. Delusions
(a) Child rearing	2. Hallucinations
(b) Child abuse	3. Symptom severity
(c) Family deviance	4. Violent fantasies
2. Work history	C. Axis II diagnosis
(a) Employment	D. Functioning
(b) Job perceptions	E. Substance abuse
3. Educational history	1. Alcohol
B. Mental hospitalization history	2. Other drugs
1. Prior hospitalizations	
2. Treatment compliance	

example, to the demographic factors of age, race, gender, and social class, as well as to personality variables (e.g., anger control and psychopathy) and neurological variables (e.g., head injury).

A second domain can be thought of as "historical." This would include significant events that have been experienced by our subjects in the past, for example, family history, work history, mental hospitalization history, history of violence, and criminal/juvenile justice history.

A third domain can be thought of as "contextual." This would refer to the indices of current social supports, social networks, and stress, as well as the presence of weapons in the environment.

A fourth and final domain can be thought of as "clinical." This would include types and symptoms of mental disorder, personality disorder, drug and alcohol abuse, and level of functioning.

This scheme is clearly not without its problems. For example, "anger control" and "psychopathy" are considered as "dispositional" variables. If one believed that these factors were more in the nature of "state" than "trait" variables, then they could with equal justification be listed in the "clinical" domain.

However, this scheme has an important virtue: It tracks both the risk assessment and risk management goals of the research. While all four of these domains are relevant to risk assessment, only two of them—the contextual and clinical domains—are relevant to risk management. There is nothing a clinician can do to "manage" the dispositional domain variables. The subject's age, race, gender, and basic personality structure must be taken as given. Likewise, a clinician cannot undo the past. If a patient has a history of being abused as a child, being arrested, being in a mental hospital, or being violent, there is, again, nothing a clinician can do to change this. These two domains are relevant to assessing risk—the existing sociological research would suggest that they are indeed the most important domains for assessing risk. But they are not relevant for managing risk. For this reason, we assess dispositional and historical variables as cues only at discharge and not repeatedly as patients are followed in the community.

The contextual and clinical domains, on the other hand, are relevant not just to assessing risk, but to managing it. They may vary "naturally," that is, independent of clinical intervention. A patient's living arrangements may change. And disorder can be more or less acute at different times. The clinician can take advantage of these "natural" variations in managing risk (e.g., only allow a home visit when the disorder is not acute or when the patient's mother is home). And the clinician can intervene directly to modify these domains (e.g., by providing treatment to reduce symptoms, or a halfway house to augment social supports). Because contextual and clinical variables change both naturally and intentionally, we are assessing them not just at discharge but repeatedly during the following up of patients in the community.

(8) Our chosen criterion variables focus on physical violence to others in the community, measured at two levels of seriousness.

We have chosen to concentrate on physical violence to others, rather than psychological harm or harm to the property of others. We have chosen to emphasize violence in the community after release from the hospital, rather than in-hospital violence. We will gather in-hospital violence data to be used as independent variables for community violence. We plan to disaggregate violence into two levels of seriousness, depending upon whether the victim was injured or a weapon was involved. Thus we define "Level 1" violence as (a) any battery accompanied by an injury, (b) any battery involving a weapon, (c) any imminent threat of battery (i.e., assault) involving a weapon, and (d) any sexual assault. All other batteries come under "Level 2" violence. We do not count verbal arguments or verbal threats without a weapon being present as being "violent."

We will also disaggregate our criterion by the type of violent act (e.g., throwing something, hitting with a fist), and the type of victim (e.g., spouse, child, stranger).

Pilot Community Follow-Up Study

Based on these assumptions, we conducted a pilot study that attempted to overcome the four methodological limitations of existing research described above. To address the cramped range of predictor variables, we administered to short-term civil hospital patients a broad array of assessment instruments. The battery included the Diagnostic Interview Schedule (DIS), the Brief Psychiatric Rating Scale (BPRS), the Global Assessment of Functioning Scale (GAF), the Personal Ideation Inventory (PII), which was used while the MADS was under development, and an exhaustive interview schedule that tapped psychiatric, criminal justice, family and employment history, alcohol and drug use, child abuse history, violent fantasies, access to weapons, and a large number of other "risk markers."

To address the weak criterion variables in prior research, we measured violent behavior in the community: (a) by record reviews of all arrests and rehospitalizations; (b) by comprehensive face-to-face interviews with each subject at 2-month intervals for up to 6 months after release from the hospital; and (c) by parallel face-to-face interviews with a collateral of each subject whom the subject reported was in the best position to know about the subject's behavior (e.g., a spouse, a parent), also for up to 6 months.

To correct for the restricted samples, we chose our subjects from consecutive admissions of both male and female voluntary and involuntary patients, between the ages of 18 and 64, unscreened for diagnosis (except to exclude a primary diagnosis of mental retardation).

Finally, to avoid the existing condition of producing results that are specific to a single site, three sites were involved in the study: (a) the Western Psychiatric Institute and Clinic (WPIC) at the University of Pittsburgh; (b) Worcester [MA] State Hospital (WSH); and (c) the Western Missouri Mental Health Center in Kansas City (WMMHC).

The pilot focused on both logistical and substantive questions. The logistical questions centered on our ability to: (a) recruit subjects at the proper pace and obtain their informed consent; (b) successfully complete the very lengthy initial battery; and (c) locate and interview subjects for follow-up in the community. The substantive questions focused on three major issues: (a) Was there sufficient frequency of violence to provide a dependent variable for the full-scale study? (b) Would the frequency of violence among women warrant their inclusion? and (c) Would the frequency of violence warrant the inclusion of all persons over the age of 18?

A total of 169 subjects completed the initial battery in the pilot study. The initial interview took an average of 4 hours to complete. Of these 169 subjects, 146 had at least one follow-up interview in the community where data on self-reported violence in the 2 months since hospital discharge (or since the prior community interview), treatment compliance, and remeasures of the state variables were obtained. One site (WPIC) did one 2-month follow-up interview. Another site (WSH) did two 2-month follow-ups, and the third site (WMMHC) did three 2-month follow-ups.

The following shows the key data for each of the logistical and substantive questions that we addressed in the pilot and the conclusions we drew from these data in regard to the final design for their full-scale study.

Subject Recruitment

Of the 393 patients sampled, 274 were approached to consent to participate. Of these, 200 (73.0%) agreed to participate in the pilot study. Of those who agreed, 31 dropped out either prior to beginning or during the initial interview. This yielded our final sample of 169 persons (see Table 3.2). The most common reason for noninclusion among the 193 who were not included was patient refusal (38.3%). Other reasons for noninclusion in the pilot study were clinician refusal or delay (28.0%), and discharge before enrolled (15.5%). The vast majority of the patients who did refuse either gave no reason for refusal or simply said that they were uninterested (21.6% and 32.4%, respectively), but some cited privacy (16.2%) or fear of subpoena (8.1%) as concerns. Only 7 persons felt (at the time of consent) that the interview was going to be too long. The only difference between the original sample ($N = 393$) and the final sample ($N = 169$) was that the males were more likely to be enrolled (55.8%) than females (44.8%).

The demographic characteristics of the available pool of subjects, as well as those completing an initial interview, varied greatly by site. The sampling strategy employed for the pilot study was to take a systematic sample using every nth eligible admission to the acute care units selected. This resulted in a sample that was disproportionately white at two sites, slightly more male at the third site, and with different distributions of legal status and diagnosis distributions across all three sites. Our final sample

TABLE 3.2 MacArthur Risk Assessment Pilot Study Sample

Sites	Initial Sample	Initial Battery Completed	Follow-Up 1 Completed	Follow-Up 2 Completed	Follow-Up 3 Completed	At Least One Follow-Up
Kansas City	118	80	63	65	58	70
Worcester	175	49	39	36	NA	40
Pittsburgh	100	40	36	NA	NA	36
Total	393	169	138	101	58	146

was disproportionately male in Kansas City (67.5%) as compared with our other two sites, Worcester and Pittsburgh, where males comprised roughly half of the sample (53.1% and 50.0%, respectively). The Worcester site was almost entirely white (91.8 %) as compared to the other two sites (Kansas City had 66.3% white subjects with random sampling and Pittsburgh had 62.5% white subjects after oversampling for blacks). These results clearly demonstrated that we needed to refine our sampling approach for the full-scale study. Our current thinking for that study is to use a computer-generated stratified sampling design, stratifying on gender, race, and age and targeting those hard-to-enroll cases (e.g., blacks in Worcester). This will eliminate some of the most obvious site differences, allowing us to combine the data across sites. By using quota sampling, we will make these descriptors close to statistically independent for analysis purposes, enabling us to test for the relationship of violence and other variables of interest (e.g., delusions, anger) beyond just patient descriptors listed above.

Initial Instrument Battery

Generally, the instruments contained in the initial battery were relatively easy to administer, but the total length of the interview session was unacceptably long. The time required to complete the hospital interview ranged from 2 to 10 hours over one to five interview sessions. Clearly, the patients became fatigued and distracted by the length of the interview. Also, it was difficult to identify large time blocks within the active hospital routines within which the initial battery could be completed.

The DIS was the most time consuming and most difficult instrument for the patients to complete, especially those who had multiple diagnoses or who were very symptomatic. Also, as we rethought why we were using the DIS, we recognized that it was mainly to establish an independent DSM-III-R diagnosis. The particular symptoms in which we were interested were being measured by other instruments so that the necessity of the entire DIS was reduced. As a result, we have decided to pare down the initial battery, eliminating the DIS and shortening the other instruments wherever possible. We will keep an instrument to establish an independent DSM-III-R diagnosis. It will probably be the DSM-III-R checklist, which will be completed by a person with substantial clinical training and be less tedious for the patient. Ideally, the initial battery in the full-scale study will require one clinical session for the diagnosis instrument and other symptom inventories (delusions, hallucinations, BPRS, GAF, neurology screen) and one session with the community interviewer to complete the remainder of the initial battery. This will involve a total of two sessions of 1½ to 2 hours each in length.

Locating Subjects in the Community

The following-up of subjects in the community at 2-month intervals after discharge from the hospital proved to be no more difficult than we had anticipated, given the prior experience in doing community follow-ups by the study teams at two of the sites (Kansas City and Pittsburgh). While our subjects were often very difficult to locate, our staff were equally resourceful in finding them. Our follow-up results reflect their efforts. Across the three sites, we have at least one follow-up on 146 of the 169 patients who completed the initial interview (86.4%). The major reason for missed follow-ups was that the subject could not be located. Very few subjects were lost because of patient refusal to participate in the follow-up interviews. We also found that once we had located a patient for the first community interview, our subsequent follow-up rate was even higher (more than 90%).

Our pilot study results strongly suggest that these persistently mentally ill persons can be successfully located and interviewed at 2- to 3-month intervals in the community. Our results also demonstrate just how important the first contact in the community is to control attrition. This suggests that in the full-scale study we need to exert a greater effort to locate the subjects initially after discharge by collecting more information before they leave the hospital about where they will go and who will know where they are, as well as allotting more staff time for locating subjects to minimize subject attrition.

Frequency of Reported Violence

Our primary substantive question was simply, would we have something to study? Prior research on community assaultiveness of cross sections of mentally disordered persons had generally found that between 2% and 5%

had records of some type of arrests for violent crimes (Hiday, 1991; Steadman, Cocozza, & Melick, 1978). Klassen and O'Connor (1988) had studied persons with prior records of violence upon presentation to a community mental health center and they found 19% had subsequent arrests for violence. Given that our subjects were a random cross section of acute inpatients not screened for prior violence, what would their self-reports produce? The results are seen in Table 3.3. Across all three sites for up to three follow-up interviews in the community, 26.7% reported at least one violent incident. In the site where all three follow-ups were attempted, 32.7% of the subjects reported at least one violent incident. Also, when official records, which have not yet been analyzed, are added to self-reports, the rates may be even higher.

In addition to the follow-up violence, of the 169 subjects who completed the initial battery, 63 (37.3%) reported an average of five incidents each in the 2 months prior to their target admission. Our conclusion from these data was that, indeed, we did have a dependent variable to study. Further, as we will see below, by stratifying our sample somewhat, we expect the rate of reported violence to increase even further.

Violence by Women

Because so much of the research on violence is done in criminal justice settings, the data on women and violence, outside of that on domestic violence, are sparse. Even studies on mentally disordered persons who have arrest rates as a dependent variable have tended to concentrate on male subjects (e.g., Klassen & O'Connor, 1988). Accordingly, the self-reports from our pilot data in which 40.8% of the subjects were women were crucial in determining the most appropriate sample for the full-scale study.

The distributions of reported violence by sex, race, and age are reported in Table 3.4. In fact, a higher proportion of women than men (32.8% vs. 22.4%) reported at least one violent incident in the community after their hospitalizations. A somewhat smaller proportion of women than men reported violence in the 2 months prior to their target admission (34.8% vs. 39.0%). Clearly, then, there is every reason to include women as well as men in the larger study.

Violence by Age

The basic question about the desirability of stratifying the sample for the full-scale study was whether to exclude persons over certain ages because of the low rates of violence. From a cost-effectiveness standpoint, if violence in any subgroup is very infrequent, there will be too few

TABLE 3.3 Reported Violence by Site and Instrument Administration*

	Initial Battery (prior)			Follow-Up 1			Follow-Up 2			Follow-Up 3			All Follow-Ups		
	People		Incidents	People		Incidents	People		Incidents	People		Incidents	People		Incidents
	#	%	#	#	%	#	#	%	#	#	%	#	#	%	#
Kansas City	37	46.3	276	11	17.2	33	10	15.4	14	6	10.3	9	23	32.9	56
Worcester	14	28.6	20	6	15.4	8	6	16.7	14	NA	NA	NA	11	27.5	22
Pittsburgh	12	30.0	97	5	13.9	15	NA	NA	NA	NA	NA	NA	5	13.9	15
Total	63	37.3	393	22	15.8	56	16	15.8	28	6	10.3	9	39	26.7	93

NOTE: *Violence includes hitting with hand/fist, threatening with a weapon, or using a weapon.

TABLE 3.4 Initial and Follow-Up Violence by Demographic Characteristics by Site

| | All Sites | | | | Kansas City | | | | Worcester | | | | Pittsburgh | | | |
| | Initial Violence | | Follow-Up Violence | | Initial Violence | | Follow-Up Violence | | Initial Violence | | Follow-Up Violence | | Initial Violence | | Follow-Up Violence | |
	#	%	#	%	#	%	#	%	#	%	#	%	#	%	#	%
Sex																
Male	39	39.0	19	22.4	25	46.3	12	26.7	8	30.8	6	28.6	6	30.0	1	5.3
Female	24	34.8	20	32.8	12	46.2	11	44.0	6	26.1	5	26.3	6	30.0	4	23.5
Race																
White	43	35.0	27	25.5	24	45.3	15	31.9	13	28.9	10	27.0	6	24.0	2	9.1
Black	16	42.1	9	26.5	10	45.5	6	31.6	0	0.0	0	0.0	6	40.0	3	21.4
Other	4	50.0	3	50.0	3	60.0	2	50.0	1	33.3	1	50.0	0	0.0	0	0.0
Legal status																
Voluntary	46	36.5	28	25.2	30	44.1	20	33.3	6	22.2	3	12.5	10	32.3	5	18.5
Involuntary	17	39.5	11	31.4	7	58.3	3	30.0	8	36.4	8	50.0	2	22.2	0	0.0
Age																
Under 25	17	45.9	11	37.9	12	63.2	8	53.3	3	33.3	2	28.6	2	22.2	1	14.3
25-40	38	39.2	25	29.4	21	42.9	15	34.9	9	31.0	7	29.2	8	42.1	3	16.7
Over 40	8	22.9	3	9.4	4	33.3	0	0.0	2	18.2	2	22.2	2	16.7	1	9.1

incidents or persons in even a medium-sized sample to study the phenomenon of interest.

As is evident in Table 3.4, the proportion of the pilot subjects who reported any violent incident either in the 2 months prior to the target admission or in any of the follow-up community interviews decreased as age increased. In the subjects over the age of 40, the proportions with reported violence were about half of those of persons aged 25 to 40 (22.9% vs. 39.2% prior to admissions and 9.4% vs. 29.4% in the community after release). The 25-40 age group was only slightly lower than the 18-25 age group. Accordingly, we will include persons between 18 and 40 years of age in the final sample, which is expected to produce a frequency of violence sufficient to ensure an adequate number of cases for statistical analysis.

Full-Scale Study

Based on the results of our pilot study and further discussion among the study group, we have made a number of decisions that have shaped the design of the full-scale study scheduled for the spring of 1992. Our decisions and their implications for the design of this study are discussed below.

(1) Our criterion variables will be measured by (a) official arrest and mental hospital records, (b) subject self-reports, and (c) collateral reports obtained every 2 or 3 months by interviewing the subject in the community five times over a one-year period after discharge from the target hospitalization.

The limitations of relying on official records (e.g., arrest) are well known. Self-report, of course, is not unproblematic, but is recognized in the field as vastly superior to official records. For the fullest reporting, however, we will also obtain arrest records, outpatient treatment records, and rehospitalization admission notes.

There is no definitive basis for selecting the optimum length of follow-up interviews. Ultimately, duration of follow-up is dictated by both the research questions and the resources available to support the research. Given that persons who are treated on the inpatient acute treatment units from which our subjects are recruited tend to cycle in and out of hospitals, over any length of time they will have periods of high and low functioning that may or may not relate to occurrences of violence. We need to have as many levels of functioning as possible to test for these factors. Given that almost all of the subjects are treated with neuroleptics, some effects of treatment linger even if the patient decides to stop taking medication after release. While clinicians focus on decisions about dangerousness that may relate to the 14- or 30-day periods of time specified in commitment statutes, ours is not a study of treatment efficacy or of clinical decision making. Were it about either of these, a 60- or 90-day follow-up might be suggested since so many patients become noncompliant (meaning treatment ceases) or since clinicians often focus their risk assessments on fairly immediate time frames. We are studying the relationships, separately and in interaction, of numerous variables with violence. Since many of our variables are state measures, they ebb and flow. This concern would suggest a longer follow-up period. Balancing a desire for a longer follow-up with the time and support available, we settled on a one-year follow-up period.

The frequency of contact with our subjects over the year was another decision with no clear-cut answer. In the pilot study, we used 2 months, since it had worked well in the prior study by Network member Edward P. Mulvey, and his colleague, Charles Lidz. That had been sufficiently frequent to find the subjects and have them remember that they had agreed to participate in the research. It also seemed to be a time span that they could recall violent incidents that had occurred with apparent accuracy and detail.

As a substudy at one pilot site, after two 2-month interviews, we assigned one set of subjects ($n = 20$) to a 1-1-1-3-month interview schedule and another set ($n = 19$) on a 3-1-1-1-month schedule. Our questions centered both on the subjects' tolerance for more frequent contacts and the improvement or diminution of recall over 1- or 3-month periods. Because of the small number of subjects in this substudy, meaningful statistical analyses were impossible. We drew our conclusions mainly on the impressions of the field staff.

The field staff found the subjects very intolerant of the 1-month interviews, especially because we used telephone calls at 2-week intervals to stay in contact. Also, since the core of the interview about the frequency and details of violent incidents was the same at every administration, we became concerned that a response set would develop. That response set might be either the subjects making up incidents so they had something to tell us or, reciprocally, underreporting incidents because they would know if they reported a violent incident, an additional set of questions would ensue and extend the interview. Accordingly, we decided against 1-month interviews.

The advisability of the 3-month interval was much less clear. The field staff had somewhat less confidence than with the 2-month interval that the subjects could clearly recall exactly when the prior interview had been done and, therefore, what the relevant reporting period was. Yet, the amount and types of violence seemed to be fairly similar to what was generated with 2-month intervals, particularly for the more serious incidents. Three months was attractive logistically since it would reduce the number of community follow-ups from six to four, which, in turn, would permit an increase in the size of the sample, increasing the statistical power of the study and better protecting against attrition compromising statistical analyses. To best balance these competing interests we decided to do five follow-up interviews over one year after the subject's hospital discharge.

(2) We will use both experienced clinicians and highly trained community interviewers to administer our research measures.

Our plan is to have experienced clinicians confirm the chart diagnosis using the DSM-III-R Checklist and to administer those instruments requiring the greatest clinical expertise (e.g., a modification of the MADS). Highly trained community interviewers will administer the remaining instruments (e.g., the self-report measures of anger control and impulsivity). The community interviewers will listen to an audiotape of the clinician interview done as part of the initial battery, so that they will be prepared to readminister selected clinical variables (e.g., the BPRS, the MADS) in the community during the follow-up interviews.

(3) Our subjects will be (a) males and females, (b) between the ages of 18 and 40, (c) of white, African-American, or Hispanic race/ethnicity, (d) able to speak English, (e) local residents, (f) of both voluntary and involuntary admission status, (g) unscreened for prior or presenting violence, and (h) excluding only those whose primary diagnosis is mental retardation.

The two principles that guided our inclusion and exclusion criteria are the desire to have as representative a sample of mental patients as possible, and the necessity that the chosen sample have a sufficiently high base rate of violence during the follow-up to permit data analysis. Our choice of subjects is a straightforward attempt to balance these two principles. In our pilot study, females had rates of violence comparable to males, and persons over 40 had much lower rates than persons under 40. Therefore, females were "in" and people over 40 were "out." Since race/ethnicity could be an important factor in the research, we wished to study as many racial/ethnic groupings as possible. But since the presence of groups other than whites, African-Americans, and Hispanics—for example, Asian-Americans—in the hospitals from which we are gathering our data is very small, any data we obtained would be uninterpretable (and, therefore, a waste of resources to gather). As it is, we do not expect that the Hispanic sample will be large enough to provide a sufficient amount of follow-up violence for independent analysis. But we will at least be able to compare Hispanics and non-Hispanics on their scores on the initial in-hospital instrument. Eventually, it could be possible to prepare a Spanish-language version of our instruments. But this is clearly premature, given the enormous cost that would be involved.

Screening for prior violence in the admission incident would clearly raise the base rate of follow-up violence. But since to do so would mean that we would miss all the follow-up violence committed by people *without* prior or presenting violence, we have decided not to do so. Also, from a policy standpoint, we want to have as typical a range of patients as actually presents for inpatient admission and for whom clinical risk assessments are regularly demanded.

(4) We plan on a total sample size of approximately 1,000 patients, selected from three civil mental hospitals: the Western Psychiatric Institute and Clinic in Pittsburgh, the Worcester (MA) State Hospital, and the Western Missouri Mental Health Center in Kansas City.

Given the level of follow-up violence expected, the number of factors we wished to control for, and the problem of subject attrition over time, we concluded that this sample size was necessary to allow meaningful analysis of our data. Our sites represent the range of settings currently providing public and private inpatient mental health care in the United States: a university-based medical center, a state mental hospital, and a metropolitan community mental health center. While the use of multiple sites makes special demands for comparability in order to pool the data, we feel we can meet this demand and the research will be substantially more generalizable as a result.

Conclusions

It can be seen from Table 3.1 that we are exploring a rich array of dispositional, historical, and clinical cues. The one domain that has been most difficult to capture is the "contextual" one. In future studies, we hope to develop instruments to better measure the "situational" and "interactional" context within which violence occurs.

One step we will be taking in these regards emerges from our pilot data. In those interviews, when violent incidents were reported, we obtained semistructured narratives of what happened. Using an approach first developed for these types of interviews by Felson and Steadman (1983) and adapted by Mulvey and Lidz in their work discussed above, we recorded subjects' descriptions of who did what to whom in what order during the violent incidents they mentioned. We had some specific points of interest such as the content of the dispute, the number and relationships of people present, and alcohol and drug use by the subject and other participant. However, we were most interested in figuring out meaningful sequences of behavioral acts and what factors might be associated with escalation to the point of violence, rather than the dispute being truncated prior to the occurrence of violence.

Data such as these are hard to quantify in meaningful ways. Also, the type of research design to test such factors fully is quite different from that which we felt best tested the other types of risk markers we have been discussing here. Accordingly, while we forge ahead with the full-scale study of the more clinically based risk markers we have described here, we will also be transcribing our pilot data, developing appropriate coding schemes, and more fully elaborating the theoretical underpinnings for a situational-contextual approach to understanding violence. The current study promises rich returns, but, even as ambitious as it is, there remain other complementary approaches to be considered. It is only by such interdisciplinary, long-term, incremental research that we can hope to develop research that impacts on theory, policy, and practice. Such goals are daunting, but they represent the intentions of our research group.

Note

1. The members are: John Monahan, Director,* the Honorable Shirley S. Abrahamson, Paul S. Appelbaum, M.D.,* Richard J. Bonnie, LL.B., Thomas Grisso, Ph.D.,* Pamela S. Hyde, J.D., Stephen J. Morse, J.D., Ph.D., Edward P. Mulvey, Ph.D.,* Loren Roth, M.D.,* Paul Slovic, Ph.D., Henry J. Steadman, Ph.D.,* and David B. Wexler, J.D. The members of the Risk Working Group are indicated with an asterisk.

References

Basaglia, F. (1980). Problems of law and psychiatry: The Italian experience. *International Journal of Law and Psychiatry, 3,* 17-37.

Brunswick, E. (1956). *Perception and the representative design of psychological experiments.* Berkeley: University of California Press.

Cocozza, J. J., & Steadman, H. J. (1978). Prediction in psychiatry: An example of misplaced confidence in experts. *Social Problems, 25,* 265-276.

Curran, W. J. (1978). Comparative analysis of mental health legislation in forty-three countries: A discussion of historical trends. *International Journal of Law and Psychiatry, 1,* 79-92.

Felson, R. B., & Steadman, H. J. (1983). Situational factors in disputes leading to criminal violence. *Criminology, 21,* 59-74.

Grisso, T., Tomkins, A., & Casey, P. (1988). Psychosocial concepts in juvenile law. *Law and Human Behavior, 12*, 403-437.

Hiday, V. A. (1991). Arrest and incarceration of civil commitment candidates. *Hospital and Community Psychiatry, 42*, 729-734.

Klassen, D., & O'Connor, W. A. (1988). A prospective study of predictors of violence in adult mental health admissions. *Law and Human Behavior, 12*, 143-158.

Link, B. G., & Cullen, F. T. (1986). Contact with the mentally ill and perceptions of how dangerous they are. *Journal of Health and Social Behavior, 27*, 289-303.

Mercy, J. A., & O'Carroll, P. W. (1988). New directions in violence prediction: The public health arena. *Violence and Victims, 3*(4), 285-301.

Monahan, J. (1988). Risk assessment of violence among the mentally disordered: Generating useful knowledge. *International Journal of Law and Psychiatry, 11*, 249-257.

Monahan, J., & Shah, S. A. (1989). Dangerousness and commitment of the mentally disordered in the United States. *Schizophrenia Bulletin, 15*(4), 541-553.

Mulvey, E. P., & Lidz, C. (1988). *What clinicians talk about when assessing dangerousness.* Paper presented at the Meeting of American Psychology Law Society, Division 41, Miami, Fl.

New York Academy of Medicine. (1986). *Homicide: The Public Health Perspective, 62*(5), 373-624.

Shah, S. A. (1978). Dangerousness: A paradigm for exploring some issues in law and psychology. *American Psychologist,* (March), 224-238.

Soothill, K. L., Harding, T. W., Adserballe, H., Berheim, J., Erne, S., Magdi, S., Panpreecha, C., & Reinhold, F. (1981). Compulsory admissions to mental hospitals in six countries. *International Journal of Law and Psychiatry, 4*, 327-344.

Steadman, H. J. (1973). Some evidence on the inadequacy of the concept and determination of dangerousness in psychiatry and law. *Journal of Psychiatry and Law, 1*, 409-426.

Steadman, H. J., & Cocozza, J. J. (1979). The dangerousness standard and psychiatry: A cross national issue in the social control of the mentally ill. *Sociology and Social Research, 63*, 649-670.

Steadman, H. J., Cocozza, J. J., & Melick, M. E. (1978). Explaining the increased arrest rate among mental patients: The changing clientele of state hospitals. *American Journal of Psychiatry, 135*, 816-820.

Steadman, H. J., & Morrissey, J. P. (1981). The statistical prediction of violent behavior: Measuring the costs of a public protectionist versus a civil libertarian model. *Law and Human Behavior, 5*, 263-274.

U.S. Department of Health and Human Services. (1991). *Healthy people 2000: National health promotion and disease prevention objectives.* Washington, DC: Government Printing Office.

4

Schizophrenia and Crime:
Distinctive Patterns in Association

PAMELA J. TAYLOR

Background

Perhaps it is a tribute to the small contribution that schizophrenia makes to officially recognized crime that, in spite of the fact that there is a substantial literature on "mental disorder" and crime, there is relatively little work focusing exclusively on schizophrenia itself, or even on the rather wider concept of psychosis. The psychoses loom large in any general or forensic psychiatric practice, and most of the relevant research has been done by psychiatrists or psychologists. So why this lack of focus? Continuing diagnostic "naïveté," confusion between legal and medical classification systems, and muddled thinking about responsibility are most likely to have limited the recognition and understanding of a modest but specific relationship between schizophrenia, or the psychoses and crime.

There is now considerable sophistication in delineating the details of clinical presentation of psychotic disorders, and established reliability in doing so. The terms *schizophrenia* and *affective psychosis* are nevertheless, even now, less diagnostic statements than operational definitions. Diagnosis should, however, be more than a descriptive statement. It implies information about cause, course, prognosis, and effective treatment for a disorder so labeled. A strong family history of a particular pattern of disorder can elevate the definitive description to diagnostic

AUTHOR'S NOTE: The study from which data for this chapter were drawn was supported by the Medical Research Council. I am extremely grateful to Professor John Gunn, without whom the study would not have been possible, to Dr. Graham Robertson for tireless statistical advice, and to Mrs. Carol Double for patience and precision in preparing the manuscript.

63

status, with implications for both etiology and prognosis. It is probably helpful to demarcate the functional psychoses from other psychiatric disorders, but more often than not, the most precise adherence to a disease classification system alone to distinguish between the various forms of the functional psychoses has yielded little to elucidate further personal etiology or even treatment or prognosis. Some representative examples from the literature illustrate this. The relapse rate for those with depressive psychosis in Copeland's (1983) study was remarkably similar to that for the women with schizophrenia, and only slightly better than that for the men as in the study by Watt, Katz, and Shepherd (1983), while among patients with a schizoaffective disorder, only those with "schizomania" were distinguished, seeming to fare better than others with a functional psychosis (Brockington, Kendell, & Wainwright, 1980; Brockington, Wainwright, & Kendell, 1980). Within the very broad group of disorders that may be called schizophrenia, Hawk, Carpenter, and Strauss (1975) confirmed little advantage for laboring to define subtypes, while Brockington, Kendell, and Leff (1978), applying 10 widely accepted but differing operational definitions of schizophrenia to 119 patients, found that the number who qualified as having schizophrenia varied from 3 to 45, depending on the definition used. Even the ICD-9 thrust that personality disturbance (described in DSM-III-R as a state "below highest level previously achieved" in more than one area of functioning) is a core disturbance in schizophrenia, but unworthy of mention in the context of affective psychosis, is probably not a practical distinction.

It is true that there may be a tautological approach to the definition of chronic schizophrenia as a state of chronic disability in conjunction with present or past positive symptoms; further, there is evidence that at least where offenders and/or poor treatment compliers are concerned, clinicians tend to emphasize the personality disorder to the exclusion of recognition of the illness. Coid (1988) found that clinicians in one health region had labeled a number of chronic psychotic men as being untreatable psychopaths, probably as a means of avoiding the burden of their care. People with affective psychoses have not, however, been immune to similar problems. Thorneloe and Crews (1981), for example, described six patients with manic-depressive illness, manic type, who had been diagnosed also as having a personality disorder, while Akiskal, Djenderadjian, and Rosenthal (1977) noted that 66% of a series of patients with cyclothymic disorder, not all amounting to psychosis, had previously been diagnosed as hysterics or sociopaths.

The principal justification for considering schizophrenia per se in relation to crime, rather than psychosis more generally, may in itself be circular, in that people who have acquired a label of schizophrenia appear more frequently in criminal or violent populations than do people with affective or, indeed, organic psychoses (e.g., among offenders: Häfner & Böker, 1973/1982; Taylor & Gunn 1984a; among hospital samples: Ekblom, 1970; Sosowsky, 1978). The important community survey of Swanson, Holzer, Ganju, and Jono (1990) differs partly in showing that those with affective disorders, including manic-depressive illness, did not have lower rates of assaultive behavior than those with other disorders, although those with manic depression may have shown a more restricted and less dangerous pattern of such behavior than the others in that all such behavior was domestic and none of them reported using a weapon. For homicide, at the most serious end of the spectrum, and indeed the form of violence probably calculated with most reliability and validity, people with schizophrenia have been shown as very much more likely to be implicated than people with an affective psychosis (Häfner & Böker, 1973/1982; Taylor & Gunn, 1984a). Further, although the risk that a person with schizophrenia will kill someone else remains tiny (Häfner and Böker estimated it to be 0.05%), he or she is likely to be overrepresented in a group of those who have committed homicide compared with the general population (Taylor & Gunn, 1984a; Wilcox, 1985).

The evaluation of possible associations between illness and crime is rendered more complex by the fact that not only is illness thought to affect responsibility for actions, but allowance may be made for this in law. Even in those countries more attached to the insanity defense than the United Kingdom, however, the matter of responsibility is rarely formally tested. Decisions to direct a particular individual into the health care or criminal justice systems are often arbitrary and at best based on very practical considerations, like places available or the doctor on duty on a particular day. This creates havoc for a researcher's sampling.

Monahan and Steadman (1983) emphasized the differences between "true" rates of mental disorder and of crime and their "treated" rates, that is, the rate at which antisocial activity—or mental disorder—really occurs, compared with that at which it is formally recorded and dealt with accordingly. Psychotic offenders undoubtedly appear in both health and criminal systems; how far exclusively in one or the other remains uncertain. Providing that a crime is substantial—in particular, homicide—it is likely to be recorded as a crime regardless of the state of health of the person committing it, but lesser crimes have lower clear-up rates. In 1 year in London, for example (Commissioner of Police of the Metropolis, 1983), the clear-up rate for notified offenses was only one in seven overall, varying from 50% for assault, to 12% for criminal damage, and less than 10% for burglary. It is very unclear whether the dark figure of unrecorded crime favors the relatively healthy or the psychotic in terms of identification.

Many of the more healthy people may be better able than those with psychosis to conceal their offending behavior. Robertson (1988) showed that among those arrested for a crime and remanded in custody, only 45% of the normal men had been arrested by a uniformed police officer, implying that some detective work had been necessary for the rest, but 90% of the ill offenders were arrested by uniformed police, 86% of them on the day of the offense, and 75% at the scene of the crime. Just one third of the normal group was arrested so quickly. Two thirds of the offenses committed by people with schizophrenia and nearly three-quarters of those committed by people with an affective psychosis were witnessed compared with less than a third of those committed by the normal group. Often, however, even violent behavior on the part of the mentally ill results in direct admission to hospital rather than the criminal justice system. Lagos, Perlmutter, and Saexinger (1977), for example, found that in one U.S. hospital, although 18% of a series of patients had been admitted following actual violence and a further 18% after threatened violence, only 1% had been arrested, suggesting that many were protected from reaching criminal statistics by virtue of their state of health. In a series of 275 people with a first episode of schizophrenia (Johnstone, Crow, Johnson, & MacMillan, 1986), 55 (20%) had been identified through police contacts and 52 had behaved in a way threatening to the life of others, but only 12 passed through the criminal justice system and sustained a conviction.

The problems generated by origin of sample are likely not only to affect attempts to estimate the frequency of association among schizophrenia, other psychoses, and crime, but also the nature of any link. Wessely and Taylor (1991) give the most recent account of the state of the art. In a hospital setting, for example, it is likely that there will be emphasis on the role of symptomatology, but in a penal setting symptoms may be missed altogether, let alone reliably evaluated with respect to their consequences. Actions by people with a partially treated psychosis in a hospital setting may well be more powerfully influenced by the petty restrictions of an institutional environment than are the actions by those with a wholly untreated disorder but minimal external limits on their behavior.

Brixton Prison, still the largest remand (pretrial/presentence) prison in Europe, was chosen to study the nature of any relationship between schizophrenia, other psychoses, and crime because of both the range of activities leading to detention and the range of disorder. The majority of people charged with a criminal offense in England are remanded on bail pending trial, but a substantial minority are remanded in custody. At the time of the study, Brixton Prison received all men remanded on a murder charge and the majority of male remands in custody for Greater London and its environs, about one third of the population of England. The sample studied may be representative of nothing other than itself, but given the range of offending behavior encountered and the variety of mental disorders, was thus a more fruitful source for comparison of psychotic and nonpsychotic offending than could be found in a hospital setting alone, an average prison alone, or indeed any context other than a massive community survey. Although detailed diagnostic formulations on the basis of standardized clinical interviews (the Present State Examination, PSE; Wing, Cooper, & Sartorius, 1974) were formulated, most of the overall illness comparisons were between men with a psychotic illness and men without, with more attention being paid to the influence of symptoms than of diagnosis. This was done partly for the reasons given above and partly because so many diagnoses based on present state alone were varied when all possible clinical and social information was available.

Method

Two samples were drawn from the prison: a small group of 203 men who were interviewed and studied in depth, and a much larger group of 1,264 men who were all the men remanded on violence charges *and* all the men who had been admitted to the hospital areas of the prison for every 3rd month of one year. Data for the latter men were collected solely from prison records, mainly to establish a context for the interview study. They are referred to hereafter as "the overview group" (see also Taylor & Gunn, 1984a, 1984b).

The Interviewed Sample

The aim of sampling was to generate equal subgroups of violent normal men and violent and nonviolent men with schizophrenia, together with smaller subgroups of violent and nonviolent men with affective psychoses. The interview group was not a representative sample of the prison population. Two hundred twelve men remanded on violence charges, sent to the hospital wing of the prison, or both, were assured of confidentiality and asked to take part in an interview and to permit supplementary data collection, being told that the aim of the study was to explore the relationship, if any, between mental state and offending and that both sick and healthy men would be interviewed.

Nine men refused to participate. All, according to prison records, were ill, and seven of them psychotic. They were not included further in the study. Over a 20-month period, every 10th man with alleged schizophrenia and approximately one in five with an affective psychosis were interviewed (further details are given in Taylor, 1985). In comparison with the overview group, the interviewed sample included more people who had committed homicide (14% compared with 4%), more people who had schizophrenia (45% compared with 6.5%), more people with an affective psychosis (12% compared with 1.2%), and very substantially fewer with alcohol or drug dependencies. Diagnostic differences were a deliberate bias of sampling. Other key features like age, country of birth, and rates of violent assaults other than homicide were, overall, remarkably similar between the samples.

The Assessment

The assessment combined three approaches to data collection: the psychiatrist's direct observations during the interview, the man's assessment of himself, and the views and facts documented by previous observers. The most important feature of the study—which distinguished it from its predecessors—was the inclusion of direct interviews by researchers, more than half of which were completed within 3 weeks of the offense and 85% within 6 weeks. Recall for both offense and mental state at the time of the offense was thus likely to be at its best and least biased, both for the proximity in time and for the minimal contamination by intervening interviews with lawyers and other medical practitioners. Most men had previously only given a brief statement to the police and to a prison medical officer. The lengthy free and structured interviews are described more fully in Taylor, 1985.

For every man there was some sort of independent data, although its extent varied in some areas with the seriousness of the offense. Police records of the offense were available, for example, for almost all of the serious offenses but few of the trivial ones. Records of previous criminal offenses were available for all but 1% of the men and full previous hospital records were available for all but 8% of those with a previous psychiatric history (independently verified through the National Mental Health Index). In addition, although friends and relatives were rarely approached, social work or probation records were available for many of the men.

Results

One hundred and twenty-one of the 203 interviewed men had a psychotic illness. Ninety of these, taking all possible information into account, were regarded as having schizophrenia, 25 as having an affective psychosis, and 6 as having "other" paranoid psychoses.

TABLE 4.1 Relationship Between Form of Violent Offenses and Psychosis

A. Interviewed Sample of Men Convicted of Inflicting Actual Violence		
	Personal Violence	Property Violence
Nonpsychotic men	49 (80%)	12 (20%)
Psychotic men	35 (48%)	38 (52%)
	$\chi^2 = 13.54$, $df = 1$, $p < .0002$	
B. Overview Sample of Men Convicted of Violent Offenses		
	Personal Violence	Property Violence
Nonpsychotic men	294 (68%)	137 (32%)
Psychotic men	34 (43%)	46 (57%)
	$\chi^2 = 18.30$, $df = 1$, $p < .0001$	

Psychotic and Nonpsychotic Offending Compared

Thirty-nine of the men with a psychosis had committed completely non-violent offenses, although a further 18 had not inflicted any physical harm, engaging in minor sexual misdemeanors or only threatening violence. In this series, the nonpsychotic offenders had, by definition, committed violent offenses, although a few were later convicted of a nonviolent offense or had been reclassified into this group when a research diagnosis of psychosis could not be established. The psychotic/nonpsychotic comparisons for offending in Table 4.1 were made only for offenses involving actual physical violence; subsequent calculations referring to victims (Tables 4.2 to 4.4) were made for all offenses with a clear victim, including the sexual offenses and threats, but excluded property and wholly nonviolent offenses.

Part (a) of Table 4.1 shows that the psychotic men were less likely to engage in personal violence than the nonpsychotic men in the highly selected interview sample. Thirty of the psychotic men engaging in personal violence had schizophrenia compared with 31 of those targeting property. The relative figures for the overview sample (part [b]) are remarkably similar, but these too have to be regarded with caution from the epidemiological point of view since a decision to remand in custody in England has almost as much to do with the likelihood of the alleged offender returning to court as with the seriousness of the offense. The mentally ill are generally seen by the courts as less reliable in this regard—not least because they are more likely to be itinerant (Gibbens, Soothill, & Pope, 1977). This could have partly accounted for the relatively high proportion of property offenders in the psychotic group.

Considerably more detail was available about the violence within the interviewed sample, for which each man was also rated on a 5-point scale

(Gunn & Robertson, 1976) for the seriousness of his index offense. Taking all the men charged with some form of violent offense, the consequences of the violence were undoubtedly more serious within the nonpsychotic than the psychotic group (mean scores 3 and 2.4, respectively, analysis of variance [ANOVA] $F = 9.89, p < .002$). This remained true if analysis were confined to men convicted of at least one offense of personal violence (means 3.2 and 2.7, respectively, $F = 6.05, p < .02$).

Historical information about violence was only reliably available for the interviewed sample. Violence over the whole lifetime, up to but not including the index offense, was considered on a similar 5-point scale. The rating for this was based on all possible information and covered both criminal violence and violence that had not been drawn to the attention of the law. The average rating for the nonpsychotic group (1.76) was not significantly different from that for the psychotic (1.56). Overall, when the data were broken into criminal and noncriminal violence, both were regular features for the psychotic and nonpsychotic alike. About 41% of the nonpsychotic men and 35% of the psychotic men had previous convictions for offenses of violence against others, and nearly a third of both groups for offenses against property. Rather more of the nonpsychotic had violence reported in their history that had not come to the attention of the law (46% compared with 35% of psychotics), but again the difference was not significant. Confining consideration of violence patterns of the 2 years leading up to the index offense similarly yielded no differences.

Although suicide has long since ceased to be a criminal offense, a consideration of the differences in violent behavior between the psychotic and the nonpsychotic would not be complete without a comment about the capacity for self-harm within the groups. Within the overview sample, seven of the men killed themselves in prison before their trial, but much information about possible suicidal histories was missing. Even in the interviewed and heavily researched sample, uncertainty remained for about 10% of the men. Seventy (nearly 40% of the interviewed sample) had previously attempted suicide, some on more than one occasion, but these men were evenly distributed between psychotic and nonpsychotic subgroups. Between 20% and 30% of each group had previously attempted suicide by overdose, while about 14% of each had used other methods. Only three with psychosis (all schizophrenic) and five without had engaged in self-mutilating behavior not considered of primarily suicidal intent.

The Impact of Illness on the Offending Career

The men with psychosis were, on average, older than those without (means 35.5 and 32 years, respectively, ANOVA $F = 4.92, p < .03$). They had also been older both at the time of their first offense involving any kind of violence, including threats and criminal damage (means 30.7 and 26.8, respectively, ANOVA $F = 5.95$, $p < .02$) and on their first offense involving personal injury to others (means 31 and 27 years, respectively, ANOVA $F = 5.41$, $p < .02$). This prompted further analysis of the offending landmarks in relation to the onset of illness for the psychotic men.

Twenty-seven of the psychotic men had no criminal record. The criminal history per se, however, bore little temporal relationship to the onset of schizophrenia, a criminal record being as likely before the onset of illness as following it. With violence, it was a different matter. Among the men with schizophrenia who had ever been violent, 79% had first acted in a way that could have been construed as aggressive after the onset of their illness. Although contemporaneous records at least dated the onset of the first admission to hospital for the majority of men, and we were not reliant for this estimate on the man's recall alone, the precise onset of a schizophrenic illness is notoriously difficult to establish. It may be that in a number of cases an insidious onset had been unremarked. In 9 of the 13 cases where the aggressive activity was contemporaneous with or preceded the onset of illness, it was within 4 years. The figures were even more striking when activity resulting in actual injury—not necessarily serious—was considered. In 88% of cases it followed the onset of schizophrenia, and of the six cases preceding the onset, five were within 3 years. Figure 4.1 shows how the first violence may long postdate the illness, but most usually occurs once the illness is well established, the peak being between 5 and 10 years after the onset.

Almost exactly similar patterns were found for the much smaller group of men with affective psychosis, with the age of a first criminal conviction evenly spread before and after the onset of illness, but violence being the successor to it. Among the 21 engaging in any identifiable aggression, 17 men (81%) did so *after* the onset of illness and only 4 men *before* it; where violence resulted in some sort of physical injury, for only the same 4 men did it precede symptoms.

Differences in the Victim Relationship Between Men With or Without Psychosis

Taking only those men convicted of completed violence against others, the men with psychosis (42%) were slightly less likely to have known their victims than the nonpsychotic (59%), but not significantly so. Further, the psychotic men overall were much more likely to be socially isolated, with only half as many (17%), for example, married or de facto married as among the nonpsychotic (40%). Where there was a marriage the spouse

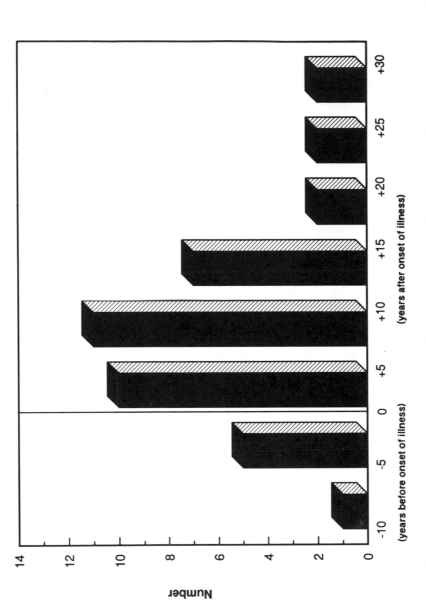

Figure 4.1. The Relationship Between Age of Onset of Schizophrenia and the First Infliction of Injury Against Another ($N = 40$)

TABLE 4.2 Feelings About the Victims of Assault Contrasted Between Psychotic and Nonpsychotic Men

	No Feelings About Victim	Liked Victim
Nonpsychotic	23 (48%)	25 (52%)
Psychotic	29 (73%)	11 (27%)
	Undecided = 2	
	Corrected χ^2 = –4.49, df = 1, p < .03	

was just as likely to be the victim of a psychotic as a nonpsychotic man (60%). There were few other victim relationship differences between the groups, although the only related child to be killed was the daughter of a depressive, and the only parent to be killed was the mother of a schizophrenic. There did, however, appear to be a considerable difference in the level of offender-victim interaction between the groups. Of the total group who completed criminal assaults on others, only one man with psychosis and five without admitted to disliking their victims. While just over half of the nonpsychotics claimed to have liked their victim, this was true for less than 30% of the psychotic men, who thus seem significantly more likely to feel indifferent to their victim, despite having attacked them (see Table 4.2).

The majority of those psychotic men who admitted positive feelings for their victims had an affective psychosis. Twenty-two of the 29 psychotic men insisting on indifference were schizophrenic, but this nevertheless meant that indifference was evenly distributed between the schizophrenic (24%) and affectively psychotic (21%) men. Two men claimed simultaneously to like and dislike their victims, but neither of them was psychotic. Claims about a history of quarreling with the victim supported the probability that the psychotic men were truly disinterested in their victims. Thirty-eight percent of the nonpsychotic men admitted quarreling, compared with only 17% of those with a psychosis (χ^2 = 4.29, df = 1, p < .04). Relative indifference of yet another kind was also suggested among the psychotic men. They were equally likely to attack males and females, whereas the nonpsychotic were slightly more likely (67%) to have female victims.

Aggressive behavior by the victim at the time of the offense was more likely to be cited by the nonpsychotic men (χ^2 = 3.66, df = 1, p < .06) as a reason for their violence, which fitted with the evidence about provocation. Table 4.3 shows that in external reality the psychotic men were indeed comparatively rarely provoked.

TABLE 4.3 The Role of Real External Provocation in Completed Personal Violence

	No Evidence of Provocation	Evidence of Provocation
Nonpsychotic	12 (29%)	29 (71%)
Psychotic	18 (60%)	12 (40%)
	Missing data: 19 cases	
	Corrected $\chi^2 = -5.51$, $df = 1$, $p < .02$	

Victims were rarely recognized as ill (only four in each group) or as sexually provocative (five in total). Alcohol use by the victim was more commonly reported by the nonpsychotic men, the impression being that offender and victim had been drinking together prior to the offense (see further in "Other Factors at the Time of the Offense" section, below). Few of the assailants in either group considered that they had given much warning of the assault to the victim, or to others (11 and 5, respectively).

Historical information about previous victims was more difficult to establish; not all violence had been documented in official records. One further interesting difference in the victims did, however, emerge in this area. Table 4.4 shows that violence, or at least criminal violence, that had been directed exclusively toward the police was almost entirely the province of the psychotic men. Fifteen of the 17 psychotic men who had been exclusively violent to the police had schizophrenia.

Other Factors at the Time of the Offense

The psychotic men were more likely to be socially isolated than their nonpsychotic peers. Among the group committing actual violence against others, only just over half were sharing homes with other people, compared

TABLE 4.4 Criminal Personal Violence Exclusively Targeted at the Police

	Previous Violence Convictions Not Confined to Police Victims	Previous Personal Violence Convictions All Against Police
Nonpsychotic men	46 (96%)	2 (4%)
Psychotic men	23 (58%)	17 (42%)
	Corrected $\chi^2 = 16.74$, $df = 1$, $p < .001$	
	Uncertain cases: 2	

TABLE 4.5 Alcohol Use in the 12 Hours Leading Up to the Offense (Violent and Nonviolent Men)

	None	*Maximum of 2 Pints of Beer or Equivalent*	*3 Pints of Beer or More or Equivalent*	*Alcohol Definitely, Quantity Uncertain*
Nonpsychotic	36 (45%)	14 (17.5%)	20 (25%)	10 (12.5%)
Psychotic	83 (79%)	11 (10.5%)	11 (10.5%)	0
	Unclear: 18 cases			
	Corrected χ^2 28.68, $df = 3$, $p < .0001$			

with 80% of the nonpsychotic men ($\chi^2 = 4.71$, $df = 1$, $p < .03$). Forty-six percent of the total sample of psychotic men were of no fixed abode of any kind—significantly more than among the others (36%) ($\chi^2 = 7.31$, $df = 1$, $p < .007$); nor were the men with a psychosis in contact with others at work. At the time of the offense, less than 20% were working, regardless of whether the whole sample was considered or merely the currently violent subgroup. In contrast, more than half of the nonpsychotic men were in regular employment (for the whole sample, $\chi^2 = 23.08$, $df = 1$, $p < .0001$). This was not a situation new to the psychotic men; 71% of them had been unemployed for more than half of the previous 5-year period, compared with 54% of the nonpsychotics ($\chi^2 = 4.92$, $df = 1$, $p < .03$).

The other major concern, in relation to the time of the offense, was the physical state of the men. Few of the men had been without food for more than 12 hours before the offense and there was no difference between the groups in this respect. It was almost impossible to calculate a fatigue factor, but offenses appear to have been evenly spread throughout the 24-hour period, and similarly so in both groups. Alcohol use, whether in small or large quantity, in the 12 hours leading up to the offense was primarily the prerogative of the nonpsychotic men ($\chi^2 = 21.48$, $df = 1$, $p < .0001$). This order of difference held true also when only the personally assaultive subgroup of the psychotic men was compared with the nonpsychotic. Table 4.5 shows a more detailed breakdown of alcohol use for the whole sample. Insofar as the men with psychosis did use alcohol, it was as often as not to a maximum of 2 pints of beer or their equivalent. In the nonpsychotic group, one third of the victims had also been drinking alcohol. This was true for only four of the psychotic incidents ($\chi^2 = 3.95$, $df = 1$, $p < .05$).

As expected, more of the men with psychosis (26%) than without (12%) had been taking prescribed drugs up to the time of the offense, but even so they were in the minority. Presumably, at least in part because of the attempt in this series to screen out offenders with physical dependence on drugs, illicit use of drugs other than alcohol, in relation to the offense, was rare. Eleven of the nonpsychotic men confessed to it, but only three of the psychotic men did. All three of the latter had schizophrenia and had merely been using cannabis, two of them in relation to alcohol use. No one admitted to the use of LSD or other psychotomimetics but otherwise the full range of "uppers" and "downers" (including barbiturates and opiates) had been sampled by the 11 nonpsychotic men in relation to their offense.

Mental State at the Time of the Offense

Among the interviewed sample of men, only 9 of the 121 with a psychotic illness were considered free of positive symptoms at the time of the offense, but almost half (49%) of the nonpsychotic men were also recognizably disturbed. It is of interest here to return briefly to the overview sample. The prison medical officers were largely responsible for the ratings of illness activity here. They produced a lower, but not very dissimilar, estimate (77%) of symptoms activity at the time of the offense for the psychotic men, but a very low estimate of symptom activity for the nonpsychotic men. Neurotic symptoms seem to have been largely disregarded by prison doctors, whether in relation to treatment or making reports.

For the interviewed sample, ratings were made on the Comprehensive Psychiatric Rating Scale (CPRS) (Åsberg, Perris, Schalling, & Sedvall, 1978) of the global severity of illness. On the 7-point rating system, a score of 2 and below is generally accepted as within the normal range and above 2 as pathological. The scores left no doubt about which group was the more disturbed—the psychotic men on average scored 4.6 and the others, 2.4 (ANOVA $F = 95.38$, $p < .001$). The presence of a psychiatric disorder at the time of an offense does not necessarily mean that the disorder directly contributed to that offense, but in a previous paper (Taylor, 1985) it was confirmed that around 40% of the psychotic men had probably been acting on psychotic symptoms, almost invariably delusions, while none of the nonpsychotic made such a claim. Psychotic as well as nonpsychotic men, however, did claim more rational motives—such as material gain for the nonviolent offenses or accident for the violent ones.

The Psychiatric Backgrounds of
the Psychotic and Nonpsychotic Men Compared

Just over one third of the nonpsychotic men had previously had psychiatric inpatient treatment, while half of them had had psychiatric care of some kind. Even so, the psychotic men were far more likely to have had treatment histories, whether as inpatients (87%) (χ^2 = 49.64, df = 1, p < .0001) or unspecified (90%) (χ^2 = 36.23, df = 1, p < .0001). Far more (82%), too, had consulted a general practitioner (GP) or primary care physician about their psychosocial problems (χ^2 = 10.20, df = 1, p < .001), but as many as 57% of the nonpsychotic men had been in touch with their GPs, and more of them (61%) had retained an actively interested GP than had the psychotic men (52%). An intriguing and unexpected finding was that, as children, the nonpsychotic men, albeit in the minority (25%), were far more likely to have been referred to a child psychiatrist than their psychotic peers (χ^2 = 7.89, df = 1, p < .0005). Of those with a psychotic illness who were known to have been seen by a child psychiatrist, all 10 had schizophrenia.

As the use of alcohol at the time of the offense had so clearly distinguished the groups, the history of alcohol and other drug abuse was examined more carefully. Few of either group had ever received a previous diagnosis of alcohol or drug dependency and, by the time of the offense, the label of alcoholism had stuck for only two of the psychotic men and one of the nonpsychotic, and of other drug addiction for only two of the latter. When rated on the criminal profile (Gunn & Robertson, 1976), however, for the severity of their past drunkenness and antisocial drinking, the nonpsychotic men were revealed as having some serious problems, and as a group were significantly worse in this respect than the psychotic men (ANOVA F = 9.31, p < .003). Other drug abuse was generally trivial for both groups.

Selected Aspects of the Personal and Social Histories of the Psychotics and Nonpsychotics

On the relatively crude measures available for statistical analysis, there were remarkably few personal or social differences between the psychotic and the nonpsychotic men. Both had suffered substantial periods of maternal loss throughout childhood (34% and 41%, respectively), and of paternal loss (43% and 47%, respectively), and a substantial minority had spent at least a year in institutional care before they were 16 (14% and 24%, respectively). A measure of uncertainty was noted about other disturbances within the family of the offenders in that up to 35 of the men said that they did not know anything about illness or violence within their families, whether considering the nuclear or extended family, and there was no independent evidence either way. Where definite ratings were possible, violence was already established as a family feature in nearly one quarter of both groups and a range of criminal behavior had occurred in about 20% of all families. While pathological drinking was more common in the families of nonpsychotic men (30%) than the psychotic men (19%), the difference was not significant. Illnesses featured strongly in all families. About 30% in both groups had experienced significant physical illness within the family of a familial (such as diabetes) or a seriously disruptive kind (such as carcinoma in an immediate relative). Mental disorder was even more prominent. Although as many as 28% of the nonpsychotics reported that a close family member had been in some kind of psychiatric treatment, significantly more of the psychotic men (48%) noted it ($\chi^2 = 5.94$, $df = 1$, $p < .01$).

Reference has already been made to how few of the psychotic men had retained homes at all, still less with other people, by the time of the offense. Fewer of the men with psychosis (28%) had ever been married compared with the nonpsychotic men (44%) ($\chi^2 = 5.05$, $df = 1$, $p < .02$), but this difference was mainly accounted for by the men with schizophrenia (21% married); of those with affective psychosis, almost half had married. Only about one third of any of the men, psychotic or nonpsychotic, had had children. By the time of the study, and for at least 5 years before it, the psychotic men were in a much less comfortable position for supporting a family, the majority being fairly consistently unemployed. By contrast, there was absolutely no difference between groups in terms of their educational records. Very few had degrees or higher college qualifications, but 27% of both groups had at least gained some national examination certificates, to the level of "O" (ordinary) level passes (roughly equivalent to the high school sophomore level).

Discussion

This study sought to establish whether any qualities of the psychotic offender are distinctive. Criminal violence by psychotic and nonpsychotic men was compared in two stages in samples from a population that was biased toward the more seriously violent, but largely unselected for the nature of mental disorder. The population included all homicide cases, most other seriously violent men and arsonists, and an unknown proportion of less seriously violent and trivial male offenders from Greater London and its surrounds. Overall, the nature and seriousness of the violence for which the men were on remand differed markedly between the psychotic and nonpsychotic men. Those with psychosis were much more likely to have offended against property and, whether offending against property or not, their violence had had less serious consequences. The risk of serious psychotic violence, however, was not negligible; we showed previously that the men with schizophrenia were probably over-represented among the criminal homicides (Taylor & Gunn, 1984a). It is not clear how far the finding of a tendency toward less serious violence among the psychotic was an artifact resulting from an increased likelihood that the police will notice the mad, and the courts will remand them into custody, particularly if they are homeless. It may equally be that insofar as psychosis does contribute to the genesis of violence the considerable impairment of drive and of many skills that often accompany it also limit the damage done in many cases.

Throughout this chapter, the psychotic and nonpsychotic men are each generally treated as an homogeneous group for purposes of statistical comparison. Numbers were too small for realistic comparisons by diagnostic subgroup on most of the factors of interest. We have some concern about this in relation to the nonpsychotic men, only 19 of whom were regarded as truly free of psychiatric disorder and the majority of whom had, between them, a heterogeneous conglomeration of neurotic disorders. As initially argued, there seemed some acceptable theoretical reasons for combining the psychotic subgroups. In the nature of their symptoms and the degree to which they were disturbed by them, the psychotic men certainly had more in common with each other than with the nonpsychotic, and vice versa. As expected, however, the men with schizophrenia accounted for more of the psychotic violence and social deviance than the other psychotics, not only because they were the larger subgroup, but also because within the psychotic group they were the most deviant. For more than half of the men with an affective psychosis the index offense amounted to no more than threatened or actual damage to property, but this was true for less than a third of the schizophrenic men. Nevertheless, only a minority of each group (21% and 31%, respectively) had been seriously violent. Their past histories showed a similar order of difference. Overall 63% of the men with schizophrenia had had one or two previous convictions for violence or had been repeatedly violent, sometimes inflicting serious injury, compared with only 39% of those with affective psychosis. Differences were less marked in the 2 years leading up to the index offense. Examples of other ways in which the men with schizophrenia were more seriously deviant included their accounting for more of the poor employment records and the anomie of being without a fixed address. Nevertheless, the affective psychotics as a group hardly fulfilled the traditional image of the respectable, middle-aged depressive man with a single terrible blemish on his career. Seventy-nine percent had hypomania, in most cases of long duration, and only 29% were without criminal records at all.

Walker and McCabe (1973) found that treated psychotic offenders (in their series, those admitted to hospital under a 1959 Mental Health Act order from the courts) tended to be considerably older (on average 8 years) than other treated psychotic patients. Häfner and Böker (1973/1982) found that mentally abnormal offenders, in particular the psychotic groups, were very much older than those without gross abnormality, on an average by 10 to 15 years. This study showed a similar, albeit less marked, age differential between psychotic and nonpsychotic offenders. It is interesting to speculate whether the change in service provision in the 10 years or more between the studies may be bringing psychotic people into conflict with the law much sooner. Taylor and Parrott (1988) showed that men with schizophrenia in the overview sample occupied an intermediate distribution, according to their age, between the prison remand group as a whole and men with schizophrenia in the general population. These age differences implied that the psychosis did indeed trigger offending in some people, and reference back to the illness and criminal careers of these men tended to confirm that.

Criminality and/or violent behavior does not render men immune from developing a psychotic illness. Many of the psychotic men in this sample, as perhaps might be expected given its origins in a prison population, were established as criminals, albeit usually very petty criminals, before their illness was manifest. Some might argue that even this showing of an element of social disintegration might be a prodrome of the illness rather than independent of it. Several authors have presented evidence that people who subsequently develop schizophrenia are more likely to show evidence of behavioral disorders before the presentation of classical symptoms than those who do not (e.g., Offord, 1974). Petty criminality would fit well in this model. The most striking impact of a psychotic illness— schizophrenia or affective psychosis—was, however, on violent behavior. Most of the psychotic men had not been violent in any way prior to the onset of their illness. That one or two had merely serves to emphasize that violent men are not immune to becoming psychotic. That in most cases the illness was well established before violence was described or recorded as having emerged suggests that the psychosis was indeed a material factor. Wessely (1992) has subsequently examined the records of a community sample of people with schizophrenia, from the Camberwell register, with similar results.

The most important clinical differentiator of the psychotic subgroup was not diagnosis. It was delusional drive. As described more fully elsewhere (Taylor, 1985), about 46% of the psychotic men had apparently offended in direct response to their psychotic symptoms; except for five men acting on hallucinations, they were responding to delusions. This latter group was significantly more likely to have been seriously violent than the other psychotic men and, in many other criminal and social ways to have had more in common with the nonpsychotic offender group than their psychotic, more rationally motivated peers. The data presented here suggest that the psychotic men as a group appeared more socially isolated than the nonpsychotic, but most of this difference was due to the psychotic group who had not, apparently, offended in response to their delusions. The delusionally driven had remained more socialized and were as likely as the nonpsychotic still to be living with other people at the time of the offense.

Across the board, by contrast, the psychotic men were less likely to have abused alcohol than the nonpsychotic. Alcohol use is often associated with violent offenses: Some researchers have remarked on its importance as a trigger of dangerous behavior, even specifically among schizophrenics (e.g., Yesevage & Zarcone, 1983). The present study again implicates alcohol as an agent at the time of the offense, whether by the offender or the victim, but exonerates the majority of psychotic men from having drunk it, either in the long term or at the time of the offense itself. This is not an isolated finding; Tardiff and Sweillam (1980) described the characteristics of all 9,365 patients admitted to public hospitals in one year in two counties on Long Island, New York. Twenty-one percent of the series showed problems with violence. The authors expressed surprise at a finding of an inverse relationship between alcohol abuse and assaultive or suicidal behavior. This was largely accounted for by the relative absence of alcohol abuse among people with schizophrenia and psychotic depression, and those with organic brain syndromes. Moving from a hospital-based sample to a criminal series, Häfner and Böker (1973/1982) made similar observations. The influence of alcohol at the time of a homicidal offense was almost exclusively a problem of male offenders. People with chronic alcoholism, epilepsy, and mental impairment had all indulged at the time of an offense (two-thirds, one-third, and one-third, respectively) but among people with schizophrenia, only about 10% had taken alcohol, as had even less of the affective psychotics (5%). Drugs other than alcohol played very little part in the backgrounds or the offenses of either psychotic or nonpsychotic men. Given our attempt to exclude those dependent on drugs from the sample, this might have been partially an artifact of the selection process, but it has been noted elsewhere that illicit drug use, including cannabis, LSD, and opiates, is rarely accompanied by violent offending (Hemphill & Fisher, 1980).

Abram and Teplin (1991) and Lindqvist and Allebeck (1990) both found substance abuse to have been a major problem within their psychotic offender samples. Abram and Teplin emphasized the co-occurrence of schizophrenia or major affective disorder with substance abuse in a sample of jail detainees. Lindqvist and Allebeck, however, also emphasized that substance abuse, particularly alcohol abuse, had been a problem at the time of an assaultive offense among the majority of people with schizophrenia. Both groups interpreted the substance abuse factor as most likely to be evidence of social disintegration among those with a serious psychotic illness. If this is so it may account for most of the apparent discrepancy in the findings on the role of alcohol in psychotic offending. The more integrated psychotic with a predominantly delusional presentation and, when violent, a tendency to inflict the most serious harm may indeed be less likely to abuse alcohol or other drugs. The more chaotic, socially disabled, rather more trivial but psychotic offender is the one prone to substance abuse.

The relationship between the psychotic man and his victim also seemed somewhat distinctive. Contrary to expectation, since they were relatively isolated, the psychotic men were not significantly more likely to attack strangers—although the habit of exclusively assaulting police officers was virtually characteristic. Nevertheless, only in part related to this, the psychotic man almost seemed to treat his victim as if he or she were a stranger; there was much less evidence of feeling about the victim, or of social interaction around the offense than with the nonpsychotic offenders. The evidence of relative lack of victim role in the event seemed indirectly to confirm the importance of the psychosis itself.

The majority of the psychotic men in this series had been psychiatric inpatients, and the majority had also served a prison sentence. More nonpsychotic than psychotic men had served a prison sentence for nonviolent offenses, and more psychotic than nonpsychotic men had been psychiatric inpatients, but both groups had substantial criminal histories. Past "treatment" for either group, whether penal or therapeutic, seemed to have had little impact on offending or on mental state at the time of the offense. For the psychotic group, only four had definitely never been in institutional care of any kind, although data were missing for a further 12. Only two were actually in hospital at the time of their offense, but a further 20 had left their last period of institutional care (hospital or prison) within only 1 month of the index offense. Eighty percent of the rest had been in an institution within 2 years, the bare majority within 6 months. Others, too, have, suggested that the gap between institutional care or treatment and offending for the mentally ill is short. In a 15-year follow-up of offender patients who had been in hospital in England or Wales under Section 60 of the Mental Health Act 1959, Gibbens and Robertson (1983) showed that half of all reconvictions occurred within 12 months of release. Häfner and Böker (1973/1982) found that the vast majority of the violent offenders in their series who had been in treatment had been discharged from previous care with the full agreement of the treating staff. In spite of a theoretical basis for optimism about the prevention of violence by psychotic people, since it usually follows the onset of illness, treatment studies give no grounds for it (e.g., Bowden, 1978; Moodley & Thornicroft, 1988; Szmukler, Bind, & Button, 1981). What is more troubling is that this may be as likely to reflect despair, or even hostility in the psychiatric profession, as the reluctance of the prospective patients. The homeless and overtly socially disabled are very demanding because they consume scarce physical and practical resources. They are materially costly patients at a time when health and social services are working with tightly constrained budgets. The superficially better adjusted but more often dangerous patients are deceptive in their veneer of preserved social skills and, not frequently with a particularly active civil rights lawyer in tow, exhausting in their "reasoned" hostility to treatment compliance. It is easier to collude with their delusions of sanity than to maintain treatment of the partly modified delusions credited by most good rating scales. These are emotionally costly patients and either group, with a little judicious diagnostic massage (Coid, 1988), can readily be rejected or discharged, not only with the full agreement of the treating staff but often under pressure from some members of the clinical team, and always with a mask of clinical common sense in the decision.

The majority of violent psychotic offenders are distinguishable from other violent offenders because their illness usually has influenced their actions and the nature of the offense. While observing nonviolent psychotic offenders, this study did not formally compare them with their nonpsychotic peers; it can be noted, however, that almost all the nonviolent offending on the part of the psychotic men was exceptionally trivial, the worst offender having tried to relieve his sister of £300 by forging a check (Taylor, 1985). Although in many cases the illness seemed relevant for the nonviolent offending, it was generally less directly so than for the violent offending.

Most violence by most psychotic people should be predictable, and preventable through treatment, given the resource. Both material provision and skilled, sensitive supervision or peer group support must be included in resource calculations.

References

Abram, K. M., & Teplin, L. A. (1991). Co-occurring disorders among mentally ill jail detainees: Implications for public policy. *American Psychologist, 46,* 1036-1045.

Akiskal, H. S., Djenderadjian, A. N., & Rosenthal, R. H. (1977). Cyclothymic disorder: Validating criteria for inclusion in the bipolar affective group. *American Journal of Psychiatry, 134,* 1227-1233.

Åsberg, M., Perris, C., Schalling, D., & Sedvall, G. (1978). The CPRS-development and applications of a psychiatric rating scale. *Acta Psychiatrica Scandinavica, 271*(Supplement).

Bowden, P. (1978). Men remanded into custody for medical reports: The outcome of the treatment recommendation. *British Journal of Psychiatry, 133,* 332-338.

Brockington, I. F., Kendell, R. E., & Leff, J. P. (1978). Definitions of schizophrenia: Concordance and prediction of outcome. *Psychological Medicine, 8,* 387-398.

Brockington, I. F., Kendell, R. E., & Wainwright, S. (1980). Depressed patients with schizophrenic or paranoid symptoms. *Psychological Medicine, 10,* 665-675.

Brockington, I. F., Wainwright, S., & Kendell, R. E. (1980). Manic patients with schizophrenia or paranoid symptoms. *Psychological Medicine, 10,* 73-83.

Coid, J. W. (1988). Mentally abnormal prisoners on remand: II comparison of services provided by Oxford and Wessex regions. *British Medical Journal, 296,* 1783-1784.

Commissioner of Police of the Metropolis. (1983). *Reports of the Commissioner of Police of the Metropolis for the year 1982.* London: HMSO Cmnd 8928.

Copeland, J. R. M. (1983). Psychotic and neurotic depression: Discriminant further analysis and five year outcome. *Psychological Medicine, 13,* 373-384.

Ekblom, B. (1970). *Acts of violence by patients in mental hospitals.* Uppsala, Sweden: Scandinavian University Books.

Gibbens, T. C. N., & Robertson, G. (1983). A survey of the criminal careers of hospital order patients. *British Journal of Psychiatry, 143,* 362-369.

Gibbens, T. C. N., Soothill, K., & Pope, P. (1977). *Medical remands in the criminal court* [Maudsley Monograph No. 25]. Oxford: Oxford University Press.

Gunn, J., & Robertson, G. (1976). Drawing a criminal profile. *British Journal of Criminology, 16,* 156-160.

Häfner, H. O., & Böker, W. (1982). *Crimes of violence by mentally abnormal offenders* (H. Marshall, Trans.). Cambridge: Cambridge University Press. (Original work published in 1973.)

Hemphill, R. E., & Fisher, W. (1980). Drugs, alcohol and violence in 604 male offenders referred for in-patient psychiatric assessment. *South African Medical Journal, 57,* 243-247.

Johnstone, E. C., Crow, T., Johnson, A. L., & MacMillan, J. F. (1986). The Northwick Park study of first episodes of schizophrenia 1. Presentation of the illness and procedures relating to admission. *British Journal of Psychiatry, 148,* 115-120.

Lagos, J. M., Perlmutter, K., & Saexinger, H. (1977). Fear of the mentally ill: Empirical support for the common man's response. *American Journal of Psychiatry, 134,* 1134-1137.

Lindqvist, P., & Allebeck, P. (1990). Schizophrenia and assaultive behavior: The role of alcohol and drug abuse. *Acta Psychiatrica Scandinavica, 82,* 191-195.

Monahan, J., & Steadman, H. J. (1983). Crime and mental disorder: An epidemiological approach. In M. Tonry & N. Morris (Eds.), *Crime and justice: An annual review of research* (Vol. 4, pp. 145-189). Chicago: University of Chicago Press.

Moodley, P., & Thornicroft, G. (1988). Ethnic group and compulsory detention. *Medicine, Science and the Law, 28,* 324-328.

Offord, D. R. (1974). School performance of adult schizophrenics, their siblings and age mates. *British Journal of Psychiatry, 125,* 12-19.

Robertson, G. (1988). Arrest patterns among mentally disordered offenders. *British Journal of Psychiatry, 153,* 313-316.

Sosowsky, L. (1978). Crime and violence among mental patients reconsidered in view of the new legal relationship between the state and the mentally ill. *American Journal of Psychiatry, 135,* 33-42.

Swanson, J. W., Holzer, C. E., Ganju, V. K., & Jono, R. T. (1990). Violence and psychiatric disorder in the community: Evidence from the Epidemiologic Catchment Area surveys. *Hospital and Community Psychiatry, 41,* 761-770.

Szmukler, G. I., Bird, A. S., & Button, E. J. (1981). Compulsory admissions in a London borough: 1. Social and clinical features and a follow-up. *Psychological Medicine, 11,* 617-636.

Tardiff, K., & Sweillam, A. (1980). Suicide and mental illness. *Archives of General Psychiatry, 37,* 164-169.

Taylor, P. J. (1985). Motives for offending among violent and psychotic men. *British Journal of Psychiatry, 147,* 491-498.

Taylor, P. J., & Gunn, J. (1984a). Violence and psychosis I—Risk of violence among psychotic men. *British Medical Journal, 288,* 1945-1949.

Taylor, P. J., & Gunn, J. (1984b). Violence and psychosis II—Effect of psychiatric diagnosis on convictions and sentencing of offenders. *British Medical Journal, 289,* 9-12.

Taylor, P. J., & Parrott, J. M. (1988). Elderly offenders. *British Journal of Psychiatry, 152,* 340-346.

Thorneloe, W. F., & Crews, E. L. (1981). Manic depressive illness concomitant with antisocial personality disorder: Six case reports and review of the literature. *Journal of Clinical Psychiatry, 42,* 5-9.

Walker, N., & McCabe, S. (1973). *Crime and insanity in England: Vol. 2. New solutions and new problems.* Edinburgh: Edinburgh University Press.

Watt, D. C., Katz, K., & Shepherd, M. (1983). The national history of schizophrenia: A 5-year prospective follow-up of a representative sample of schizophrenics by means of a standardized clinical and social assessment. *Psychological Medicine, 13,* 663-670.

Wessely, S. (1992, February). *The criminal careers of people in one London borough with and without schizophrenia.* Presentation to the Winter Workshop on Schizophrenia, Badgastein, Austria.

Wessely, S., & Taylor, P. J. (1991). Madness and crime: Criminology versus psychiatry. *Criminal Justice and Mental Health, 1,* 193-228.

Wilcox, D. E. (1985). The relationship of mental illness to homicide. *American Journal of Forensic Psychiatry, 6,* 3-15.

Wing, J. K., Cooper, J. E., & Sartorius, N. (1974). *The measurement and classification of psychiatric symptoms.* Cambridge: Cambridge University Press.

Yesevage, J. A., & Zarcone, V. (1983). History of drug abuse and dangerous behavior in inpatient schizophrenics. *Journal of Clinical Psychiatry, 44,* 259-261.

5

The Role of Mental Disorder and Substance Abuse in Predicting Violent Crime Among Released Offenders

LINDA A. TEPLIN

GARY M. McCLELLAND

KAREN M. ABRAM

There is a longstanding stereotype that the mentally ill are particularly prone to violence (Fracchia, Canale, Cambria, Ruest, & Sheppard, 1976; Monahan, 1992; Olmstead & Durham, 1976; Rabkin, 1979; Shah, 1975; Steadman & Cocozza, 1978). This image is perpetuated by the news and entertainment media (Gerbner, Gross, Morgan, & Signorielli, 1981; Shain & Phillips, 1991).

Researchers have investigated this stereotype by comparing the incidence of violence (measured either by arrest rates or self-report) among the mentally ill (most often prior psychiatric patients) with general population rates. Some find a relationship between mental disorder and violence (Lindqvist & Allebeck, 1990; Schuerman & Kobrin, 1984; Sosowsky, 1978, 1980; Swanson, Holzer, Ganju, & Jono, 1990). Other studies find that, after controlling for demographic variables such as age, sex, and arrest history, persons with serious mental disorders (schizophrenia or major affective illnesses) are no more violent than the non-mentally ill (Monahan & Steadman, 1983; Rabkin, 1979; Steadman, Cocozza, & Melick, 1978; Steadman & Ribner, 1980; Teplin, 1985). Overall, a number of recent reviews conclude that, at worst, mental disorder poses only a slightly elevated risk for violence (Monahan, 1992; Swanson et al., 1990; Wessely & Taylor, in press).

Because most research investigated only state hospital psychiatric patients, however, we have little knowledge concerning the violence potential of other populations. One critical group—jail detainees—has received relatively little attention. Jail detainees are important to study because, regardless of their psychiatric status, they are at risk for committing violent crimes post-release (U.S. Department of Justice, 1991a).

Does mental disorder increase the risk of violent crime among jail detainees? This question is particularly timely: Because jails are so over-crowded (U.S. Department of Justice, 1991b), more arrestees are being released into the community than ever before (U.S. Department of Justice, 1988). It is thus critical to know if mental disorder is a significant risk factor for committing violent crimes postrelease.

This chapter examines the following question: Does mental disorder predict violent crime among jail detainees?

The Literature

There is little doubt that the prevalence of mental disorder among jail detainees is high compared to general population rates.[1] Recent reviews conclude that rates of severe mental illness (sometimes defined as schizo-phrenia; other times defined as "any psychosis") range from 4%-5% to 12% (Teplin, 1990b). The range of rates most likely results from inconsis-tencies across studies in sampling and measurement techniques (Teplin, 1990b). Despite the variation in rates, one solid trend emerges: Even the lowest estimates of severe mental disorder are 2 to 3 times higher than general population rates (Teplin, 1990b).

Given that the number of mentally ill jail detainees is disproportionately high, information concerning their criminal careers is critical. Prior re-search has investigated this issue in two ways. Some researchers have compared the prevalence of mental disorder of violent jail detainees with those who are nonviolent. Other studies have compared the criminal careers of mentally ill jail detainees with nonmentally ill jail detainees. A summary of each research approach follows.

(1) *Comparing the prevalence of mental illness between "violent" and "nonviolent" jail detainees.* Two studies found greater psychopathology among detainees who had a history of violence than among those who did not (cf. Langevin, Ben-Aron, Wortzman, Dickey, & Handy, 1987; Taylor & Gunn, 1984). Unfortunately, neither of these studies sampled the entire range of offenders. Langevin et al. (1987), for example, compared mur-derers to property offenders. Taylor and Gunn (1984) used a somewhat broader sampling design, but still did not sample the entire range of offenders: They compared offenders arrested for violent crimes to all forensic patients. They omitted inmates who were not recognized as being

ill by jail medical personnel as well as persons who were arrested for nonviolent index offenses. To date, no study of jail detainees has sampled the breadth of offender categories. Our knowledge of the mental disorder-violence relationship is thus limited.

Other studies have provided descriptive data on specific populations such as sex offenders (Packard & Rosner, 1985) or forensic patients (Roman & Gerbing, 1989; Rosner, Wiederlight, & Wieczorek, 1985). All found that a large proportion of subjects exhibited severe psychopathology. These studies suffer from a major limitation, however: None included a control group. Without a control group, we do not know if the prevalence of severe mental disorder is greater among violent offenders than among nonviolent offenders. These studies thus provide interesting data but do not address the role of mental disorder in predicting violence.

(2) *Comparing the criminal careers of jail detainees who have severe mental disorders with those who do not.* Research in this area is equivocal. One study of jail detainees found that mental disorder and violence were correlated (Ashford, 1989), while another found they were not (Valdiserri, Carroll, & Hartl, 1986). Collins and Bailey (1990) found that it depends on the disorder; only some disorders were associated with selected measures of violence.

Part of the reason for the discrepancy may be methodological. Most investigators have not used random samples. Phillips, Wolf, and Coons (1988), for example, studied only forensic patients. They found that the forensic patients were responsible for a very small proportion of violent crime. While their finding is provocative, we cannot know if their results would be the same had they sampled nonforensic patients as well. Other studies have used samples of jail detainees who were *referred* for mental health services (see, e.g., Valdisseri et al., 1986) and did not sample from the jail's general population. Such treatment samples are biased because, by definition, they are limited to detainees whom jail personnel define to be in need of mental health services. Unfortunately, the jail's treatment decision is imperfectly correlated with the true presence or absence of mental disorder (Teplin, 1990a) and results in incalculable biases. Other studies sampled from the jail's general population but limited their focus to only one or two disorders. Collins and Bailey (1990), for example, studied the effect of mood disorders on violence, finding several intriguing relationships: Dysthymia and recurrent depression were associated with robbery and fighting; manic symptoms were sometimes associated with "expressive" violence. While their results are extremely interesting, we cannot generalize their findings to other disorders.

Perhaps the most relevant studies pertaining to our question are those by Ashford (1989) and Valdisseri et al. (1986). Both studies sampled a range of diagnostic categories. Ashford sampled the jail's general population, and found that mentally ill inmates were more likely to have a history of violence than "the average" inmate. Unfortunately, Ashford's definition of mental illness may have biased his results. He relied on the jail's identification of severe mental disorder. Such samples probably overrepresent the mentally ill who are disruptive (Teplin, 1990a) and are more likely to be violent, and underrepresent those who have less disruptive disorders such as depression (Teplin, 1990a). Valdisseri et al. (1986) sampled only persons referred for treatment, categorizing them as psychotic or nonpsychotic. They found that psychotic inmates were 4 times more likely to have been incarcerated for less serious charges (such as disorderly conduct and threats) than the nonpsychotic inmates. Their study, however, had two problems: Like the Ashford study, their referred sample was biased. In addition, they relied on the current charge as the sole indicator of violence. Using current charge to measure violent behavior yields only a "snapshot" of the detainee's criminal career.

In sum, several studies have found a relationship between mental disorder and violent crime among jail detainees, while others have not. The source of the confusion may be methodological: To date no study has used an unbiased sample of jail detainees, an appropriate control group, and at the same time used reliable measures of mental disorder and violence.

The data presented here are part of a larger project investigating the prevalence and treatment of mentally disordered jail detainees (cf. Abram, 1989, 1990; Abram & Teplin, 1991; Teplin, 1990a, 1990b). For this epidemiologic study, we administered psychiatric interviews to a random sample of 728 jail detainees. The extensive diagnostic data we collected provide an ideal opportunity to compare the criminal careers of mentally ill and non-mentally ill jail detainees. In this chapter we present longitudinal arrest data for 3 years post-interview to see if arrest rates for violent crime differed as a function of psychiatric diagnosis.

Method

Subjects. Diagnostic data were collected between November 1983 and November 1984 at the Cook County Department of Corrections (CCDC) in Chicago. CCDC is used solely for pretrial detention and for offenders sentenced on misdemeanor charges for less than one year.

Subjects were male detainees, randomly selected directly from pretrial arraignment; $N = 728$. In order that the study include a sufficient number of detainees accused of serious crimes, the sample was stratified by category of charge (one half misdemeanants, one half felons). Persons charged with both misdemeanors and felonies were categorized as felons. Data were then weighted to reflect the jail's actual misdemeanor/felony distribution.

All detainees, excluding persons with gunshot wounds or other traumatic injuries, were part of the sampling pool. Personnel at the jail referred all persons targeted for participation in the project regardless of their mental state, potential for violence, or fitness to stand trial. Since virtually no detainee was a priori ruled ineligible, the sample was unbiased in relation to the characteristics of the larger jail population.

Subjects ranged in age from 16 to 68, with mean and median ages of 26.3 and 25, respectively. The majority were African American (80.8%), 12% were non-Hispanic white, and 6.5% were Hispanic. Most of the remaining (0.8%) subjects were Asian or Native American. Fewer than half of the detainees were employed at the time of their arrest (42.6%). Education level ranged from 2 to 16 years, with mean and median being 10.6 and 11.0 years, respectively. These demographic characteristics are consistent with those of many large urban jails nationwide (U.S. Department of Justice, 1991c).

Procedure. Interviewers were three Ph.D. clinical psychologists, extensively trained in interviewing techniques, psychopathology, and the data collection instrument. Persons targeted by the random sampling procedure (a random numbers table) were approached during the routine jail intake process by the research interviewer. The potential subjects were told that the goal of the project was "to find out more about the people who come to CCDC." The interviewer stressed that the detainees' participation would not affect their treatment while in jail nor shorten their incarceration. Subjects who agreed to participate signed a consent form and were paid $5 for taking part. Persons who declined to participate proceeded through intake.

Of 767 detainees approached, only 35 (4.6%) declined to participate. The low refusal rate was probably due to the detainees' viewing the research project as a way of avoiding the crowded and dismal conditions of the regular intake area. Two subjects were excluded because the interviewer felt they were inventing their responses. Two others were "duplicate" subjects; they were rearrested sometime after their initial interview and again randomly selected. The final N is 728.

Subjects were interviewed in a soundproof, private glass booth in the central receiving and processing area. Diagnostic assessments were made using the National Institute of Mental Health Diagnostic Interview Schedule (NIMH-DIS) (Robins, Helzer, Croughan, Williams, & Spitzer, 1981). Empirical tests have documented the reliability of the NIMH-DIS in both institutionalized samples and the general population (Burke, 1986; Helzer et al., 1985; Robins, Helzer, Croughan, & Ratcliff, 1981; Robins, Helzer, Ratcliff, & Seyfried, 1982; in contrast, see Anthony et al., 1985). The DIS systematically differentiates between disorders that were ever manifest, even if currently remitted ("lifetime" disorders), and disorders in which symptoms have been recently experienced ("current" disorders).

The NIMH-DIS provides diagnostic categories rather than global psychopathology scores. Because of subject variance over time and the rarity of many disorders, it is difficult to assess the reliability and validity of psychiatric assessments such as the DIS (Robins, 1985). Nevertheless, a test-retest consistency check of 20 cases yielded results that compare favorably with other studies (Robins, 1985): 93% agreement across all diagnoses and 95% agreement for the severe disorders. Two independent interviewers gave nearly identical profiles to 85% of the cases. Interviewer consistency was scrupulously maintained after the initial 3-month training period via mock interviews with live subjects, spot checks, and videotape training.

The interview lasted 1 to 3 hours, depending on the number of positive symptoms of the detainee. After the interview, the detainee was thanked for his participation and escorted by jail staff back to the intake area.

Arrest data were obtained from Chicago Police Department records. Each file contains the detainee's "rap sheet" itemizing his arrest and conviction history. Charges incurred outside the county are routinely transcribed from FBI and IBI (Illinois Bureau of Investigation) records onto the rap sheet so that this procedure resulted in a relatively complete data set. For each subject, we obtained data on arrests incurred during the 3 years post-interview.

The criminal history data involve mostly objective variables that require low levels of coder inference. Nevertheless, two research assistants coded the same data for 2 weeks to confirm the interrater reliability of the coding procedures. Analysis of the reliability of the coding instrument revealed interrater reliability consistently above .90.

Definition of Terms and Data Management

Diagnostic Variables. Diagnostic categories were determined conservatively. In order to meet criteria for a particular disorder, the subject had to attain the "definite" or "severe" category (whichever was applicable); all "possible" or "mild" cases were scored as absent.

In no case does the presence of one of the disorders preclude the diagnosis of another disorder via "exclusionary" criteria (see Boyd et al.,

1984). Because most serious disorders tend to reoccur, we used lifetime diagnosis for these analyses.

Final Sample Size. We omitted subjects who met criteria for severe cognitive impairment ($n = 2$) because there were too few cases. The 3-year follow-up data were unavailable for 35 of the subjects. We excluded 2 dead subjects because we were unable to determine the date of death. An additional 55 subjects were omitted because they were in jail or prison (but never mental hospitals) for the entire 3-year follow-up. Of these 55 cases, 9.1% had a severe mental disorder (either schizophrenia, manic episode, or major depressive episode), 41.8% had a drug or alcohol use disorder only (no major mental disorder), and 49.1% had no disorder. Our final sample size was 634.

Units of Analysis. Because subjects may have more than one disorder, we analyzed the data in two complementary ways: (a) *Disorder as the Unit of Analysis.* These tables show the effect of each disorder on the dependent variable. Because subjects may have more than one disorder, columns sum to more than 100%. (b) *The Subject as the Unit of Analysis.* These tables demonstrate what proportion of the sample was violent. For these analyses, we had to categorize each person into one diagnostic group. Given our interest in severe disorders and the purported relationship between manic episode, schizophrenia, and violence (Davis, 1991; Krakowski, Volavka, & Brizer, 1986), we developed the following hierarchy: schizophrenia/ schizophreniform disorders, manic episode, major depressive episode, drug and alcohol use disorder, drug use disorder only, alcohol use disorder only, no disorder. For example, persons who had both schizophrenia and an alcohol use disorder would be categorized as "schizophrenic." Persons who had both manic episode and schizophrenia were categorized as "schizophrenic." Persons categorized as "alcoholic" have neither drug use disorders, major depressive episode, manic episode, nor schizophrenia. This scheme is necessitated by our sample size: Although larger than prior studies (728) it is still too small to allow us to categorize persons into more specific categories reflecting their comorbidity.

Defining and Measuring Violence. Violent crime included both felony and misdemeanor crimes against persons: murder, manslaughter, kidnap, aggravated battery, unlawful restraint, aggravated assault, assault, battery, robbery, rape, and deviant sexual assault.

A common problem in longitudinal research is controlling for the time spent "at risk," in other words, the time that the subject is available to commit crime during the follow-up period (cf. Blumstein & Cohen, 1979; Blumstein, Cohen, Roth, & Visher, 1986). For example, a detainee who is in jail or in a mental hospital or dies during the 3 follow-up years would ceteris paribus be less likely to be rearrested than a person who was available the entire time. Although 85% of our subjects were available for at least 90% of the follow-up period, we nevertheless adjusted both variables for the following factors:

(1) Hospital Stays: the number of days spent in Illinois state mental hospitals;
(2) Jail Stays: the number of days spent in jail post-interview corresponding to the current arrest. (These data were available from jail records.) Once a detainee was released from the jail, either after being found not guilty, bonding out, or after having completed his sentence, his time available for rearrest began;
(3) Prison Stays: incarceration sentences (in days) received for any arrest taking place during the 3-year follow-up period. (These data are noted on the rap sheet.) This period of time was an estimate since detainees were routinely released before their sentences elapsed. Because data on actual time served by detainees were unavailable, we weighted sentences by the calculated average sentence served by inmates in Illinois prisons based on Illinois sentencing law for a 10-year sentence, .475 (Illinois Criminal Justice Information Authority, 1989). This figure is consistent with the national average percentage of time served in prison (Jamieson & Flanagan, 1989);
(4) Death. Using the date of death, we adjusted time at risk for three subjects who died during the follow-up period.

Results

Probability of Arrest for Violent Crime During 3-Year Follow-Up

Using the "time at risk" data, we calculated the probability of being arrested for a violent crime for each diagnostic group by dividing the number of persons in each group who had a rearrest for violent crime by "time at risk" (expressed in months). This probability represents the chances of being arrested for a violent crime in any given month. The 3-year probabilities reported in Table 5.1 are calculated as: $1 - (1 - p)^{36}$. We estimated variances and confidence intervals using Cochran's (1977) technique for combined ratio estimates.

Table 5.1 reports the probability of arrest for a violent crime by diagnostic group. As noted above, the ns sum to more than 100% because many subjects have more than one disorder. We used two-tailed difference of proportions tests to compare each of the diagnostic groups with the "no disorder" group. There were no significant differences between any of the diagnostic groups and the no disorder group.

TABLE 5.1 Probability of Being Arrested One or More Times During 3-Year Follow-Up Period by Diagnosis, Adjusted for Time at Risk*

Psychiatric Disorder	3-Year Probability of Arrest	Lower 95% Confidence Interval	Upper 95% Confidence Interval	n
Severe disorder	0.352	0.171	0.494	58
Schizophrenia	0.399	0.082	0.608	23
Manic episode	0.467	—**	—**	15
Depression	0.305	0.048	0.494	35
Any substance abuse or dependence disorder	0.385	0.288	0.468	390
Drug and alcohol	0.364	0.199	0.495	139
Drug	0.367	0.224	0.484	209
Alcohol	0.387	0.286	0.474	320
No disorder	0.383	0.141	0.558	240
Totals	0.383	0.282	0.470	634

NOTES: *No significant differences between the No Disorder Group and each Psychiatric Disorder Group at the .05 level.
**Due to sample size, we are unable to compute a confidence interval for this group.

Because the diagnostic groups in Table 5.1 are not independent, we cannot calculate significance tests to test for differences between them. Nevertheless, the heterogeneity of persons in the "severe disorder" group is notable. While the probability of arrest for a violent crime in the severe disorder group is .352, the rates for each of the severe diagnoses are quite disparate: depressives have a low probability of arrest (.305) during the follow-up period, compared to those with schizophrenia (.399) and manic episode (.467). Probabilities for the substance abuse disorders were fairly similar to the no disorder rate.

Table 5.2 presents the same data, but by hierarchical group (by subject as opposed to disorder). Results are substantially similar to Table 5.1. Because the hierarchical groups in Table 5.2 are independent, we were able to calculate significance tests between the schizophrenic and major depressive groups. The difference was not significant, possibly because of the small n.

Number of Arrests for Violent Crime

For each group, we calculated the ratio of the total number of arrests for violent crime to the time at risk, a Poisson procedure (Mendenhall, 1987). Table 5.3 presents this measure of violence. As with Table 5.1, the ns sum to more than 100% because subjects may have more than one disorder.

TABLE 5.2 Probability of Being Arrested One or More Times During 3-Year Follow-Up Period by Hierarchical Psychiatric Disorder Group, Adjusted for Time at Risk*

Psychiatric Disorder	3-Year Probability of Arrest	Lower 95% Confidence Interval	Upper 95% Confidence Interval	n
Severe disorder	0.352	0.171	0.494	58
Schizophrenia	0.399	0.082	0.608	23
Manic episode	0.454	—**	—**	10
Depression	0.243	0.002	0.427	25
Any substance abuse or dependence disorder	0.389	0.285	0.478	336
Drug and alcohol	0.357	0.167	0.505	112
Drug	0.391	0.060	0.608	64
Alcohol	0.409	0.267	0.524	160
No disorder	0.383	0.141	0.558	240
Totals	0.383	0.282	0.470	634

NOTES: *No significant differences between the No Disorder Group and each Psychiatric Disorder Group at the .05 level.
**Due to sample size, we are unable to compute a confidence interval for this group.

Interestingly, the median and mode for all groups were zero, indicating that more detainees did not commit a violent crime 3 years post-arrest than did. There were no significant differences between the disordered groups and the no disorder group. The difference between the schizophrenia group and the no disorder group, however, was marginally significant ($p = .08$), and probably would be significant had the sample of schizophrenics been larger.

Once again, when we separate the severe disorder group into specific diagnostic categories, we see disparities between the rates. Because the severe disorder groups in Table 5.3 are not independent, we cannot calculate significance tests between them. Nevertheless, it is interesting that major depressive episode and manic episode have lower rates than the group with schizophrenia. Rates for the substance abuse groups—whether alcohol and drug combined or alcohol or drug alone—are substantially similar to the no disorder group.

We also calculated the same dependent variable using the hierarchical groups (the individual subject as the unit of analysis). These results are in Table 5.4 and confirm those presented in Table 5.3. The rates of violence for the severe disorder group as a whole are not significantly different than the no disorder group. Nor are there any significant differences between the three severely disordered groups, probably because of the relatively

TABLE 5.3 Number of Arrests for Violent Crimes Per 3-Year Period by Diagnosis, Adjusted for Time at Risk*

Psychiatric Disorder	Number of Violent Arrests	Lower 95% Confidence Interval	Upper 95% Confidence Interval	n
Severe disorder	0.975	0.531	1.419	58
Schizophrenia	1.419	0.557	2.282	23
Manic episode	0.779	—**	—**	15
Depression	0.845	0.310	1.380	35
Any substance abuse or dependence disorder	0.839	0.682	0.997	390
Drug and alcohol	0.912	0.636	1.188	139
Drug	0.821	0.608	1.034	209
Alcohol	0.882	0.703	1.060	320
No disorder	0.788	0.593	0.983	240
Totals	0.819	0.697	0.942	634

NOTES: *No significant differences between the No Disorder Group and each Psychiatric Disorder Group at the .05 level.
**Due to sample size, we are unable to compute a confidence interval for this group.

small n. Nevertheless, we must note the diversity within the severe disorder category. Persons with manic episode and major depression have lower rates of arrests for violent crime than persons with schizophrenia. Again, persons with substance abuse—whether drug only, alcohol only, or both—have rates of violent arrests substantially similar to the no disorder group.

The raw data showed that the schizophrenia and major depression groups are quite heterogeneous. For example, despite the small n of the schizophrenia group, the range was 0-6 arrests for violent crimes. While more than one half of the schizophrenia group was never arrested for a violent crime during the follow-up period, three persons (13%) were arrested four or more times. In contrast, less than 2% of the no disorder group was arrested four or more times. The major depression group displayed similar diversity. While more than three quarters had no arrests, 2 out of the 35 subjects were arrested for a violent crime four or more times. This suggests that while most mentally ill detainees are not any more likely to become violent than the no disorder group, those who did sometimes did so repeatedly.

It is instructive to explore whether the mentally ill groups were disproportionately arrested for the most serious violent crimes (rape, murder, manslaughter, kidnapping, aggravated battery, etc.). The schizophrenia group is important because it had the highest rate of arrests for violence. The raw data showed that, of the 27 violent crimes allegedly perpetrated

TABLE 5.4 Number of Arrests for Violent Crimes Per 3-Year Period by Hierarchical Psychiatric Disorder Group, Adjusted for Time at Risk*

Psychiatric Disorder	Number of Violent Arrests	Lower 95% Confidence Interval	Upper 95% Confidence Interval	n
Severe disorder	0.975	0.531	1.419	58
Schizophrenia	1.419	0.557	2.282	23
Manic episode	0.599	—**	—**	10
Depression	0.608	0.068	1.148	25
Any substance abuse or dependence disorder	0.813	0.646	0.981	336
Drug and alcohol	0.809	0.519	1.099	112
Drug	0.657	0.311	1.004	64
Alcohol	0.871	0.619	1.122	160
No disorder	0.788	0.593	0.983	240
Totals	0.819	0.697	0.942	634

NOTES: *No significant differences between the No Disorder Group and each Psychiatric Disorder Group at the .05 level.
**Due to sample size, we are unable to compute a confidence interval for this group.

by the schizophrenic subjects, 22 (81.48%) were for less serious violent crimes such as battery or simple assault. Only 5 (18.52%) were for the most serious violent acts (murder, manslaughter, etc.)

Discussion

Among this sample of jail detainees, neither severe mental disorder nor substance abuse/dependence predicted the probability of arrest for violent crime, or the number of violent arrests. Only the schizophrenia group had a higher number of violent arrests compared to the no disorder group, albeit not significantly so. In the schizophrenia subgroup, this trend was a result of high rates of violent crimes perpetrated by a few individuals; the median and mode were zero. Overall, our findings do not support the commonly held presumption that mentally ill persons will commit violent crimes if they are released.

Unfortunately, television continues to present this image. One study of prime-time television dramas found that 73% of the mentally ill television characters were portrayed as violent and/or homicidal compared to 40% of the "normal" television characters (Gerbner et al., 1981). As Monahan (1992) has pointed out, news media are not much better: A content analysis of United Press International news stories found that 86% of all print stories dealing with former mental patients focused on the issue of violent crime, "usually murder or mass murder" (Shain & Phillips, 1991). The image of mentally ill persons as crazed and violent psychotics may make intriguing movie plots but is not supported by our data. A few of our mentally ill jail detainees committed violent crimes post-release; most did not. Unfortunately, the stereotype of the invariably violent mentally ill person is ultimately harmful to the deinstitutionalized mental patient who has no choice but to live within the community (Teplin, 1985).

How do our findings fit into the ongoing debate on the relationship between mental disorder and violence? Because our sample included only jail detainees, our results cannot be generalized to the deinstitutionalized mentally ill within the community. Nevertheless, this study has major public policy implications. If the violence potential of arrestees with severe mental disorder or substance abuse/dependence is substantially similar to their non-mentally ill counterparts, probation and parole decisions for mentally ill offenders could be based on similar decision rules used with non-mentally ill offenders. Ideally, such decision rules would allow us to discriminate between the majority of mentally ill jail detainees who do not commit violent acts post-release, and those few who commit multiple violent acts. Our major finding—most mentally ill jail detainees do not become violent, but a few may become repeatedly violent—confirms that one of the best predictors of future violence is prior violence (Monahan & Steadman, 1983).

We found substantial diversity among the three severe disorder groups (schizophrenia, manic episode, and major depression). These results demonstrate the pitfalls inherent in the practice of combining diverse disorders into one "psychotic" or "severely ill" group and comparing them to a "nonpsychotic" group. Heterogeneity within a "severely ill" group could obfuscate important differences between diagnostic categories.

It is interesting that alcohol and drug use disorders did not predict violence. This failure of alcohol use disorder to be related to violence is particularly striking because it has been assumed to play a strong role in violence (Collins, 1988, 1989; Fagan, 1990). There are two plausible explanations for the inconsistency between our findings on alcohol and the extant literature. First, alcohol intoxication may be a better predictor of violence than alcoholism per se. Second, the link between alcohol and crime found in other studies may be an artifact of the association between alcohol and a third correlated variable such as antisocial personality disorder (Abram, 1989).

One potential threat to validity should be highlighted: Perhaps mental disorder failed to predict the probability of arrest for violent crime because our subjects were diverted to mental hospitals instead of arrested (Klassen & O'Connor, 1988). This is unlikely. In Illinois, persons charged with felonies must be arrested first, and then treated for their mental disorder (Teplin, 1984). In practice, even mentally ill misdemeanants are usually arrested before being treated (Teplin & Pruett, 1992). Our present study also confirmed this. Of the 37 severely ill persons who were never arrested for a violent crime during the 3-year follow-up (possible false negatives), only 4 (10.84%) were hospitalized one or more times during the follow-up. Because of their arrest history, released jail detainees may be more likely to be rearrested than hospitalized when they are violent.

Several limitations of this study should be kept in mind. First, our generalizability is limited to other large urban jails. Second, our sample included only criminal "failures": All had been caught. Thus our data may be more generalizable of the mental disorder-violence relationship among failed criminals than among the universe of offenders. Third, the dependent variable—violence—incorporated only detected crime. This variable has a built-in bias because relatively few crimes are detected; even fewer culminate in an arrest. Moreover, the criminal acts that do become "crimes" are clearly not a random sample of all violent acts. Finally, our sample of persons with severe mental disorder was relatively small and did not allow us to control for variables thought to influence violence, such as age and comorbidity, with other psychiatric disorders.

Notwithstanding the need for further refinements, our results demonstrate the importance of further research in this area, in particular exploring violence within a broader context. For example, studies should use a multi-indicator cross-validated approach where self-reported violent activity is compared with arrest rates. This approach would provide a fuller picture of the relationship between mental disorder and violence. Future studies should also use larger samples and test whether combinations of disorders—for example, schizophrenia coupled with drug abuse/dependence—interact to produce greater violence than either disorder alone. Larger samples would also allow researchers to control for demographic factors that are known to affect violence predictions. Finally, the tremendous diversity within the schizophrenia group (most were never violent; a few were very violent) suggests that diagnosis per se may not be a meaningful predictor of violence. A new study suggests that psychotic symptoms may be more accurate predictors of violence than diagnosis per se (Link, Andrews, & Cullen, 1992).

Additional research on the violence potential of the mentally ill is vital to dispel inaccurate stereotypes. It is also vital, however, because mental health professionals will continue to be required to assess the violence potential of the mentally ill (Monahan, 1981). New research designed to improve violence prediction holds promise (Steadman et al., Chapter 3 in this volume). By learning to predict violence more accurately, both among the mentally ill and nonmentally ill, we may balance our need to provide treatment for the mentally disordered offender with our obligation to protect the safety and welfare of the public.

Note

1. Studies using prison samples (e.g., Guze, Tuason, Gatfied, Stewart, & Picken, 1962; Guze, Woodruff, & Clayton, 1974; Sutker & Moan, 1973) are not discussed because recent research has shown that the rate of mental disorder among prison detainees in the United States is actually lower than that in the general population (Collins & Schlenger, 1983). This is because most seriously ill offenders are diverted to mental health facilities at some point during the adjudication process.

References

Abram, K. M. (1989). The effect of co-occurring disorders on criminal careers: Interaction of antisocial personality, alcoholism, and drug disorders. *International Journal of Law and Psychiatry, 12,* 133-148.

Abram, K. M. (1990). The problem of co-occurring disorders among jail detainees: Antisocial disorder, alcoholism, drug abuse, and depression. *Law and Human Behavior, 14,* 333-345.

Abram, K. M., & Teplin, L. A. (1991). Co-occurring disorders among mentally ill jail detainees: Implications for public policy. *American Psychologist, 46,* 1036-1045.

Anthony, J. C., Folstein, M., Romanoski, A. J., Von Korff, M. R., Nestadt, G. R., Cahal, R., Merchant, A., Brown, H., Shapiro, S., Kramer, M., & Gruenberg, E. M. (1985). Comparison of the lay Diagnostic Interview Schedule and a standardized psychiatric diagnosis. *Archives of General Psychiatry, 42,* 667-675.

Ashford, J. B. (1989). Offense comparisons between mentally disordered and nonmentally disordered inmates. *Canadian Journal of Criminology, 31,* 35-48.

Blumstein, A., & Cohen, J. (1979). Estimation of individual crime rates from arrest records. *Journal of Criminal Law and Criminology, 70,* 561-585.

Blumstein, A., Cohen, J. M., Roth, J. A., & Visher, C. A. (Eds.). (1986). Methodological issues in criminal career research. In *Criminal careers and "career criminals"* (Vol. I, pp. 97-108). Washington, DC: National Academy Press.

Boyd, J. H., Burke, J. D., Gruenberg, E., Holzer, C. E., Rae, D. S., George, L. K., Karno, M., Stoltzman, R., McEvoy, L., & Nestadt, G. (1984). Exclusion criteria of DSM-III. *Archives of General Psychiatry, 41,* 983-989.

Burke, J. D. (1986). Diagnostic categorization by the Diagnostic Interview Schedule (DIS): A comparison with other methods of assessment. In J. Barrett & R. Rose (Eds.), *Mental disorders in the community* (pp. 255-285). New York: Guilford.

Cochran, W. G. (1977). *Sampling techniques* (3rd ed.) (pp. 153-167). New York: John Wiley.

Collins, J. J. (1988). Suggested explanatory frameworks to clarify the alcohol use/violence relationship. *Contemporary Drug Problems,* Spring, 107-121.

Collins, J. J. (1989). Alcohol and interpersonal violence: Less than meets the eye. In A. Weiner & M. E. Wolfgang (Eds.), *Pathways to criminal violence* (pp. 49-67). Newbury Park, CA: Sage.

Collins, J. J., & Bailey, S. L. (1990). Traumatic stress disorder and violent behavior. *Journal of Traumatic Stress, 3,* 203-220.

Collins, J. J., & Schlenger, W. E. (1983). *The prevalence of psychiatric disorder among admissions to prison.* Paper presented at the annual meeting of the American Society of Criminology, Denver, CO.

Davis, S. (1991). Violence by psychiatric inpatients: A review. *Hospital and Community Psychiatry, 42,* 585-590.

Fagan, J. (1990). Intoxication and aggression. In M. Tonry & J. Q. Wilson (Eds.), *Crime and justice: A review of research: Vol. 13. Drugs and crime* (pp. 241-320). Chicago: University of Chicago Press.

Fracchia, J., Canale, D., Cambria, E., Ruest, E., & Sheppard, C. (1976). Public views of ex-mental patients: A note on perceived dangerousness and unpredictability. *Psychiatric Reports, 38,* 495-498.

Gerbner, G., Gross, L., Morgan, M., & Signorielli, N. (1981). Health and medicine on television. *New England Journal of Medicine, 305,* 901-904.

Guze, S. B., Tuason, V. B., Gatfied, P. D., Stewart, M. A., & Picken, B. (1962). Psychiatric illness and crime with particular reference to alcoholism: A study of 223 criminals. *The Journal of Nervous and Mental Disease, 134,* 512-521.

Guze, S. B., Woodruff, R., & Clayton, P. (1974). Psychiatric disorders and criminality. *Journal of the American Medical Association, 227,* 641-642.

Helzer, J. E., Robins, L. N., McEvoy, L. T., Spitznagel, E. L., Stoltzman, R. K., Farmer, A., & Brockington, I. F. (1985). A comparison of clinical and Diagnostic Interview Schedule diagnoses. *Archives of General Psychiatry, 42,* 657-666.

Illinois Criminal Justice Information Authority. (1989). *Trends and issues 89: Criminal and juvenile justice in Illinois* (p. 146). Chicago: The Authority.

Jamieson, K. M., & Flanagan, T. J. (Eds.). (1989). *Sourcebook of criminal justice statistics, 1989* (U.S. Department of Justice, Bureau of Justice Statistics). Washington, DC: Government Printing Office.

Klassen, D., & O'Connor, W. A. (1988). Crime, inpatient admissions, and violence among male mental patients. *International Journal of Law and Psychiatry, 11,* 305-312.

Krakowski, J., Volavka, J., & Brizer, D. (1986). Psychopathology and violence: A review of the literature. *Comprehensive Psychiatry, 27,* 131-148.

Langevin, R., Ben-Aron, M., Wortzman, G., Dickey, R., & Handy, L. (1987). Brain damage, diagnosis and substance abuse among violent offenders. *Behavioral Sciences and the Law, 5,* 77-94.

Lindqvist, P., & Allebeck, P. (1990). Schizophrenia and crime: A longitudinal follow-up of 644 schizophrenics in Stockholm. *British Journal of Psychiatry, 157,* 345-350.

Link, B. G., Andrews, H., & Cullen, F. (1992). The violent and illegal behavior of mental patients reconsidered. *American Sociological Review, 57,* 275-292.

Mendenhall, W. (1985). *Introduction to probability and statistics* (7th ed.) (pp. 162-166). Boston: PWS-Kent.

Monahan, J. (1981). *Predicting violent behavior. An assessment of clinical techniques.* Beverly Hills, CA: Sage.

Monahan, J. (1992). Mental disorder and violent behavior: Perceptions and evidence. *American Psychologist, 47,* 511-521.

Monahan, J., & Steadman, H. J. (1983). Crime and mental disorder: An epidemiological approach. In M. Tonry & N. Morris (Eds.), *Crime and justice: An annual review of research* (Vol. 4, pp. 145-189). Chicago: University of Chicago Press.

Olmstead, D. W., & Durham, K. (1976). Stability of mental health attitudes: A semantic differential study. *Journal of Health and Social Behavior, 17,* 35-44.

Packard, W. S., & Rosner, R. (1985). Psychiatric evaluations of sexual offenders. *Journal of Forensic Sciences, 30,* 715-720.

Phillips, M. R., Wolf, A. S., & Coons, D. J. (1988). Psychiatry and the criminal justice system: Testing the myths. *American Journal of Psychiatry, 145,* 605-610.

Rabkin, J. (1979). Criminal behavior of discharged mental patients: A critical appraisal of the research. *Psychological Bulletin, 86,* 127.

Robins, L. N. (1985). Epidemiology: Reflections on testing the validity of psychiatric interviews. *Archives of General Psychiatry, 9,* 918-924.

Robins, L. N., Helzer, J. E., Croughan, J., & Ratcliff, K. (1981). National Institute of Mental Health Diagnostic Interview Schedule: Its history, characteristics and validity. *Archives of General Psychiatry, 38,* 381-389.

Robins, L. N., Helzer, J. E., Croughan, J., Williams, J., & Spitzer, R. (1981). *NIMH Diagnostic Interview Schedule: Version III.* Rockville, MD: National Institute of Mental Health, Division of Biometry and Epidemiology.

Robins, L. N., Helzer, J. E., Ratcliff, K., & Seyfried, W. (1982). Validity of the Diagnostic Interview Schedule, Version II: DSM-III diagnoses. *Psychological Medicine, 12,* 855-870.

Roman, D. D., & Gerbing, D. W. (1989). The mentally disordered criminal offender: A description based on demographic, clinical and MMPI data. *Journal of Clinical Psychology, 45,* 983-990.

Rosner, R., Wiederlight, M., & Wieczorek, R. R. (1985). Forensic psychiatric evaluations of women accused of felonies: A three year descriptive study. *Journal of Forensic Sciences, 30,* 721-728.

Schuerman, L. A., & Kobrin, S. (1984). Exposure of community mental health clients to the criminal justice system: Client/criminal or patient/prisoner. In L. A. Teplin (Ed.), *Mental health and criminal justice* (pp. 87-118). Beverly Hills, CA: Sage.

Shah, S. A. (1975). Dangerousness and civil commitment of the mentally ill: Some public policy considerations. *American Journal of Psychiatry, 132,* 501-505.

Shain, R., & Phillips, J. (1991). The stigma of mental illness: Labeling and stereotyping in the news. In L. Wilkins & P. Patterson (Eds.), *Risky business: Communicating issues of science, risk. and public policy* (pp. 61-74). Westport, CT: Greenwood Press.

Sosowsky, L. (1978). Crime and violence among mental patients reconsidered in view of the new legal relationships between the state and the mentally ill. *American Journal of Psychiatry, 135,* 33-42.

Sosowsky, L. (1980). Explaining the increased arrest rate among mental patients: A cautionary note. *American Journal of Psychiatry, 137,* 1602-1605.

Steadman, H. J., & Cocozza, J. (1978). Selective reporting and the public's misconceptions of the criminally insane. *Public Opinion Quarterly, 41,* 523-533.

Steadman, H. J., Cocozza, J. J., & Melick, M. E. (1978). Explaining the increased arrest rate among mental patients: The changing clientele of state hospitals. *American Journal of Psychiatry, 135,* 816-820.

Steadman, H. J., & Ribner, S. A. (1980). Changing perceptions of the mental health needs of inmates in local jails. *American Journal of Psychiatry, 137,* 1115-1116.

Sutker, P., & Moan, A. (1973). A psycho-social description of penitentiary inmates. *Archives of General Psychiatry, 29,* 663-667.

Swanson, J. W., Holzer, C., Ganju, V., & Jono, R. (1990). Violence and psychiatric disorder in the community: Evidence from the Epidemiologic Catchment Area surveys. *Hospital and Community Psychiatry, 41,* 761-770.

Taylor, P., & Gunn, J. (1984). Violence and psychosis I—Risk of violence among psychotic men. *British Medical Journal, 288,* 1945-1949.

Teplin, L. A. (1984). *Mental disorder in an urban jail.* Grant application.

Teplin, L. A. (1985). The criminality of the mentally ill: A dangerous misconception. *American Journal of Psychiatry, 142,* 593-599.

Teplin, L. A. (1990a). Detecting disorder: The treatment of mental illness among jail detainees. *Journal of Consulting and Clinical Psychology, 58,* 233-236.

Teplin, L. A. (1990b). The prevalence of severe mental disorder among male urban jail detainees: Comparison with the Epidemiologic Catchment Area program. *American Journal of Public Health, 80,* 663-669.

Teplin L. A., & Pruett, N. S. (1992). Police as streetcorner psychiatrist: Managing the mentally ill. *International Journal of Law and Psychiatry, 15,* 139-156.

U.S. Department of Justice, Bureau of Justice Statistics. (1988). Our crowded jails: A national plight (NCJ-110643). Washington, DC: Author.

U.S. Department of Justice, Bureau of Justice Statistics. (1991a). Profile of jail inmates, 1989 (NCJ-129097). Washington, DC: Author.

U.S. Department of Justice, Bureau of Justice Statistics. (1991b). Jail inmates, 1990 (NCJ-129756). Washington, DC: Author.

U.S. Department of Justice, Bureau of Justice Statistics. (1991c). *Census of local jails. 1988: Volumes I-V.* Washington, DC: Author.

Valdisseri, E. V., Carroll, K. R., & Hartl, A. J. (1986). A study of offenses committed by psychotic inmates in a county jail. *Hospital and Community Psychiatry, 27,* 163-166.

Wessely, S., & Taylor, P. (1991). Madness and crime: Criminology versus psychiatry. *Criminal Justice and Mental Health, 1,* 193-228.

6

Psychopathy, Mental Disorder, and Crime

ROBERT D. HARE

STEPHEN D. HART

In this chapter, we review research looking at the association between psychopathy and crime, particularly violent crime. Next, we review the association between psychopathy and other mental disorders. Finally, we outline some directions for research on criminal offending as an interaction between psychopathy and other mental disorders.

Before we begin, two issues require clarification. First, by *psychopathy* we mean the specific form of personality disorder described by North American clinicians, including Cleckley (1976), Arieti (1967), and McCord and McCord (1964). This conceptualization is similar in many respects to the category antisocial personality disorder as described in the DSM-III and DSM-III-R (American Psychiatric Association, 1980, 1987) and to the category sociopathic personality disorder as described in ICD-9 (International Classification of Diseases; World Health Organization, 1978) (or dyssocial personality disorder in the forthcoming ICD-10). We do not use the term *psychopathy* as a synonym for personality deviation in general, or as a medicolegal category of the sort defined in the Mental Health Act of England and Wales (see Blackburn, 1990, for a critique of this category). We define psychopathy in terms of a cluster of personality traits and socially deviant behaviors: a glib and superficial charm; egocentricity; selfishness; lack of empathy, guilt, and remorse; deceitfulness and manipulativeness; lack of enduring attachments to people, principles, or goals; impulsive and irresponsible behavior; and a tendency to violate explicit social norms. The disorder is usually first evident in childhood, worsens in adolescence, and persists into late adulthood.

AUTHORS' NOTE: Preparation of this chapter was generously supported by the MacArthur Research Network on Mental Health and the Law (John Monahan, Director).

TABLE 6.1 Items in the Hare Psychopathy Checklist-Revised (PCL-R)

Item
1. Glibness/superficial charm[1]
2. Grandiose sense of self-worth[1]
3. Need for stimulation/proneness to boredom[2]
4. Pathological lying[1]
5. Conning/manipulative[1]
6. Lack of remorse or guilt[1]
7. Shallow affect[1]
8. Callous/lack of empathy[1]
9. Parasitic life-style[2]
10. Poor behavioral controls[2]
11. Promiscuous sexual behavior
12. Early behavior problems[2]
13. Lack of realistic, long-term goals[2]
14. Impulsivity[2]
15. Irresponsibility[2]
16. Failure to accept responsibility for actions[1]
17. Many short-term marital relationships
18. Juvenile delinquency[2]
19. Revocation of conditional release[2]
20. Criminal versatility

SOURCE: From Hare, 1991. Reprinted with permission of Multi-Health Systems, 908 Niagara Falls Blvd., North Tonawanda, NY 14120-2060. (800) 456-3003.
NOTE: 1 Loads on Factor 1; 2 Loads on Factor 2.

Second, those familiar with our research know that in the past we have been—and continue to be—highly critical of self-report methods for assessing psychopathy (as well as of the DSM-III and DSM-III-R diagnostic criteria for antisocial personality disorder) for focusing on overt delinquent and antisocial symptoms of psychopathy (social deviance) to the neglect of the disorder's interpersonal and affective symptoms (e.g., Hare, 1985; Hare, Hart, & Harpur, 1991). At present, the best validated procedure for assessing psychopathy in forensic populations is the recent revision of the Psychopathy Checklist (PCL-R; Hare, 1991). Because our review focuses primarily on research using the PCL-R (or its predecessor, the 22-item PCL; Hare, 1980), we describe it briefly here.

The PCL-R is a 20-item symptom-construct rating scale, scored on the basis of an interview with the subject and a review of case history information. Table 6.1 presents the PCL-R items.

Each item is scored, according to explicit criteria, on a 3-point scale reflecting the degree to which it applies to the individual (0 = does not apply; 1 = uncertain, applies somewhat; 2 = definitely applies). The total score can range from 0 to 40, and represents the degree to which an individual resembles the prototypical psychopath. For diagnostic purposes, a score of 30 or above is considered to be indicative of psychopathy. There is a substantial body of evidence attesting to the reliability and validity of the PCL-R (see Hare, 1991; Hare et al., 1990; Harpur, Hare, & Hakstian, 1989; Hart, Hare, & Harpur, 1992). With respect to reliability, Hart et al. (1992) reported that the internal consistency (alpha) for the PCL-R, aggregated over seven samples of male prison inmates from Canada, the United States, and England ($N = 1,192$), was .87; the interrater reliability (intraclass correlation) was .83 for single ratings and .91 for the average of two ratings. More detailed information about the PCL and PCL-R can be found in Hare (1985, 1991); Hare et al. (1991); and Hart, Hare, and Harpur (1992).

For present purposes, it is important to note that the PCL-R provides a *dimensional* measure of psychopathy. Although it is possible that the underlying construct is categorical, PCL-R Total scores provide a useful indication of the number of psychopathic traits and behaviors exhibited by a given individual.

Psychopathy and Crime

Given the characteristics of psychopathy listed in Table 6.1, it comes as no surprise that the disorder is implicated in a disproportionate amount of serious repetitive crime and violence. Previous reviews of research on incarcerated offenders have concluded that psychopaths are more criminally active throughout much of their life span than are other offenders (e.g., Hare, 1991; Hare, Strachan, & Forth, in press); some key studies are described below.

Hare (1981) analyzed the violent behaviors of 243 male prison inmates. Psychopaths, diagnosed according to clinical global ratings (which preceded development of the PCL), were generally more violent than nonpsychopaths. Specifically, 97% of the psychopaths and 74% of the other inmates had received at least one conviction for a violent offense.

Hare and Jutai (1983) compared the criminal behaviors of 97 psychopaths and 96 nonpsychopaths, also diagnosed using clinical global ratings. The mean number of charges per-year-free for all offenses was 5.06 for the psychopaths and 3.25 for the nonpsychopaths. The mean number of charges per-year-free for violent offenses was more than 3 times higher for the psychopaths than for the nonpsychopaths (0.91 and 0.27, respectively).

Hare and McPherson (1984) investigated the association between violence and psychopathy, as measured by the PCL, in a sample of 227 male inmates. Because two of the PCL items (poor behavioral controls; criminal versatility) directly reflect violent or criminal behaviors, they were deleted to avoid overlap between the PCL and the dependent variables. The sample was divided into groups with high, medium, and low PCL scores. Inmates with high PCL scores (psychopaths) were significantly more likely to have been convicted for a violent offense than were other inmates. Other analyses indicated that the mean number of convictions per-year-free for violent offenses was considerably greater for inmates with high PCL scores (1.00) than it was for those with medium (0.36) or low (0.27) PCL scores.

There is good evidence that psychopaths' propensity for violence is not inhibited during incarceration. For example, Hare and McPherson (1984) also examined the institutional violence and aggression of the same subjects described above. Psychopaths were more likely to have engaged in a variety of different types of aggressive acts (e.g., threats, fighting) than were other inmates. The PCL also correlated significantly with global ratings of institutional violence ($r = .46$).

Wong (1984) analyzed the criminal records of a random sample of 315 male inmates from minimum, medium, and maximum security institutions in Canada. Psychopaths were defined by a PCL score of at least 30 and nonpsychopaths by a score of 20 or less. Compared with the nonpsychopaths, the psychopaths committed more than twice as many offenses per-year-free (mean of 4.4 and 1.9, respectively), almost 9 times as many institutional offenses (6.3 and 0.73), and had their first formal contact with the law at an earlier age (17.8 and 24.1). He also found that psychopaths committed almost 4 times as many institutional offenses and engaged in significantly more threatening behavior and acts of violence than did nonpsychopaths.

In a sample of 80 consecutive male admissions to a forensic psychiatric hospital (Hart & Hare, 1989; see Hare, 1991), PCL-R scores correlated .30 with number of prior violent offenses, .35 with number of prior nonviolent offenses, .37 with number of prison terms served (corrected for age), and .33 with months spent in prison (corrected for age).

Kosson, Smith, and Newman (1990) investigated the association between psychopathy and crime in 230 white inmates and 70 black inmates of a state correctional facility. The PCL-R was used for the assessment of psychopathy; item 20 (criminal versatility) was deleted to avoid circularity and the scores were prorated to a 20-item scale. Psychopaths of both races generally had more extensive criminal histories than did nonpsychopaths. Thus, for the white inmates the mean numbers of charges for violent and nonviolent offenses were, respectively, 1.96 and 9.06 for psychopaths, and 1.23 and 4.08 for nonpsychopaths. For the black inmates the corresponding values were 3.09 and 8.00 for psychopaths, and 1.80 and 5.40 for non-psychopaths. In addition, the psychopaths committed a greater variety of offenses than did the nonpsychopaths. Using raw data provided by the authors we determined that the correlation between PCL-R scores and the total number of charges (violent and nonviolent) was .40 for whites and .30 for blacks. The correlation between PCL-R scores and the number of different types of charges was .46 for whites and .35 for blacks.

Forth, Hart, and Hare (1990) found a similar, though weaker, association between psychopathy and crime in a sample of 75 young offenders assessed using an 18-item modification of the PCL-R. PCL-R scores were significantly correlated with the number of prior violent offenses ($r = .27$), and with the number of institutional charges for violent or aggressive behavior ($r = .46$).

In a study of psychopathy and violence, Serin (1991) analyzed the criminal histories of 87 male inmates assessed with the PCL-R. He found that all of the psychopaths ($n = 21$) and 68% of the other inmates ($n = 66$) had been convicted of a violent offense. Psychopaths were more than twice as likely as other inmates to have used a weapon, threats, or instrumental aggression, both inside and outside of prison.

Although psychopathy is generally considered to be a disorder that persists across much of the life span, there is evidence that the antisocial and criminal activities of at least some male psychopaths decrease in frequency and severity with age. Hare, McPherson, and Forth (1988) reported that the criminal activities of male psychopaths were more extensive than were those of other persistent offenders until around age 35 or 40, after which they decreased sharply. These age-related changes were much more dramatic for nonviolent crimes than for violent crimes. That is, the violent activities of psychopaths appeared to remain relatively constant even after there had been a sharp drop in nonviolent criminal activities. Their capacity for violence apparently did not change with age nearly as much as did their readiness to engage in other forms of illegal and antisocial behavior.

The studies described up to this point have all looked at the postdictive validity of psychopathy assessments. However, the PCL and PCL-R have also proven useful in the prediction of recidivism following release from prison and following treatment in forensic psychiatric hospitals. Hart, Kropp, and Hare (1988) administered the PCL to 231 male inmates prior to their release from prison on parole or mandatory supervision. (In Canada, *parole* is early release granted to selected inmates, typically after they have served at least one third of their sentence, whereas *mandatory supervision* is a form of early release contingent on good behavior during incarceration, and is usually granted after two thirds of a sentence has been served.) The PCL assessments and decisions about release were completely independent. Following release, each inmate's progress was followed until: (a) he had his release revoked; (b) he was convicted of a new offense; (c) he successfully reached the end of the period of supervised release; or (d) the end of the study period was reached. An unsuccessful release (failure) was defined as revocation or conviction for a new offense during the period of supervision. Overall, 46.3% of the releases, 56.4% of the mandatory supervisions, and 25.3% of the paroles ended in failure. Outcome (0 = success, 1 = failure) was correlated .33 with PCL scores. A series of regression analyses demonstrated that the PCL made a significant contribution to the prediction of outcome over and beyond that made by relevant criminal-history and demographic variables. Psychopaths not only violated the conditions of release faster and more often than did nonpsychopaths, they also received more suspensions and presented more supervisory problems during the release period.

Several group analyses were also performed. The sample was subdivided into groups with high (H), medium (M), and low (L) PCL scores, using the cutoffs described by Hare (1985). The percentage of criminals in Groups H, M, and L that violated the conditions of release was 65.2, 48.9, and 23.5, respectively. Survival analysis indicated that the probability of remaining out of prison for at least one year was .80, .54, and .34, Groups L, M, and H, respectively. In addition, those in Group H received more suspensions and presented more supervisory problems during the release period than did those in the other groups. During the release period, inmates in Group H were almost 3 times more likely to violate the conditions of release, and almost 4 times more likely to commit a violent crime, than were those in Group L.

Serin, Peters, and Barbaree (1990) administered the PCL-R to 93 male inmates prior to release from a federal prison on unescorted temporary absence (UTA). Six (37.5%) of the 16 psychopaths in the study, defined by a PCL-R score greater than 31, violated the conditions of UTA, whereas none of the 16 nonpsychopaths, defined by a score less than 17, did so. Subsequently, 77 of the 93 inmates were released on parole; follow-up data were available for 74 of these inmates, including 11 psychopaths and 13 nonpsychopaths. The failure (recommittal) rate on parole was 27% for the entire sample, 7% for the nonpsychopaths, and 33% for the psychopaths. Moreover, the mean time to failure was significantly shorter for the psychopaths (8.0 months) than it was for the nonpsychopaths (14.6 months). The PCL-R predicted outcome better than did a combination of criminal-history and demographic variables, and several standard actuarial risk instruments.

Psychopathy also predicted violent recidivism in young male offenders. Forth et al. (1990) found that PCL-R scores in sample of 75 young offenders were significantly correlated with the number of charges or convictions for violent offenses ($r = .26$) after release. Though the correlation was small, it is important to note that it was obtained with a relatively homogeneous sample—all but two of the offenders met the DSM-III-R criteria for conduct disorder—that consisted of some of the most seriously criminal and persistent young offenders in the province of British Columbia.

In a long-term follow-up study of 166 male patients released from a forensic psychiatric unit, Harris, Rice, and Cormier (1991) reported that 77% of 52 psychopaths, defined by a PCL-R score of at least 25, committed a violent crime subsequent to their release from an intensive therapeutic community program. In comparison, the violent recidivism rate for the other 114 patients was only 21%. In a stringent test of the predictive ability of the PCL-R, the four best criminal history variables (selected from a list of traditionally important predictor variables) were entered into a hierarchical multiple regression analysis. The PCL-R was allowed to enter the analysis only if it produced a significant improvement in the prediction of violent outcome. The addition of the PCL-R increased the multiple correlation with outcome (0 = success, 1 = failure) from .31 to .45, a significant improvement.

Finally, Rice, Harris, and Quinsey (1990) studied 54 rapists released from a maximum security psychiatric hospital. During the follow-up period, which averaged 46 months, 28% of the patients committed a sexual offense and 43% committed a violent offense (all sexual offenses were coded as violent). PCL-R scores were predictive of postrelease sexual offenses ($r = .31$) and of violent offenses ($r = .35$). A combination of PCL-R scores and a phallometric measure of sexual arousal (as measured by penile plethysmography) was as effective (77% correct) at predicting sexual offenses as was a battery of demographic, psychological, and criminal history variables.

Psychopathy and Mental Disorder

Most research on the association between psychopathy and other mental disorders has been plagued by methodological problems. Perhaps the single biggest problem has been a reliance on diagnostic criteria of unknown—or even poor—reliability and validity (e.g., Howard, Bailey, & Newman, 1984). However, it is now apparent that the psychometric properties of the PCL and PCL-R are just as high in forensic psychiatric populations as they are in correctional populations (Harris et al., 1991; Hart & Hare, 1989; Hart, Hare, & Heilbrun, 1992; Ogloff, Wong, &

Greenwood, 1990; Rice & Harris, in press). Recently, Hart and Hare (1989) studied a sample of 80 men remanded in custody for inpatient assessment of fitness to stand trial. These subjects were consecutive admissions to a provincial forensic psychiatric hospital over a 6-month period. Psychopathy was assessed using the PCL-R, and other mental disorders were diagnosed according to DSM-III Axis I and II criteria (American Psychiatric Association, 1980). Subjects were also given clinical global ratings for schizophrenia and for the Axis II personality disorders. PCL-R Total scores were uncorrelated with all Axis I disorders other than drug abuse/dependence ($r = .31$). Total scores were correlated with several Axis II disorders: histrionic ($r = .30$) and antisocial personality ($r = .45$). Categorical analyses indicated that psychopaths were significantly *less* likely than nonpsychopaths to have any Axis I disorder other than substance use and significantly *more* likely to have antisocial personality disorder.

Interesting findings emerged when dimensional ratings of mental disorders were analyzed. Consistent with the results described above, PCL-R scores were uncorrelated with Axis I ratings of schizophrenia. PCL-R scores were correlated with several Axis II ratings: positively with histrionic, narcissistic, antisocial personality disorder ($r = .33$, .39, and .71, respectively), and negatively with avoidant personality disorder ($r = -.30$).

We concluded, on the basis of these results, that psychopathy was either unassociated or negatively associated with most Axis I mental disorders, other than substance use disorders. However, psychopathy had a significant and clinically meaningful pattern of associations with a number of Axis II disorders.

A number of studies have replicated and extended these findings. Hart, Hare, and Heilbrun (1992) looked at the association between PCL scores and DSM-III-R diagnoses of functional psychotic disorders in a sample of 218 men, consecutive admissions to a state forensic psychiatric hospital in Florida. A subsample of 175 men was administered structured diagnostic interviews to assess Axis I disorders. There was no difference between psychopaths and nonpsychopaths in the prevalence, type, or severity of schizophrenia-related disorders; the correlation between the PCL and psychotic diagnoses was $r = .04$.

There have been several studies of psychopathy and substance use. Smith and Newman (1990) assessed substance use disorder with a structured diagnostic interview in 360 male prison inmates. Correlational and categorical analyses revealed that psychopathy, as measured by the PCL-R, was significantly associated with both alcohol and drug abuse/dependence disorders. In two other studies (Hart et al., 1992; Hemphill, Hart, & Hare, 1990), PCL/PCL-R scores were significantly correlated with drug abuse/

dependence diagnoses; however, correlations with alcohol abuse/ dependence diagnoses were nonsignificant.

Hart, Forth, and Hare (1991) recently examined the prevalence of global neuropsychological impairment, assessed using a brief screening battery of clinical tests, in two large samples of prison inmates (N = 90 and 167). They found no increased prevalence of dysfunction or impairment in psychopaths, using either dimensional or categorical analyses. These findings were consistent with an earlier study, conducted by Hare (1984), who looked specifically at measures of frontal lobe functioning in prison inmates.

Finally, we should note that the pattern of correlations between psychopathy and other mental disorders described above is not method-specific. The pattern appears to be similar regardless of whether mental disorder is assessed by clinical interview and chart review, structured clinical interview, or self-report inventory (e.g., Hart, Forth, & Hare, 1991).

Psychopathy, Mental Disorder, and Crime

Although the interactive effects of psychopathy and mental disorder, with respect to crime, have received little scientific attention, the results of several recent studies are suggestive.

Rasmussen and Levander (1991) selected 13 DSM-III schizophrenics from a maximum-security psychiatric ward for chronically aggressive patients. These patients were compared with a group of 13 nonaggressive schizophrenics—matched on the basis of age and time spent in institutions—selected from nearby civil psychiatric facilities. Variables studied were PCL scores and scores on two standardized rating scales of psychiatric symptomatology. The best discriminator between the two groups was the PCL score; aggressive patients had a mean PCL score of 26.6 (SD = 8.50), compared with a mean of 14.5 (SD = 4.68) for the nonaggressive patients.

Rice and Harris (in press) looked at recidivism rates in 96 male schizophrenics found not guilty by reason of insanity and remanded to a forensic psychiatric facility. A control group consisted of 96 nonschizophrenic male forensic patients remanded for brief pretrial psychiatric assessments. The two groups were matched on a number of variables, including age, index offense, and criminal history. Schizophrenics had lower rates of general and violent recidivism than did the other forensic patients, although only the difference for general recidivism was significant. However, psychopathy predicted general recidivism equally well in both groups:

the correlation between the PCL-R and general recidivism was $r = .33$ in schizophrenics and $r = .30$ in nonschizophrenics. PCL-R scores were predictive of violent recidivism in schizophrenics ($r = .20$), but not in nonschizophrenics ($r = -.05$).

Heilbrun, Gustaffson, Hart, and Hare (1992) looked at the associations among psychopathy, schizophrenia, and violence in consecutive admissions to a forensic psychiatric hospital; these subjects were also used in the Hart et al. (1992) study, described above. The index of inpatient violence was the number of verbal and physical assaults, computed for the first and last 3 months of hospitalization. For the 208 patients who were subsequently released from hospital, we also coded *violent recidivism,* defined as any arrest for a violent offense that appeared on the patients' FBI criminal record during the follow-up period. All variables were coded dichotomously (0 = no, 1 = yes).

The PCL was significantly correlated $r = .30$ with assaults during the first 3 months of hospitalization, but only $r = .03$ with assaults in the last 3 months. The PCL was also significantly correlated with violent recidivism ($r = .16$).

The base rate for schizophrenia and related disorders was 41% among the 177 patients who completed a structured diagnostic interview. The correlation between the PCL and schizophrenia (absence vs. presence) was .06. Schizophrenia was not correlated with either inpatient violence ($r = -.12$) or with violent recidivism ($r = .09$). The association between psychopathy and violence was similar in both schizophrenics and nonschizophrenics: the correlation between the PCL and inpatient violence was $r = .19$ in schizophrenics and $r = .32$ in nonschizophrenics (a nonsignificant difference); for violent recidivism, the correlations were $r = .25$ and .11, respectively (also a nonsignificant difference).

Conclusions

The research reviewed in this chapter strongly suggests that psychopathy is associated with an increased risk for criminal and violent behavior in male offenders. In addition, it appears that psychopathic traits predict violence even in those suffering from serious mental disorder (i.e., psychosis).

We should emphasize that any conclusions concerning the link between psychopathy, mental disorder, and violence must be treated with caution in light of the relative lack of solid empirical data available. Also, no study to date has looked at the *interactive* effects of psychopathy and mental disorder on criminal behavior. Such research would require large samples and sophisticated statistical procedures (such as logistic regression or log-linear modeling). It may be that some disorders, such as psychosis, tend either to inhibit or potentiate the behavioral manifestations of psychopathic traits.

References

American Psychiatric Association. (1980). *Diagnostic and statistical manual of mental disorders* (3rd ed.). Washington, DC: Author.

American Psychiatric Association. (1987). *Diagnostic and statistical manual of mental disorders* (3rd ed., rev.). Washington, DC: Author.

Arieti, S. (1967). *The intrapsychic self.* New York: Basic Books.

Blackburn, R. (1990). Treatment of the psychopathic offender. In K. Howells & C. R. Hollin (Eds.), *Clinical approaches to working with mentally disordered and sexual offenders* [Issues in Criminological and Legal Psychology, No. 16] (pp. 54-66). Leicester, England: British Psychological Society.

Cleckley, H. (1976). *The mask of sanity* (5th ed.). St. Louis: C. V. Mosby.

Forth, A. E., Hart, S. D., & Hare, R. D. (1990). Assessment of psychopathy in male young offenders. *Psychological Assessment: A Journal of Consulting and Clinical Psychology, 2,* 342-344.

Hare, R. D. (1980). A research scale for the assessment of psychopathy in criminal populations. *Personality and Individual Differences, 1,* 111-119.

Hare, R. D. (1981). Psychopathy & violence. In J. R. Hayes, T. K. Roberts, & K. S. Solway (Eds.), *Violence and the violent individual* (pp. 53-74). Jamaica, NY: Spectrum.

Hare, R. D. (1984). Performance of psychopaths on cognitive tasks related to frontal lobe function. *Journal of Abnormal Psychology, 93,* 133-140.

Hare, R. D. (1985). Comparison of procedures for the assessment of psychopathy. *Journal of Consulting and Clinical Psychology, 53,* 7-16.

Hare, R. D. (1991). *The Hare Psychopathy Checklist-Revised.* Toronto: Multi-Health Systems.

Hare, R. D., Harpur, T. J., Hakstian, A. R., Forth, A. E., Hart, S. D., & Newman, J. P. (1990). The Revised Psychopathy Checklist: Reliability and factor structure. *Psychological Assessment: A Journal of Consulting and Clinical Psychology, 2,* 338-341.

Hare, R. D., Hart, S. D., & Harpur, T. J. (1991). Psychopathy and the DSM-IV criteria for antisocial personality disorder. *Journal of Abnormal Psychology, 100,* 391-398.

Hare, R. D., & Jutai, J. W. (1983). Criminal history of the male psychopath: Some preliminary data. In K. T. Van Dusen & S. A. Mednick (Eds.), *Prospective studies of crime and delinquency* (pp. 225-236). Boston: Kluwer-Nijhoff.

Hare, R. D., & McPherson, L. M. (1984). Violent and aggressive behavior by criminal psychopaths. *International Journal of Law and Psychiatry, 7,* 35-50.

Hare, R. D., McPherson, L. M., & Forth, A. E. (1988). Male psychopaths and their criminal careers. *Journal of Consulting and Clinical Psychology, 56,* 710-714.

Hare, R. D., Strachan, K. E., & Forth, A. E. (in press). Psychopathy and crime: A review. In K. Howells & C. Hollin (Eds.), *Clinical approaches to mentally disordered offenders.* New York: John Wiley.

Harpur, T. J., Hare, R. D., & Hakstian, A. R. (1989). Two-factor conceptualization of psychopathy: Construct validation and assessment implications. *Psychological Assessment: A Journal of Consulting and Clinical Psychology, 1,* 6-17.

Harris, G. T., Rice, M. E., & Cormier, C. A. (1991). Psychopathy and violent recidivism. *Law and Human Behavior, 15*, 625-637.

Hart, S. D., Forth, A. E., & Hare, R. D. (1991). The MCMI-II as measure of psychopathy. *Journal of Personality Disorders, 5*, 318-327.

Hart, S. D., & Hare, R. D. (1989). Discriminant validity of the Psychopathy Checklist in a forensic psychiatric population. *Psychological Assessment: A Journal of Consulting and Clinical Psychology, 1*, 211-218.

Hart, S. D., Hare, R. D., & Harpur, T. J. (1992). The Psychopathy Checklist-Revised (PCL-R): An overview for researchers and clinicians. In J. Rosen & P. McReynolds (Eds.), *Advances in psychological assessment, 8* (pp. 103-130). New York: Plenum.

Hart, S. D., Hare, R. D., & Heilbrun, K. (1992). *Assessment of psychopathy in forensic psychiatric patients.* Manuscript in preparation.

Hart, S. D., Kropp, P. R., & Hare, R. D. (1988). Performance of male psychopaths following conditional release from prison. *Journal of Consulting and Clinical Psychology, 56*, 227-232.

Heilbrun, K., Gustaffson, D., Hart, S. D., & Hare, R. D. (1992). *Psychopathy and the prediction of violence in forensic patients.* Manuscript in preparation.

Hemphill, J. F., Hart, S. D., & Hare, R. D. (1990, May). *Self-reported frequency and age at first substance use in criminal psychopaths.* Paper presented at the Annual Meeting of the Canadian Psychological Association, Ottawa.

Howard, R., Bailey, R., & Newman, A. (1984). A preliminary study of Hare's "Research Scale for the Assessment of Psychopathy" in mentally-abnormal offenders. *Personality and Individual Differences, 5*, 389-396.

Kosson, D. S., Smith, S. S., & Newman, J. P. (1990). Evaluating the construct validity of psychopathy on black and white male inmates: Three preliminary studies. *Journal of Abnormal Psychology, 99*, 250-259.

McCord, W., & McCord, J. (1964). *The psychopath: An essay on the criminal mind.* Princeton, NJ: Van Nostrand.

Ogloff, J. R., Wong, S., & Greenwood, A. (1990). Treating criminal psychopaths in a therapeutic community program. *Behavioral Sciences and the Law, 8*, 81-90.

Rasmussen, K., & Levander, S. (1991). *Comparison of aggressive and nonaggressive schizophrenics.* Manuscript submitted for publication.

Rice, M. E., & Harris, G. T. (in press). Violent recidivism in schizophrenic and non-schizophrenic forensic psychiatric patients. *International Journal of Law and Psychiatry.*

Rice, M. E., Harris, G. T., & Quinsey, V. L. (1990). A follow-up of rapists assessed in a maximum security psychiatric facility. *Journal of Interpersonal Violence, 4*, 435-448.

Serin, R. C. (1991). Psychopathy and violence in criminals. *Journal of Interpersonal Violence, 6*, 423-431.

Serin, R. C., Peters, R., & Barbaree, H. E. (1990). Predictors of psychopathy and release outcome in a criminal population. *Psychological Assessment: A Journal of Consulting and Clinical Psychology, 2*, 419-422.

Smith, S. S., & Newman, J. P. (1990). Alcohol and drug abuse/dependence disorders in psychopathic and nonpsychopathic criminal offenders. *Journal of Abnormal Psychology, 99*, 430-439.

Wong, S. (1984). Criminal and institutional behaviours of psychopaths. *Programs Branch Users Report.* Ottawa: Ministry of the Solicitor-General of Canada.

World Health Organization. (1978). *Mental disorders: Glossary and guide to their classification in accordance with the Ninth Revision of the International Classification of Diseases.* Geneva: Author.

II

Risk Factors
for Violent Behavior

7

Childhood Precursors of Aggressive Offending in Personality-Disordered Adults

BARBARA MAUGHAN

As longitudinal studies of mental disorder and crime accumulate, so our understanding of the childhood roots of these severe adult difficulties is gradually expanding. This chapter examines developmental evidence on one particular aspect of this broad field: the childhood precursors of offending, especially aggressive offending, in personality-disordered adults. Personality disorders are among the most frequent diagnoses found in offender populations; and aggressive tendencies, when they occur in these groups, have often been evident from an early age (Hodgins & von Grunau, 1989). Both theoretically and practically, a developmental perspective is especially important in this area.

Although many different types of personality problems have been identified in serious offender samples (Hollander & Turner, 1985), most could be broadly characterized as "dramatic." Antisocial personality and explosive or impulsive character disorders are among the most clearly distinguishable groups in those convicted of violent or aggressive crimes. There is an extensive developmental literature in these areas, dating from Robins's (1966) classic follow-ups of conduct-disordered children. Many differing early correlates have been identified, and one of the main challenges in this field is to come to some integration of the varying strands of existing evidence. An overview of recent findings on the antecedents of antisocial personality and aggressive offending forms the main focus for this chapter.

Childhood conduct problems and seriously aggressive behaviors in adulthood have also, however, been noted in groups showing very different patterns of general personality functioning. Although these are generally less well recognized than the dramatic personality disorders, and have been much less extensively studied, any comprehensive account of childhood precursors must eventually take them into account. To illustrate these varying patterns, we begin with a brief description of one such group, of particular concern because of the unpredictability of their aggressive acts: individuals diagnosed as showing schizoid personality problems, or Asperger's syndrome.

Asperger's Syndrome and Aggressive Offending

The first account of Asperger's syndrome (Asperger, 1944) appeared shortly after early descriptions of autism (Kanner, 1943), and the condition resembles autism in a number of clinical features. It is marked by solitariness and severe impairments in social interaction; a profound lack of empathy; the inability to recognize and respond to social cues; a lack of pretend or fantasy play in childhood; and an unusual and repetitive repertoire of interests in later life. As in autism, boys are more likely to be affected than girls, and many features of the disorder are evident very early in childhood, often from the second year. Unlike autism, however, children with Asperger's syndrome are not usually seriously intellectually impaired, and give little evidence of language delay, though their expressive language may be odd and pedantic.

This clinical picture of severe social isolation and eccentricity shows considerable continuity at least into early adulthood. Despite uncertainties over its nosological status (Howlin & Yule, 1990; Tantum, 1988a; Wing, 1981; Wolff & Chick, 1980), much current opinion in child psychiatry favors its retention as a separate syndrome. Wolff (1984) has argued that "schizoidness," as related to this group, contributes specific features to conduct problems in childhood and to personality disorder in adult life. A number of individual case studies (e.g., Baron-Cohen, 1988; Everall & Le Couteur, 1990; Mawson, Grounds, & Tantum, 1985) and clinical accounts of larger series of patients support these suggestions. Wolff and Cull (1986) conducted a retrospective case note study of "schizoid" boys and matched "non-schizoid" clinic attenders, supplemented by clinical descriptions of the antisocial behavior of both boys and girls from a larger schizoid cohort. The matched groups did not differ in *rates* of conduct symptoms or aggression in childhood, nor in levels of police contact after age 16, but the nature of their problems did seem to vary. Conduct-disordered children in the comparison group showed the expected patterns of stealing in childhood and alcohol problems post age 16. Neither of these features emerged among the schizoid boys: instead, their conduct problems were of a different type, less dependent on adverse environmental circumstances, and possibly more associated with their unusual fantasy life.

Of the 20 seriously antisocial boys in the larger cohort, the majority had been physically aggressive or had threatened violence. Their behavior was impulsive and involved persistent and apparently unprovoked expressions of hostility to others. Parents were often targets for attacks, and if provoking circumstances could be identified, they seemed to center on what were experienced as intrusive interpersonal contacts. Among affected individuals proportionately more girls than boys were seriously antisocial, and girls were more likely to put their fantasies into action.

A not dissimilar picture has emerged from accounts of adult psychiatric patients receiving help because of lifelong social isolation and eccentricity (Tantum, 1988b). Assaults on family members and children were also common in this group, and (unlike the pattern found in some autistic individuals), none of their crimes was associated with their special interests. Unpredictability and unaccountability were again frequent and disturbing features of their offenses: One instance is cited of a 16-year-old boy, visiting a shopping center, picking up an infant from a stroller and dropping him 30 feet to a concrete walkway below. Finally, subjects in this violent minority appeared to have no grasp of their victim's distress: Tantum notes that "it was not uncommon for the subject to criticize the victim for making too much of a fuss" (1988b, p. 782).

We know very little about the etiology of this pattern of severe childhood difficulties. From a developmental perspective, it is important in suggesting that conduct symptoms not only cluster together as specific disorders, but also appear as elements of the symptomatology of a range of other conditions, and are likely, when they do, to persist into adult life. Asperger's individuals do not appear to show a seriously increased likelihood of violent or aggressive acts in adulthood, and will make up only a very small proportion of adjudicated violent offenders. But they are of concern because of the unusual, unpredictable, and distressing pattern of their aggressivity, and, in the context of assessments of dangerousness, their apparent inability to consider the effects of their actions on others. Further work on the etiology of their problems and the precipitants of their aggressive acts is clearly extremely important.

Antisocial Personality Disorders and Aggressive Crime

In the main, however, the dramatic types of personality disorder, especially antisocial personality and psychopathy, are most usually associated with aggressive offending. Antisocial personality is heavily represented in offender populations, with rates as high as 45% reported in jail groups (Petrich, 1976), in contrast to the lifetime prevalence of just over 7%

estimated in men in the general population (Robins, Tipp, & Przybeck, 1990). Childhood antecedents of these conditions have been extensively investigated from a variety of different perspectives. Later chapters provide detailed discussions of three issues of particular importance: conduct problems (Robins, Chapter 9 in this volume), bullying (Olweus, Chapter 17 in this volume), and the role of parenting difficulties in the genesis of antisocial behavior in childhood (Patterson and Yoerger, Chapter 8 in this volume). This chapter sets these more detailed accounts in the broader context of related evidence on behavioral and other precursors in the child.

Some Methodological Issues

A wide range of both criminological and more psychiatrically oriented studies provides evidence on the childhood precursors of antisocial personality and aggressive offending. Because these problems are relatively rare in adulthood, retrospective studies and prospective investigations of high-risk childhood groups make up a large part of the literature. Prospective studies of general population samples (in many ways the most powerful designs from a developmental perspective), however, are becoming increasingly available. Much work in the area is methodologically sophisticated, but the evidence is still not without its shortcomings: Many studies lack appropriate comparison groups or provide only a limited basis for generalization, and the measurement (and at times conceptualization) of some important childhood characteristics has varied over time and between investigators. Synthesizing findings across quite disparate studies is always hazardous, and these difficulties need to be borne in mind throughout.

Other issues arise in relation to adult outcomes. Our particular concern here is with links between mental disorder and crime. Most longitudinal studies, however, have taken either one or the other of these outcomes as their prime focus of interest. As the Epidemiological Catchment Area (ECA) studies have confirmed, they are by no means synonymous; violence is a frequent characteristic of those meeting criteria for antisocial personality, but repeated offending was found in fewer than half of those receiving the diagnosis (Robins et al., 1990). Our interest here thus centers on a subgroup of both aggressive offenders on the one hand, and antisocial personality disorders on the other. In many instances we can do no more than note that possible precursors show links with one or the other condition separately, but that data are limited at this stage on the specificity of predictions to the joint adult pattern.

More detailed questions then require attention in each area. In relation to personality disorders, there are continuing debates over the links between *antisocial personality* as defined in DSM-III-R (American Psychiatric Association, 1987) and *psychopathy* (Hare, Hart, & Harpur, 1991). To date, the great majority of developmental studies have used DSM criteria in assessing adult outcomes, and we shall do so here. There are suggestions, however, that some aspects of the childhood picture may differ in important ways between these two groups, and we note these possible variations as they arise. Next, rates of comorbidity in adulthood, especially with alcohol and drug-related disorders, are high in offender populations of this kind. Drug disorders in general show stronger links with income-generating than with violent crime (Gandossy, Williams, Cohen, & Harwood, 1980), but alcohol use is clearly strongly associated with the commission of aggressive offenses, though the precise nature of the causal mechanisms involved is still not well understood (Fagan, 1990; Pihl & Peterson, Chapter 14 in this volume). The role of more long-standing alcohol problems is also unclear. Buydens-Branchey, Branchey, and Noumair (1989) report much increased rates of incarceration for violent offenses in patients with an early onset of alcoholism, but Abram (1989) found no associations between alcohol disorders and either property or aggressive offenses in an incarcerated population once comorbidity with antisocial personality had been taken into account. In the light of these uncertainties, we have not attempted to examine the implications of comorbid adult disorders here; this will clearly be an important area of investigation in future studies.

In relation to offending, the majority of the evidence on childhood correlates is relatively unspecific in terms of later offense types. In general, longitudinal evidence on aggressive crime relates to chronic "versatile" offenders, who engage in aggressive acts as part of a pattern of high-rate offending of all kinds. The peak age for the commission of most violent crime in Western societies appears to be in the early to mid twenties (Wilson & Herrnstein, 1985). Prospective studies thus need to extend well into the twenties to cover the full risk period. At present, several important prospective follow-ups have either not yet reached this age range or are only able to provide partial data, covering the beginning of the main risk period. Where data on adjudicated aggressive offenses are still limited in this way, we have noted findings on other potentially informative indicators: self-reports of undetected but illegal confrontative behaviors, and other features of the criminal career pattern typical of many violent offenders—an early onset of offending, and a high-rate, persistent pattern of both aggressive and nonaggressive crime. Finally, because longitudinal evidence on the small groups of aggressive female offenders is extremely limited, this discussion is confined very predominantly to studies of men.

Childhood Precursors

With these cautions in mind, we turn to an overview of current evidence on childhood precursors. Aggressive tendencies (Olweus, 1979) and the disregard for social norms typical of conduct disorder (Robins, 1966, 1978) have been widely viewed as the core childhood features, but many other hypotheses have also been advanced: Quay (1965) has argued for the centrality of a propensity for sensation-seeking; Ellis (1982) for lack of empathy; Smetana (1990) for impaired moral development; Eysenck (1977) for the failure to learn from experience; Pulkinnen (1988) for inadequate impulse control; Venables (1987) for a reduced capacity to experience fear; Gray (1987) for a two-factor model involving neurological systems of behavioral activation and inhibition; Farrington, Loeber, and Van Kammen (1990) for a behavioral constellation focusing on hyperactivity-impulsivity-inattentiveness; and Dodge (1986) and others for a deficit in interpersonal relationship skills reflecting problems in social cognition.

On current evidence, it seems likely that a range of factors, including aggressive conduct problems, hyperactivity, biological markers, neuropsychological deficits, and difficulties in relationships with peers, all form part of the predictive picture from childhood. Comprehensive reviews have recently been undertaken in a number of these areas (Loeber, 1990; Moffitt, 1990b; Robins, 1991; Schachar, 1991). Here, we highlight just a few key findings in each area to provide a background for discussion of their possible interrelationships.

Child Behaviors

Childhood conduct problems have long been established as central predictors of antisocial personality disorder (Robins, 1966, 1978), and conduct disorder and aggressiveness have consistently been associated with later aggressive offending. Looking backwards from adulthood, continuities between these adult outcomes and early aggression and conduct problems are strong. This conclusion has been confirmed in retrospective investigations of groups of adjudicated offenders (Lewis et al., 1985), in follow-back studies of clinic samples (Robins, 1978), and in prospective studies of general population groups (Farrington, 1978). In the great majority of cases, recurrent adult violence appears to have been preceded by a clear pattern of aggressiveness in childhood or early adolescence, and antisocial personality disorder by a range of childhood conduct problems.

As with all other childhood predictors, continuities looking forward are less complete, but nonetheless substantial. Loeber and Stouthamer-Loeber (1987) reviewed prospective evidence in relation to offending and used a measure of relative improvement over chance (RIOC) to compare predictors across studies. They found median RIOC values of 38.3 and 52.5 for childhood aggression and general problem behaviors, respectively, in predicting recidivism, and 66.3 for the prediction of serious offending from the general problem behavior cluster. In relation to conduct problems, findings from the ECA studies confirm the picture emerging from earlier clinical populations: More than a quarter of children meeting childhood criteria for antisocial personality were found to show the full disorder in adulthood (Robins et al., 1990).

These figures accord well with the wider literature confirming conduct disorder as highly stable across childhood, with long-term sequelae in a range of domains of adult functioning (Robins, 1991), and aggression as among the most stable of individual traits (Eron & Huesmann, 1990; Olweus, 1979). Predictions to persistent or recidivist offending appear to be strongest in the case of conduct disorder of early onset, high frequency, involving antisocial behaviors, and evident in a variety of settings (Loeber, 1990). The ECA studies (Robins, 1991; Robins et al., 1990) suggest a similar picture for antisocial personality: The total number of childhood symptoms, rather than any particular pattern of problems, was the strongest predictor of adult difficulties. Age of onset contributed additional effects, with a very early onset (before age 6) being particularly associated with an increased likelihood of persistence into adult life. Antisocial behavior beginning in the teens shows both different correlates (Rutter, Tizard, Yule, Graham, & Whitmore, 1976) and an apparently more benign course. In the case of aggression, however, the picture may be rather different, with the strongest associations with adult offending emerging for measures of aggression taken later, in the early teens, when aggressiveness is in general much less common than in early childhood (Loeber & Stouthamer-Loeber, 1987). In both cases, then, predictions are strongest for the more extreme, relatively atypical patterns of behavior.

Persistence has also been associated with various subtypes of conduct problems. Henn, Bardwell, and Jenkins (1980) found undersocialized aggressive juveniles more likely to have adult arrests for violent crime, and Loeber and Schmalling (1985a) have argued for the utility of distinctions based on "overt" and "covert" antisocial behaviors. "Versatile" boys, engaging in both of these types of behavior, were more likely to become multiple offenders over a 5-year follow-up than those showing either type of problem alone at initial assessment (Loeber & Schmalling, 1985b). A further subgroup of particular interest in this context is children showing a mixture of both shy and aggressive behaviors. Shyness has been argued to act as a protective factor against delinquency in nonaggressive boys (Ensminger, Kellam, & Rubin, 1983), but the combination of shyness and aggression appears to be associated with especially poor outcomes. A number of studies (Farrington, Gallagher, Morley, St. Ledger, & West, 1988; Kellam, Simon, & Ensminger, 1983; McCord, 1981; Moskowitz & Schwartzman, 1989) have identified this unusual pattern as a strong predictor of later arrest, drug use, and other problems. To date, however, the meaning of this pattern in childhood and the mechanisms underlying continuities with adult difficulties raise many queries. Rubin, LeMare, and Lollis (1990) have recently postulated two possibly different routes to the development of social withdrawal in childhood, one associated with insecure or hostile early relationships with caregivers, the other with temperamental inhibition in the child. It will clearly be important to link work in these areas with findings on longer term outcomes, to extend our understanding of the implications of this unusual childhood pattern.

In addition to conduct disorder, pervasive hyperactivity/attention deficit is also strongly associated with aggression in childhood. It shows a marked tendency to lead on to later conduct problems, and has well-established associations with offending (see e.g., Mednick & Kandel, 1988; Moffitt, 1990a; Offord, Sullivan, Allen, & Abrams, 1979; Satterfield, Hoppe, & Schell, 1982) and antisocial personality (Manuzza et al., 1991). The high rate of comorbidity between hyperactivity and conduct disorder (Schachar, 1991) may have confounded results in earlier studies, but more recent work has been designed specifically to take this into account. In a follow-up of diagnosed ADDH clinic attenders, screened to exclude those with associated conduct problems at the time of the initial assessment (Manuzza, Klein, Konig, & Giampino, 1989), probands were found to have more multiple convictions than nonproblem controls by ages 16 to 23, longer arrest histories, and more arrests for aggressive crimes. Poor outcomes in terms of offending were almost entirely concentrated on the subset of subjects who had developed conduct disorder or antisocial personality by the time of the follow-up; indeed, those probands showing no disorder at follow-up differed very little from controls on a range of indicators of early adult adjustment (Manuzza, Klein, Bonagura, Konig, & Shenker, 1988). A second study has recently replicated these findings in relation to continuities with antisocial personality (Manuzza et al., 1991). Hyperactivity clearly needs to be included alongside conduct problems as a potentially important precursor.

Biological Factors

There is a considerable body of evidence that abnormalities in biological functioning, centering on markers of autonomic hyporesponsivity, characterize male offenders meeting criteria for antisocial personality. Similar patterns have also been found in aggressive, conduct-disordered children and adolescents (Venables, 1987). Abnormally low plasma adrenalin levels have been identified in aggressive adolescents who went on to offend in adulthood (Magnusson, Stattin, & Dunér, 1983), consistent with the view that a lessened fear response may be central to many cases of antisocial personality disorder. Recent psychophysiological work (Raine, Venables, & Williams, 1990) has identified prospective links between reduced electrodermal, cardiovascular, and cortical arousal in adolescence, and offending (relatively serious, but not specifically aggressive in nature) in early adulthood. Finally, there is evidence that men with a diagnosis of explosive or intermittent personality disorder metabolize sugar abnormally (Virkkunen, 1983), and that, when exacerbated by alcohol, this can lead to confusion and violent behavior. Recent studies of incarcerated juvenile offenders (Gans et al., 1990) have confirmed this picture among 14- to 19-year-olds, but failed to find consistent performance deficits after sucrose ingestion; indeed, delinquents rated as hyperactive in this sample (Bachorowski et al., 1990) showed improved, rather than impaired, performance on a range of psychological tests. Hyperactive groups performed especially poorly after a no-sucrose meal; as the authors note, these findings may also be consistent with a model of poor performance in such groups reflecting suboptimal arousal.

Neuropsychological Abnormalities

The possibility that brain dysfunction might show specific relations with violence, perhaps through defects in impulse control, has been of interest for many years. Hodgins, de Bray, and Brown (1989) found poor brain functioning, as reflected in low neuropsychological test scores, to be differentially associated with criminal histories of violence in a sample of mentally disordered adult offenders. Similar specific links between neuropsychological deficits and violent, but not property, crimes have been reported in nondisordered offender samples (Bryant, Scott, & Golden, 1984). Current evidence from neuropsychological studies of juveniles is less conclusive, partly because of general methodological weaknesses, and also very probably because of the difficulty of identifying repeat offenders at this early stage (Moffitt, 1990b). There is, however, evidence that neuropsychological deficits, in combination with attention deficits and other problems, show short-term predictive links with self-reports of aggressive offending within the juvenile period (Moffitt, 1990a). We return to a more detailed discussion of these results later.

The interpretation of the neuropsychological findings has been the subject of much debate. In the delinquency literature, impairments in intellectual functioning have been assumed to contribute to offending only indirectly, with factors such as poor school achievement and feelings of status deprivation constituting the more immediate causal influences. Neuropsychological theories suggest a more direct role for neurological impairments on the early development of temperament, personality, and psychopathology (Moffitt, 1990b). Links with problems in the modulation of attention, in the development of impulsive behavioral styles, or more specifically in the perception and interpretation of social cues, have all been proposed here. Such models suggest much earlier influences on the development of social behavior and interactions, likely to cumulate across childhood in the context of relationships with both family members and peers.

Peer Relations

Children who are rejected or neglected by their peers have consistently been found to be at risk for a variety of later difficulties, including both juvenile and adult offending, and adult psychopathology (Kupersmidt, Coie, & Dodge, 1990; Parker & Asher, 1987). Peer relations have been argued to make unique contributions to the development of social competence in childhood, and in particular to the socialization of aggression (Hartup, 1978, 1983). From the empirical literature, however, it is difficult to assess how far the documented associations with later outcomes do in fact reflect independent causal influences. Poor peer relations are characteristic of a number of childhood disorders and are strongly associated with aggression after the preschool period. Links with adult outcomes might thus reflect independent causal processes or multiplier effects, or simply show that measures of peer relations act as correlated lead indicators for other problems. To date, it is difficult to choose between these various possibilities, though there is some evidence that peer rejection adds little to predictions of delinquency once peer-perceived aggression is taken into account (Kupersmidt & Coie, 1985). Further studies examining peer status alongside other potential predictors of later outcomes are clearly needed. At present, it seems likely that limited or aberrant peer relations at the least compound other difficulties, and may well contribute in more specific ways: One obvious route would be through elevating risks of deviant peer group membership.

Alongside these findings, a related literature has explored the social cognitions of children with low peer status. Aggressive children have been found to show particular forms of attributional bias in interpreting social cues: They are much more likely to attribute hostile intent to a hypothetical peer in ambiguous conditions (Dodge, 1980), and to misinterpret benign intentions as hostile (Dodge & Newman, 1981). In a recent study of incarcerated adolescent offenders (Dodge, Price, Bachorowski, & Newman, 1990), a hostile attributional style was especially associated with undersocialized, but not socialized, aggression. These links held when controlled for race, SES, and IQ, suggesting that they were not simply a reflection of cultural factors or general information-processing difficulties.

As with the wider data on peer relations, the causal status of these social-cognitive findings is still unclear; much current evidence is correlational, making it uncertain how far biases in attributions contribute to, are a consequence of, or act primarily to maintain aggressive behaviors. The findings are of interest, however, in suggesting that deficits in social learning, especially centering on the recognition and interpretation of social cues, may be particularly characteristic of aggressive offenders.

Integrating the Childhood Findings

Identifying these various associations is only the first step in setting forward a developmental account of aggressive offending and problems in adult personality functioning. Even at this level, many questions still remain. Are links between childhood factors and later outcomes dimensional or categorical in form, reflecting continuously distributed traits or differential syndromes? Are particular childhood features associated with particular aspects of an aggressive criminal career (Blumstein, Cohen, Roth, & Visher, 1986; Farrington & Hawkins, 1991)? Do these childhood difficulties lead directly, or only in more indirect ways, to deviant behaviors in adult life? And, perhaps most important, how are the various predictors related together, and what is the central nature of the predispositions or deficits that may underlie them?

At present, these questions are difficult to answer. Most prospective studies have focused on one or at the most two childhood factors, and, so far as we are aware, none has yet included them all. In many instances their interrelations in childhood remain poorly understood, so that extending the focus to adult outcomes inevitably involves speculation. Where several predictors have been studied together, however, results are consistent in suggesting that a constellation of factors, rather than individual traits, is likely to be important in predicting the persistence of difficulties over time. Each of the elements outlined above seems likely to be involved here, and, although the evidence is far from complete, there are a number of pointers that a hyperactivity-impulsivity-inattention constellation may well be central to the overall picture.

Various different lines of evidence point in this direction. Some of the most persuasive come from studies of the developmental associations among hyperactivity, conduct disorder, and aggression in childhood. Rates of comorbidity between hyperactivity and conduct disorder are high, and there has been considerable debate (Hinshaw, 1987; Robins, 1991) over whether they are best viewed as separate disorders or as age-related manifestations of the same underlying construct. On balance, many investigators currently favor their retention as separate disorders, and they note that, when viewed in this way, two important conclusions emerge. First, hyperactivity in general predates, and appears to predispose to the development of, conduct problems. Second, it is the joint pattern that appears most ominous in terms of later outcomes.

To date, follow-up studies of "pure" groups showing each separate pattern, as well as the combined disorders, are extremely limited, so these conclusions must remain tentative. In childhood, however, Taylor, Sandberg, Thorley, and Giles (1991) found that 28% of conduct disordered only, 51% of hyperactive only, but 81% of comorbid cases showed continuing disorder at a 9-month follow-up. Follow-ups into adolescence (Barkley, Fischer, Edelbrock, & Smallish, 1990) and into early adulthood (Manuzza et al., 1989) have reported a similar pattern: The most serious antisocial outcomes occurred in groups where the original ADDH syndrome persisted, and was accompanied by conduct disorder/antisocial personality.

In terms of links with aggression, more severely aggressive conduct problems have been noted in comorbid groups in a number of studies (Hinshaw, 1987; Offord et al., 1979). In early childhood, hyperactivity shows strong links with aggression, and may be of equal importance in predicting difficulties in peer relations. Pope, Bierman, and Mumma (1989), in a school-based study of boys in Grades 1 to 6, found only a very small proportion showing aggressiveness alone, in the absence of hyperactivity, at these ages. While levels of hyperactivity were similar in groups with and without accompanying aggression, aggressivity was much higher in the mixed group. In addition, hyperactivity made independent contributions to the prediction of peer status. Inattentiveness, rather than motor activity per se, seemed most important here, underlining suggestions that insensitivity to social and interpersonal cues might lie at the heart of these children's difficulties with their peers.

At older ages, Moffitt (Moffitt, 1990a; Moffitt & Henry, 1989) has provided evidence for the discriminant validity of a comorbid ADD/delinquent subgroup in the Dunedin prospective study. Cross sectionally at 13, this small group ($N = 19/435$) did not differ from other ADD boys in terms of hyperactivity or inattentiveness, nor from other delinquents in severity of self-reported delinquency. They had worse neuropsychological deficits than other groups, however. They faced the worst family adversity and received aggression ratings more than 2 standard deviations higher than other self-report offenders. Developmentally, they also showed a distinct profile, with the lowest scores on motor skills in early childhood, the lowest IQ scores from ages 5 to 13, and consistently the most serious antisocial behavior up until age 13, when other delinquents first began to show problems in a similar range. Prospectively, results for these groups have only been reported to age 15; at that point, the ADD/delinquent group, along with other delinquents identified at 13, reported much higher levels of continuing delinquency than other boys. The ADD/delinquent group did not differ from other delinquents in levels of self-reported theft, but scored 1.5 standard deviations higher on self-reports of illegal aggressive acts. This particular combination of difficulties may thus be of special importance in terms of later aggressive offending.

Many elements of the constellation of interest here have been examined in the Swedish general population cohort studied by Magnusson and colleagues (Magnusson & Bergman, 1988, 1990). Cross sectionally at 13, cluster analyses showed that of a range of behaviors—aggressiveness, motor restlessness, lack of concentration, low school motivation, poor peer relations, and underachievement—only poor peer relations and underachievement emerged separately as single-problem factors. For all other behaviors, the much more usual pattern was one of clusters of difficulties occurring together, with the most severe scores concentrated in the multiproblem groupings. Physiological data, available on subsamples of these adolescents, lent further support to this conclusion: Adrenalin excretion was significantly lower in multiproblem than in well-adjusted clusters (Magnusson & Bergman, 1990), and particularly associated with hyperactivity and inattention (af Klinteberg & Magnusson, 1989). By early adolescence, then, many of the factors outlined in earlier sections showed a marked tendency to occur together.

Prospectively, analyses based on the adolescent clusters showed that associations with later offending occurred largely in the multiproblem groups; if these were removed from the analyses, individual traits no longer showed links with later outcomes. Aggression alone, for example, in the absence of other problems, did not predict to later criminality (Magnusson & Bergman, 1988) or to alcohol abuse (Andersson, Bergman, & Magnusson, 1989). In addition, the biological markers of reduced autonomic reactivity showed no associations with aggression in the absence of hyperactivity and inattention.

Across a range of ages, and in terms of different developmental connections, there are thus a number of pointers that the comorbid pattern of hyperactivity and conduct disorder may be at the core of the wider range of factors identified in earlier sections. Loeber (1990) reached similar conclusions in a discussion of evidence for differing developmental pathways to adult offending. He postulated separate nonaggressive and "aggressive-versatile" paths, primarily distinguished by age of onset (the aggressive-versatile path beginning earlier), and the more marked presence of hyperactivity, aggressive conduct problems, poor peer relations, and academic problems in the versatile-aggressive route.

If confirmed, these findings in their turn raise further questions. Does the postulated constellation reflect a distinct clinical syndrome in childhood, a subtype of either hyperactivity or conduct disorder, or perhaps the conjunction of extremes on a number of continuously distributed traits? To date, evidence on these questions is limited. Conduct disorder has been shown to predict to antisocial personality in a dimensional way (Robins, 1991), and there appear to be few childhood differences between hyperactive children who do and do not show comorbid conduct disorder (Schachar, 1991). In contrast, some follow-ups of hyperactive children have suggested that poor adult outcomes are largely concentrated in particular subgroups, which may be qualitatively distinct in nature. Much further evidence is clearly needed to resolve these questions.

A second set of queries arises from the early adolescent findings of associations between biological markers of reduced autonomic reactivity and measures of hyperactivity and inattention. In adulthood, comparable biological measures are especially characteristic of psychopaths, but they are a group known not to show evidence of neuropsychological impairment or inattentiveness. This is clearly an important issue: The disjunction between the childhood and adult findings suggests either that early deficits may remit in some cases, so that they are no longer evident in adulthood, or that there may be different developmental pathways to different types of serious adult offending, not yet distinguished in the developmental literature. Once again, more detailed evidence is required before these issues can be resolved.

Yet further questions concern the underlying predispositions involved in a more widely defined behavioral constellation. If hyperactivity forms a core element in this picture along with conduct problems, then difficulties in the modulation of attention and in information-processing may be key elements in the underlying pattern. These suggestions are not inconsistent with current evidence, but raise further particular queries: Is a general information-processing deficit implicated or, as the social-cognitive work suggests, are the problems more specific to the recognition and interpretation of social cues? How could the findings on the poor prognosis for shy-aggressive children be understood in terms of this type of model? And would it imply that the childhood constellation operates as a direct risk factor for later difficulties, or in some more indirect way, perhaps by increasing vulnerability to the effects of adverse environmental circumstances?

There are suggestions from a number of studies that interactive effects of this kind may be important. Raine and Mednick (1989) have recently proposed that biological factors predispose to nonviolent antisocial behavior in individuals with benign home backgrounds, but to violence or seriously recidivistic crime in those experiencing adverse early rearing. Mednick and Kandel (1988) found differential effects of this kind in a study of perinatal abnormalities: Minor physical abnormalities were associated with later violence in individuals raised in unstable, nonintact families, but carried no increased risk for those brought up in more favorable environments. In the Dunedin study, the ADD/delinquent group had the highest family adversity scores: Comparable levels of attention deficit in children from more favorable home backgrounds were not associated with poor later outcomes. In a similar way, a number of studies in the hyperactivity field have indicated that poor outcomes are predicted by poor family relationships, maternal depression, parental divorce, and paternal antisocial behaviors (Barkley et al., 1990; Hechtman, Weiss, Perlman, & Amsel, 1984; Lambert, 1988; Wallander, 1988).

The role of very early deficits may thus be to convey increased vulnerability to stressful home background conditions, rather than to act as direct risk factors per se. Later, reciprocal influences of the child's behavior on caregivers, peers, and others doubtless contribute to the maintenance of continuities in behavior over time. Impulsive antisocial children are more likely to elicit negative responses from those around them; at older ages, similar processes may act to maintain them in environments that elevate the possibility of continuing risk. While models of this kind have been examined in relation to other aspects of childhood-adulthood continuities (Caspi, Elder, & Herbener, 1990), their specific operation in the context of later offending and personality disorder requires much further elaboration.

A number of important methodological implications also follow from these proposals. First, we need a great deal more evidence on developmental linkages between the variables of interest in childhood to substantiate or refine the suggestions outlined thus far. In terms of behavioral indicators, we need to know more about the course of both "pure" and mixed problem groups in general population and clinical samples. In a similar way, adult outcome measures in prospective studies could include a range of differing criteria and their interrelationships, to allow both for assessments of risk for comorbid adult patterns, and for more refined specification of the links with particular adult disorders. And last, as Magnusson and his colleagues have argued, if constellations of factors rather than individual variables are of predictive importance, different styles of analysis will be required in longitudinal investigations. Traditionally, prediction analyses have been variable-oriented, examining associations between individual indicators at different points in time. If combinations of these factors show the most discriminating power, then analyses of single variables need to be complemented by other approaches: in particular, more "person-oriented" methods such as those outlined above, focusing on subgroups defined in terms of combinations of risk factors.

Conclusions

Aggressive offending in adulthood can arise in the context of differing types of personality disorder. Our understanding of possible childhood precursors varies markedly: Very little is known of the factors underlying the aggressive behavior of individuals with conditions such as Asperger's syndrome, but there is a complex and constantly expanding literature on the antecedents of offending and antisocial personality disorder.

In these latter areas, integrating existing findings into a coherent developmental account presents major challenges. It is clear that the patterns of childhood difficulty most likely to persist to adulthood are those that begin early in childhood, and involve a wide range of antisocial behaviors. We have suggested, however, that the underlying predisposition may be one that turns on a behavioral constellation of hyperactivity-impulsivity-inattentiveness in early childhood, from which aggressive conduct symptoms develop in a number of cases. This suggestion can only be tentative at present. If correct, it argues in turn for the possible role of deficits in social learning as among the central predisposing factors. Adverse family circumstances, poor parenting practices, genetic factors, and minor neurological damage all seem likely to contribute etiologically. What makes for the persistence of early childhood difficulties in some cases but not others is less clear: Continued family adversities and the self-perpetuating effects of the individual's own behavior doubtless both play a part, but our understanding of key intervening stages in the developmental process from childhood to adulthood, and the potential role of continuing life stressors or opportunities, needs much fuller explication.

References

Abram, K. M. (1989). The effect of co-occurring disorders on criminal careers: Interaction of antisocial personality, alcoholism, and drug disorders. *International Journal of Law and Psychiatry, 12,* 133-148.

American Psychiatric Association. (1987). *Diagnostic and statistical manual of mental disorders* (3rd ed., rev.). Washington, DC: Author.

Andersson, T., Bergman, L. R., & Magnusson, D. (1989). Patterns of adjustment problems and alcohol abuse in early adulthood: A prospective longitudinal study. *Development and Psychopathology, 1,* 119-131.

Asperger, H. (1944). Die autischen Psychopathen im Kinder. *Archiv für Psychiatrie und Nervenkrankheiten, 117,* 76-146.

Bachorowski, J.-A., Newman, J. P., Nichols, S. L., Gans, D. A., Harper, A. E., & Taylor, S. L. (1990). Sucrose and delinquency: Behavioral assessment. *Pediatrics, 86,* 244-253.

Barkley, R. A., Fischer, M., Edelbrock, C. S., & Smallish, L. (1990). The adolescent outcome of hyperactive children diagnosed by research criteria. I. An 8-year prospective follow-up study. *Journal of the American Academy of Child and Adolescent Psychiatry, 29,* 546-557.

Baron-Cohen, S. (1988). An assessment of violence in a young man with Asperger's syndrome. *Journal of Child Psychology and Psychiatry, 29,* 351-360.

Blumstein, A., Cohen, J. M., Roth, J. A., & Visher, C. A. (Eds.). (1986). *Criminal careers and "career criminals."* Washington, DC: National Academy of Sciences.

Bryant, E. T., Scott, M. L., & Golden, C. (1984). Neuropsychological deficits, learning disability and violent behavior. *Journal of Consulting and Clinical Psychology, 52,* 323-324.

Buydens-Branchey, L., Branchey, M. H., & Noumair, D. (1989). Age of alcoholism onset. I. Relationship to psychopathology. *Archives of General Psychiatry, 46,* 225-230.

Caspi, A., Elder, G. H., & Herbener, E. S. (1990). Childhood personality and the prediction of life-course patterns. In L. Robins & M. Rutter (Eds.), *Straight and devious pathways from childhood to adulthood.* Cambridge: Cambridge University Press.

Dodge, K. A. (1980). Social cognition and children's aggressive behavior. *Child Development, 51,* 162-170.

Dodge, K. A. (1986). A social information processing model of social competence in children. In M. Perlmutter (Ed.), *Minnesota Symposia on Child Psychology* (Vol. 18, pp. 75-127). Hillsdale, NJ: Lawrence Erlbaum.

Dodge, K. A., & Newman, J. P. (1981). Biased decision-making processes in aggressive boys. *Journal of Abnormal Psychology, 90,* 375-379.

Dodge, K. A., Price, J. M., Bachorowski, J.-A., & Newman, J. P. (1990). Hostile attributional biases in severely aggressive adolescents. *Journal of Abnormal Psychology, 99,* 385-392.

Ellis, P. L. (1982). Empathy: A factor in antisocial behavior. *Journal of Abnormal Child Psychology, 10,* 123-134.

Ensminger, M. E., Kellam, S. G., & Rubin, B. R. (1983). School and family origins of delinquency. In K. T. Van Dusen & S. A. Mednick (Eds.), *Prospective studies of crime and delinquency* (pp. 73-97). Boston: Kluwer-Nijhoff.

Eron, L. D., & Huesmann, L. R. (1990). The stability of aggressive behavior—Even unto the third generation. In M. Lewis & S. M. Miller (Eds.), *Handbook of developmental psychopathology* (pp. 147-156). New York: Plenum.

Everall, I. P., & Le Couteur, A. (1990). Firesetting in an adolescent boy with Asperger's syndrome. *British Journal of Psychiatry, 157,* 284-287.

Eysenck, H. J. (1977). *Crime and personality.* London: Routledge & Kegan Paul.

Fagan, J. (1990). Intoxication and aggression. In M. Tonry & J. Q. Wilson (Eds.), *Crime and justice: A review of research: Vol. 13. Drugs and crime* (pp. 241-314). Chicago: University of Chicago Press.

Farrington, D. P. (1978). The family background of aggressive youths. In L. A. Hersov, M. Berger, & D. Schaffer (Eds.), *Aggression and antisocial behavior in childhood and adolescence* (pp. 73-93). Oxford: Pergamon.

Farrington, D. P., Gallagher, B., Morley, L., St. Ledger, R. J., & West, D. J. (1988). Are there any successful men from criminogenic backgrounds? *Psychiatry, 50,* 116-130.

Farrington, D. P., & Hawkins, D. J. (1991). Predicting participation, early onset and later persistence in officially recorded offending. *Criminal Behavior and Mental Health, 1,* 1-33.

Farrington, D. P., Loeber, R., & Van Kammer, W. B. (1990). Long-term criminal outcomes of hyperactivity-impulsivity-attention deficit and conduct problems in childhood. In L. N. Robins & M. Rutter (Eds.), *Straight and devious pathways from childhood to adulthood* (pp. 62-81). Cambridge: Cambridge University Press.

Gandossy, R. P., Williams, J. R., Cohen, J., & Harwood, H. J. (1980). *Drugs and crime: A survey and analysis of the literature.* Washington, DC: National Institute of Justice.

Gans, D. A., Harper, A. E., Bachorowski, J.-A., Newman, J. P., Shrago, E. S., & Taylor, S. L. (1990). Sucrose and delinquency: Oral sucrose tolerance test and nutritional assessment. *Pediatrics, 86,* 254-262.

Gray, J. A. (1987). *The psychology of fear and stress.* Cambridge: Cambridge University Press.

Hare, R. D., Hart, S. D., & Harpur, T. J. (1991). Psychopathy and the DSM-IV criteria for antisocial personality disorder. *Journal of Abnormal Psychology, 100,* 391-398.

Hartup, W. W. (1978). Children and their friends. In H. McGurk (Ed.), *Issues in childhood social development* (pp. 130-170). London: Methuen.

Hartup, W. W. (1983). Peer relationships. In E. M. Hetherington (Ed.), *Handbook of child psychology: Vol. 4. Socialization, personality and social development* (pp. 103-196). New York: John Wiley.

Hechtman, L., Weiss, G., Perlman, T., & Amsel, R. (1984). Hyperactives as young adults: Initial predictors of adult outcome. *Journal of the American Academy of Child Psychiatry, 23,* 250-260.

Henn, F. A., Bardwell, R., & Jenkins, R. L. (1980). Juvenile delinquents revisited: Adult criminal activity. *Archives of General Psychiatry, 37,* 1160-1163.

Hinshaw, S. P. (1987). On the distinction between attention deficits/hyperactivity and conduct problems/aggression in child psychopathology. *Psychology Bulletin, 101,* 636-643.

Hodgins, S., de Bray, G., & Braun, C. (1989). *Patterns of brain functioning of mentally abnormal offenders.* Quebec: Institut Philippe Pinel de Montreal.

Hodgins, S., & Grunau, M. von. (1989). Biology, mental disorder, aggression and violence: What do we know? In T. E. Moffitt & S. A. Mednick (Eds.), *Biological contributions to crime causation* (pp. 161-182). Dordrecht, The Netherlands: Matinus Nijhoff.

Hollander, H. E., & Turner, F. D. (1985). Characteristics of incarcerated delinquents: Relationship between developmental disorders, environmental and family factors, and patterns of offenses and recidivism. *Journal of the American Academy of Child Psychiatry, 2,* 221-226.

Howlin, P., & Yule, W. (1990). Taxonomy of major disorders in childhood. In M. Lewis & S. M. Miller (Eds.), *Handbook of developmental psychopathology* (pp. 371-383). New York: Plenum.

Kanner, L. (1943). Autistic disturbances of affective contact. *Nervous Child, 2,* 217-250.

Kellam, S. G., Simon, M. B., & Ensminger, M. E. (1983). Antecedents in first grade of teenage substance use and psychological well-being: A ten-year community-wide prospective study. In D. F. Ricks & B. S. Dohrenwend (Eds.), *Origins of psychopathology* (pp. 17-42). Cambridge: Cambridge University Press.

Klinteberg, B. af, & Magnusson, D. (1989). Aggressiveness and hyperactive behavior as related to adrenaline excretion. *European Journal of Personality, 3,* 81-93.

Kupersmidt, J. B., & Coie, J. D. (1985). *The prediction of delinquency and school-related problems from childhood peer status.* Unpublished manuscript, Duke University, Durham, NC.

Kupersmidt, J. B., Coie, J. D., & Dodge, K. A. (1990). The role of poor peer relationships in the development of disorder. In S. R. Asher & J. D. Coie (Eds.), *Peer rejection in childhood* (pp. 217-249). Cambridge: Cambridge University Press.

Lambert, N. M. (1988). Adolescent outcomes for hyperactive children. Perspectives on general and specific patterns of risk for adolescent educational, social and mental health problems. *American Psychologist, 43,* 786-799.

Lewis, D. O., Moy, E., Jackson, L. D., Aaronson, R., Restifo, N., Serra, S., & Simos, A. (1985). Biopsychosocial characteristics of children who later murder: A prospective study. *American Journal of Psychiatry, 142,* 1161-1167.

Loeber, R. (1990). Development and risk factors of juvenile antisocial behavior and delinquency. *Clinical Psychology Review, 10,* 1-41.

Loeber, R., & Schmalling, K. B. (1985a). Empirical evidence for overt and covert patterns of antisocial conduct problems: A meta analysis. *Journal of Abnormal Child Psychology, 13,* 337-352.

Loeber, R., & Schmalling, K. B. (1985b). The utility of differentiating between mixed and pure forms of antisocial child behavior. *Journal of Abnormal Child Psychology, 13,* 315-336.

Loeber, R., & Stouthamer-Loeber, M. (1987). Prediction. In H. C. Quay (Ed.), *Handbook of juvenile delinquency* (pp. 325-382). New York: John Wiley.

Magnusson, D., & Bergman, L. (1988). Individual and variable-based approaches to longitudinal research on early risk factors. In M. Rutter (Ed.), *Studies of psychosocial risk: The power of longitudinal data* (pp. 45-61). Cambridge: Cambridge University Press.

Magnusson, D., & Bergman, L. (1990). A pattern approach to the study of pathways from childhood to adulthood. In L. Robins & M. Rutter (Eds.), *Straight and devious pathways from childhood to adulthood* (pp. 101-115). Cambridge: Cambridge University Press.

Magnusson, D., Stattin, H., & Dunér, A. (1983). Aggression and criminality in a longitudinal perspective. In K. T. Dusen & S. A. Mednick (Eds.), *Antecedents of aggression and antisocial behavior* (pp. 277-302). Boston: Kluwer-Nijhoff.

Manuzza, S., Klein, R. G., Bonagura, N., Konig, P. H., & Shenker, R. (1988). Hyperactive boys almost grown up. II. Status of subjects without a mental disorder. *Archives of General Psychiatry, 45,* 13-18.

Manuzza, S., Klein, R. G., Bonagura, N., Malloy, P., Giampino, T. L., & Addalli, K. A. (1991). Hyperactive boys almost grown up. V. Replication of psychiatric status. *Archives of General Psychiatry, 48,* 77-83.

Manuzza, S., Klein, R. G., Konig, P. H., & Giampino, T. L. (1989). Hyperactive boys almost grown up. IV. Criminality and its relationship to psychiatric status. *Archives of General Psychiatry, 46,* 1073-1079.

Mawson, D. C., Grounds, A., & Tantum, D. (1985). Violence and Asperger's syndrome: A case study. *British Journal of Psychiatry, 147,* 566-569.

McCord, J. (1987, April). *Another perspective on aggression and shyness as predictors of problems.* Paper presented at the Biannual Meeting of the Society for Research in Child Development, Baltimore, MD.

Mednick, S. A., & Kandel, E. S. (1988). Cognitive determinants of violence. *Bulletin of the American Academy of Psychiatry Law, 16,* 101-109.

Moffitt, T. E. (1990a). Juvenile delinquency and attention deficit disorder: Developmental trajectories from age 3 to age 15. *Child Development, 61,* 893-910.

Moffitt, T. E. (1990b). The neuropsychology of juvenile delinquency: A critical review. In M. Tonry & N. Morris (Eds.), *Crime and justice: A review of research* (Vol. 12, pp. 99-169). Chicago: University of Chicago Press.

Moffitt, T. E., & Henry, B. (1989). Neuropsychological deficits in executive function in self-reported delinquents. *Development and Psychopathology, 1,* 105-118.

Moskowitz, D. S., & Schwartzman, A. E. (1989). Painting group portraits: Assessing life outcomes for aggressive and withdrawn children. *Journal of Personality, 57,* 723-746.

Offord, D. R., Sullivan, K., Allen, N., & Abrams, N. (1979). Delinquency and hyperactivity. *Journal of Nervous and Mental Disorders, 167,* 734-741.

Olweus, D. (1979). Stability of aggressive reaction patterns in males: A review. *Psychology Bulletin, 86,* 852-875.

Parker, J. G., & Asher, S. R. (1987). Peer relations and later personal adjustment: Are low-accepted children at risk? *Psychological Bulletin, 102,* 357-389.

Petrich, J. (1976). Rate of psychiatric morbidity in a metropolitan county jail population. *American Journal of Psychiatry, 133,* 1439-1444.

Pope, A. W., Bierman, K. L., & Mumma, G. H. (1989). Relations between hyperactive and aggressive behavior and peer relations at three elementary grade levels. *Journal of Abnormal Child Psychology, 17,* 253-267.

Pulkinnen, L. (1988). Delinquent development: Theoretical and empirical considerations. In M. Rutter (Ed.), *Studies of psychosocial risk: The power of longitudinal data* (pp. 184-199). Cambridge: Cambridge University Press.

Quay, H. C. (1965). Psychopathic personality as pathological stimulation-seeking. *American Journal of Psychiatry, 122,* 180-183.

Raine, A., & Mednick, S. A. (1989). Biosocial longitudinal research into antisocial behavior. *Revue Epidemiologie Sante Publique, 37,* 515-524.

Raine, A., Venables, P., & Williams, M. (1990). Relationships between central and autonomic measures of arousal at age 15 years and criminality at age 24 years. *Archives of General Psychiatry, 47,* 1003-1007.

Robins, L. N. (1966). *Deviant children grown up: A sociological and psychiatric study of sociopathic personality.* Baltimore, MD: Williams & Wilkins.

Robins, L. N. (1978). Sturdy childhood predictors of adult antisocial behavior: Replications from longitudinal studies. *Psychological Medicine, 8,* 611-622.

Robins, L. N. (1991). Conduct disorder. *Journal of Child Psychology and Psychiatry, 32,* 193-212.

Robins, L. N., Tipp, J., & Przybeck, T. R. (1990). Antisocial personality. In L. N. Robins & D. A. Reiger (Eds.), *Psychiatric disorders in America* (pp. 258-290). New York: Free Press.

Rubin, K. H., LeMare, L. J., & Lollis, S. (1990). Social withdrawal in childhood: Developmental pathways to rejection. In S. R. Asher & J. D. Coie (Eds.), *Peer rejection in childhood* (pp. 217-249). Cambridge: Cambridge University Press.

Rutter, M., Tizard, J., Yule, W., Graham, P., & Whitmore, K. (1976). Isle of Wight studies, 1964-1974. *Psychological Medicine, 6,* 313-332.

Satterfield, J. M., Hoppe, C. M., & Schell, A. M. (1982). A prospective study of delinquency in 110 adolescent boys with attention deficit disorder and 88 normal adolescent boys. *American Journal of Psychiatry, 139,* 795-798.

Schachar, R. (1991). Childhood hyperactivity. *Journal of Child Psychology and Psychiatry, 32,* 155-191.

Smetana, J. (1990). Morality and conduct disorders. In M. Lewis & S. M. Miller (Eds.), *Handbook of developmental psychopathology* (pp. 157-179). New York: Plenum.

Tantum, D. (1988a). Asperger's syndrome. *Journal of Child Psychology and Psychiatry, 29,* 245-255.

Tantum, D. (1988b). Lifelong eccentricity and social isolation I. Psychiatric, social and forensic aspects. *British Journal of Psychiatry, 153,* 777-782.

Taylor, E., Sandberg, S., Thorley, G., & Giles, S. (1991). *The epidemiology of childhood hyperactivity.* Institute of Psychiatry Maudsley Monographs, 33. London: Oxford University Press.

Venables, P. H. (1987). Autonomic nervous system factors in criminal behavior. In S. A. Mednick, T. E. Moffitt, S. A. Stack (Eds.), *The causes of crime: New biological approaches* (pp. 110-136). Cambridge: Cambridge University Press.

Virkkunen, M. (1983). Insulin secretion during the glucose tolerance test in antisocial personality. *British Journal of Psychiatry, 142,* 598-604.

Wallander, J. L. (1988). The relationship between attention problems in childhood and antisocial behavior eight years later. *Journal of Child Psychology and Psychiatry, 29,* 53-61.

Wilson, J. Q., & Herrnstein, R. J. (1985). *Crime and human nature.* New York: Simon & Schuster.

Wing, L. (1981). Asperger's syndrome: A clinical account. *Psychological Medicine, 11,* 115-129.

Wolff, S. (1984). Annotation: The concept of personality disorder in childhood. *Journal of Child Psychology and Psychiatry, 25,* 5-13.

Wolff, S., & Chick, J. (1980). Schizoid personality disorder in childhood: A follow-up study. *Psychological Medicine, 10,* 85-100.

Wolff, S., & Cull, A. (1986). Schizoid personality and antisocial conduct: A retrospective case note study. *Psychological Medicine, 16,* 677-687.

8

Developmental Models
for Delinquent Behavior

GERALD R. PATTERSON

KAREN YOERGER

This chapter examines two different routes to delinquency. Each path is defined by a different set of determinants and a different set of long-term outcomes. The critical variable defining one path or the other is when the child is first arrested. If the child is arrested before the age of 14, he or she is an *early starter*; if arrested after the age of 14, he or she is a *late starter*. It is assumed that disrupted parenting practices directly determine children's antisocial behavior and that these, in turn, place children at significant risk for early arrest (Patterson, Debaryshe, & Ramsey, 1989). It is also assumed that the bulk of adult career offenders are early starters. The present report provides a summary of those findings of the Oregon Youth Study (OYS) relating to the key hypotheses about an early start model.

There is a substantial group of nonproblem children who are arrested after the age of 14; this is the late start group. Presumably, disruptions in family process lead some young adolescents to become heavily involved with deviant peers. For this model, family process is indirectly involved, and the deviant peer group is viewed as the direct determinant. The late starters are also thought to be less at risk for adult offending. This chapter briefly examines data relevant to the first component of the late start model.

AUTHORS' NOTE: Support for this project was provided by Grant No. MH 37940, NIMH, U.S. Public Health Service. The writers gratefully acknowledge the contributions of Lynn Crosby, Lew Bank, and Mike Stoolmiller to the data analysis and formulation for many of these problems.

The Early Start Model

The core idea is that, for younger children, antisocial behaviors emerge directly as a result of the reinforcement provided by family members and peers (Patterson, 1982). The general formulation was developed as a means for understanding aggressive children referred for treatment. It was always assumed, however, that childhood patterns of antisocial behavior were prototypic of adolescent delinquency. This chapter reviews findings that relate to a number of the questions underlying such a model. For example, to what extent do family process variables covary with measures of antisocial child behavior? What is the evidence for parenting skills being causes rather than effects? Do childhood measures of antisocial behavior predict the onset of first police arrest? Are they best for predicting overall frequency of arrests? If not, then what variable(s) serve this function? Do parenting skill variables predict age of onset for police arrest? What is the relation between early onset and chronicity? Is the annual rate for arrests a constant after the first arrest? In the discussions that follow, findings will be reviewed that relate to these questions.

A Contingency Theory

Many children's aversive and antisocial acts are acquired and maintained by reinforcements supplied by the immediate social environment. Our coercion model is a general formulation that describes how this comes about (Patterson, Capaldi, & Bank, 1991; Patterson & Reid, 1984).[1] The general formulation was tested by observation data collected in several hundred homes of normal boys and more than 500 homes of antisocial boys, and suggests that parents in our clinical samples were noncontingent in three very important ways: (a) they usually did not positively reinforce the child's prosocial behaviors, (b) they usually did not use effective punishment for coercive behaviors, and (c) they provided a *rich supply of reinforcement for coercive behaviors*. The most important reinforcement consists of a three-step sequence. First, there is the aversive behavior of a family member directed to the target child. This is followed by a counterattack from the child, which will very often "turn off" the aversive intrusion. So, coercive child behaviors "work" in families, in that they effectively terminate aversive behaviors by other family members. Systematic observations in homes have shown the expected differences in contingencies supplied by normal and clinical families (Patterson, 1982). Patterson, Dishion, and Chamberlain (in press) showed that the aversive behaviors that occur most frequently, such as arguing, are also the behaviors that are most likely to be reinforced. The observation studies of Patterson (1984) and Snyder and Patterson (1986, 1992) have shown that children's relative rates of deviant behaviors are delicately matched to the relative payoffs provided by the family (i.e., what works the best is used the most).

What is the relation between the trivial coercive behaviors shaped in interactions at home and adolescent assault, theft, and vandalism? Our coercion model asserts that, as the frequency of antisocial acts increases, there is a move from trivial to severe acts (Patterson, 1982). Presumably, this shift toward increasing severity is transitive; if a more severe act is recorded, the individual engages in the less severe acts as well. Both cross-sectional (Patterson & Dawes, 1975) and longitudinal (Patterson, 1988; Patterson & Bank, 1989) analyses have provided support for the transitivity hypothesis.

One of the key ideas in the coercion model is that training for antisocial behaviors at home generalizes to other settings and across time. Ramsey, Patterson, and Walker (1990) examined this hypothesis and found a path coefficient of .73 between a latent construct measuring antisocial behavior at home and a construct based only on measures collected at school one year later.

The findings support the hypothesis that parents of antisocial children are essentially noncontingent in many of their interactions with their children. They use less effective discipline for deviant behaviors: They also use fewer positive reinforcers for prosocial behaviors. As a result, the child has two problems: He or she is antisocial, and he or she is lacking in prosocial survival skills.

The general assumption for our coercion model is that effective parenting skills control the kinds of contingencies occurring in families. Several decades of work were devoted to training parents to be more contingent (i.e., to use more effective praise and support as well as more effective discipline and problem solving skills) (Forgatch & Patterson, 1989). Three random assignment design studies have been carried out that show a significant interaction term for pre- and posttreatment comparisons (the experimental group improved and the comparison group did not) (Bank, Marlowe, Reid, Patterson, & Weinrott, 1991; Dishion, Patterson, & Kavanagh, in press; Patterson, Chamberlain, & Reid, 1982). The outcomes from the field observation studies and the clinical trials were encouraging enough for us to develop a longitudinal study examining the relation between family variables, boys' antisocial behavior, and delinquency as it developed over time.

Building the Coercion Model

The coercion model emphasizes poor parenting skills as a main determinant for antisocial behavior in young children. How does one measure parenting practices? In the late 1970s, efforts to measure parenting practices based on interviews or questionnaires accounted for less than 10% of the variance in measures of child antisocial behavior. Worse yet, the two major studies of this covariation failed to replicate (Schuck, 1974). But a single method of assessing parenting practices is biased. (The impact of shared method variance and some techniques for controlling it have been considered in detail in reports such as the one by Bank, Dishion, Skinner, & Patterson, 1990.) We decided to use variables from multimethod, multiagent ratings to define all key concepts of the coercion model. Extensive data were collected from a substantial planning sample of normal families, and those data were used to build most of the constructs central to the coercion model. The analyses provided a solid basis for revising many of the measures as well as some of the constructs. Based on these studies, we initiated a longitudinal design with the goal of building models contributing to the understanding of delinquency and to our ability to predict it. The resulting study, the Oregon Youth Study (OYS), began in 1984 and is supported by the National Institute of Mental Health. The sample ($N = 206$) consists of two cohorts of boys living in the highest crime neighborhoods of a small metropolitan area. From a list of elementary schools in the 10 highest crime neighborhoods, 4 were randomly selected to define Cohort I. A new list was prepared the following year, and seven of those schools were randomly selected to define Cohort II. Capaldi and Patterson (1987) described in detail the recruitment process. Of the families contacted, 74% agreed to participate in more than 20 hours of assessment. They participated in the full assessment battery (home observations, interviews, questionnaires, telephone interviews, videotapes of family problem solving, peer nominations, and teacher questionnaires) at Grades 4, 6, 8, and 10. Each family was paid about $300 for participating in the assessment. Families that left the area after the study began were also included in the follow-up assessment (traveling assessors). Ninety-eight percent of the families are still participating.

Each of the constructs defining the coercion model was identified by at least three indicators. Capaldi and Patterson (1989) detailed the sequence and the psychometric analyses for 14 of the constructs. Before the parenting model could be constructed, several questions needed to be addressed. For instance, can parenting practices actually be differentiated from one another, or do they fall along a single dimension (i.e., from good to bad parenting)? Five parenting constructs have been built: discipline, monitoring, family problem solving, involvement, and positive reinforcement. Patterson and Bank (1987) were able to differentiate a monitoring construct and a discipline construct. The confirmatory factor analysis showed that the two-factor solution was significantly better than the one-factor solution. Thus, these two constructs sampling parenting practices were defining more than just "bad parenting." A confirmatory factor analysis also showed that positive reinforcement, problem solving, and involvement were three distinctly different parenting practices (Patterson, Reid, & Dishion, 1992).

The next question addressed a key assumption of the coercion model. Do the measures of parent monitoring and discipline practices covary significantly with child antisocial behavior? Structural equation modeling (SEM) showed that the parenting practices model provided a good fit to the data sets for both cohorts of the OYS (Patterson, 1986). The two measures of parenting practices accounted for about 30% of the variance in a latent construct for antisocial behavior (defined by ratings from teachers, parents, peers, and child telephone interviews). The data fit for both cohorts, suggesting that the replication problem noted in the earlier studies by Schuck (1974) had been overcome. Forgatch (1991) examined the fit for a divorced sample of boys and for a clinical sample of boys and girls. Again the a priori model provided a good fit to the data sets. The amount of variance accounted for ranged from 31% to 52%.

Family processes obviously take place in a societal matrix. How do contextual variables such as social status or parent pathology impact family process? Contextual variables significantly impact child adjustment; in each case, the effect is thought to be indirect. The child is affected only if the contextual variables covary with altered parenting practices such as monitoring and discipline. Laub and Sampson (1988) carried out one of the first tests of the mediational hypothesis in their reanalyses of the Glueck and Glueck (1959) data sets. Their analyses provided solid support for a mediational hypothesis and their findings were replicated by an analysis of the OYS data by Larzelere and Patterson (1990). Whereas social disadvantage covaried significantly with child adjustment problems, the contribution became nonsignificant after measures of parenting practices were partialled out.

How do we demonstrate that parent discipline may be a primary determinant for the maintenance of antisocial behavior? Though structural equation models are replicated, the correlations do not establish causal connections; only experimental manipulations can test this assumption. We see the primary function of multivariate models of longitudinal data sets as identifying which sets of variables are worthy of experimental manipulation. Forgatch (1991) described how clinical interventions can be used as experimental manipulations to test for the causal status of key variables in the coercion model. Planned experiments could be carried out that randomly assign some parents to experimental training groups and other parents to alternative groups. Forgatch and Toobert (1979) and Dishion et al. (in press) carried out the random assignment design manipulations to test the causal status of parent discipline practices for child antisocial behavior. Both studies provided support for the hypothesis.

Some Developmental Shifts: The Cascade Model

We believe that antisocial behaviors produce a cascade of secondary problems. In this section, we review data relating to the hypothesis that antisocial behaviors directly determine school failure, rejection by peers, and involvement with deviant peers, and indirectly determine depressed mood and substance use. To understand the qualitative shifts occurring in the antisocial individual's trajectory, we must start with a consideration of the trait.

Noncompliance is at the core of the antisocial trait. It is typically accompanied by a wide range of aversive behaviors, including whining, yelling, losing one's temper, using threats, and hitting. Together, these behaviors define an extremely aversive interpersonal style used to guide, shape, and manipulate the behavior of others. This style makes it difficult to give corrective feedback, to monitor, or to discipline a difficult child. Over time, the child's faltering social skills become increasingly apparent. Skill deficits in peer relations and academic failure become qualitative additions to the child's problems. The repertoire of coercive and antisocial acts gradually expands to include new forms of antisocial acts such as fighting, stealing, fire setting, and delinquency (Patterson, 1982, 1991).

Qualitative Shifts. From the perspective of the coercion model, the antisocial trait is merely the first step in a dynamic process (Patterson, Dishion, & Chamberlain, in press). The sequence is analogous to a series of actions and reactions. The child entering school initiates coercive actions, producing a predictable set of reactions from peers and teachers. The peers' and teachers' reactions produce predictable reactions from the problem child, and the sequence continues into adulthood. As shown in Figure 8.1, the initial determinant is antisocial behavior. Each new problem in the sequence causes new reactions, which in turn form a new problem; hence, the term *cascade*. For problems produced at later stages, antisocial behavior is only an indirect determinant.

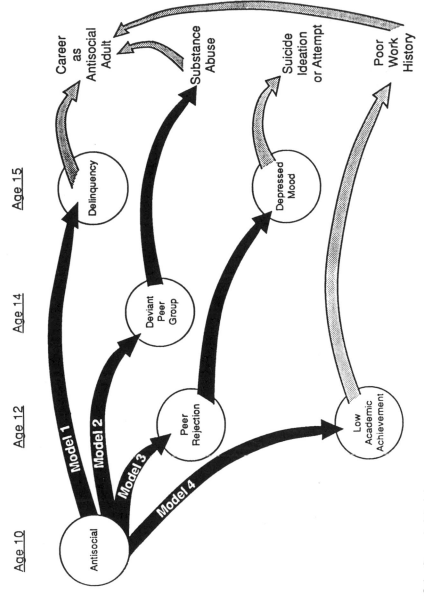

Figure 8.1. Cascade Models

Model No. 1: Antisocial Behavior

The hypothesis is that children scoring above the median on measures of the antisocial trait define a group at risk for early age of onset for delinquency and chronicity. The SEM by Patterson et. al. (1991) tested this hypothesis. The latent antisocial construct assessed at age 10 accounted for 40% of the variance in the latent delinquency construct (based on self-report and official records) assessed at age 14. The model assessing the antisocial trait at age 10 and again at age 12 accounted for 60% of the variance.

Model No. 2: Deviant Peers and Substance Use

The developmental literature suggests that problem children tend to be selected as friends by isolated or rejected children. Snyder, Dishion, and Patterson (1986) showed that earlier measures of the antisocial trait and rejection by peers related to later involvement in a deviant peer group. Dishion (1990) demonstrated that rejection by peers contributed to later involvement with deviant peers. This held even after partialling out the prior contributions of parent monitoring and involvement with deviant peers. This finding underscores that peer rejection makes a strong contribution to the drift toward deviant peers. By early adolescence, the concepts of antisocial trait and deviant peer are almost the same. For example, Patterson et al. (1991) showed in a confirmatory factor analysis a correlation between antisocial and deviant peer constructs of .89!

Dishion (personal communication, January 1992) examined the links between involvement with deviant peers, antisocial behavior, and polysubstance use. He considered five different levels each for tobacco, alcohol, and drug use assessed at ages 15 and 16. The levels ranged from exploration to daily use. As hypothesized, earlier measures of antisocial behavior and involvement with deviant peers were both uniquely and significantly related to the more extreme practices for each of the three substances.

Models No. 3 and No. 4: Peer Rejection and Academic Failure

It is hypothesized that antisocial behavior in the elementary grades increases the child's risk for peer rejection and academic failure. In systematic studies over the past 10 years, developmental psychologists have established that an abrasive/explosive interpersonal style causes rejection by normal peers (Coie & Kupersmidt, 1983; Dodge, 1983). In groups comprising strangers, the children's ratings indicated that they had identified and rejected the aggressive child after only one or two meetings. This suggests that most extremely antisocial children are rejected shortly after entering school. The close relation between antisocial behavior and peer rejection is reflected in the path coefficient of .51, shown by Dishion (1990) in his studies of Grade 4 OYS boys.

Patterson (1986) and Patterson et al. (1989) extensively reviewed classroom studies showing that antisocial boys spend less time on task in the classroom, fail to complete homework, and are at grave risk of being held back at least one grade by the age of 11 (Walker, Shinn, O'Neill, & Ramsey, 1987). Their noncompliance and explosive temper make it difficult for parents, siblings, teachers, or peers to teach them anything. For example, longitudinal data have shown that antisocial preschoolers were at significant risk for academic failure 2 years later (Tremblay, 1988).

From a social interactional perspective, peer rejection and academic failure represent yoked failures having powerful consequences for the antisocial boy (Patterson & Capaldi, 1991). Each failure is associated with increased rates of aversive experience and reduced rates of positive reinforcement. The resulting imbalance should correlate with increased risk for dysphoric mood. Patterson and Capaldi (1990) tested this model using SEM to define three constructs: peer relations, academic achievement, and depressed mood. The dual failure model showed a good fit to the data. There was a significant path from rejection by peers to dysphoric mood; the contribution of academic failure was borderline. A systematic comparison of the models from three different samples showed both structural and factor invariance (Patterson & Stoolmiller, 1991).

Capaldi (1991) showed that 14-year-old boys who are antisocial and depressed are at increased risk for suicide ideation during the following 2 years. Thirty-one percent of the boys who are at the extreme for both kinds of problems report that they have occasional thoughts of suicide. Thirteen percent of boys who are only depressed and 12% of those who are only antisocial have such thoughts. The findings are in keeping with the results from the large-scale survey of adolescents by Cairns and Cairns (1991). They found that suicide ideation and suicide attempts were significantly related to both aggression and depression.

The findings from studies modeling longitudinal data from the OYS provide consistent support for the metaphorical cascade of effects. None of the analyses directly tests the assumption that an event at one point in time may serve as a causal variable for the next event in the sequence, but the findings emphasize the idea of an expanding definition of the problems attending antisocial behavior. The problem child's difficulties are expanding in a systematic way described by a second-order deviancy factor evaluated at several points in time (Patterson, 1991).

Predictive Utility of the Model

The prior discussion informs the reader of a possible developmental history for aggressive children. Most of the antisocial acts described in parents' and teachers' ratings for young children are not of major concern to police. To be useful, the general coercion model must move to the next developmental stage. This means shifting the setting from the home and classroom to the streets. It also requires that we account for how children's antisocial acts change to become of concern to the police and the community at large.

Street Time

If problem children continued to practice their antisocial trade only in the home and the school, it is doubtful that many arrests would result. To become delinquents, they must first expand their theater of operations to the streets, where they are relatively free of adult supervision and are free to shop for social groups that match their own proclivities. It is in this context that their new mentors can assist in the transformation of childish antisocial behaviors into delinquent acts worthy of police attention.

Consistent with this idea, Dishion, Andrews, and Patterson (1990) showed that antisocial boys tended to select antisocial peers as confidantes. In keeping with the formulation by Elliott, Huizinga, and Ageton (1985), we believe that members of these deviant peer groups directly train the problem children in new forms of antisocial acts. The analyses of the longitudinal data set by Patterson (1991) show that intraindividual changes into new forms can be used to define a latent construct. The covariate that was significantly associated with these changes was shown to be involvement with deviant peers: Youths demonstrating the most growth in new forms of antisocial behavior tend to be those most committed to deviant peers.

Parents determine when their children can begin spending more time on the street. For example, the survey of parents of normal families (Patterson & Stouthamer-Loeber, 1984) showed that Grade 4 boys experienced an average of 0.78 unsupervised hours per day, but by Grade 10 the average was 2.06 hours per day. In the case of extremely antisocial children, however, it seems likely that they may overwhelm parental efforts to control them, and be out on the streets by age 6 or 7 (OYS data set). As a test of this hypothesis, Stoolmiller (1990) used a latent growth model to examine the relation between intraindividual changes in antisocial behavior and changes in wandering (i.e., time the child spends outside the home without adult supervision). He found the relationship to be reciprocal: The sooner the antisocial child is out on the streets, the more exposed he or she is than his or her contemporaries to higher levels of antisocial behavior.

Farrington, Gallagher, Morley, St. Ledger, and West (1986) found that, of boys arrested between ages 10 and 13, 75% of their crimes were committed in the presence of one or more peers. The comparable figure for crimes committed at ages 21 through 24 is only 43%. This indicates that early onset crimes may reflect a group process to a greater extent than do adult crimes. This is in keeping with the idea that the major function of street time is to bring the antisocial child into greater contact with antisocial peers.

Onset

The utility of the coercion model as a potential theory of delinquency rests partly on its ability to predict which boys will be arrested at an early age. From this perspective, one police arrest is only the tip of a theoretical iceberg, contributing the total number of antisocial acts observed across settings over a period of several months. Multimethod and -agent defined reports of antisocial behavior are estimates of this underlying absolute true score (Bank & Patterson, 1992). From this perspective, the children who are the most extreme on measures estimating total frequency of antisocial acts would be among the youngest to be on the street. The reason for this is that the more deviant the children, the sooner they will overpower parental efforts to keep them off the street. The highest-rate performers are also most at risk of being caught. It follows that a composite measure of the childhood trait for antisocial behavior should significantly predict age at first police arrest. The hypothesis was tested using longitudinal data from the OYS (Patterson, Crosby, & Vuchinich, in press). An event history analysis showed that distribution of hazard rates for first arrest varied significantly as a function of age of the youth. At age 10, for example, the risk was modest; only 2.6% of those boys still at risk were arrested. At age 13, however, 11% of those still at risk were arrested. The distribution of hazard rates peaked between ages 12 and 13. Continuous time regression analyses showed that measures of parental monitoring and discipline accounted for significant increases in risk through age 14. As expected, boys from families characterized by inept discipline and monitoring practices were at significantly greater risk. According to the model, the effect of poor parenting skills on future delinquency should be mediated by the child's level of antisocial behavior (Patterson et al., 1989). When the antisocial trait score was added to the model, the contributions of parenting practices were no longer significant. The mediational role of the child's antisocial trait was strongly supported. Each unit of increase (standard deviation) in the trait score increased the risk for arrest by 22.1%.

A multiple regression was also carried out only for those boys arrested between ages 10 through 15. The findings showed that boys who had high antisocial trait scores and who were from socially disadvantaged families were at significant risk for early arrest. The multiple correlation was .552 ($p < .001$). The findings support the idea that a measure of the childhood antisocial trait can be used to predict who is at risk for early arrest. The findings are consistent with those from the longitudinal study of Finnish adolescents by Pulkkinen (1988). She demonstrated a significant relation between adult convictions and both peers' and teachers' ratings for aggression collected at age 8. Contributions of social disadvantage were also consistent with those from the longitudinal study of Swedish children showing the variable to covary significantly with age of onset (Wikström, 1987).

It is assumed that the distribution of risk scores for first arrest based on the OYS has a form that is reasonably generalizable across samples. For example, the analyses of hazard rates from four samples by Blumstein, Cohen, Roth, and Visher (1986) showed that the samples displayed a general increase in hazard rates from age 10 through early adolescence, and then peaked between the ages of 16 and 18. Figure 8.2 summarizes Blumstein et al.'s reanalysis of Farrington's (1983) data, as well as data from the OYS. For both distributions, there was a general increase in hazard rate from preadolescence through early adolescence, with the first peak in hazard rates occurring in early adolescence. Notice that although the general shape of the distribution of hazard rates might be similar across samples, the mean level is not. The OYS sample consistently showed higher levels of risk. The findings are consistent with the idea that the OYS is based on at-risk families.

Prediction and Chronicity

There were 100 ten-year-old boys in the OYS who scored above the median on the composite score for the antisocial trait. If a boy was in this at-risk group, the likelihood of him being arrested by age 13 years 11 months was .47. An examination of the data set showed that 90.4% of the boys who were arrested by this age also tested above the median on the composite antisocial trait score measured at age 10 (i.e., the false negative errors were quite small). For the group of 52 early arrests, 34 had been arrested 3 or more times by age 15 (i.e., the conditional likelihood was .654). Starting with a high value for the childhood trait score, the likelihood is that .307 will be arrested 3 or more times by age 16. In the total OYS, we can expect that the risk for three arrests by this age is .165 (base rate). Farrington's (1981) findings showed that about two thirds of the

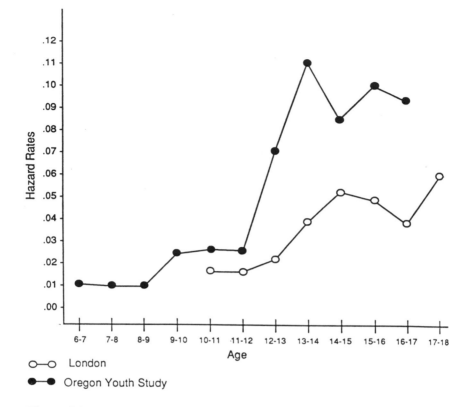

Figure 8.2. Hazard Rates for First Arrest by Age for Two Samples

chronic offenders in his sample had committed their first offense before age 15. Based on these findings, we assume that about 50% of the chronic juvenile offenders in the OYS will be early starters.

Capaldi and Patterson (1992) demonstrated that chronic offenders (three or more arrests) significantly covaried with violent offending. Given three or more offenses, the likelihood of them committing a violent offense by age 16 to 17 was .55. This compares to the comparable value of .49 calculated from the London data set (Farrington, 1991).

The concept of chronicity is a reflection of the fact that these young boys are being arrested every year or so. Loeber (1982) adapted the findings from the Farrington study to demonstrate that boys who began their careers early tend to maintain higher mean annual frequencies of convictions through age 24. As shown in Figure 8.3, boys who were first

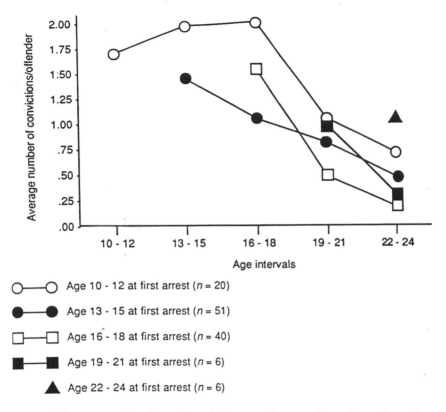

Figure 8.3. Average Number of Convictions per Year as a Function of Onset for London Sample
SOURCE: From Loeber, 1982.

arrested from ages 10 through 12 showed the highest annual mean frequency, and those first arrested at ages 13 to 15 showed the next highest. Those who began in late adolescence showed the lowest mean annual frequency.

It follows from these findings that chronicity would be related to early age of onset. Farrington (1982) found that of 23 youths who had six or more convictions, 11 had been first arrested between the ages of 10 and 12. Six of the chronic offenders were first arrested between ages 13 and 14, and the other 6 before age 16. Loeber (1982) cited findings from McCord (1981) and Hamparian, Schuster, Dinitz, and Conrad (1978) as further support for this hypothesis.

We hypothesize that the majority of early starters are at risk for status as chronic offenders. The data base from the OYS consisted of the official records of police arrests collected for the 206 boys each year, beginning at age 10 and continuing until most of the boys reached age 16. Arrests for traffic offenses or driving while uninsured were not included in the analyses. The findings show that 10 boys had been arrested prior to the age of 10, 5 boys were first arrested at 10, and so forth. Those arrested at a given age were then used to calculate the conditional likelihood of a second, a third, and a fourth arrest occurring by age 16. For boys arrested by age 9, the likelihood of a second arrest was 1.0, a third arrest .90, and a fourth arrest .80. A regular pattern to the chronicity probability values emerges even though the sample sizes are small. Boys arrested at or before age 13 have a substantial risk (.54 to .80) of three additional arrests by age 16. The conditional values fall off appreciably for age of onset beyond age 14 or 15 (i.e., the risk for four arrests was only .15 and .13 respectively). The rank order correlation between age of onset and likelihood of a fourth arrest was .93 ($p < .01$). The findings offer strong support for early onset as increased risk for chronicity; however, it is really too early to say that the risk increases as a linear function of age of onset.

Even though the findings offer strong support for the onset-chronicity hypothesis, it could be that covariation simply reflects the fact that more data were collected for the early starters than for the late starters. For example, the probability value for those arrested at age 10 included 7 years of data as compared to 2 years of data for boys first arrested at age 16. The risk for a second arrest was recalculated based on 2 years of data for all ages of onset. To make all the calculations equivalent to those made at age 16, the frequency data include only the year of arrest and the year immediately following. The results are summarized in the parentheses in the first column of figures in Table 8.1. The use of data based on only 2 years of sampling leads to underestimates in five of the seven calculations. Even with these shifts, the correlation between onset and chronicity is still significant (.74, $p < .05$).

The chronicity correlations based on brief intervals of 2 to 5 years seem to support the onset-chronicity hypothesis. If the interval between arrests lengthens during midadolescence, then an adequate test for chronicity would require a longer time span when evaluating later age of onset. We examine this alternative in a section that follows.

Learning to Avoid the Police. It was noted earlier that while on the street, youths add new forms of antisocial behavior to their repertoires. In this section, we consider the possibility that they also learn some skills for avoiding arrest. This is a difficult hypothesis to test directly. First, it would

TABLE 8.1 Chronicity as Function of Age of Onset

		Likelihood of Rearrest[a]	
Age of Onset	PO_2/O_1	PO_3/O_1	PO_4/O_1
Prior to 10	1.00	.90	.80
($n = 10$)	$(.40)^b$		
Age 10	1.00	.60	.60
($n = 5$)	(.80)		
Age 11	.80	.80	.80
($n = 5$)	(.80)		
Age 12	.77	.70	.54
($n = 13$)	(.46)		
Age 13	.58	.47	.42
($n = 19$)	(.37)		
Age 14	.31	.15	.15
($n = 13$)	(.15)		
Age 15	.33	.13	.13
($n = 15$)	(.33)		

Notes: a. Through age 16.
b. Based only on data from arrest year and one-year follow-up.

require a significant drop in arrest frequency as a function of age. For example, Loeber's (1982) reanalyses of Farrington's data from the London sample showed that early starters (first conviction at ages 10 to 12) averaged about 1.5 to 2.0 convictions per year through early adolescence (see Figure 8.3). After the age of 16, there was a precipitous drop in annual arrest frequencies for both early and late starters. Le Blanc and Frechette (1989) hypothesized that there was a gradual decrease in frequency in the year or two immediately prior to the youth dropping out of the crime process.

Decreasing arrest frequencies or some combination of three very different processes could reflect any of the following: (a) some youths drop out of the process altogether at around age 16; (b) no one drops out, but around age 16 they perform delinquent behaviors at a lower rate; or (c) no one drops out at age 16—they perform delinquent behaviors at the same rate or at an increased rate. They have learned to avoid detection, so the interval between arrests lengthens. As Le Blanc and Frechette point out, it is most likely that the decreases apparent at age 16 or 17 reflect all three mechanisms.

The emphasis on a drop in arrest frequency at midadolescence for early starters is surprising given the recent emphasis on the age-crime-frequency distribution by Gottfredson and Hirschi (1990). Hirschi and Gottfredson (1983) emphasized that there is a steady increase in crime frequency during midadolescence. We believe that boys who start early show a decrease in arrests at midadolescence, but there are many new participants (late starters) who are now being arrested. The net effect is an overall increase in arrest frequency by age. We will return to the problem of the age-crime-frequency distribution in a later section.

The hypothesis put forth in the present report is that the performance of delinquent acts remains steady through age 16, but those boys who are arrested gradually become more skilled at avoiding detection. The hypothesis of a sustained level of performance is in accord with the self-report data from Elliott, Ageton, Huizinga, Knowles, and Canter (1983). Their data showed a *positive slope* between ages 16 and 20 for general delinquency. The increases held for estimates of both participation and frequency. Analyses of the same data set showed a decrease in more serious crimes in terms of participation and frequency. Notice in Loeber's (1982) analyses that the decrease in arrests for early starters was evident between ages 15 and 19. As a further test, OYS data were used to determine whether decreases in annual arrest frequencies occurred during the same interval when self-report data showed a stable level of performance. If the annual arrest frequencies decrease during the same interval that the youths report stable levels of performance, this would be presumptive evidence for the possibility that 16-year-old offenders are learning to avoid detection.

The findings from the OYS for annual arrest frequencies are summarized in Figure 8.4. Because of the small sample sizes, the data are presented for the early start groups, combined ages 10 to 11 and 12 to 13, and for the late start group, combined ages 14 and 15. For each group, the mean arrest frequency was calculated separately for each year through age 16. Because several boys were not yet 16 at the last data collection, that data point should be viewed as a somewhat conservative estimate. There was about a 30% drop in mean annual arrest rates for the early start groups. For the late start group, decrease in annual rate from age 14-15 to age 16 was more precipitous.

That rates are decreasing is consistent with the idea that at around age 15 or 16 the intervals between arrests increase for all three groups. As previously shown in Figure 8.3, the London data set also showed a similar decrease for both early and late starters. What was different for the London sample was that the decrease started 2 years later than the decrease for the OYS sample. Presently, we can only guess why these differences occurred.

The decrease in annual arrest and conviction frequency during midadolescence appears to hold across the London and OYS samples. Does this represent an actual dropping out, a general reduction in antisocial activity, and/or greater skill in avoiding arrest? All are plausible alternatives. If a different measure of delinquency, such as self-report, showed

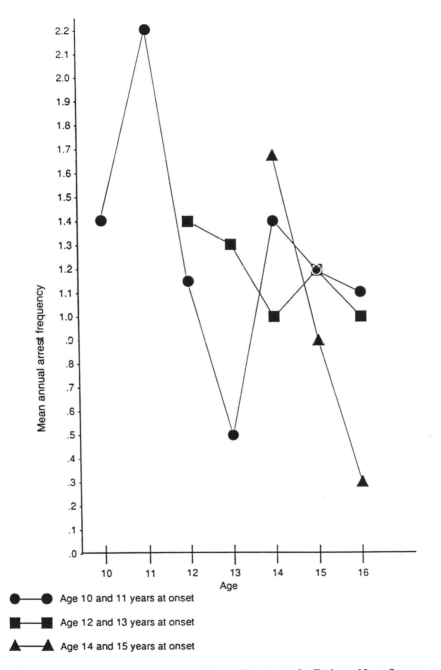

Figure 8.4. Decrease in Mean Annual Arrest Frequency for Early and Late Starters

the rates of criminal activity were unchanged while arrests decreased in frequency, we might conclude that the youths were learning to avoid detection.

To address these questions, the self-report data were analyzed for each wave of data collection from the OYS. The self-report instrument was based on Elliott et al. (1985). Items signifying index crimes were scored at each of the four waves of data collection separately for the early and the late starters. By way of comparison, data were also included for boys who had never been arrested. The findings are summarized in Figure 8.5. The 51 early starters reported increases in activities involving serious crimes during the very intervals that their police arrests were dropping in frequency. The measure of general delinquency showed a pattern of findings similar to this. The dramatic surge in offending reported by the OYS early starters between ages 14 and 16 is remarkable. Notice that the data for the 41 late starters were similar to never-arrested boys; neither group showed high frequencies of index crimes. The self-reported crimes for the late starters did show a decrease, which is consistent with an accompanying decrease in the criminal arrests for frequency during the same interval. Unless there is very high false positive error in self-reported crimes, the findings suggest that early starters may actually be increasing their criminal activity during the period that police arrests are decreasing. We believe that age and increasing experience both contribute to a lengthening interval between police arrests that is apparent at about age 16.

Age-Crime-Frequency Distribution. The decrease in annual arrest frequencies for the various samples did not fit well with our general expectations based on Hirschi and Gottfredson's (1983) well-known age-crime-frequency distribution. The shape of the distribution suggests an increase in crime as a function of age through late adolescence and then a drop. How do our findings fit with this? As Hirschi and Gottfredson (1983) point out, the particular shape of age-crime-frequency distribution is invariant across time (19th to 20th century), across cultures (Europe and the United States), and across types of criminal acts. The data in Figure 8.6 summarize the total crime frequencies at each age from the OYS and from the Blumstein et al. (1986) analyses for the London sample. Both distributions show a characteristic noted by Hirschi and Gottfredson: a sharp increase from age 10 through early adolescence to midadolescence in total frequency of arrests and convictions. How is it that during the interval when the annual arrest frequencies are decreasing, the age-crime-frequency distribution shows an increase?

The reason for the seeming discrepancy is that the age-crime-frequency distribution masks several important developmental changes that occur in

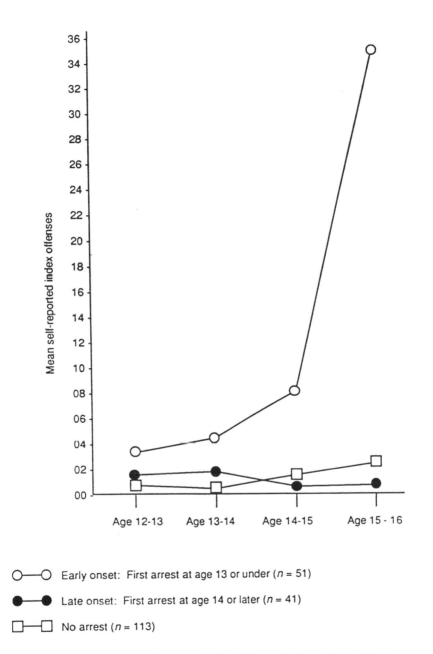

Figure 8.5. Self-Reported Frequency Index Crimes: Early and Later Starters

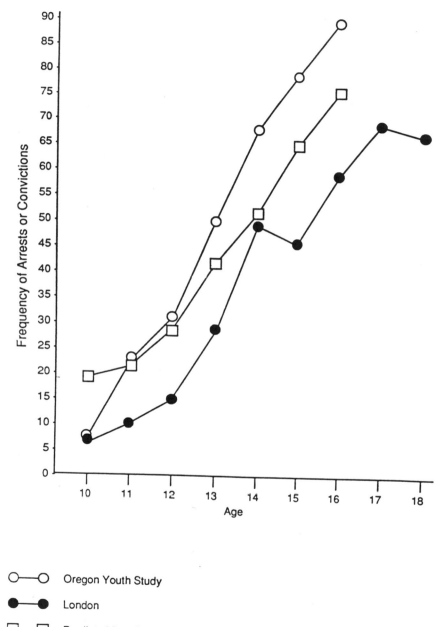

Figure 8.6. Expected and Obtained Age-Crime-Frequency Distributions

early adolescence. Combining estimates of participation and frequency at each age provides a misleading picture of what is really occurring. For both the London and the OYS samples, for example, those who are arrested early tend to be rearrested repeatedly; then their rate declines in mid-adolescence. On the other hand, those who start later tend to show abrupt decreases in arrest rates. At any given age, the age-crime-frequency curve summary may combine new arrivals, prior offenders who continue at high rates, and a few prior offenders who are decreasing their rates. Knowing this may be useful for some policy decisions, but it is confusing in the context of theory building.

We propose that the general shape of the age-crime-frequency distribution may be generated simply from estimates of the expected number of participants at each age and their expected annual arrest frequencies by age of onset. For example, the data showing changes in hazard rate as a function of age would be an appropriate measure of participation. The key idea would be that there is a reasonable degree of generalizability in these estimates across samples. What is generalizable across samples is the *shape* of this distribution of hazard rates (i.e., the risk increases markedly immediately prior to adolescence). If most samples show this characteristic, then we can think of it as a known set of values (i.e., at age 10, 2% or 3% of the boys will experience their first arrest, but at age 12, 3 or 4 times as many will be arrested). The analyses of hazard rates for four samples by Blumstein et al. (1986), and the findings summarized in Figure 8.2, show that this is a reasonable assumption. We should be able to use the distribution of hazard rates from one sample as a constant set of values in calculating the age-crime-frequency distribution for another sample.

The data from Figure 8.2 show that, starting at age 10, an increasing number of boys will be added each year. The only other piece of information required to build an age-crime-frequency distribution would be an estimate of how many crimes on the average they will commit each year once they start (e.g., what is the mean annual arrest frequency for each age of onset?). We also assume that the shape for the distribution of mean annual arrest frequencies by age is similar across samples. In this instance, the characteristic that generalizes across samples would be the tendency to show higher annual arrest frequencies for those arrested in early adolescence as compared to those arrested later on. The information about participation and frequency should make it possible to trace out the cumulative contribution from each age-of-onset group over the interval through midadolescence. In effect, there are two sets of constant values. If we have these estimates, we should be able to reproduce the shape of the age-crime-frequency distribution. If this is so, it should be possible to use the two pieces of information based on the London sample to estimate the age-crime-frequency distribution obtained for the OYS data set. The first constant would be the hazard rate for each age group from the London data. For example, the hazard rate for age 12 was .021. Multiplying this by the 190 OYS boys who are still at risk generates an estimate that 4 OYS boys will be first arrested at age 12. Notice the N contains only the number of boys still at risk for first arrest at each age level. The second constant would be the estimate of mean annual arrest frequency for early and for late starters based on the London data. Based on data from Figure 8.3 for the London sample, a mean of 1.85 arrests per year would be a very rough approximation for boys beginning their careers at age 13 or younger. The figure 1.45 would be a rough estimate of the mean annual frequency of arrests for the late start group. With the London-based estimate of how many Oregon boys should be involved in a first arrest at each age, the data can be used in the following way to estimate the OYS age-crime-frequency distribution. First, the London hazard rate was used to obtain the estimate that 3 boys would be arrested at age 10. The London data suggest that early starters would have about 1.85 arrests per year; multiplying 3 (participants) by 1.85 arrests (frequency) gives the number of arrests expected during each of the ensuing years. From this group, we can expect 5.5 arrests when the boys are 10, another 5.5 when they are 11, and so on through age 16. Completing this simple arithmetic separately for each age of onset generates the predicted distribution shown in Figure 8.6. The age-crime-frequency distribution based on calculations from the London sample gives a reasonable fit to distributions obtained for the OYS and London samples. It also provides a reasonable fit to the curves reported in Gottfredson and Hirschi (1990) as examples of culturally invariant data. We believe this comes about because the distributions are the outcome of combining information from two sets of constant values that are themselves reasonably invariant across samples.

In that age-crime-frequency distribution confounds participation with frequency, it is not very useful for describing involvement in crime. It masks the important fact that each age of onset is characterized by quite different intraindividual growth curves for arrest.

Late Starters

Patterson et al. (1989) and Patterson et al. (1991) hypothesized that late starters have three defining characteristics: (a) They are not perceived as being antisocial when assessed at Grade 4 (i.e., they test below the median on a composite measure of the trait); (b) during their early adolescence there are significant family conflicts accompanied by disrupted parental supervision; and (c) they begin actively wandering and becoming involved with the deviant peer group at around age 13 or 14. Because their training for delinquency takes place on the street, the direct cause for the ensuing delinquent behavior is the deviant peer group. The indirect causes are in the family processes resulting in their being on the street and unsupervised.

We hypothesize that the youths who begin their delinquent careers after age 13 remain involved with crime for only a short time, and that they are less at risk for chronic juvenile offending. We also hypothesize that a larger proportion of early, rather than late, starters will become adult chronic offenders. In keeping with the hypothesis, Blumstein et al. (1986) showed that adult offenders were most likely the outcome of juvenile chronic offending. For example, with four juvenile offenses, the likelihood of becoming an adult offender ranged from .92 in one longitudinal study, to .55 in a second study, and to .90 in a third study.

Based on the findings from DiLalla and Gottesman (1989) and others, the assumption is that the late starters tend not to be identified as problem children. Their large-scale survey data did suggest that these *transitory delinquents* were moderately troublesome and marginally skilled in achievement and IQ in comparison to nonoffenders. We also assume that teachers, parents, and peers identify them as only moderately troubled and at least marginally skilled in relationships with peers and in academic achievement. Processes present in the family during early adolescence are what lead to their involvement in a deviant peer group.

Contacts with deviant peers are readily available to most adolescents. Cairns and Cairns (1991) showed that most adolescents develop support networks of some kind. Elliott and Menard (in press) found that for most normal adolescents, the peer group is really a set of subgroups. The majority of these subgroups are likely to include at least one deviant individual, and they vary in the density of deviant peers. As shown by Dishion, Patterson, Stoolmiller, and Skinner (1991), childhood antisocial behavior, academic failure, and peer rejection place children at risk for later involvement with deviant peers. The data showed that the frequency of contacts with deviant peers increased sharply through midadolescence. This suggests that the opportunity for contact with deviant peers actually increases during the high school years. It is hypothesized that at ages 13 through 15, late starters move into increasing amounts of unsupervised time. The second hypothesis is that their marginal status at school and lack of monitoring by parents increase their access to the deviant members of their peer group.

The late start model bears a close resemblance to the well-known factor, Socialized Delinquent, that appeared in the earliest studies of both clinical and normal samples (Jenkins & Hewitt, 1944). Quay (1987) provided a thoughtful review of findings that emerged over the next 40 years. He noted that about 28% of institutionalized delinquents would fit into the Socialized Delinquent category. He cited several studies showing significantly better peer relations for this group than for the group labeled Unsocialized Aggressive. Pulkkinen (1988) has identified a group of Revelers that also seems very similar to the group we have identified as early starters.

Quay (1987) cited several studies showing a significantly reduced risk of arrest for the socialized delinquent group. In keeping with our own position, he also noted that the unsocialized aggressors more likely reflect biological risk factors than do the socialized aggressors. Based on the factor analytic studies, he speculated that many of the delinquent acts engaged in by the socialized aggressors tend to be more covert (e.g., truancy, drug use, and stealing) than overt.

Model for Late Starters. Youths at risk for a late start in crime were identified as nonantisocial when tested in Grade 4 of the OYS. The 105 boys who tested below the median on the antisocial construct comprised the sample used to examine the late start model.

It was hypothesized that disrupted monitoring would contribute significantly to involvement with deviant peers. This hypothesis had previously been supported by data from a sample of normal adolescents (Patterson & Dishion, 1985), but it had never been examined specifically for samples of nonantisocial boys as required for the present model. As shown in Figure 8.7, the path coefficient of .71 between monitoring and deviant peers measured a year later provided strong support for this hypothesis.

The formulations about late starters raise the question of why some families would permit more unsupervised time than others (Patterson et al., 1989). The idea of disrupters was introduced as a possible explanation. To test this idea, 10 potential disrupters were considered, including change of residence, pubescence, unemployment or financial loss, severe illness or death, and family transition (e.g., divorce, marital conflict). The disrupter risk score described events that occurred when the boys were ages 11-12.

Findings from studies by Montemayor and Flannery (1989) and Paikoff and Brooks-Gunn (1990) suggest the need to add one more construct to the late start model. The Paikoff and Brooks-Gunn review showed that adolescents spent less time with their parents than they did when the adolescents were younger. They also found that there was increasing conflict between adolescents and their parents and that adolescents perceived their parents as being less accepting of them. These findings are reminiscent of the earlier findings of Elder (1980), who suggested that

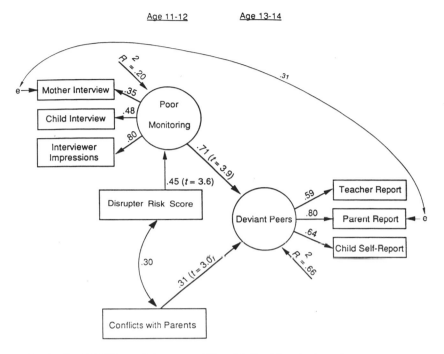

Figure 8.7. The OYS Late Start Model

family conflict might initiate a "flight to peers." To test these ideas, a risk score based on seven measures of family conflict was developed. The hypothesis was that continual conflicts with parents and siblings would accelerate the boy's increasing involvement with members of the peer group. Indicators included questionnaires filled out by parents, videotaped family problem solving of "hot interchanges," telephone interviews, and ratings by home observers. As shown in Figure 8.7, there was a modest but significant relation (path .31) between the family conflict score and the deviant peers construct. This value reflects the relation remaining after the contribution of inept monitoring was partialled out. The combination of family conflict and the inept monitoring construct accounted for 72% of the variance in measures of deviant peer involvement.

The chi-square test showed a good fit between the data and the a priori model outlined earlier by Patterson et al. (1989). The findings from the structural equation model are viewed as support for the first stage in testing the late start formulation. The next crucial stage will require a demonstration that the model predicts the arrest histories for those who begin their careers after the age of 14.

Implications

There may be two very different developmental paths leading to juvenile delinquency. Presumably, they differ both in terms of the determinants that bring them about and in terms of the long-term outcomes of following one path or the other. In this chapter, both paths were framed in a social interactional perspective. As predicted by this model, latent constructs assessing parenting practices were shown to relate to measures of both antisocial and delinquent behavior. As predicted by the mediational model, however, measures of the child antisocial trait provided the best predictor of age for first arrest. For the early start group, age of onset was in turn closely related to risk for repeated arrests over the next few years. Inspection of the early onset group's intraindividual growth curves for police arrests showed a marked drop by midadolescence. In that the self-report data for these same groups showed marked increases in severe crimes during the same interval, it was hypothesized that these experienced youths might be learning to avoid detection.

The findings suggest that the coercion model can be effectively used to understand and predict some important aspects of the early start group. One of the major implications provided by this perspective concerns how one thinks about the nature of crime and criminal behavior. Thinking of crime as a subset of antisocial behaviors that carefully match reinforcing contingencies provided by the social environment is very different from considering delinquent behavior to be a failure of internal controls. Both formulations are eminently plausible, but the ease with which they can be falsified varies enormously. Many types of children's antisocial acts are directly observable; such data can readily be used to falsify claims about reinforcement or punishment effects. How does one test a hypothesis about internal controls or attributional processes? Typically, one asks the youths about their acceptance of societal values or about the nature of the attributions they hold about others. Such variables have been shown to correlate significantly (.42) with self-reported involvement (Elliott et al., 1985), but the contribution of shared method variance is unknown. The key problem, of course, is to demonstrate that these verbal reports have some causal effect on antisocial behavior. There are very few social control studies that effectively attempt to do this (e.g., do self-reports about normlessness contribute to later involvement with deviant peers given that the current level of involvement has been partialled out?). Although one can imagine experimental or appropriate cross-lagged panel tests for the causal status of such variables, social control theories appear to have mounted few efforts along these lines. We suspect that part of the challenge lies in the difficulty of measuring what one means by "internal states."

The delineation between early and late starters also has direct implications for prevention policy. Because of limited resources, it would seem reasonable to focus on reducing the number of children at risk of becoming early starters. Findings from the literature suggest that the identification of at-risk youths might be carried out as early as Grade 2 or 3. In keeping with these speculations, our colleague John Reid has recently initiated field trials for the prevention of conduct disorders; one of his experimental groups includes first-grade children and their families.

There is one further implication that might easily be overlooked because of the restricted scope of this chapter. The strategy of analyzing annual arrest frequencies separately by age of onset showed a general decrease around age 16. This has direct implications for the design of intervention studies. If 10- to 14-year-old chronically offending delinquents were randomly assigned to treatment or comparison groups, *both groups* would be expected to show a decrease in offending, regardless of what the treatment is. As experienced by some recent investigators, this is a most unfortunate outcome. For example, Bank et al. (1991) found that the effect of parent training therapy was significant as measured by police offenses and institutionalization; the reduced mean levels were maintained during follow-up. A year after the intervention, however, the comparison group showed a commensurate drop. As we have speculated here, the chronic offenders in the comparison group may have been learning to avoid arrest (i.e., a maturational decrease in arrest frequencies). It is equally plausible, however, that the decrease after the experimental period reflected a delayed treatment effect. But one effect cannot be disentangled from the other, making this an unfortunate situation for investigators studying the outcome of treatment for chronic offenders.

The most important fallout from this report is that we must develop not one, but two theories of juvenile delinquency. If there are different determinants and outcomes for early and late starters, implications for prediction and prevention are straightforward. One model is needed to predict early starters, and a very different model is needed for late starters. It will be 3 or 4 years before our longitudinal data are available to address this issue in a systematic fashion. Findings available at the present time suggest that the structural equation model for early starters is quite different from that for the late start model. In the former, poor parenting directly determines antisocial behavior. In the latter, the deviant peer group directly provides the training for delinquent acts but the youth is never really antisocial in his style of interacting with others. We believe this difference has fundamental implications for the youth's long-term adjustment.

Note

1. The effort to build a preliminary assessment battery tailored to the coercion model was supported from 1979-1980 by MH No. 32857 from the Center for Studies of Antisocial and Violent Behavior, National Institute of Mental Health, U.S. Public Health Service.

References

Bank, L., Dishion, T., Skinner, M., & Patterson, G. R. (1990). Method variance in structural equation modeling: Living with "glop." In G. R. Patterson (Ed.), *Depression and aggression in family interaction* (pp. 247-279). Hillsdale, NJ: Lawrence Erlbaum.

Bank, L., Marlowe, J. H., Reid, J. B., Patterson, G. R., & Weinrott, M. R. (1991). A comparative evaluation of parent-training interventions for families of chronic delinquents. *Journal of Abnormal Child Psychology, 19,* 15-33.

Bank, L., & Patterson, G. R. (1992). The use of structural equation modeling in combining data from different types of assessment. In J. C. Rosen & P. McReynolds (Ed.), *Advances in psychological assessment: Vol. 8.* New York: Plenum.

Blumstein, A., Cohen, J., Roth, J. A., & Visher, C. A. (Eds.). (1986). *Criminal careers and career criminals* (Vols. 1-2). Washington, DC: National Academy Press.

Cairns, R. B., & Cairns, B. D. (1991). Social cognition and social networks: A developmental perspective. In D. J. Pepler & K. H. Rubin (Eds.), *The development and treatment of childhood aggression* (pp. 249-274). Hillsdale, NJ: Lawrence Erlbaum.

Capaldi, D. M. (1991). Co-occurrence of conduct problems and depressive symptoms in early adolescent boys: 1. Familial factors and general adjustment at Grade 6. *Development and Psychopathology, 3,* 277-300.

Capaldi, D. M., & Patterson, G. R. (1987). An approach to the problem of recruitment and retention rates for longitudinal research. *Behavioral Assessment, 9,* 169-177.

Capaldi, D. M., & Patterson, G. R. (1989). *Psychometric properties of fourteen latent constructs from the Oregon Youth Study.* New York: Springer.

Capaldi, D. M., & Patterson, G. R. (1992). *Is violence a selective trajectory or part of a deviant life style?* Oregon Social Learning Center, Eugene. Manuscript in preparation.

Coie, J. D., & Kupersmidt, J. B. (1983). A behavioral analysis of emerging social status in boys' groups. *Child Development, 54,* 1400-1416.

DiLalla, L. F., & Gottesman. I. I. (1989, April). *Early predictors of delinquency and adult criminality.* Paper presented at the meeting of the Society for Research in Child Development, Kansas City, MO.

Dishion, T. J. (1990). The family ecology of boys' peer relations in middle childhood. *Child Development, 61,* 874-892.

Dishion, T. J., Andrews, D. W., & Patterson, G. R. (1990, January). *The microsocial peer interactions of adolescent boys and their relation to delinquent behaviors.* Paper presented at the conference of the Society for Research in Child and Adolescent Psychopathology, Costa Mesa, CA.

Dishion, T. J., Patterson, G. R., & Kavanagh, K. (in press). An experimental test of the coercion model: Linking theory, measurement, and intervention. In J. McCord & R. Tremblay (Eds.), *The interaction of theory and practice: Experimental studies of intervention.* New York: Guilford.

Dishion, T. J., Patterson, G. R., Stoolmiller, M., & Skinner, M. L. (1991). Family, school, and behavioral antecedents to early adolescent involvement with antisocial peers. *Developmental Psychology, 27,* 172-180.

Dodge, K. A. (1983). Behavioral antecedents: A peer social status. *Child Development, 54,* 1386-1399.

Elder, G. H. (1980). *Family structure and socialization.* New York: Arno Press.

Elliott, D. S., Ageton, S. S., Huizinga, D., Knowles, B. A., & Canter, R. J. (1983) *The prevalence and incidence of delinquent behavior 1976-1980. National estimates of delinquent behavior by sex, race, social class, and other selected variables* (National Youth Survey Report No. 26). Boulder, CO: Behavioral Research Institute.

Elliott, D. S., Huizinga, D., & Ageton, S. S. (1985). *Explaining delinquency and drug use.* Beverly Hills, CA: Sage.

Elliott, D. S., & Menard. S. (in press). Delinquent behavior and delinquent peers: Temporal and developmental patterns. In D. Hawkins (Ed.), *Current theories of crime and deviance.* Newbury Park, CA: Sage.

Farrington, D. P. (1981, November). *Delinquency from ages 10 to 25.* Paper presented at the conference Antecedent Aggression and Antisocial Behavior, of the Society for Life History Research, Monterey, CA.

Farrington, D. P. (1982, July). *Stepping stones to adult criminal careers.* Paper presented at the conference on the Development of Antisocial and Prosocial Behavior, Voss, Norway.

Farrington, D. P. (1983). Offending from 10 to 25 years of age. In K. T. Van Dusen & S. A. Mednick (Eds.), *Prospective studies of crime and delinquency* (pp. 11-38). Boston: Kluwer-Nijhoff.

Farrington, D. P. (1991). Childhood aggression and adult violence: Early precursors and later-life outcomes. In D. J. Pepler & K. H. Rubin (Eds.), *The development and treatment of childhood aggression* (pp. 5-29). Hillsdale, NJ: Lawrence Erlbaum.

Farrington, D. P., Gallagher, B., Morley, L., St. Ledger, R. J., & West, D. J. (1986, September). *Cambridge study in delinquent development: Long term follow-up.* Unpublished annual report, Cambridge University Institute of Criminology, Cambridge, UK.

Forgatch, M. S. (1991). The clinical science vortex: A developing theory of antisocial behavior. In D. Pepler & K. H. Rubin (Eds.), *The development and treatment of childhood aggression* (pp. 291-315). Hillsdale, NJ: Lawrence Erlbaum.

Forgatch, M. S., & Patterson, G. R. (1989). *Parents and adolescents living together: II. Family problem solving.* Eugene, OR: Castalia.

Forgatch, M. S., & Toobert, D. (1979). A cost-effective parent training program for use with normal preschool children. *Journal of Pediatric Psychology, 4,* 129-143.

Glueck, S., & Glueck, E. (1959). *Predicting delinquency and crime*. Cambridge, MA: Harvard University Press.

Gottfredson, M. R., & Hirschi, T. (1990). *A general theory of crime*. Stanford, CA: Stanford University Press.

Hamparian, D. M., Schuster, R., Dinitz, S., & Conrad, J. P. (1978). *Violent few: A study of dangerous juvenile offenders*. Lexington, MA: D. C. Heath.

Hirschi, T., & Gottfredson, M. (1983). Age and the explanation of crime. *American Journal of Sociology, 89*, 552-584.

Jenkins, R. L., & Hewitt, L. (1944). Types of personality structure encountered in child guidance clinics. *American Journal of Orthopsychiatry, 14*(1), 84-94.

Larzelere, R. E., & Patterson, G. R. (1990). Parental management: Mediator of the effect of socioeconomic status on early delinquency. *Criminology, 28*, 301-323.

Laub, J. H., & Sampson. R. J. (1988). Unraveling families and delinquency: A reanalysis of the Gluecks' data. *Criminology, 26*, 355-380.

Le Blanc, M., & Frechette, M. (1989). *Male criminal activity from childhood through youth: Multilevel and developmental perspectives*. New York: Springer.

Loeber, R. (1982). The stability of antisocial and delinquent child behavior: A review. *Child Development, 53*, 1431-1446.

McCord, J. A. (1981). A longitudinal perspective on patterns of crime. *Criminology, 19*, 211-218.

Montemayor, R., & Flannery, D. (1989). A naturalistic study of the involvement of children and adolescents with their mothers and friends: Developmental differences in expressive behavior. *Journal of Adolescent Research, 4*, 3-14.

Paikoff, R. L., & Brooks-Gunn, J. (1990). Physiological processes: What role do they play during the transition to adolescence? In R. Montemayor, G. R. Adams, & T. P. Gullotta (Eds.), *From childhood to adolescence: A transitional period?* (pp. 310-348). Newbury Park, CA: Sage.

Patterson, G. R. (1982). *A social learning approach: III. Coercive family process*. Eugene, OR: Castalia.

Patterson, G. R. (1984). Siblings: Fellow travelers in coercive family processes. In R. J. Blanchard & D. C. Blanchard (Eds.), *Advances in the study of aggression* (Vol. 1, pp. 173-215). Orlando, FL: Academic Press.

Patterson, G. R. (1986). Maternal rejection: Determinant or product for deviant child behavior? In W. W. Hartup & Z. Rubin (Eds.), *Relationships and development* (pp. 73-94). Hillsdale, NJ: Lawrence Erlbaum.

Patterson, G. R. (1988). Family process: Loops, levels, and linkages. In N. Bolger, A. Caspi, G. Downey, & M. Moorehouse (Eds.), *Persons in context: Developmental processes* (pp 114-151). Cambridge: Cambridge University Press.

Patterson, G. R. (1991, April). *Interaction of stress and family structure, and their relation to child adjustment: An example of across-site collaboration*. Paper presented at the meeting of the Society for Research in Child Development, Seattle.

Patterson, G. R., & Bank, L. (1987). When is a nomological network a construct? In D. R. Peterson & D. B. Fishman (Eds.), *Assessment for decision* (pp. 249-279). New Brunswick, NJ: Rutgers University Press.

Patterson, G. R., & Bank, L. (1989). Some amplifying mechanisms for pathologic process in families. In M. R. Gunnar & E. Thelem (Eds.), *Systems and development: The Minnesota Symposia on Child Psychology*, (Vol. 22, pp. 167-210). Hillsdale, NJ: Lawrence Erlbaum.

Patterson, G. R., & Capaldi, D. M. (1990). A mediational model for boys' depressed mood. In J. Rolf, A. S. Masten, D. Cicchetti, K. H. Neuchterlein, & S. Weintraub (Eds.), *Risk and protective factors in the development of psychopathology* (pp. 141-163). Cambridge: Cambridge University Press.

Patterson, G. R., & Capaldi, D. M. (1991). Antisocial parents: Unskilled and vulnerable. In P. A. Cowan & E. M. Hetherington (Eds.), *Family transitions* (pp. 195-218). Hillsdale, NJ: Lawrence Erlbaum.

Patterson, G. R., Capaldi, D. M., & Bank, L. (1991). An early starter model for predicting delinquency. In D. Pepler & K. H. Rubin (Eds.), *The development and treatment of childhood aggression* (pp. 139-168). Hillsdale, NJ: Lawrence Erlbaum.

Patterson, G. R., Chamberlain, P., & Reid, J. B. (1982). A comparative evaluation of parent training procedures. *Behavior Therapy, 13,* 638-650.

Patterson, G. R., Crosby. L., & Vuchinich, S. (in press). Predicting risk for early police arrest. *Journal of Quantitative Criminology.*

Patterson, G. R., & Dawes, R. M. (1975). A Guttman scale of children's coercive behaviors. *Journal of Consulting and Clinical Psychology, 43,* 594.

Patterson, G. R., DeBaryshe, B. D., & Ramsey, E. (1989). A developmental perspective on antisocial behavior. *American Psychologist, 44,* 329-335.

Patterson, G. R., & Dishion, T. J. (1985). Contributions of families and peers to delinquency. *Criminology, 23*(1), 63-79.

Patterson, G. R., Dishion, T. J., & Chamberlain, P. (in press). Outcomes and methodological issues relating to treatment of antisocial children. In T R Giles (Ed.), *Effective psychotherapy: A handbook of comparative research.* New York: Plenum.

Patterson, G. R., & Reid, J. B. (1984). Social interactional processes within the family: The study of moment-by-moment family transactions in which human social development is imbedded. *Journal of Applied Developmental Psychology, 5,* 237-262.

Patterson, G. R., Reid, J. B., & Dishion, T. J. (1992). *A social learning approach: IV. Antisocial boys.* Eugene, OR: Castalia.

Patterson, G. R., & Stoolmiller. M. (1991). Replications of a dual failure model for boys' depressed mood. *Journal of Consulting and Clinical Psychology, 59,* 491-498.

Patterson, G. R., & Stouthamer-Loeber, M. (1984). The correlation of family management practices and delinquency. *Child Development, 55,* 1299-1307.

Pulkkinen, L. (1988). Delinquent development: Theoretical and empirical considerations. In M. Rutter (Ed.), *Studies of psychosocial risk: The power of longitudinal data* (pp. 184-199). Cambridge: Cambridge University Press.

Quay, H. C. (1987). Patterns of delinquent behavior. In H. C. Quay (Ed.), *Handbook of juvenile delinquency* (pp. 118-138). New York: John Wiley.

Ramsey, E., Patterson, G. R., & Walker, H. M. (1990). Generalization of the antisocial trait from home to school settings. *Journal of Applied Developmental Psychology, 11,* 209-223.

Schuck, G. R. (1974). The use of causal nonexperimental models in aggression research. In J. DeWit & W. W. Hartup (Eds.), *Determinants and origins of aggressive behavior* (pp. 381-389). The Hague, The Netherlands: Mouton.

Snyder, J. J., Dishion, T. J., & Patterson, G. R. (1986). Determinants and consequences of associating with deviant peers during preadolescence and adolescence. *Journal of Early Adolescence, 6,* 29-43.

Snyder, J. J., & Patterson, G. R. (1986). The effects of consequences on patterns of social interaction: A quasi experimental approach to reinforcement in natural interaction. *Child Development, 57,* 1257-1268.

Snyder, J. J., & Patterson, G. R. (1992). *Covariation of the relative rate of child behavior and the relative rate of maternal reinforcement in natural family interactions.* Manuscript in preparation.

Stoolmiller, M. (1990). *Latent growth model analysis of the relation between antisocial behavior and wandering.* Unpublished doctoral dissertation, University of Oregon, Eugene.

Tremblay, R. (1988, June). *Some findings from the Montreal studies.* Paper presented at the Earlscourt Symposium on Childhood Aggression, Toronto.

Walker, H. M., Shinn, M. R., O'Neill, R. E., & Ramsey, E. (1987). A longitudinal assessment of the development of antisocial behavior in boys: Rationale, methodology, and first-year results. *Remedial and Special Education, 8*(4), 7-16.

Wikström, P.-O. (1987). *Patterns of crime in a birth cohort: Age, sex, and class differences* (Project Metropolitan: A longitudinal study of a Stockholm cohort No. 24.) Department of Sociology, University of Stockholm.

9

Childhood Conduct Problems, Adult Psychopathology, and Crime

LEE N. ROBINS

S tudies attempting to predict crime on the basis of psychopathology have focused on conduct disorder in childhood (Robins, 1966/1974) and in adolescence and adulthood on substance abuse (Cloninger & Guze, 1970; Guze, Woodruff, & Clayton, 1974; Martin, Cloninger, & Guze, 1982; Petrich, 1976; Robinson, Patten, & Kerr, 1965), and on antisocial personality (Baker, 1986; Guze, 1976; Guze, Wolfgram, McKinney, & Cantwell, 1967; Piotrowski, Losacco, & Guze, 1916; Widom, 1978; Woodside, 1962). No study has yet treated all three of these disorders together to ask whether conduct disorder has a direct effect on crime, or only an indirect effect through engendering substance abuse and adult antisocial behavior.

Moreover, conduct problems have recently been shown to predict adult disorders other than substance abuse and antisocial personality, particularly in women (Robins & Price, 1991), while family members of children with attention deficit disorder, a frequent precursor of conduct problems, have been shown to have an increased rate of affective disorder (Biederman, Faraone, Keenan, & Tsuang, 1991), whether or not the index child had an affective disorder. If there is a relationship between conduct disorder and crime not explained by its effects on substance abuse and antisocial personality, it becomes necessary to ask whether it occurs through conduct disorder's effect on other psychiatric disorders. That such a pathway might exist is suggested by the fact that manic-depressive disorders and anxiety are common in prisoners (Good, 1978; Gunn, 1978) and schizophrenia has sometimes been found to be associated with violence (Giovannoni & Gurel, 1967; Rabkin, 1979).

It is also well known that juvenile delinquency is generally preceded by conduct disorder (Loeber & LeBlanc, 1990), and that juvenile delinquents have a greatly increased risk of becoming adult offenders. Yet previous studies have not asked to what extent conduct problems and juvenile delinquency are independent predictors of crime or whether instead delinquency may merely act as a marker for severe conduct disorder. It is also possible that conduct disorder's only role in adult crime is to introduce youngsters to the courts, at which time the criminal career runs an independent course into adulthood.

Another issue of interest is whether the prediction of crime by behavior in childhood and later is best served by following the guidance of the official nomenclature in defining the syndromes of conduct disorder and antisocial personality, or whether only certain of the symptoms used to construct these syndromes are relevant.

This chapter is an effort to explore these previously overlooked issues in an unusual data set—the Epidemiological Catchment Area project. To do so, we ask the following succession of questions:

(1) What adult disorders does conduct disorder predict in addition to substance abuse and the syndrome of adult behaviors used to diagnose antisocial personality?

(2) Do predicted disorders other than substance abuse and adult antisocial behaviors in turn predict crime?

(3) Is the relation of these disorders to crime merely a consequence of their relation to conduct disorder?

(4) Is the relation of these disorders to crime merely a consequence of their association with antisocial behavior or substance abuse?

(5) If we set aside the effect of conduct disorder on psychiatric disorder, does it have an additional effect on crime?

(6) How do substance use and antisocial behavior compare as predictors of crime?

(7) Does conduct disorder have an effect on crime beyond its effect on juvenile delinquency?

(8) If we consider all the disorders conduct disorder predicts *plus* its effect on juvenile delinquency, does it still contribute directly to crime?

(9) How much of the arrest history do childhood behavior and adult diagnosis explain?

(10) Can the dimensional measurement of conduct problems and antisocial behavior be improved?

Methods

The source of data with which we attempt to answer these questions is the Epidemiologic Catchment Area (ECA) study. This study was done in

TABLE 9.1 Definitions of Crime and Conduct Disorder

Crime Reported in Either Interview
0 = None
1 = 1 arrest, no felony
2 = 2 arrests, no felony
3 = 1 felony, no other arrest
4 = 2 or more arrests, and at least 1 felony

Conduct Disorder in First Interview
Count of symptoms beginning before 18:
Truancy
Runaway
Lying
Stealing
Vandalism
Fighting

five sites, but we will use data from only three: St. Louis, Durham, and Los Angeles, because in the other two sites questions about crime were asked only of persons who had at least three childhood behavior problems. In the three usable sites, 10,711 persons residing in the community or in institutions were interviewed between 1981 and 1985. Two of the sites included rural as well as urban residential areas. In 80% to 84% of those interviewed, a second interview was carried out a year later, when the questions about crime and adult psychiatric disorders were repeated. The questions on childhood behavior were not repeated. We accepted reports of crime and psychiatric symptoms from either interview, to obtain as large an affected sample as possible.

The sample was weighted inversely to the probability of selection and to represent the sex, age, and ethnic structure of the nation as of 1980. The probability of selection varied with household size, with the fact that institutional residents were sampled at 10 times the rate of household residents, and with the fact that blacks were oversampled in one site and the elderly in another site. In calculating significance of differences, the sample was downweighted to compensate for the increase in variance resulting from cluster sampling and weighting. The significance of differences was reduced to levels that would be found in a simple random sample of 6,378.

The variables constructed for this chapter are shown in Tables 9.1 and 9.2. Table 9.1 shows the definitions of *crime* and *conduct disorder* used. Crime is measured by reported arrest and conviction history, not by actual crimes committed. It is a four-level scale varying from no arrest to multiple nontraffic arrests, at least one of which resulted in a felony conviction. Traffic offenses are not included.

The conduct symptoms include most of those listed in the definition of conduct disorder in the current official nomenclature of the American Psychiatric Association (1987), DSM-III-R. Missing are cruelty to animals, cruelty to people, and forced sex. Use of weapons in a fight is included in fighting, break-ins are included either in stealing or in vandalism, fire-setting is included in vandalism. (Missing symptoms are explained by the fact that questions about childhood behavior were included in order to assess Antisocial Personality according to the earlier DSM-III nomenclature, not conduct disorder.) These symptoms are counted as present if they appeared before age 18. Rather than using an improper categorical diagnosis of conduct disorder, given the fact that not all of the symptoms are available, we treat conduct problems as a dimension varying from none to six symptoms.

In all analyses involving conduct disorder or crime, it will be important to control for both age and sex. For conduct disorder, age is a powerful predictor, with highest rates in those under 40, and men have considerably higher rates than women (see Figure 9.1). For crime, sex is the major factor, with very low rates for women, particularly at a more serious level (see Figure 9.2). There is also a tendency for more young than older people to have had an arrest. Thus, we would expect a relationship between conduct problems and crime on the basis of their demographic distributions alone, even if conduct disorder were not causal.

Table 9.2 shows the adult symptoms of antisocial personality covered. These include all the symptoms in DSM-III-R with the exception of failing to meet financial obligations and lacking remorse, which were not covered in the interview, and failing to conform to social norms through illegal behavior, which was omitted because it is so closely linked to arrests that it could not be considered independent. Marital problems, which include multiple divorces, multiple affairs, and desertion, substitute for absence of a totally monogamous relationship for one year. Because we are interested in childhood behavior problems as predictors of these adult behaviors, we will not use the categorical diagnosis of antisocial personality in this chapter, since it requires at least three childhood symptoms before age 15, making impossible the study of the relation of childhood problems to adult behavior. Instead, we will treat the occurrence since age 18 of the adult symptoms of antisocial personality exclusive of criminal behavior as a dimension, with values varying from none to seven different types of antisocial behavior.

Substance abuse includes diagnoses at any time in life according to DSM-III criteria of alcohol abuse or dependence and abuse of or dependence

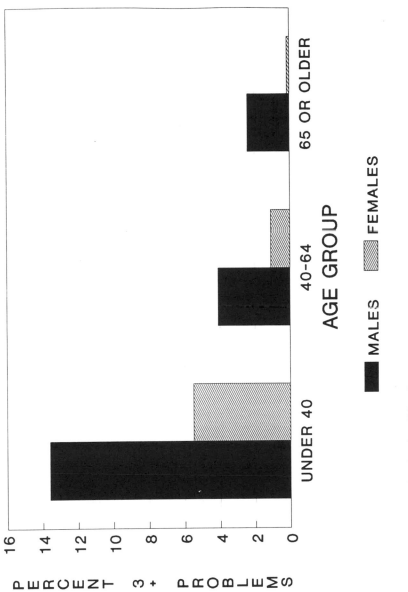

Figure 9.1. Age and Sex Predict Conduct Disorders

177

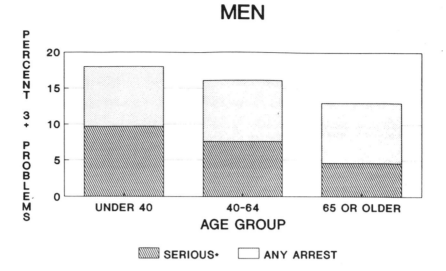

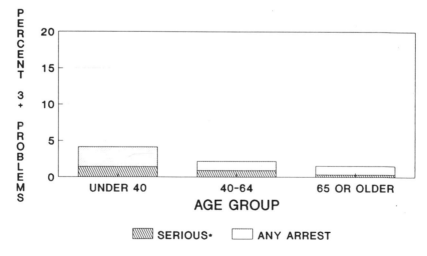

•FELONY OR MORE THAN ONE ARREST

Figure 9.2. Age and Sex Predict Crime

TABLE 9.2 Definitions of Psychiatric Disorder

Antisocial Symptoms Other Than Crime in Either Interview

Count of: Work problems
            Lying
            Vagrancy
            Violence
            Speeding
            Child neglect
            Marital/relationship problems

Substance Abuse in Either Interview

---

0 = None
1 = Alcohol abuse or dependence
2 = Illicit drug abuse or dependence
3 = Both

Mania/Psychosis in Either Interview
    Manic episode, delusions, or hallucinations
Depression in Either Interview
    Major depressive episode or dysthymia
Panic/Agoraphobia in Either Interview
    Panic attack or agoraphobia

---

on cannabis, stimulants, sedatives, tranquilizers, cocaine, opiates, hallucinogens, and inhalants. It is analyzed as a four-point scale, starting with neither an alcohol nor drug diagnosis, and ending with dependence on or abuse of both alcohol and one or more illicit drugs.

Other disorders are grouped into three categories, representing psychosis, depression, and anxiety. *Psychosis* includes a manic episode or any of the hallucinations and delusions used to diagnosis schizophrenia, schizophreniform, or schizoaffective disorders. We will call this category *mania/psychosis*. *Depression* includes a major depressive episode or dysthymia. *Anxiety* includes panic attacks (as defined in DSM-III, whether or not full criteria for panic disorder are met) and agoraphobia (as defined in DSM-III, when full criteria are met). We will refer to this category as *panic/agoraphobia*. Each of these definitions accepts occurrence at any time in the life history.

These definitions provide us with substantial numbers of both men and women with crime, conduct disorder, and each adult disorder (see Table 9.3). The smallest group is the mania/psychosis group, with 665 cases.

Juvenile delinquency is assessed by asking respondents whether they had ever been arrested as a juvenile or appeared in juvenile court.

TABLE 9.3 The Sample

From Three ECA Sites Surveyed Twice, a Year Apart Between 1981 and 1985:
St. Louis (Including Two Rural Counties)
Los Angeles (Hispanic and Anglo Areas)
Durham, North Carolina (Including Four Rural Counties)
Number = 10,737 Weighted to Represent the Nation as of 1980

| | *Males* | *Females* |
	4,707	*6,030*
Any crime	1,160	290
Any conduct problem	2,339	1,549
Any antisocial behavior	3,476	3,421
Substance abuse	1,683	581
Mania/psychosis	296	369
Depression	370	832
Panic/agoraphobia	476	1,062

Because conduct problems and juvenile delinquency were counted only if they occurred in childhood or adolescence and crime was defined as adult arrests, we can be reasonably certain that any causal relationships are in the direction of conduct problems and delinquency causing crime, not the reverse. We are not certain about the temporal order between crime and the other psychiatric disorders. Because both disorders and crime typically begin in early adulthood, it is possible that some of the disorders were responses to arrest, rather than its cause. By assuming that they are causal in our analyses, we are putting the early-appearing conduct problems and delinquency to a particularly stringent test when they are asked to compete with disorders that may have appeared only subsequent to the criminality.

Data analysis is by multiple regression. With so large a sample, most findings are significant at the $p < .0001$ level. To give a better sense of the relative contribution of these variables to crime, we compare their F values initially and subsequent to adding in other predictors.

Results

(1) What adult disorders does conduct disorder predict in addition to substance abuse and the syndrome of adult behaviors used to diagnose antisocial personality?

Asking this question requires controlling for age and sex. In the ECA data, both conduct disorder and specific diagnoses are strongly correlated with both demographic factors. Conduct disorder is more commonly reported in each successively younger cohort, as are substance abuse, mania, and schizophrenia, while depression is somewhat more common in the middle-aged. All disorders (except two we are not considering—dementia and somatization disorder) are rarely reported by the elderly. Men predominate among those with conduct disorder, substance abuse, and antisocial personality; women predominate among those with depression, panic attacks, and agoraphobia. The two sexes are about equally represented among persons reporting manic episodes and psychotic symptoms.

When we control for age and sex, we find (as expected) a strong relationship between conduct disorder and both adult antisocial behavior and substance abuse (see Table 9.4). Relationships of conduct disorder to the other three diagnoses, although much weaker, are still highly significant and similar in strength. Their weakness compared to the relation with substance abuse can be seen in Figure 9.3. Not only are the base rates of psychosis mania, depression, and panic/agoraphobia low compared with substance abuse, particularly in men, but rates are less responsive to number of conduct problems. Nonetheless, there is a definite positive gradient for both sexes as the number of conduct problems increases.

(2) Do predicted adult disorders other than substance abuse and adult antisocial behavior in turn predict crime?

All three of these disorders are positively related to crime, although the relationship is stronger for mania/psychosis (F value approximately 86) than for panic/agoraphobia or depression, which have similar F values of 27 and 39 (see Table 9.5 and top bars of Figure 9.4). The relation of each of these disorders to crime is much weaker than the relation of antisocial symptoms or substance abuse to crime (F values of 1,108 and 934 respectively).

(3) Is the relation of these disorders to crime merely a consequence of their relation to conduct disorder?

When we control for number of conduct problems, the strength of the relationship of these disorders to crime diminishes, but it remains statistically significant (Figure 9.4, second group of bars.)

(4) Is the relation of these disorders to crime merely a consequence of their association with antisocial behavior or substance abuse?

It has often been noted that there is a relationship between substance abuse and depression. This relationship might be explained either by persons becoming addicted as a result of attempts to self-medicate or becoming depressed in response to the social problems caused by their antisocial behavior or substance abuse or perhaps as a response to chemical

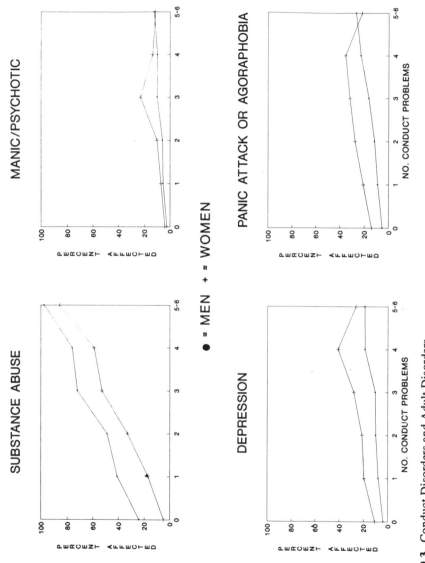

SUBSTANCE ABUSE

MANIC/PSYCHOTIC

● = MEN   + = WOMEN

PANIC ATTACK OR AGORAPHOBIA

DEPRESSION

Figure 9.3. Conduct Disorders and Adult Disorders

182

TABLE 9.4 What Psychiatric Disorders Do Conduct Disorders Predict? (Multiple Regression, Controlling for Sex)

	F Values Controlling for Age and Sex
Antisocial symptoms (other than criminal behavior)	1,886.1
Substance abuse	1,382.4
Panic/agoraphobia	159.0
Depression	158.7
Mania/psychosis	138.0

changes in the nervous system caused by the drugs. It has also been noted that drinking excessively is common during a manic episode, and that many schizophrenics abuse drugs and alcohol. These observations are confirmed in this study (see Table 9.6). Even controlling for conduct disorder and antisocial behavior, substance abuse is strongly related to each of these "legal" disorders. However, these disorders are also strongly related to antisocial behaviors, controlling for conduct disorder and substance abuse. The relationship between antisocial behavior and depression is particularly strong (F value = 213).

We note that the relationship of conduct disorder to these disorders must be largely mediated through its relation to substance abuse and antisocial personality (see Table 9.6). When controls for both those disorders are entered, conduct disorder is no longer significantly related to depression, and its relation to mania/psychosis and panic/agoraphobia is greatly reduced (F values drop to between 2% and 6% of their initial value).

It seems possible, then, that while the association between "legal" disorders and crime cannot be explained by their common roots in conduct problems, it might be secondary to the association of antisocial behavior or substance abuse with these disorders (Martin et al., 1985).

When we control for either antisocial behavior or substance abuse, only mania/psychosis remains significantly related to crime (Figure 9.4, sections 3 and 4). Adding conduct disorder to either controlled disorder does not change the situation (see sections 5 and 6). However, when controls are introduced for both antisocial behavior and substance abuse (section 7), there is no further impact of mania/psychosis on crime, whether or not conduct problems are also controlled for (section 8).

We conclude then that the association of disorders *other* than antisocial personality and substance abuse with crime is not direct, but occurs when these disorders are secondary to antisocial personality and substance abuse.

184

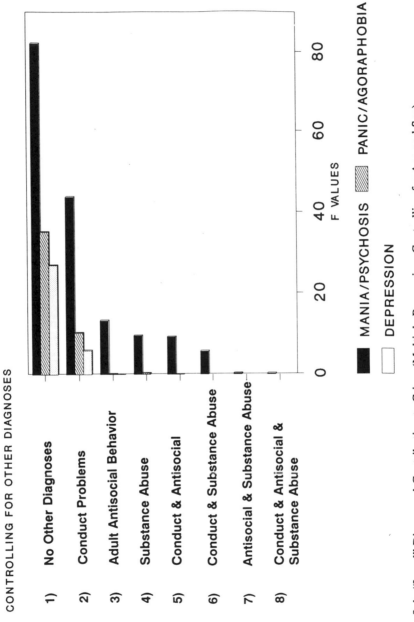

Figure 9.4. "Legal" Diagnoses' Contribution to Crime (Multiple Regression, Controlling for Age and Sex)

TABLE 9.5 Psychiatric Disorder Predicts Crime (Multiple Regression)

Controlling for Sex and Age:	*F Values*
Antisocial symptoms (other than crime)	1,107.7
Substance abuse	934.2
Mania/psychosis	85.8
Panic/agoraphobia	39.1
Depression	27.1

(5) If we set aside the effect of conduct disorder on psychiatric disorder, does it have an additional effect on crime?

Conduct disorder had a much stronger initial relationship to crime (*F* value = 578) than did depression, mania/psychosis, or panic/agoraphobia, even though symptoms typically occur well prior to the arrests while the other disorders may be contemporaneous with the arrests, subsequent to them, or precursors. However, conduct disorder was less strongly associated with crime initially than either antisocial behavior (*F* value = 1,108) or substance abuse (*F* value = 934), both of which were predicted by conduct problems. Was the contribution of conduct disorder to crime only through its ability to predict antisocial behavior and substance abuse?

We find that conduct disorder continued to have a substantial effect (*F* value = 54) in the prediction of crime even when both adult antisocial behavior and substance abuse were controlled for (see Table 9.7). Adding the other three diagnoses, depression, panic/agoraphobia, and mania/psychosis, did not further reduce the predictive value of conduct problems.

(6) How do substance abuse and antisocial behavior compare as predictors of arrest?

TABLE 9.6 Prediction of Adult Diagnoses by Conduct Disorder Versus Adult Antisocial Symptoms and Substance Abuse (Multiple Regression, Controlling for Sex, Age, and the Other Two Predictors)

	Conduct Disorder *F*	*Antisocial Behaviors* *F*	*Substance Abuse* *F*
Depression	3.2	213.1***	70.3***
Mania or psychosis	4.4*	113.8***	109.6***
Panic or agoraphobia	9.2**	122.3***	67.9***

NOTE: *p < .05; **p < .01; ***p < .001

TABLE 9.7 Contribution of Conduct Disorder to Crime Controlling for Sex, Age, and Adult Diagnoses (Multiple Regression)

Controlling for:	F Values
Sex and age only	577.9
One diagnosis:	
Depression (D)	555.6
Panic/agoraphobia (P)	551.5
Mania/psychosis (M)	537.7
Antisocial behavior (except crime) (A)	165.9
Substance abuse (S)	164.5
Two diagnoses:	
S + A	53.7
Three diagnoses:	
S + A + M	53.6+
Four diagnoses:	
S + A + M + D	54.7*
Five diagnoses:	
S + A + M + D + P	55.3+

NOTES: * Adding depression is *protective*, with $p < .001$.
+ Adding this disorder has no significant effect.

We noted above that when the only controls were for age and sex, antisocial behavior was the best predictor of crime among the psychiatric disorders we examined, lending support to the view that antisocial personality and crime are intimately connected. Once conduct problems in childhood are controlled for, however, substance abuse is as strongly associated with crime as is antisocial behavior (F value = 441 vs. 437) (Table 9.8). Of course, use of illicit drugs is grounds for arrest, but so are several of the behaviors listed as antisocial, including violence, vagrancy, and drunk driving.

TABLE 9.8 Comparing Conduct Disorder, Antisocial Disorder, and Substance Abuse as Predictors of Crime (Multiple Regression Controlling for Sex and Age)

		F Values	
	Conduct	Antisocial	Substance Abuse
Age and sex only	577.9	1,107.6	934.2
Also controlling for:			
Conduct	—	675.1	576.3
Antisocial	164.9	—	441.1
Substance abuse	164.5	437.2	—
Both other variables	53.7	320.5	341.0

TABLE 9.9 Does Conduct Disorder Have an Effect on Crime Beyond Contributing to Its Chief Predictors?

Contribution of Conduct Disorder After Introducing Age, Sex, and:	*F Value for Conduct Disorder*
Delinquency	280.6****
+ Antisocial behavior	63.6****
+ Substance abuse	12.5***

NOTE: ***p < .001; ****p < .0001

Antisocial behavior, then, appears no more intimately associated with arrest than is substance abuse, after the contribution of the childhood behavior required for a diagnosis of antisocial personality is taken into account.

(7) Does conduct disorder have an effect on crime beyond its effect on juvenile delinquency?

We have found that conduct problems continue to have an effect on crime, even taking into account the disorders that they predict best—substance abuse and antisocial personality. Conduct problems also predict delinquency. Indeed, the association between conduct disorder and delinquency has been called "one of the main tenets of developmental criminology" (Loeber & LeBlanc, 1990, p. 387).

That there is a strong tendency toward continuity of arrests from adolescence to adulthood is also well known. Perhaps, then, the only reason that conduct problems continue to predict crime even when the adult disorders it predicts are controlled for is simply the fact that conduct-disordered youngsters are more likely already to have had police contacts by the time they reach adulthood.

However, this does not seem to be the case. When delinquency is controlled for, conduct problems continue to have a strong effect on crime (*F* value = 281) (Table 9.9).

(8) If we consider all the disorders conduct disorder predicts *plus* its effect on juvenile delinquency, does it still contribute directly to crime?

When we also add antisocial behavior and substance abuse to the equation, conduct disorder still has a significant, but diminished, role in predicting crime (Table 9.9). We conclude, therefore, that while the chief effects of conduct disorder on crime are through its effect on delinquency, substance abuse, and adult antisocial behavior, this does not exhaust its impact.

TABLE 9.10 How the Chief Contributors Rank in Predicting Crime

	F Value, Net of Age and Sex	
	Initially	Controlling for Three Other Contributors
Delinquency	885	326
Substance abuse	934	295
Antisocial behavior	1,108	273
Conduct disorder	578	13

Strongest of the four predictors, controlling for all others, is delinquency (Table 9.10), with substance abuse and antisocial behavior not far behind. Thus there appears to be a major independent effect of early contacts with the justice system on the risk of later arrest if arrestable behaviors such as substance abuse and aggression occur in adult life.

(9) How much of the arrest history do childhood behavior and adult diagnosis explain?

The awesome size of the F values in the results presented so far is a tribute not so much to the relevance of the variables studied as to the size of the sample. In fact, these variables explain only a small part of the arrest history (Table 9.11). Conduct problems alone explain 10% and delinquency adds another 4%. Thus, at the end of childhood, we can explain 14% of the variance in future arrest careers. Adding adult antisocial behavior and substance abuse raises our explanatory power to 22%. Many other factors likely remain unaccounted for, but part of the indeterminacy undoubtedly lies also in the error with which the available variables are measured when the only source of information is retrospective self-report. We do not know how great that error rate is, but it is presumably substantial.

TABLE 9.11 How Much Do the Main Predictors of Crime Explain? (Multiple Regression, Controlling for Sex and Age)

	R^2
Conduct problems	.10
+	
Delinquency	.14
+	
Antisocial behavior	.19
+	
Substance abuse	.22

TABLE 9.12 Which Individual Conduct Problems Contribute Most to Crime? (Controlling for Sex, Age, and Number of Conduct Problems)

	F Value
Truancy	14.9****
Running away	13.9***
Vandalism	6.0*
Fighting	5.8*
Not significant: lying, stealing	

NOTE: $*p < .05$; $***p < .001$; $****p < .0001$

(10) Can the dimensional measurement of conduct problems and antisocial behavior be improved?

The items that we included in our measure of conduct problems and adult antisocial behavior are based on the criteria for conduct disorder and antisocial personality in DSM-III-R. These criteria were chosen for the Manual because they appeared to cluster in persons seen in clinical settings, not because they could predict crime. It is possible that the strength of prediction by these dimensional measures lies not in their relation to the latent variables of conduct disorder and antisocial personality, but because some of their individual items are good predictors of crime. If only some of their elements are relevant, the predictive power of these dimensional scales might be strengthened by dropping items that are not making a contribution.

Because the dimensional measures we have used for conduct problems and antisocial behavior have been shown to be strong predictors of crime (Figure 9.5), it is important that we use number of positive items on that dimension as a control variable when looking at the impact of a specific item. Otherwise, the effect of that particular behavior is likely to be confused with the nonspecific effect of adding any one behavior to the total number of other behaviors present.

Among the six conduct problems we investigated, four made a significant contribution to crime, even after controls for the number of conduct problems were instituted (Table 9.12). The two strongest predictors were truancy and running away from home. Lying and stealing were not significant, perhaps because they were so common.

Among the seven adult antisocial behaviors, all except child neglect made a significant contribution (Table 9.13). Four of the seven were of particular and similar importance—violence, drunk driving, job problems, and lying (including use of aliases).

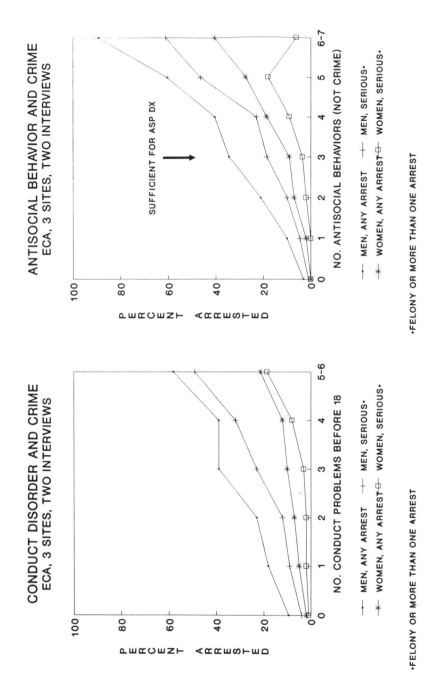

Figure 9.5. Conduct Disorders and Adult Antisocial Behavior as Predictors of Adult Arrests

190

TABLE 9.13 Which Individual Antisocial Behaviors Best Predict Crime? (Controlling for Sex, Age, Conduct Problems, Substance Abuse, and Number of Antisocial Problems)

	F Value (p < .0001)
Violence	25.0
Drunk driving	24.5
Job trouble	23.6
Aliases, lying	21.0
Marital problems	12.8
Vagrancy	10.5
Not significant: Child neglect	

We repeated the analysis with conduct disorder and adult antisocial behaviors, omitting the nonsignificant items to see whether that increased the strength of either dimension as a predictor. The only change from results in Table 9.11 was that the initial contribution of conduct disorder dropped from 10% to 9%. The explained variance when both conduct disorder and adult antisocial behavior were entered along with substance abuse remained at 22%.

We conclude then that it is probably conduct disorder and antisocial personality that predict crime, not specific behaviors that happen to be part of this psychiatric constellation.

Conclusions

This effort to understand the role of psychopathology in crime made use of self-reported lifetime symptoms and criminal history in a very large sample of the general population aged 18 and over. The fact that this sample included institutional residents as well as those in households means that it did not exclude the more seriously criminal, as household surveys typically do.

Definitions of psychopathology were based on the standard nomenclatures of the American Psychiatric Association, DSM-III and DSM-III-R. Six types of psychopathology were considered: childhood conduct disorder, the adult symptoms of antisocial personality, substance abuse, psychosis, depression, and anxiety.

Controlling for age and sex, the first three, conduct disorder, antisocial personality, and substance abuse, were associated with criminal history initially and when all other disorders were controlled for. The other three disorders were initially significant, but none remained so when antisocial personality and substance abuse were controlled for, suggesting that their chief importance in predicting crime is as indicators for the more immediately relevant disorders with which they are associated.

More predictive than any single disorder was the experience of official juvenile delinquency, although all three types of psychopathology further added to the prediction of crime.

Although the contribution of conduct disorder was diminished substantially when delinquency and the disorders it predicted were controlled for, it still made an additional contribution. Thus it has effects even greater than its effects on delinquency and the measured adult disorders. Perhaps if we had had a more complete accounting of the adult symptoms of antisocial personality, including the missing symptoms of financial irresponsibility and lack of remorse, conduct disorder would not have retained its direct effect. There may also be other types of adult antisocial behavior, not included in the DSM-III-R criteria for antisocial personality, that could use up the variance conduct disorder accounts for. In any case, a large part of the effect of conduct disorder on crime is mediated through its effect on delinquency, adult antisocial behavior, and substance abuse.

Some authors have complained that the DSM-III-R definition of antisocial personality is virtually redundant with criminality. Clearly, this is not the case in these data. In Figure 9.5 we noted the cutoff point for adult antisocial behavior at which the addition of criminal behavior would qualify the person for the diagnosis if he or she had sufficient childhood problems. At this cutoff point, less than 40% of adults also had an arrest. In fact, adult antisocial behaviors were no more related to criminality than was substance abuse, although no one has suggested that substance abuse and criminality are one and the same. Indeed, while our results support a substantial association between psychopathology and crime, criminality is clearly something other than a psychiatric syndrome. Along with age and sex, conduct disorder, antisocial behavior, and substance abuse (with or without the other three disorders) together explained only 19% of the variance in criminal history, while delinquency alone explained 12%.

References

American Psychiatric Association. (1987). *Diagnostic and statistical manual of mental disorders* (3rd ed., rev.). Washington, DC: Author.

Baker, L. A. (1986). Estimating genetic correlations among discontinuous phenotypes: An analysis of criminal convictions and psychiatric-hospital diagnoses in Danish adoptees. *Behavior Genetics, 16*(1), 127-142.

Biederman, J., Faraone, S. V., Keenan, K., & Tsuang, M. T. (1991). Evidence of familial association between attention deficit disorder and major affective disorders. *Archives of General Psychiatry, 48*(7), 633-642.

Cloninger, C. R., & Guze, S. B. (1990). Psychiatric illness and female criminality: The role of sociopathy and hysteria in the antisocial woman. *American Journal of Psychiatry, 127,* 303-311.

Giovannoni, J. M., & Gurel, L. (1967). Socially disruptive behavior of ex-mental patients. *Archives of General Psychiatry, 17,* 146-153.

Good, M. I. (1978). Primary affective disorder, aggression, and criminality: A review and clinical study. *Archives of General Psychiatry, 35,* 954-960.

Gunn, J., Robertson, G., Dell, S., & Way, C. (1978). *Psychiatric aspects of imprisonment.* London: Academic Press.

Guze, S. B. (1976). *Criminality and psychiatric disorders.* New York: Oxford University Press.

Guze, S. B., Wolfgram, E. D., McKinney, J. K., & Cantwell, D. P. (1967). Psychiatric illness in the families of convicted criminals: A study of 519 first-degree relatives. *Diseases of the Nervous System, 28,* 651-659.

Guze, S. B., & Woodruff, R. A., Jr., & Clayton, P. J. (1974). Psychiatric disorders and criminality. *Journal of the American Medical Association, 227*(6), 641-642.

Loeber, R., & LeBlanc, M. (1990). Toward a developmental criminology. In M. Tonry & N Morris (Eds.), *Crime and justice: A review of research* (Vol. 12, pp. 375-473). Chicago: University of Chicago Press.

Martin, R. L., Cloninger, C. R., & Guze, S. B. (1982). Alcoholism and female criminality. *Journal of Clinical Psychiatry, 43,* 400-403.

Petrich, J. (1976). Rate of psychiatric morbidity in a metropolitan county jail population. *American Journal of Psychiatry, 133,* 1439-1444.

Piotrowski, K. W., Losacco, D., & Guze, S. B. (1976). Psychiatric disorders and crime: A study of pretrial psychiatric examinations. *Diseases of the Nervous System, 37*(5), 309-311.

Rabkin, J. G. (1979). Criminal behavior of discharged mental patients: A critical appraisal of the research. *Psychological Bulletin, 86,* 1-27.

Robins, L. (1974). *Deviant children grown up: A sociological and psychiatric study of sociopathic personality.* Huntington, NY: Robert E. Krieger. (Original work published in 1966.)

Robins, L. N., & Price, R. (1991). Adult disorders predicted by childhood conduct problems: Results from the NIMH Epidemiologic Catchment Area Project. *Psychiatry, 54,* 116-132.

Robinson, C. B., Patten, J. W., & Kerr, W. S. (1965). A psychiatric assessment of criminal offenders. *Medicine, Science and the Law,* (July), 140-146.

Widom, C. S. (1978). An empirical classification of female offenders. *Criminal Justice and Behavior, 5,* 35-52.

Woodside, M. (1962). Instability in women prisoners. *Lancet, 2,* 928-930.

10

Bridges From the Animal Laboratory to the Study of Violent or Criminal Individuals

BURR EICHELMAN

The use of animal model systems to explore biology has been a long-standing approach toward understanding problems in human pathology. In the area of violence research and research into "criminality" there exists a potentially useful body of research focusing on aggressive behavior in various animal model systems. Many of these studies illustrate potentially useful concepts or principles that should be applicable to future human research. As the sophistication of human research has progressed, some of the discoveries appear to be analogous to human situations. Presumably, greater awareness of this body of animal research by clinical investigators should enhance the construction of successful biological research in criminal or violent individuals.

Genetics

Behaviors are, in part, the end product of a neurochemistry and neurophysiology that are, themselves, the products of a genetic substrate. Any breeder of dogs is well aware of the inbred behaviors that distinguish the aggressiveness of pit bulls or Doberman pinschers from collies or cocker spaniels (Scott & Fuller, 1965). In both mice (Southwick & Clark, 1968) and rats (Eichelman, 1980), strain differences breed true for high or low levels of both affective and predatory aggression. Such behavioral variability is coupled to substantial differences in neurotransmitter (Slater, Blizard, & Pohorecky, 1977) and second messenger systems (Orenberg, Renson, Elliott, Barchas, & Kessler, 1975). Moreover, through repeated selection both high and low aggressive populations can be generated from one gene pool. This has been done with mice (Lagerspetz & Lagerspetz, 1971) as well as with foxes (Popova, Voitenko, Kulikov, & Agustinovich, 1991).

Such clear preclinical genetic research on temperament has been only sparsely applied to the human condition. Initial studies of the XYY chromosome suggested the possibility of increased aggressive behavior in this population (Jacobs et al., 1965) which has not been substantiated (Meyer-Bahlburg, 1981). However, there does appear to be a greater than expected incidence of this disorder in the prison population (Kessler, 1975).

Adoption studies, particularly in Scandinavian countries where a registry is kept, have provided some opportunity to begin to explore genetic loading for criminal or violent behavior. Such studies, (e.g., Hutchings & Mednick, 1975; Mednick, Gabrielli, & Hutchings, 1984) suggest a genetic diathesis for "criminal behavior" that persists despite cross-fostering into noncriminal families. These studies, however, did not demonstrate a heritable predisposition for violent behavior, but rather criminal behavior predominantly characterized by nonviolent crime. Nevertheless, future research targeted on criminal or violent populations, perhaps those meeting psychiatric criteria for personality disorders and tied to biological markers (e.g., a hyporesponsive central serotonin system) might begin to yield a clearer picture of heritable elements in human criminal/violent behavior or temperament. This research should also be further enhanced by a clearer understanding of the molecular genetics and concomitant neurochemistry of animal strains bred selectively for high and low levels of aggressive behavior.

Electrophysiology

Illustrated by rabies (Viets, 1926) and classical cases of brain tumors (Alpers, 1937; Reeves & Plum, 1969), pathology of the brain's limbic system (Eichelman, 1983) has been linked to violent or socially dysfunctional behavior. Mark and Ervin (1970) argued compellingly that much of clinical violence was the result of epilepsy, most undetected. Monroe (1970) argued that a seizure diathesis existed for individuals now diagnosable as having an intermittent explosive disorder (DSM-III-R). Clearly, criminal offenders appear to have a higher incidence of grand mal epilepsy than the general population (Gunn, 1969). Violent prisoners have a higher incidence of abnormal EEGs than the general population (D. Williams, 1970). However, temporal lobe seizures do not appear to be associated with well-directed violent behaviors (Delgado-Escueta et al., 1981). Nevertheless, anticonvulsant drugs like phenytoin (Maletzky & Klotter, 1974; Simoupoulis et al., 1974; Stephens & Shaffer, 1970), mysoline (Monroe,

1975), and carbamazepine (Hakola & Laulamaa, 1982; Luchins, 1983; Neppe, 1982) have been effective in reducing violent behavior in various clinical populations.

Animal research has demonstrated that electrical stimulation of key brain regions such as the hypothalamus (Hess, 1957) or periaqueductal grey (Shaikh, Barrett, & Siegel, 1987) can induce rage and attack behaviors (even without the induction of seizures). Limbic seizures induced by cholinergic stimulation in the cat's amygdala induce a rage-like syndrome (Grossman, 1963). However, neither animal research nor human research has carried out functional studies of the electrical activity and concomitant metabolic activity of limbic brain regions in aggressive human subjects. The kindling animal model developed by Post (1981) may be useful. In this model, rats are injected chronically with lidocaine. This establishes a kindling phenomenon traced (by 2-deoxyglucose studies) to the rat's amygdala and other limbic structures that leads eventually to generalized seizures (Post et al., 1984). Such kindled rats show a marked hyperirritability at the onset of their development of generalized seizures (Post, 1981). Interestingly, such irritability to handling, however, is not reflected in a total increase in aggressive behavior as neither predatory aggression (measured by mouse killing) or intraspecific affective aggression (as measured by shock-induced fighting) is increased in this model (Eichelman, Hegstrand, & Hind, n.d.).

While such rats demonstrate increased limbic cerebral metabolism (Post et al., 1984), studies of aggressive human subjects still remain to be researched using SPECT or PET technology. Application of such technology could theoretically detect limbic "hot spots" that would be indicative of undetected seizure foci that could be responsible for inducing violent behavior, but also amenable to anticonvulsant treatment.

Hormones

Since ancient times, the practical behavioral scientist has learned that the gelding is safer to ride and the ox safer to plow with in the field. Male hormones, specifically testosterone, have been repeatedly linked to increased agonistic behavior in nonhuman species. Interestingly, however, their social value has been to assist in the dispersal of male populations and in the natural selection of strong breeding stock. Little, if any, scientific literature exists to show that testosterone or testosterone "excess" is responsible for socially destructive behavior in nonhuman species. It does suggest that in most species males are more aggressive than females and that testosterone is responsible for this effect (Svare, 1982).

In the human, clearly, male behavior also appears more aggressive, whether linked to the preponderance in males of violent behavior (*Statistical Abstracts*, 1991) or to the socially sanctioned exhibition of violent behavior in the sports arena or on the battlefield. Paradoxically, however, while testosterone levels have been reported to correlate positively with aggressive behavior in certain male populations (Kreuz & Rose, 1972; Olweus, Mattsson, Schalling, & Löw, 1988; Rada, Laws, & Kellner, 1976) such levels account for relatively little of the variance in the amount of aggressive or violent behavior and essentially have minimal clinical utility (Olweus et al., 1988).

Animal research may offer an explanation for this puzzling observation if testosterone is seen as a neural organizer and not just as a behavior-modifying hormone. An experiment by Connor, Levine, Wertheim, and Cummer (1969) illustrates this point. Male rats castrated at birth, when mature, are hypoaggressive in the shock-induced fighting paradigm. Male rats castrated at weaning, 10 days after birth, and after further brain development, are also hypoaggressive. The first group remains hypoaggressive, even if given exogenous testosterone in adulthood. The second group becomes "normally aggressive" when given exogenous testosterone. Thus the presence of testosterone during the preweaning period allowed for a central organization of the brain that provided for the effect—in adulthood—of testosterone. Perhaps in violent male humans, the level of circulating testosterone is much less important than the sensitivity, the "priming," of the brain to this circulating hormone. Thus measuring levels would be futile, whereas experiments to detect sensitivity to hormone (i.e., perhaps to measure the sensitivity of the pituitary to exogenous hormone) might be a more potent research methodology. At least some support for perinatal hormonal organization of the brain is gained from the literature describing the development of infants with the adrenogenital syndrome (Money & Ehrhardt, 1972) and the development of altered behavior patterns in male children treated *in utero* with diethylstilbestrol (Yalom, Green, & Fisk, 1973).

Neurotransmitters

Just as neurophysiological research and brain lesion studies illustrated that there is no single "aggression center" (Eichelman, 1971), neurochemical research has illustrated that no single neurotransmitter is responsible for aggressive behavior. An extensive review of this literature is beyond the scope of this chapter but available elsewhere (Eichelman, 1987, 1990). Briefly, and perhaps somewhat simplistically, neurotransmitters such as acetylcholine, dopamine, and probably norepinephrine appear to play a predominantly facilitating role in affective (Eichelman, 1987) aggressive behavior. For example, central cholinergic enhancement in rats (Rodgers & Brown, 1976) increases pain-induced aggression. This behavior is suppressed with muscarinic blockade (Powell, Mulligan, & Walters, 1973). Relevance of the cholinergic system to human aggressive behavior has yet to be ascertained.

Enhancing central gamma aminobutyric acid (GABA) activity in rodents reduces isolation-induced fighting (Puglisi-Allegra & Mandel, 1980) and pain-induced fighting (Puglisi-Allegra et al., 1981). Central GABA activity is enhanced by benzodiazepines (Costa, Guidott, & Mao, 1976). This class of drugs has generally, across species and animal models, been effective at suppressing affective aggression (Christmas & Maxwell, 1970; Randall et al., 1960; Valzelli, 1973) although exceptions to this observation exist in rodents chronically treated with low doses of benzodiazepines in social situations (Fox & Snyder, 1969; Fox, Tuckosh, & Wilcox, 1970). While abnormalities in the GABA system have not been demonstrated in violent individuals, treatment of patients with benzodiazepines, particularly lorazepam (Salzman et al., 1986) and oxazepam (Lion, 1979) has been reported as successful in open studies (Eichelman, 1986).

In animal models, the central enhancement of dopamine (DA) stimulation is correlated with increased aggressive behavior. L-DOPA treatment induces aggressive behavior in the rat intruder model (Miczek, 1977). The DA agonist apomorphine induces defensive "boxing" behavior in rats (Senault, 1970) and the infusion of DA into rat cerebroventricles increases pain-induced fighting (Geyer & Segal, 1974). Although dopamine antagonists have been a mainstay in the treatment of aggressive behavior in psychiatric patients (Itil & Seaman, 1979; Itil & Wadud, 1975; Leventhal & Brodie, 1981), there has not been a successful linkage of an impaired DA system and aggressive behavior in humans. For example, Brown, Goodwin, Ballenger, Goyer, and Major (1979) found no correlation between the cerebrospinal fluid levels of the DA metabolite homovanillic acid (HVA) and ratings of violent behavior in a military population.

Perhaps the two most useful neurochemical "handles" for manipulating aggressive behavior in animal models with relevance to humans are the neurotransmitters norepinephrine and serotonin. Early in the 1970s these two neurotransmitters were hypothesized as key neurotransmitters in the understanding of aggressive behavior (Eichelman & Thoa, 1972). Subsequently, more supportive evidence has been compiled and new studies in humans suggest that these neurotransmitters may have comparable relevance in humans as well.

Many correlative studies point to a facilitating role for the neurotransmitter NE. Drugs that enhance central noradrenergic activity like tricyclic antidepressants and monoamine oxidase inhibitors (Eichelman & Barchas, 1975) or the alkali metal cation rubidium (Eichelman, Thoa, & Perez-Cruet, 1973; Stolk, Conner, & Barchas, 1970) all increase rodent aggressive behavior.

Rats experimentally made supersensitive to norepinephrine (NE) through treatment with the neurotoxin 6-hydroxydopa (Thoa, Eichelman, Richardson, & Jacobowitz, 1972) or with chronic propranolol treatment and sudden withdrawal (Hegstrand & Eichelman, 1983) are more aggressive than controls. REM sleep-deprived rats show increased brainstem tyrosine hydroxylase activity (suggesting increased NE synthesis) and a down-regulation of cortical beta adrenergic receptor density (Eichelman & Hegstrand, 1982) correlated with increased pain-induced fighting. Conversely, rodents treated with lithium—which decreases the functional availability of NE (Schildkraut et al., 1967)—manifest a decrease in aggressive behavior (Eichelman, Thoa, & Perez-Cruet, 1973; Sheard, 1970).

Neurochemically, there is a positive correlation in cats between the frequency of sham rage attacks and the disappearance of brainstem NE (Reis & Fuxe, 1969). A similar correlation between NE metabolism and shock-induced fighting has been reported in the rat (Stolk et al., 1974).

Examination of NE's role in human aggressive behavior has been, in part, consistent with animal studies. In at least one study of human spinal fluid, a positive correlation was found between the concentration of the NE metabolite 3-methoxy-4-hydroxyphenylglycol (MHPG) and a lifetime aggression score (Brown et al., 1979). Provocative testing of central noradrenergic responsiveness with the release of growth hormone to the infusion of the alpha$_2$-adrenergic agonist clonidine in personality-disordered patients has suggested a positive correlation between receptor responsiveness (measured by growth hormone release) and measures of irritability and impulsiveness (Coccaro et al., 1991). Clinically, in open studies, beta adrenergic antagonists such as propranolol have been reported effective in treating the violent behavior of schizophrenics (Sorgi, Ratey, & Polakoff, 1986), organically impaired adults (Yudofsky, Williams, & Gorman, 1981), and children (D. T. Williams et al., 1982).

In contrast to the facilitating effect of NE, serotonin appears to function in an inhibitory role regarding aggressive behavior in both animal studies and in the now developing clinical literature. Affective aggression is enhanced through the decrease of central serotonin levels and, presumably, activity. This can be accomplished by blocking the synthesis of 5HT through the use of tryptophan hydroxylase inhibition with a drug such as para-chlorophenylalanine (Sheard & Davis, 1976), or by lesioning the serotonin-containing raphe nuclei (Jacobs & Cohen, 1976), or by treating rats centrally with the 5HT neurotoxin 5,7 dihydroxytryptamine (Kantak,

Eichelman, & Hegstrand, 1981) or even by withholding dietary trypto-phan, the amino acid precursor of 5HT (Kantak, Hegstrand, Whitman, & Eichelman, 1980). Conversely, enhancement of brain 5HT following brain injury by lesions or neurotoxin treatment (which ordinarily would lead to increased aggressive behavior) attenuates the anticipated aggression pre-cipitated by these procedures (Kantak, Hegstrand, & Eichelman, 1981).

Human studies have proved to show comparable results. Cerebrospinal fluid levels of the 5HT metabolite 5-hydroxyindoleacetic acid (5-HIAA) are inversely correlated with lifetime ratings of violent behavior in mili-tary personnel (Brown et al., 1979) and lower than control values in a population of impulsively violent prisoners (Linnoila et al., 1983). This observation has also been identified in aggressive children and adolescents (Kreusi et al., 1990). Using central probes such as fenfluramine to release prolactin through a serotonergic mechanism, Coccaro et al. (1989) have also shown an inverse correlation between serotonergic responsiveness and measures of impulsiveness and aggressiveness. Such findings have suggested that serotonin-enhancing drugs might attenuate human aggres-sive behavior. This might be the mechanism through which lithium re-duces aggressive behavior in adults (Sheard, Marini Bridges, & Wagner, 1976) and children (Campbell et al., 1984). Other putative serotonin-enhancing treatments such as tryptophan-loading (Morand, Young, & Ervin, 1983), trazodone treatment (O'Neil et al., 1986; Simpson & Foster, 1986), or buspirone treatment (Ratey, Sovner, Parks, & Rogentine, 1991) have all been reported in open studies to attenuate human aggressive behavior. On the basis of their effect in animal studies, a new class of drugs (serotonin 5HT1 agonists) labeled "serenics" is currently under clinical study and offers the potential of a fairly selective effect on agonistic behavior without suppressing more prosocial behaviors (Bradford et al., 1984; Olivier, vanDalen, & Hartog, 1986).

Pathological Models of Aggressive Behavior

Animal research has illustrated that "normal" laboratory animals may not be the best research models for studying aggressive behavior. For example, dietary tryptophan enhancement has no effect on the level of pain-induced aggressive behavior of normal laboratory rats (Kantak, Hegstrand, & Eichelman, 1981). Yet it is markedly effective in blocking the increased aggressive behavior induced in rats that are made "patholog-ically aggressive" through the use of neurotoxins or with brain lesions (Kantak, Hegstrand, & Eichelman, 1981). The implication for human research seems clear. Those individuals manifesting "pathological" aggressive behavior may provide the best clinical starting point for the understanding of deviant human violent behavior. Indeed, careful neurological examination of murderers awaiting execution in the United States demonstrated a very high incidence of soft neurological signs suggestive of central neuropathology (Lewis et al., 1988).

Animal studies also point toward mechanisms by which central nervous system pathology can develop. In the rodent literature, neurotoxins that injure the dopaminergic (Eichelman, Thoa, & Ng, 1972) and noradrenergic systems (Thoa et al., 1972) (e.g., 6-hydroxydopamine and 6-hydroxydopa) as well as the serotonergic system (Kantak, Eichelman, & Hegstrand, 1981) (e.g., 5,7 dihydroxytryptamine) all markedly enhance affective aggression. The role of environmental toxins, lead, and maternal drug exposure in introducing potential neurotoxins to the human fetus might well benefit from greater study based on the animal literature.

Stress can also increase aggressive behavior, presumably through the alteration of central neurochemical metabolism. For example, rats immobilized 2 hours daily for 1 month show a dramatic increase in pain-induced aggressive behavior that is correlated with peripheral sympathetic arousal and a central enhancement in tyrosine hydroxylase (TH) activity (TH is the rate-limiting enzyme for the synthesis of central NE) (Lamprecht et al., 1972). What is more remarkable is that both the increased aggressive behavior and the central enzymatic abnormality persist at least 1 month after the stressor is removed and peripheral sympathetic activity has returned to normal. Such an experiment—as a model—raises the possibility that humans stressed during critical periods of development (e.g., children physically abused) might develop persisting abnormal brain metabolism that could then in adulthood increase their propensity for aggressive, violent, or socially deviant behaviors.

Social Interactions

Finally, animal models illustrate the obvious: Aggressive or violent behavior takes place in a social milieu and may take different forms or have different chemical or social consequences depending upon the social context. In studying pathological or criminally violent behavior in humans, the implication is that such behavior is maladaptive. Certainly, animal models suggest that much agonistic behavior, quite the contrary, is adaptive. Attack behavior may even serve as a "coping strategy" to "inescapable" stress and could attenuate the deleterious physiological effects of unavoidable stressors. One illustration of this is seen when rats are subjected to inescapable footshock. When alone these rats show a significant increase in tail blood pressure. However, if paired with another rat, the pair frequently fight in response to the footshock but also manifest a *decrease* in tail blood pressure after the block of footshocks (Williams & Eichelman, 1971) and a lesser increase in plasma ACTH than when footshocked alone (Conner, Vernikos-Danellis, & Levine, 1971). Even rats trained to escape the footshock through manipulanda may "choose" to fight rather than escape (Ulrich, 1967), suggesting a powerful reinforcing component of the agonistic behavior. Such positive elements to human aggressive behavior must be considered and assessed.

Animal studies also illustrate that the biological effects of aggressive behavior differ between the dominant and submissive animal in a confrontation. Adrenal enzyme induction (phenylethanolamine-N-methyltransferase), indicative of significant stress, only occurs in the "loser" or subsequently submissive mouse following bouts of fighting between socially isolated mice (Maengwyn-Davies et al., 1973). The dominant, alpha male macaque in a free-roving monkey colony has an elevated blood serotonin level (Raleigh, Brammer, McGuire, & Yuwiler, 1984). This elevation disappears if the alpha male is removed from the colony and isolated. Moreover, as the beta male of the colony establishes dominance, his blood serotonin level rises. Social hierarchy affects biogenic amine levels. Social hierarchy can also determine drug effects. In one study of the effect of alcohol on mice, dominant mice treated with a given concentration of alcohol became sedated. Conversely, mice lower in the social hierarchy, treated with the same dose of alcohol, became more aggressive (Krsiak, 1976). Thus subsequent study of dyssocial human aggressive behaviors must also take into account the social (and perhaps physiological) utility of the behaviors, the role of dominance or submission in the agonistic encounters, and the level within the social hierarchy of the subjects under study. Animal experiments point to all of these elements as being relevant.

Conclusion

In conclusion, the wealth of experiments and findings from animal laboratories have provided many constructs that can be applied to the study of human violent or socially deviant (criminal) behavior. Most of these constructs remain to be studied in humans as research sophistication and effort improves. Some constructs, particularly examining the role of 5HT and NE in human aggressive behavior, appear to have borne fruit both in offering increased understanding of the neurochemistry of such behaviors and also in raising the possibility of biological therapeutic interventions.

References

Alpers, P. J. (1937). Relation of the hypothalamus to disorders of personality. *Archives of Neurology, 38*, 291-303.

American Psychiatric Association. (1987). *Diagnostic and statistical manual of mental disorders* (3rd ed., rev.). Washington, DC: Author.

Bradford, L. D., Olivier, B,. van Dalen, D., & Schipper, J. (1984). "Serenics": The pharmacology of fluprazine and DU 2812. In K. A. Miczek, M. R. Kruk, & B. Olivier (Eds.), *Ethopharmacological aggression research* (pp. 191-207). New York: Alan R. Liss.

Brown, G. L., Goodwin, F. K., Ballenger, J. C., Goyer, P. F., & Major, L. F. (1979). Aggression in humans correlates with cerebrospinal fluid amine metabolites. *Psychiatry Research, 1*, 131-139.

Campbell, M., Small, A. M., Green, W. H., Jennings, S. J., Perry, R., Bennett, W. G., & Anderson, L. (1984). Behavioral efficacy of haloperidol and lithium carbonate: A comparison in hospitalized aggressive children with conduct disorder. *Archives of General Psychiatry, 41*, 650-656.

Christmas, A. J., & Maxwell, D. R. (1970). A comparison of the effects of some benzodiazepines and other drugs on aggressive and exploratory behaviour in mice and rats. *Neuropharmacology, 9*, 17-29.

Coccaro, E. F., Lawrence, T., Trestman, R., Gabriel, S., Klar, H. M., & Siever, L. J. (1991). Growth hormone responses to intravenous clonidine challenge correlate with behavioral irritability in psychiatric patients and healthy volunteers. *Psychiatry Research, 39*, 129-139.

Coccaro, E. F., Siever, L. J., Klar, H. M., Maurer, G., Cochrane, K., Cooper, T. B., Mohs, R. C., & Davis, K. L. (1989). Serotonergic studies in patients with affective and personality disorders: Correlates with suicidal and impulsive aggressive behavior. *Archives of General Psychiatry, 46*, 587-599.

Conner, R. L., Levine, S., Wertheim, G. Z., & Cummer, J. F. (1969). Hormonal determinants of aggressive behavior. *Annals of the New York Academy of Science, 159*, 760-776.

Conner, R. L., Vernikos-Danellis, J., & Levine, S. (1971). Stress, fighting and neuroendocrine function. *Nature, 234*, 565-566.

Costa, E., Guidotti, A., & Mao, C. C. (1976). A GABA hypothesis for action of benzodiazepines. In E. Roberts, T. N. Chase, & D. B. Tower (Eds.), *GABA in nervous system function* (pp. 413-426). New York: Raven Press.

Delgado-Escueta, A., Mattson, R. H., King, L., Goldensohn, E. S., Speigel, H., Madsen, J., Crandal, P., Dreifuss, F., & Porter, R. J. (1981). The nature of aggression during epileptic seizures. *New England Journal of Medicine, 305*, 711-716.

Eichelman, B. (1971). Effect of subcortical lesions on shock-induced aggression in the rat. *Journal of Comparative and Physiological Psychology, 74*, 331-339.

Eichelman, B. (1980). Variability in rat irritable and predatory aggression. *Behavioral Neural Biology, 29*, 498-505.

Eichelman, B. (1983). The limbic system and aggression in humans. *Neuroscience Behavioral Reviews, 7*, 391-394.

Eichelman, B. (1986). The biology and somatic experimental treatment of aggressive disorders. In H. K. H. Brodie & P. A. Berger (Eds.), *The American handbook of psychiatry* (Vol. 8, pp. 651-678). New York: Basic Books.

Eichelman, B. (1987). Neurochemical and psychopharmacologic aspects of aggressive behavior. In H. Meltzer (Ed.), *Psychopharmacology: The third generation of progress* (pp. 697-704). New York: Raven Press.

Eichelman, B. (1990). Neurochemical and psychopharmacologic aspects of aggressive behavior. *Annual Review of Medicine, 41*, 149-158.

Eichelman, B., & Barchas, J. (1975). Facilitated shock-induced aggression following antide-
    pressive medication in rats. *Pharmacology Biochemistry and Behavior, 3*, 601-604.
Eichelman, B., & Hegstrand, L. (1982). *Stress-induced alterations in aggression and brain
    biochemistry*. Paper presented at the 13th Collegium International Neuropsycho-
    pharmacologium, Jerusalem, Israel.
Eichelman, B., Hegstrand, L., & Hind, J. [Unpublished observations.]
Eichelman, B., & Thoa, N. B. (1972). The aggressive monoamines. *Biological Psychiatry,
    6*, 143-164.
Eichelman, B., Thoa, N. B., & Ng, K. Y. (1972). Facilitated aggression in the rat following
    6-hydroxydopamine administration. *Physiology and Behavior, 8*, 1-3.
Eichelman, B., Thoa, N. B., & Perez-Cruet, J. (1973). Alkali metal cations: Effects on
    aggression and adrenal enzymes. *Pharmacology Biochemistry and Behavior, 1*, 121-123.
Fox, K. A., & Snyder, R. L. (1969). Effect of sustained low doses of diazepam on aggression
    and mortality in grouped male mice. *Journal of Comparative and Physiological Psychol-
    ogy, 69*, 663-666.
Fox, K. A., Tuckosh, J. R., & Wilcox, A. (1970). Increased aggression among grouped male
    mice fed chlordiazepoxide. *European Journal of Pharmacology, 5*, 119-121.
Geyer, M. A., & Segal, D. S. (1974). Shock-induced aggression: Opposite effects of in-
    traventricularly infused dopamine and norepinephrine. *Behavioral Biology, 10*, 99-104.
Grossman, S. P. (1963). Chemically induced epileptiform seizures in the cat. *Science, 142*,
    409-411.
Gunn, J. C. (1969). The prevalence of epilepsy among prisoners. *Proceedings of the Royal
    Society of Medicine, 62*, 60-63.
Hakola, H. P., & Laulamaa, V. A. (1982). Carbamazepine in treatment of violent schizo-
    phrenics. *Lancet, 1*, 1358.
Hegstrand, L., & Eichelman, B. (1983). Increased shock-induced fighting with super-sensitive
    ß-adrenergic receptors. *Pharmacology Biochemistry and Behavior, 19*, 313-320.
Hess, W. R. (1957). *The functional organization of the diencephalon*. New York: Grune & Stratton.
Hutchings, B., & Mednick, S. A. (1975). Registered criminality in the adoptive and biological
    parents of registered male criminal adoptees. In R. R. Fieve, D. Rosenthal, & H. Brill
    (Eds.), *Genetic research in psychiatry* (pp. 105-116). Baltimore, MD: Johns Hopkins
    University Press.
Itil, T. M., & Seaman, P. (1979). Drug treatment of human aggression. *Progress in Neuro-
    psychopharmacology, 2*, 659-669.
Itil, T. M., & Wadud, A. (1975). Treatment of human aggression with major tranquilizers,
    antidepressants and newer psychotropic drugs. *The Journal of Nervous and Mental
    Disease, 160*, 83-99.
Jacobs, B. L., & Cohen, A. (1976). Differential health effects of lesions of the median or
    dorsal raphe nuclei in rats: Open field and pain-elicited aggression. *Journal of Compara-
    tive and Physiological Psychology, 90*, 102-108.
Jacobs, P. A., Brunton, M., Melville, M. M., Brittain, R. P., & McClemont, W. F. (1965).
    Aggressive behaviour, mental sub-normality, and the XYY male. *Nature, 208*, 1351-1352.
Kantak, K. M., Eichelman, B., & Hegstrand, L. (1981). Facilitation of shock-induced fighting
    following intraventricular 5, 7-dihydroxytryptamine and 6-hydroxydopa. *Psychopharma-
    cology, 74*, 157-160.
Kantak, K. M., Hegstrand, L., Whitman, J., & Eichelman, B. (1980). Effects of dietary
    supplements and a tryptophan-free diet on aggressive behavior in rats. *Pharmacology
    Biochemistry and Behavior, 15*, 343-350.
Kessler, S. (1975). Extra chromosomes and criminality. In R. R. Fieve, D. Rosenthal, & H.
    Brill (Eds.), *Genetic research in psychiatry* (pp. 66-73). Baltimore, MD: Johns Hopkins
    University Press.

Kreusi, M. J., Rapoport, J. L., Hamburger, S., et al. (1990). Cerebrospinal fluid monoamine metabolites, aggression, and impulsivity in disruptive behavior disorders of children and adolescents. *Archives of General Psychiatry, 47,* 419-426.

Kreuz, L. E., & Rose, R. M. (1972). Assessment of aggressive behavior and plasma testosterone in a young criminal population. *Psychosomatic Medicine, 34,* 321-332.

Krsiak, M. (1976). Effect of ethanol on aggression and timidity in mice. *Psychopharmacology, 51,* 75-80.

Lagerspetz, K. M. J., & Lagerspetz, K. Y. H. (1971). Changes in the aggressiveness of mice resulting from selective breeding, learning, and social isolation. *Scandinavian Journal of Psychology, 12,* 241-248.

Lamprecht, F., Eichelman, B., Thoa, N. B., Williams, R. B., & Kopin, I. J. (1972). Rat fighting behavior: Serum dopamine-beta-hydroxylase and hypothalamic tyrosine hydroxylase. *Science, 177,* 1214-1215.

Leventhal, B. L., & Brodie, H. K. H. (1981). The pharmacology of violence. In D. A. Hamburg & M. B. Trudeau (Eds.), *Biobehavioral aspects of aggression* (pp. 85-106). New York: Alan R. Liss.

Lewis, D. O., Pincus, J. H., Bard, B., Richardson, E., Prichep, L. S., Feldman, M., & Yaeger, C. (1988). Neuropsychiatric, pschoeducational and family characteristics of 14 juveniles condemned to death in the United States. *VAM. Journal of Psychiatry, 145,* 584-589.

Linnoila, M., Virkkunen, M., Scheinin, M., Nuutila, A., Rimon, R., & Goodwin, F. (1983). Low cerebrospinal fluid 5-hydroxy-indoleacetic acid concentration differentiates impulsive from non-impulsive violent behavior. *Life Sciences, 33,* 2609-2614.

Lion, J. (1979). Benzodiazepines in the treatment of aggressive patients. *Journal of Clinical Psychiatry, 40,* 70-71.

Luchins, D. J. (1983). Carbamazepine for the violent psychiatric patient. *Lancet, 2,* 766.

Maengwyn-Davies, G. D., Johnson, D. G., Thoa, N. B., Weise, V. K., & Kopin, I. J. (1973). Influence of isolation and of fighting on adrenal tyrosine hydroxylase and phenylethanolamine-n-methyltransferase activities in three strains of mice. *Psychopharmacologia, 28,* 339-350.

Maletzky, B. M., & Klotter, J. (1974). Episodic dyscontrol: A controlled replication. *Diseases of the Nervous System, 35,* 175-179.

Mark, V. H., & Ervin, F. R. (1970). *Violence and the brain.* New York: Harper & Row.

Mednick, S. A., Gabrielli, W. H., & Hutchings, B. (1984). Genetic influences in criminal convictions: Evidence from an adoption cohort. *Science, 224,* 891-894.

Meyer-Bahlburg, W. F. L. (1981). Sex chromosomes and aggression in humans. In P. F. Brain & D. Benton (Eds.), *The biology of aggression* (pp. 109-123). Alphen aan den Rijn, The Netherlands: Sijthoff & Noordhoff.

Miczek, K. A. (1977). Effects of L-DOPA, d-amphetamine and cocaine on intruder-evoked aggression in rats and mice. *Progress in Neuropsychopharmacology, 1,* 271-277.

Money, J., & Ehrhardt, A. A. (1972). Gender dimorphic behavior and fetal sex hormones. In E. B. Astwood (Ed.), *Recent progress in hormone research* (Vol. 28, pp. 735-754). New York: Academic Press.

Monroe, R. (1970). *Episodic behavioral disorders.* Cambridge, MA: Harvard University Press.

Monroe, R. (1975). Anticonvulsants in the treatment of aggression. *Nervous and Mental Diseases, 160,* 119-126.

Morand, C., Young, S. N., & Ervin, F. (1983). Clinical response of aggressive schizophrenics to oral tryptophan. *Biological Psychiatry, 18,* 575-578.

Neppe, V. M. (1982). Carbamazepine in the psychiatric patient. *Lancet, 2,* 334.

Olivier, B., vanDalen, D., & Hartog, J. (1986). A new class of psychotropic drugs: Serenics. *Drugs of the Future, 11,* 473-494.

Olweus, D., Mattsson, Å., Schalling, D., & Löw, H. (1988). Circulating testosterone levels and aggression in adolescent males: A causal analysis. *Psychosomatic Medicine, 50,* 261-272.

O'Neil, M., Page, N., Adkins, W. N., & Eichelman, B. (1986). Tryptophan-trazodone treatment of aggressive behavior. *Lancet, 2,* 859-860.

Orenberg, E. K., Renson, J., Elliott, G. R., Barchas, J. D., & Kessler, S. (1975). Genetic determination of aggressive behavior and brain cyclic AMP. *Psychopharmacology Communications, 1,* 99-107.

Popova, N. K., Voltenko, N.N., Kulikov, A. V., & Avgustinovich, D. F. (1991). Evidence for the involvement of central serotonin in mechanism of domestication of silver foxes. *Pharmacology Biochemistry and Behavior, 40,* 751-756.

Post, R. M. (1981). Lidocaine-kindled limbic seizures: Behavioral implications. In J. A. Wada (Ed.), *Kindling 2* (pp. 149-160). New York: Raven Press.

Post, R. M., Kennedy, C., Shinohara, M., Squillace, K., Miyaoka, M., Suda, S., Ingvar, D. H., & Sokoloff, L. (1984). Metabolic and behavioral consequences of lidocaine-kindled seizures. *Brain Research, 324,* 294-303.

Powell, D. A., Milligan, W. L., & Walters, K. (1973). The effects of muscarinic cholinergic blockage upon shock-elicited aggression. *Pharmacology Biochemistry and Behavior, 1,* 389-394.

Puglisi-Allegra, S., & Mandel, P. (1980). Effects of sodium dipropylacetate, muscimol hydrobromide and (R. S.) nipecotic acid amide on isolation-induced aggressive behavior in mice. *Psychopharmacology, 70,* 287-290.

Puglisi-Allegra, S., Simler, S., Kempf, E., & Mandel, P. (1981). Involvement of the GABAergic system on shock-induced aggressive behavior in two strains of mice. *Pharmacology Biochemistry and Behavior, 14*(Suppl. 1), 13-18.

Rada, R. T., Laws, D. R., & Kellner, R. (1976). Plasma testosterone levels in the rapist. *Psychosomatic Medicine, 38,* 257-268.

Raleigh, M. J., Brammer, G. L., McGuire, M. T., & Yuwiler, A. (1984). Social and environmental influences on blood serotonin concentrations in monkeys. *Archives of General Psychiatry, 41,* 405-410.

Randall, L. O., Schallek, W., Heise, G. A., Keith, E. F., & Bagdon, R. E. (1960). The psychosedative properties of methaminodiazepoxide. *Journal of Pharmacology and Experimental Therapeutics, 129,* 163-171.

Ratey, J., Sovner, R., Parks, A., & Rogentine, K. (1991). Buspirone treatment of aggression and anxiety in mentally retarded patients. A multiple-baseline, placebo lead-in study. *Journal of Clinical Psychiatry, 52,* 159-162.

Reeves, A. G., & Plum, F. (1969). Hyperphagia, rage and dementia accompanying a ventromedial hypothalamic neoplasm. *Archives of Neurology, 20,* 616-624.

Reis, D. J., & Fuxe, K. (1969). Brain norepinephrine: Evidence that neuronal release is essential for sham rage behavior following brainstem transection in cat. *Proceedings of the National Academy of Science USA, 64,* 108-112.

Rodgers, R. J., & Brown, K. (1976). Amygdaloid function in the central cholinergic mediation of shock-induced aggression in the rat. *Aggressive Behavior, 2,* 131-152.

Salzman, C., Green, A. L., Rodriguez-Villa, F., & Jaskiw, G. (1986). Benzodiazepines combined with neuroleptics for management of severe disruptive behavior. *Psychosomatics, 27*(Suppl.), 17-21.

Schildkraut, J. J., Schanberg, S. M., Breese, G. R., & Kopin, I. J. (1967). Norephinephrine metabolism and drugs used in the affective disorders: A possible mechanism of action. *American Journal of Psychiatry, 124,* 600-608.

Scott, J. P., & Fuller, J. (1965). *Genetics and the social behavior of the dog.* Chicago: University of Chicago Press.

Senault, B. (1970). Comportement d'aggressivite intraspecific induit par l'apomorphine chez le rat. *Psychopharmacologia, 18,* 271-287.

Shaikh, M. B., Barrett, J. A., & Siegel, A. (1987). The pathways mediating affective defense and quiet biting attack behavior from the midbrain central gray of the cat: An autoradiographic study. *Brain Research, 437,* 9-25.

Sheard, M. H. (1970). Effect of lithium on footshock aggression in rats. *Nature, 228,* 284-285.

Sheard, M. H., & Davis, M. (1976). Shock-elicited fighting in rats: Importance of intershock interval upon the effect of p-chlorophenylalanine (PCPA). *Brain Research, 111,* 433-437.

Sheard, M. H., Marini, J. L., Bridges, C. I., & Wagner, E. (1976). The effect of lithium on impulsive aggressive behavior in man. *American Journal of Psychiatry, 133,* 1409-1413.

Simoupoulis, A. M., Pinto, A., Uhlenhuth, E. H., McGee, J. J., & De Rosa, E. R. (1974). Diphenylhydantoin effectiveness in treatment of chronic schizophrenics. *Archives of General Psychiatry, 30,* 106-111.

Simpson, D. M., & Foster, D. (1986). Improvement in organically disturbed behavior with trazodone treatment. *Journal of Clinical Psychiatry, 47,* 191-193.

Slater, J., Blizard, D. A., & Pohorecky, L. A. (1977). Central and peripheral norepinephrine metabolism in rat strains selectively bred for differences in response to stress. *Pharmacology Biochemistry and Behavior, 6,* 511-520.

Sorgi, P. J., Ratey, J. J., & Polakoff, S. (1986). Beta-adrenergic blockers for the control of aggressive behaviors in patients with chronic schizophrenia. *American Journal of Psychiatry, 143,* 775-776.

Southwick, C. H., & Clark, L. H. (1968). Interstrain differences in aggressive behavior and exploratory activity of inbred mice. *Communications in Behavioral Biology, 1,* 49-59.

Statistical abstracts of the United States. (1991). (111 ed., p. 183). Washington, DC: National Data Book.

Stephens, J. H., & Shaffer, J. W. (1970). Controlled study of the effects of diphenylhydantoin anxiety, irritability and anger in neurotic outpatients. *Pharmacologia, 17,* 169-181.

Stolk, J. M., Conner, R. L., & Barchas, J. (1970). Rubidium-induced increase in shock-elicited aggression in rats. *Psychopharmacologia, 22,* 250-260.

Stolk, J. M., Conner, R. L., Levine, S., et al. (1974). Brain norepinephrine metabolism and shock-induced fighting behavior in rats: Differential effects of shock and fighting on the neurochemical response to a common footshock stimulus. *Journal of Pharmacology and Experimental Therapeutics, 190,* 193-209.

Svare, B. (Ed.). (1982). *Hormones and aggressive behavior.* New York: Plenum.

Thoa, N. B., Eichelman, B., Richardson, J. S., & Jacobowitz, D. (1972). 6-hydroxydopa depletion of brain norepinephrine and the facilitation of aggressive behavior. *Science, 178,* 75-77.

Ulrich, R. (1967). Interaction between reflexive fighting and cooperative escape. *Journal of the Experimental Analysis of Behavior, 10,* 311-317.

Valzelli, L. (1973). Activity of benzodiazepines on aggressive behavior in rats and mice. In S. Garattini, E. Mussini, & L. O. Randall (Eds.), *The benzodiazepines* (pp. 405-417). New York: Raven Press.

Viets, H. R. A. (1926). A case of hydrophobia with Negri bodies in the brain. *Archives of Neurological Psychiatry, 15,* 737-737.

Williams, D. (1970). Neural factors related to habitual aggression. *Brain, 92,* 503-520.

Williams, D. T., Mehl, R., Yudofsky, et al. (1982). The effect of propranolol on uncontrolled rage outbursts in children and adolescents with organic brain dysfunction. *Journal of the American Academy of Child Psychiatry, 143,* 775-776.

Williams, R. B., & Eichelman, B. (1971). Social setting: Influence on the physiological response to electric shock in the rat. *Science, 174,* 613-614.

Yalom, I., Green, R., & Fisk, N. (1973). Prenatal exposure to female hormones. *Archives of General Psychiatry, 28,* 554-561.

Yudofsky, S., Williams, D., & Gorman, J. (1981). Propranolol in the treatment of rage and violent behavior in patients with chronic brain syndromes. *American Journal of Psychiatry, 138,* 218-220.

11

Neurochemical Correlates of Personality, Impulsivity, and Disinhibitory Suicidality

DAISY SCHALLING

This chapter reviews some clusters of temperamental and biological variables that are related to different types of disinhibitory psychopathology (Gorenstein & Newman, 1980). The biological measures are monoamine oxidase activity in platelets, and measures related to serotonergic neurotransmission and to certain neuroendocrine functions, such as the release of cortisol. They are all related to suicidal and homicidal behavior. *Impulsivity* is a key concept. A large clinical literature deals with impulse control deficiency. However, an increasing interest is devoted to assessment of different types of trait impulsivity in nonclinical samples. Impulsivity has been studied in relation to anxiety and hostility. It may be that anxiolytic drugs have their effects partly by increasing impulsivity. This chapter starts with a brief overview of some of the psychobiological approaches to personality structure.

Psychobiological Approaches to Personality Structure

The development of methods for measuring aspects of neurobiological functions has brought with it new ideas about the biological bases of mental disorders. Early broad theories of connections between the mental disorders and biological dysfunction have been substituted with more specific

AUTHOR'S NOTE: Financial support has been given by the Swedish Medical Research Council and the Bank of Sweden Tercentary Foundation. Thanks are due to Marie Åsberg and Lars Oreland for ideas and support, and to Gunnar Edman, Britt af Klinteberg, and J. Petter Gustavsson who have contributed to the research reviewed. Special thanks are due to J. Petter Gustavsson for valuable help in the preparation of the chapter.

theories of vulnerability of different subsystems. Neurochemical deviations in major mental disorders have been shown to be more associated with basic underlying personality dimensions and psychobiological vulnerability than with nosological categories (Apter et al., 1990; Claridge, 1985). Neurochemistry has made important contributions to psychopathology, and research on neurotransmitters and hormones has given inspiration for development of new personality models. One of the goals of this personality research is to identify underlying dispositional attributes that give structure to behavior. Self-report inventories have been the major instruments in connecting dimensional models for personality and their biological bases (H. Eysenck, 1981; Zuckerman, 1983, 1989).

Biologically oriented personality theories tend to use a dimensional framework to classify and explain human behavior, rather than categorical models. A classical example is the three-dimensional personality theory by H. Eysenck, which is the most widely used model, including extraversion, neuroticism, and psychoticism. Extraversion is based on an arousal theory according to which extraverts are prone to have low cortical arousal, be sociable, and seek varied and intense stimulation in order to attain an optimal level of arousal. Neuroticism concerns differences in emotional stability-lability, high scores reflecting a disposition to negative affectivity. Psychoticism was intended to measure unusual ways of reacting and feeling, assumedly underlying a proneness to psychosis (H. Eysenck & Eysenck, 1976). Later research, however, has shown that this scale is more associated with psychopathy and lack of conformity to social norms (Robinson & Zahn, 1985).

An alternative structural model of personality has been proposed by Gray (Gray, 1981; Gray, Owen, Davis, & Tsaltas, 1983) in which the lines of causal influence were rotated by 45° from H. Eysenck's dimensions. The two new dimensions were Anxiety, running from stable extravert (low anxiety) to neurotic introvert (high anxiety), and Impulsivity, running from stable introvert (low impulsivity) to neurotic extravert (high impulsivity).

An older and less well-known dimensional system is that described by the Swedish psychiatrist Sjöbring (1913, 1973). Sjöbring assumed that certain types of personality predispose to different types of functional mental disorder, each representing a constitutionally low or high degree of development of specific degrees of mental functioning, Validity corresponding to a factor of energy, Solidity to a degree of firmness and consistency of nervous processes, and Stability to a degree of habituation and automatization attainable. Sjöbring described hypothetical personality traits in terms of under- ("sub") and over- ("super") development of Validity, Solidity, and Stability, and profiles of personality based on these.

A more recent psychobiological personality theory is that described by Cloninger, who has tried to bridge the gap between theoretical personality dimensions and categorical clinical psychiatric personality disorders. The personality model proposed by Cloninger (1987) comprises three genetic dimensions: Novelty Seeking, Harm Avoidance, and Reward Dependence. He describes interactions between these dimensions leading to integrated behavioral patterns of response to novel, dangerous, or rewarding situations. According to Cloninger, personality disorders are constituted of various combinations of high and low developments of these traits, similar to the Sjöbring "sub" and "super" concepts. The possible three-dimensional combinations of extreme variants correspond to descriptions of personality disorders, whereas normal personality traits are measured along continuous dimensions. *Novelty Seeking* is an innate tendency toward excitement and pursuit of potential rewards and avoidance of monotony. *Harm Avoidance* is an innate tendency to inhibit behavior and to avoid punishment and frustration. *Reward Dependence* is an innate tendency to respond intensively to signals of reward, for example, social approval. Cloninger (1987) has described an intricate system of interactions among these dimensions and among the underlying monoamine neuromodulating effects.

Another psychobiological approach to personality is that developed by Zuckerman (1979, 1991), who has extrapolated biological research on animals and developed an arousal theory of sensation seeking as a main component in disinhibitory behavior. Zuckerman (1983, 1989, 1991) has constructed scales for a general factor of Sensation Seeking and various subscales, relating these to biological dimensions.

Constructs derived from theories of biologically based temperament dimensions underlying various psychiatric disorders have been the framework for constructing the Karolinska Scales of Personality (KSP). The purpose was to operationalize and measure theoretical constructs defining vulnerability for different forms of psychopathology (see Schalling, 1978; Schalling, Åsberg, Edman, & Oreland, 1987; Schalling, Cronholm, & Åsberg, 1975; Schalling, Edman, & Åsberg, 1983). Some scales have been constructed by Schalling and coworkers in connection with different research projects, whereas others have been adapted and modified from published scales. Descriptions of high scorers in the various KSP scales are given in Table 11.1. These descriptions will allow the reader to make interpretations and comparisons between scales. Some of the scales are influenced by the corresponding traits in the Sjöbring model (Schalling & Åsberg, 1985). *Impulsivity* is related to "subsolidity," *Detachment* to "superstability" (schizoidia), and *Psychasthenia* to "subvalidity." A scale related to the Zuckerman Sensation Seeking scales was also constructed (Monotony Avoidance). Anxiety scales were designed on the basis of a two-factor theory of anxiety (Schalling, 1978; Schalling et al., 1975). One

TABLE 11.1 The Karolinska Scales of Personality (KSP): Classification of Scales and Description of High Scorers

KSP	Description of High Scorers
1. Impulsivity, sensation seeking and social withdrawal scales:	
Impulsiveness	Acting on the spur of the moment, nonplanning, impulsive.
Monotony avoidance	Avoiding routine, need for change and action (Sensation Seeking).
Detachment	Avoiding involvement with others, withdrawn, "schizoid."
2. Psychopathy versus conformity scales:	
Socialization	Positive childhood experiences, good school and family adjustment.
Social desirability	Socially conforming, friendly, helpful (or "faking good").
3. Anxiety-related scales:	
a. Nervous tension and distress:	
Somatic anxiety	Autonomic disturbances, restless, panicky.
Muscular tension	Tense and stiff, not relaxed.
b. Cognitive-social anxiety:	
Psychic anxiety	Worrying, anticipating, lacking self-confidence, sensitive.
Psychasthenia	Easily fatigued, feeling uneasy when urged to speed up and when facing new tasks.
Inhibition of aggression	Nonassertive, sad rather than angry when scolded, cannot speak up.
4. Hostility-related scales:	
Suspicion	Suspicious, distrusting people's motives.
Guilt	Remorseful, ashamed of bad thoughts.
5. Aggressivity-related scales:	
Indirect aggression	Sulking, slamming doors when angry.
Verbal aggression	Getting into arguments, telling people off when annoyed.
Irritability	Irritable, lacking patience.

SOURCE: Schalling, Åsberg, & Oreland, 1987.

factor, Somatic Anxiety, refers to autonomic symptoms, vague distress, panic, and concentration difficulties. Another factor, Psychic Anxiety (or Cognitive-Social Anxiety) is concerned with anticipatory anxiety, worrying, insecurity, and social anxiety. The Hostility- and Aggressivity-related scales consist of short scales, for which items were selected from the corresponding Buss factors (Buss, 1961).

These scales have been used in a series of studies in our group, with the purpose of exploring the relationships between temperamental vulnerability and biological dysfunction. The following discusses some of the findings concerning three psychobiological systems, all of which have been associated with disinhibitory psychopathology and suicidal behavior.

In exploring associations between personality dimensions and biological markers, simple linear correlations are generally used. It is not always realized, however, that a negative correlation between a personality scale (e.g., Extraversion) and a biological measure (e.g., 5-hydroxyindoleacetic acid [5-HIAA]) may mean that extraverts tend to have low 5-HIAA *or* that introverts tend to have high 5-HIAA. These two interpretations have a clearly different emphasis. Other methodological difficulties in this research are that simple correlations are very sensitive to the presence of "misfits" and "outliers," and that the linear correlation may conceal a real nonlinear association between the phenomena. An interesting discussion of such problems in the application of neurochemical variables to personality variables is given in Schooler, Zahn, Murphy, and Buchsbaum (1978). In our psychobiological research, the relationships among phenomena have often been illustrated by a categorization of the distribution of the biological variable into low, intermediate, and high levels, using this transformed variable as the independent variable in a one-way analysis of variance of personality scales (see Schalling, Åsberg, Edman, & Oreland, 1987).

Impulsivity: Models and Measures

Impulsivity is one of the most important traits in psychobiological personality research. It was originally part of the Eysenck extraversion concept. According to Carrigan (1960), there are two identifiable components, sociability and impulsivity. U.S. researchers tend to emphasize the sociability part of the concept, whereas impulsivity is used more in Europe. In order to explore these traits, two subscales were constructed from the Eysenck Extraversion Scale, Sociability and Impulsivity, which were compared to the Sjöbring variables, Stability and Solidity. Consistent relations were found between subsolidity and extraversion-impulsivity and between substability and extraversion-sociability (Schalling & Åsberg, 1985). H. Eysenck and Levey (1972) noted early that any differentiation between extraverts and intraverts on eyeblink conditioning was due entirely to the impulsivity component and not at all to the sociability component.

Impulsivity has been measured by methods such as inventories and also by strategy and style measures such as preference for speed versus accuracy (Schalling, Edman, & Åsberg, 1983). Three broad impulsivity factors were revealed from an analysis of a large number of impulsivity scales: "Spontaneous," "Not Persistent," and "Carefree" (Gerbig, Ahandi, & Patton, 1987). Clinically relevant subtraits of impulsivity of three types have been identified by Barratt (1985): "Motor Impulsivity" (acting without thinking), "Cognitive Impulsivity" (making up one's mind quickly), and "Nonplanning Impulsivity" (being present-oriented as opposed to future-oriented). S. Eysenck and Eysenck (1977, 1978) found that different subscales of Impulsivity are differentially correlated to the Extraversion and Psychoticism factors. Impulsivity in a narrow sense (e.g., Do you often buy things on impulse? Do you generally do and say things without stopping to think?) and Nonplanning (e.g, Do you like planning things carefully, well ahead of time?) tend to load in Psychoticism. Liveliness (e.g., Do you usually make up your mind quickly?) tends to load in Extraversion, and Risk Taking (e.g., Do you often long for excitement?) relates to both Extraversion and Psychoticism.

There is evidence for a strong genetic influence for impulsivity. Eaves, Martin, and Eysenck (1977) studied the heritability of impulsivity factors for males and females separately and found particularly high values for the Nonplanning factor (.88 and .91, respectively). These authors conclude that virtually all the detectable specific environmental variation is due to sampling errors in the scores. A recent study on a large sample of twins, including monozygotic (MZ) and dizygotic (DZ) twins reared apart (a) and a matched sample reared together (t) (Pedersen, Plomin, McClearn, & Friberg, 1988) verified the importance of genetic factors for the KSP Impulsiveness Scale (intraclass correlations MZa = .40, MZt = .45 vs. DZa = .15, DZt = .09).

Impulsivity is a core trait in some types of disinhibitory psychopathology, such as alcoholism, suicidal behavior, hyperactivity, and psychopathy (Gorenstein & Newman, 1980). Childhood hyperactivity is highly related to adult impulsivity. Teacher ratings of motor restlessness and concentration difficulties at age 13 in a group of normal schoolboys, used as indicators of hyperactive behavior, were found to be strongly correlated with KSP Impulsiveness scores 14 years later (af Klinteberg, Schalling, & Magnusson, 1989).

Impulsivity has been shown to have neuropsychological as well as neurobiological correlates (Åsberg, Schalling, Träskman-Bendz, & Wägner, 1987; Schalling & Åberg, 1985; Wallace, Newman & Bachorowski, 1991). One important factor has been assumed to be frontal lobe dysfunction (see Schalling, Edman, & Åsberg, 1983). Students with high scores on the KSP Impulsiveness Scale have shown fast responses and many errors in a reaction time task (Edman, Schalling, & Levander, 1983), which may reflect an impulsive life-style. A large amount of the variance in number of errors (36%) could be predicted from three personality scales: the KSP Impulsiveness and Muscular Tension scales and the EPQ Psychoticism.

In the last few years, impulsivity scales have given interesting results when related to neurochemical measures; for example, significant correlations with platelet serotonin uptake (C. Brown et al., 1989), with the serotonin CSF metabolite (5-HIAA) in suicide attempters (Regnéll et al.,

TABLE 11.2 Percentage of Agreement Responses in Items From the Impulsiveness Scale of the Impulsiveness-Venturesomeness-Empathy (IVE) Inventory in Male Subjects With Low, Intermediate, and High MAO Activity (n = 12, 34, and 12, respectively)

| | | MAO Subgroup | |
Item	Low	Intermediate	High
Do you often get into a jam because you do things without thinking? ($p < .01$)	33	3	8
Do you often do things on the spur of the moment? ($p < .01$)	83	41	8
Do you mostly speak before thinking things out? ($p < .01$)	75	44	8
Are you often surprised at people's reactions to what you say? ($p < .01$)	25	0	50
Would you often like to get high (drinking liquor or smoking marijuana)? ($p < .05$)	16	0	0
Are you an impulsive person? ($p < .05$)	83	47	33
Do you often get involved in things you later wish you could get out of? ($p < .05$)	42	15	0
Do you think an evening out is more successful if it is unplanned or arranged at the last moment? ($p < .05$)	58	47	92

SOURCE: Schalling, Edman, Åsberg, & Oreland, 1988.

1991) and with plasma cortisol levels (King, Jones, Scheuer, Curtis, & Zarcone, 1990). In one of our recent studies, the KSP Impulsiveness Scale from the Eysenck IVE inventory was used in a group of blood donors, in whom platelet monoamine oxidase (MAO) activity had been assessed (Schalling, Edman, Åsberg, & Oreland, 1988). Impulsiveness was negatively correlated with MAO ($r = -.32$). Table 11.2 shows the response patterns on item level for subgroups of MAO subjects. The items that differentiated most consistently between the MAO subgroups belonged to the "narrow impulsivity" group of items, for example, doing things on the spur of the moment, talking and doing things without forethought. Thus rapid decision making as well as lack of inhibitory control was implied.

Personality and Neurochemical Measures

Personality and Platelet Monoamine Oxidase Activity

Monoamine oxidase (MAO) is an enzyme related to the central monoamine transmitter systems. Many studies have established associations between platelet MAO activity and behavior. It is interesting that these associations are similar to those found for the serotonin system. Platelet MAO activity is probably genetically linked to some property of the central serotonin system, being regulated by some common factor (Oreland & Hallman, 1988). The existence of an association is supported by correlations obtained between the concentration of the serotonin metabolite in the cerebrospinal fluid and platelet MAO activity, both in healthy volunteers and chronic pain patients (von Knorring et al., 1986; Oreland et al., 1981).

Vulnerability

Platelet MAO activity was among the first neurochemical personality correlates to be explored in normal populations. Early studies provided support for the hypothesis that low platelet MAO was indicative of a constitutional vulnerability for disinhibitory psychopathology characterized by inability to control impulses and anticipate negative future consequences of behavior (Buchsbaum, Coursey, & Murphy, 1976; Buchsbaum, Haier, & Murphy, 1977). In a group of criminal offenders hospitalized for forensic psychiatric assessment, a remarkably low level of platelet MAO activity was found in a subgroup of patients diagnosed as psychopathic personality (Lidberg, Modin, Oreland, Tuck, & Gillner, 1985). Thus disinhibitory psychopathology has been proven to be linked to low MAO activity in such areas as psychopathy, suicidality, alcoholic addiction, and hyperactivity (for reviews see Oreland & Hallman, 1988; Oreland, von Knorring, & Schalling, 1984).

Personality

Several studies indicate an association between platelet MAO activity and personality variables in healthy volunteers (for reviews see Oreland & Hallman, 1988; Oreland et al., 1984). Sensation Seeking scales have shown negative correlations with MAO in many studies (see Zuckerman, 1991). As noted above, the relationships with personality are sometimes nonlinear, giving near zero correlations but interesting subgroup trends, when analysis of variance has been applied (Schalling et al., 1987; Schalling et al., 1988). This was especially evident when subjects were women (af Klinteberg, Schalling, Edman, Oreland, & Åsberg, 1987). Male subjects in that study showed negative correlations among MAO and Impulsiveness and Monotony Avoidance.

In our subgroup comparisons, the low MAO group tended to have high Impulsiveness, Somatic Anxiety, and Irritability as well as low Socialization, whereas the high MAO group had low Sensation Seeking. Different anxiety scales were differently associated with high and low platelet MAO activity, low MAO being more associated with Somatic Anxiety and high MAO with Muscular Tension (Schalling et al., 1987). In another study (Schalling et al., 1988), the low MAO subgroup had high scores in Impulsiveness and Irritability, whereas the high subgroup had high scores in Detachment (high schizoidia) and low scores in Monotony Avoidance, Muscular Tension, and Suspicion. The personality profile characteristic of the high MAO subgroup is consistent with clinical links between high platelet MAO activity, and anxiety and paranoia. Thus the different extreme groups with low and high MAO scores were characterized by different kinds of personality deviations.

Neuropsychology

Platelet MAO activity has an interesting relationship to impulsivity both as shown in inventory scales and in neuropsychological performance. In a reaction time task with auditory signals for response inhibition, performance was related to platelet MAO activity in two studies from our group (af Klinteberg, Levander, Oreland, Åsberg, & Schalling, 1987; af Klinteberg et al., 1990-1991). There was a strong negative relationship between platelet MAO activity and number of "failed inhibitions" in this motor disinhibition task (which has similarities to passive avoidance tasks). This may be seen as a neuropsychological link between CNS systems and enzymes.

Another example of a possible link is provided by recent studies by Bertilsson et al. (1989) and Llerena et al. (1991), who reported a relationship between debrisoquine hydroxylation capacity and personality. For example, poor metabolizers appeared to be less successfully socialized. The results give evidence for an endogenous neuroactive substrate of this polymorphic enzyme. The authors suggest that the mechanism behind this finding may be a connection between the cytochrome P450II06 and dopamine neurotransmission in the brain.

Personality and Serotonin

Serotonin, Suicide, and Homicide

During studies of the serotonin metabolite 5-HIAA measured in the lumbar cerebrospinal fluid (CSF) in depressed patients, several important observations were made (Åsberg, Thorén, Träskman, Bertilsson, & Ringberger, 1976; Åsberg, Träskman, & Thorén, 1976; Träskman, Åsberg, Bertilsson, & Sjöstrand, 1981). It was found that the distribution of levels of 5-HIAA was bimodal, and that significantly more of the patients in the low CSF 5-HIAA group had made a suicide attempt. CSF 5-HIAA levels tended to be lower among patients who had made a "violent" suicide attempt (hanging, shooting, drowning, deep cuts) (Åsberg, Träskman, & Thorén, 1976). The relationship between violent suicidal behavior and low level of CSF 5-HIAA was later extended to violence against others. Linnoila et al. (1983) studied neurochemical measures in a group of 36 male offenders who had committed or attempted murder. The 27 offenders who had attacked without provocation or had not known the victim were classified as "impulsive." These offenders had lower CSF 5-HIAA levels than the remaining 9 ("nonimpulsive") offenders. Lower 5-HIAA was also found in those who had committed more than one crime and who had made a suicide attempt. In the continued research on homicide and serotonin, negative correlations were found between concentration of 5-HIAA in CSF and number of reported hostile acts and previous suicide attempts. However, there were no significant correlations between levels of 5-HIAA and the Buss aggression scales, with the exception of the Irritability scale (Brown & Goodwin, 1987).

Decreased availability of central serotonin has thus been interpreted to be related both to suicidal auto-aggression and to interpersonal aggression. However, Soubrié (1986) suggested another interpretation of serotonergic decrease, conceptualized as "precipitation into action" or "lack of behavioral constraint," implying facilitation of expression of aggressive impulses rather than increase of aggression. An overall interpretation of these findings may be that serotonin deficiency is involved in the control of behavior in emergency situations, for example, in the presence of appropriate trigger stimuli for defensive aggression, which can release impulsive behavior. Coccaro et al. (1989) suggested that "reduced central 5-HT function may be more specifically related to physically aggressive behaviors of an irritable-impulsive nature than to physically aggressive behaviors in general" (p. 596).

Personality Correlates of Serotonin

In a study from our group (Schalling, Åsberg, Edman, & Levander, 1984), low CSF 5-HIAA was associated with high Impulsivity and Sensation Seeking and low Socialization in groups of patients and with high Psychoticism and Assertiveness in healthy male volunteers. In our most recent study (Schalling et al., 1992) many different aspects of personality were studied in healthy volunteers. CSF 5-HIAA was positively correlated to fear and anxiety scales, and negatively to assertiveness and dominance scales and to Extraversion. A subgroup with high CSF 5-HIAA levels was characterized by low Extraversion and high Detachment, as well as low Dominance and Assertiveness. Two Swedish studies (Lindström, 1985; Sedvall et al., 1980) have reported a higher level of the serotonin CSF metabolite, 5-HIAA, in subjects with a family history of schizophrenia. It is thus noteworthy that a tendency to schizoid personality has been found in our group in normal subjects with higher levels of CSF 5-HIAA.

Limson et al. (1991) conducted a large study on alcoholics, measuring the monoamine metabolites in CSF and administering personality scales (EPQ and IVE, Cloninger TPQ, and MMPI). All correlations between the CSF monoamine metabolites and the personality scales were low and nonsignificant. However, there were negative correlations with interview-derived lifetime aggression scores. This is consistent with earlier findings of connections between history of lifetime aggression and CSF 5-HIAA (G. Brown, Goodwin, Ballenger, Goyer, & Major, 1979; G. Brown et al., 1982). In a study by Roy, Adinoff, and Linnoila (1988) on alcoholics, a scale "Acting out hostility" showed a significant negative correlation (−.53) with CSF 5-HIAA. This is interesting in view of the type of items included; some of them are related to the Psychoticism construct, and others to Irritability.

The relation between serotonin and anxiety is a complicated issue, partly due to the different anxiety measures and concepts used. In our earlier studies there were no significant correlations between CSF 5-HIAA and anxiety scales in patients (Schalling et al., 1984), but in healthy males low 5-HIAA has been associated with low anxiety and high assertiveness. In a Rorschach study from our group (Rydin, Schalling, & Åsberg, 1982), patients with low 5-HIAA were compared with patients with normal or high 5-HIAA, matched for sex, age, and body height. Higher anxiety and hostility ratings and lower anxiety tolerance were observed in the low 5-HIAA group. However, the anxiety ratings were made without regarding effectiveness of defenses, "a constricted neurotic can score equally high as a subject in a state of panic" (p. 238). Thus the type of anxiety was not taken into account (see Schalling, 1986).

Personality and Cortisol

Generally, elevated cortisol levels (together with epinephrine and nor-epinephrine) have been associated with acute stress. However, large individual differences in response amplitude/degree as well as response direction have been reported (Mason, 1968, 1975). A psychopathological characteristic often accompanied by rise in adrenal cortical levels is negative emotion.

An association between increased cortisol and suicidal behavior in depressed patients has been reported (Krieger, 1974; Träskman et al., 1980). However, low cortisol levels have also been associated with psychopathology (Mason, 1968; Mason, Kosten, Southwick, & Giller, 1990). Mattson, Gross, and Hall (1971) made a long-term study of urinary free cortisol levels in hemophilic boys in relation to adjustment to the illness. One subgroup of well-adjusted boys who made efforts to adapt had higher cortisol levels, whereas poor adapters ("rule breakers") were consistent low cortisol excreters. Low urinary cortisol levels were also found in a group of young offenders, living in a reform school, in a stressful environment (Levander, Mattsson, Schalling, & Dalteg, 1986), and in a group of violent habitual offenders (Virkkunen, 1985).

In an exploratory study on biochemical correlates of personality traits (Ballenger et al., 1983), interesting associations were found between low CSF cortisol and nonconformity scales. A relationship between high Impulsivity and low plasma cortisol has also been reported in healthy volunteers (King et al., 1990). In a recent study on healthy male subjects (Schalling et al., 1992) a subgroup with low CSF cortisol levels was characterized by high Anger, Impulsivity, Dominance, and by low Fear. These results indicate that individuals with low cortisol tend to manifest a personality profile similar to that reported in some groups showing nonconformity and disinhibitory psychopathology.

Disinhibitory Suicidality

Some types of suicidal behavior may be classified as belonging to disinhibitory syndromes (Gorenstein & Newman, 1980). In the past decade it has become evident that an important aspect of suicidality is the method used in a suicide attempt. As noted above, this interest in method of attempt has its origin in research by Åsberg and colleagues (Åsberg, Thorén, et al., 1976; Åsberg et al., 1976) and Träskman et al. (1981). A search for possible differences between patients having low versus normal or high 5-HIAA led to the discovery that the low 5-HIAA group had a higher frequency of suicide attempts in their history (40% vs. 15%). Further, the low CSF 5-HIAA patients used violent methods (hanging, drowning, gas, poison, and several deep cuts) whereas patients with higher 5-HIAA had applied the most frequent method, drug overdose. This difference has been replicated in other series of studies of suicide attempts (classified according to degree of violence). In some earlier studies violent suicide attempts have also been associated with low platelet MAO activity. Gottfries, von Knorring, and Oreland (1980) found that six patients who had attempted suicide by violent "active" methods had lower MAO activity than those nine patients who had used "passive" methods or those who had made no previous suicide attempt.

In view of the findings of relationships between CSF 5-HIAA and violent suicidal attempts, it is of interest to examine personality traits and psychophysiological characteristics in patients who have committed violent suicide attempts, as compared to patients who have been admitted after a drug overdose type of attempt and to patients who report suicidal ideation only. A study was carried out in our group (Edman, Åsberg, Levander, & Schalling, 1986) on 35 suicidal patients, comprising psychophysiological measures. The rate of habituation of skin conductance responses to a series of tones was tested. The result was surprising. All violent attempters were fast habituators, as were all 4 patients who, in a 1-year follow-up, were found to have completed a suicide (all by violent methods). The violent suicide attempters thus had a more rapid habituation than the other groups. An association between suicidality and habituation has since been replicated in two independent studies (Keller, Wolfersdorf, Straub, & Hole, 1991; Thorell, 1987). There are many possible interpretations of this finding. One of them implies a more superficial processing of new information by violent attempters. This may also be true for their evaluation of internal impulses—possibly implying less anticipatory anxiety and less planning. Thus the impulsive character of their suicide attempts and the rapid habituation to new information may be intimately connected phenomena.

Personality scales given to these patients are now being analyzed. The most striking differences among the suicidal groups were the higher Psychoticism, Impulsiveness, and Monotony Avoidance scores in the violent attempters. It is noteworthy that temperament measures that are associated with violence toward others (e.g., Psychoticism) are also related to violent suicidal behavior. It is also interesting that in a recent study (Lolas, Gomez, & Suarez, 1991), Psychoticism was the only EPQ scale that showed a strong association with number of previous suicide attempts.

The personality of violent suicide attempters has also been explored in our group using the Rorschach technique. A study was carried out on Rorschach records from 20 patients who had made active, violent suicide attempts, compared with records from 20 patients who had taken drug overdoses and 20 psychiatric control patients who had not made a suicide attempt (Rydin, Åsberg, Edman, & Schalling, 1990). Ego function ratings showed that the violent attempters were more paranoid than both other groups. The most important characteristic was their lack of differentiation between reality and imagination ("reality testing"). Violent attempters tended to produce fabulized combination responses, suggesting cognitive slippage, and distorted human content responses, indicating pathological object relationships. Interestingly, nonviolent attempters did not differ from controls. There was an interesting similarity between the Rorschach performance of the violent suicide attempters in that study and the performance by borderline patients in an earlier study (Singer & Larsson, 1981). A comparison between a group of murderers and a group of suicide attempters did not yield any significant differences in Rorschach suicidal "signs" (Lester & Perdue, 1974). The interpretation was not clear—it was suggested that the method was measuring general aggression rather than suicidality.

Conclusions

In an analysis of the findings on suicidal patients, it was suggested that aggressiveness, or a decreased ability to handle aggressive impulses, may be an intervening variable for the association between violent suicide attempts and a low concentration of 5-HIAA in CSF (Åsberg et al., 1976; Åsberg, Träskman, & Thorén, 1976). Classical psychoanalytic theories have assumed links between anger and suicide (Menninger, 1938). Some studies have found excessive hostility in suicide attempters (Weissman, Fox, & Klerman, 1973).

As noted above, however, a study of violent offenders by Linnoila et al. (1983) indicates that low CSF 5-HIAA may be a marker of impulsivity rather than aggression or violence per se. They subdivided their group of offenders into those who had killed or attempted to kill their victims "impulsively" (without provocation or premeditation) and those who had committed the act after some premeditation. The former group had significantly lower concentrations of the serotonin metabolite. It is noteworthy that they all had a history of suicide attempts and they had all shown behavior disturbances at school (a diagnosis of attention deficit or conduct disorder). This finding seems to confirm the hypothesis advanced by Soubrié (1986) suggesting that deficiency in central serotonin neurons may be more related to precipitation into action or lack of behavioral constraints than to increase of aggression. In the presence of appropriate trigger stimuli for aggression, a low serotonin turnover may contribute to facilitation of expression of aggression. It appears that the degree of impulsivity in the act is crucial both for suicide attempts and for homicidal acts. It is interesting that impulsivity has been one of the most consistent correlates to our different neurochemical measures.

As noted above, there is an intriguing similarity between Rorschach records obtained from suicidal patients and those obtained from homicidal individuals (Lester & Perdue, 1974). Lidberg and coworkers are presently examining Rorschach records from violent offenders with the same methodology as the one used by Rydin and colleagues (Rydin et al., 1982; Rydin et al., 1990) on suicidal patients. It appears to be a promising approach to compare suicidal and homicidal individuals, and to distinguish between suicidal patients having chosen drastic and violent methods in their attempts and those who have used a more conventional method.

Further, another interesting comparison is that between individuals who have made a suicide attempt and those who described suicidal thoughts only. As noted above, these different types of suicidality may differ in their biological bases, and probably also in their psychological characteristics. In this connection, impulsivity both as a psychological state and as a personality trait deserves more attention than it has received.

References

Apter, A., van Praag, H. M., Plutchik, R., Sevy, S., Korn, M., & Brown, S. L. (1990). Interrelationships among anxiety, aggression, impulsivity, and mood—A serotonergically linked cluster? *Psychiatric Research, 32,* 191-199.

Åsberg, M., Schalling, D., Träskman-Bendz, L., & Wägner, A. (1987). Psychobiology of suicide, impulsivity, and related phenomena. In H. Y. Meltzer (Ed.), *Psychopharmacology—The third generation of progress* (pp. 655-668). New York. Raven Press.

Åsberg, M., Thorén, P., Träskman, L., Bertilsson, L., & Ringberger, V. (1976). "Serotonin depression"—a biochemical subgroup within the affective disorders? *Science, 191,* 478-480.

Åsberg, M., Träskman, L., & Thorén, P. (1976). 5-HIAA in the cerebrospinal fluid—a biochemical suicide predictor. *Archives of General Psychiatry, 33,* 1193-1197.

Ballenger, J. C., Post, R. M., Jimerson, D. C., Lake, R., Murphy, D., Zuckerman, M., & Cronin, C. (1983). Biochemical correlates of personality traits in normals: An exploratory study. *Personality and Individual Differences, 4,* 615-625.

Barratt, E. S. (1985). Impulsiveness subtraits: Arousal and information processing. In J. T. Spence & C. E. Izard (Eds.), *Motivation, emotion, and personality* (pp. 137-146). New York: Elsevier-North Holland.

Bertilsson, L., Alm, C., De Las Carreras, C., Widén, J., Edman, G., & Schalling, D. (1989). Debrisoquine hydroxylation polymorphism and personality. *The Lancet, ii,* 555.

Brown, C. S., Kent, T. A., Bryant, S. G., Gevedon, R. M., Campbell, J. L., Felthous, A. R., Barratt, E. S., & Rose, R. M. (1989). Blood platelet uptake of serotonin in episodic aggression. *Psychiatry Research, 27,* 5-12.

Brown, G. L., Ebert, M. H., Goyer, P. F., Jimerson, D. C., Klein, W. J., Bunney, W. E., & Goodwin, F. K. (1982). Aggression, suicide, and serotonin: Relationships to CSF amine metabolites. *American Journal of Psychiatry, 139,* 741-746.

Brown, G. L., & Goodwin, F. K. (1987). Cerebrospinal fluid correlates of suicide attempts and aggression. In J. J. Mann & M. Stanley (Eds.), *Psychobiology of suicidal behavior* (pp. 175-187). New York: Annals of the New York Academy of Sciences.

Brown, G. L., Goodwin, F. K., Ballenger, J. C., Goyer, P. F., & Major, L. F. (1979). Aggression in humans correlates with cerebrospinal fluid amine metabolites. *Psychiatry Research, 1,* 131-139.

Buchsbaum, M. S., Coursey, R. D., & Murphy, D. L. (1976). The biochemical high-risk paradigm: Behavioral and familial correlates of low platelet monoamine oxidase activity. *Science, 194,* 339-341.

Buchsbaum, M. S., Haier, R. J., & Murphy, D. L. (1977). Suicide attempts, platelet MAO and the averaged evoked response. *Acta Psychiatrica Scandinavica, 56,* 69-79.

Buss, A. (1961). *The psychology of aggression.* New York: John Wiley.

Carrigan, P. M. (1960). Extraversion-introversion as a dimension of personality: A reappraisal. *Psychological Bulletin, 57,* 329-360.

Claridge, G. (1985). *Origins of mental illness.* Oxford: Basil Blackwell.

Cloninger, C. R. (1987). A systematic method for clinical description and classification of personality variants. *Archives of General Psychiatry, 44,* 573-588.

Coccaro, E. F., Siever, L. J., Klar, H. M., Maurer, G., Cochrane, K., Cooper, T. B., Mohs, R. C., & Davis, K. L. (1989). Serotonergic studies in patients with affective and personality disorders. *Archives of General Psychiatry, 46,* 587-599.

Eaves, L. J., Martin, N. G., & Eysenck, S. B. G. (1977). An application of the analysis of covariance structure to the psychological study of impulsiveness. *British Journal of Psychiatry, 30,* 185-197.

Edman, G., Åsberg, M., Levander, S., & Schalling, D. (1986). Skin conductance habituation and cerebrospinal fluid 5-hydroxyindoleacetic acid in suicidal patients. *Archives of General Psychiatry, 43,* 586-592.

Edman, G., Schalling, D., & Levander, S. E. (1983). Impulsivity and speed and errors in a reaction time task: A contribution to the construct validity of the concept of impulsivity. *Acta Psychologia, 53,* 1-8.

Eysenck, H. J. (Ed.). (1981). *A model for personality.* New York: Springer.

Eysenck, H. J., & Eysenck, S. B. G. (1976). *Psychoticism as a dimension of personality.* London: Hodder & Stoughton.

Eysenck, H. J., & Levey, A. (1972). Conditionability and extraversion. In V. D. Nebylitsyn & J. A. Gray (Eds.), *Biological bases of individual behavior* (pp. 206-219). New York: Academic Press.

Eysenck, S. B. G., & Eysenck, H. J. (1977). The place of impulsiveness in a dimensional system of personality description. *British Journal of Social and Clinical Psychology, 16,* 57-68.

Eysenck, S. B. G., & Eysenck, H. J. (1978). Impulsiveness and venturesomeness: Their position in a dimensional system of personality description. *Psychological Reports, 43,* 1247-1255.

Gerbig, D. W., Ahandi, S. A., & Patton, J. H. (1987). Toward a conceptualization of impulsivity: Components across the behavioral and self-report domains. *Multivariate Behavioral Research, 22,* 357-379.

Gorenstein, E. E., & Newman, J. P. (1980). Disinhibitory psychopathology: A new perspective and a model for research. *Psychological Review, 87,* 301-315.

Gottfries, C. G., von Knorring, L., & Oreland, L. (1980). Platelet monoamine oxidase activity in mental disorders: II. Affective psychoses and suicidal behaviour. *Progress in Neuropsychopharmacology, 4,* 185-192.

Gray, J. A. (1981). Critique of Eysenck's theory of personality. In H. J. Eysenck (Ed.), *A model for personality.* New York: Springer.

Gray, J. A., Owen, S., Davis, N., & Tsaltas, E. (1983). Psychological and physiological relations between anxiety and impulsivity. In M. Zuckerman (Ed.), *Biological bases of sensation seeking, impulsivity, and anxiety* (pp. 181-217). Hillsdale, NJ: Lawrence Erlbaum.

Keller, F., Wolfersdorf, M., Straub, R., & Hole, G. (1991). Suicidal behaviour and electrodermal activity in depressive inpatients. *Acta Psychiatrica Scandinavica, 83,* 324-328.

King, R. J., Jones, J., Scheuer, J. W., Curtis, D., & Zarcone, V. P. (1990). Plasma cortisol correlates of impulsivity and substance abuse. *Personality and Individual Differences, 11*, 287-291.

Klinteberg, B. af, Levander, S., Oreland, L., Åsberg, M., & Schalling, D. (1987). Neuropsychological correlates of platelet monoamine oxidase MAO activity in female and male subjects. *Biological Psychology, 24*, 237-252.

Klinteberg, B. af, Oreland, L., Hallman, J., Wirsén, A., Levander, S. E., & Schalling, D. (1990-1991). Exploring the connections between platelet monoamine oxidase activity and behavior: Relationships with performance in neuropsychological tasks. *Neuropsychobiology, 23*, 188-196.

Klinteberg, B. af, Schalling, D., Edman, G., Oreland, L., & Åsberg, M. (1987). Personality correlates of platelet monoamineoxidase (MAO) activity in female and male subjects. *Neuropsychobiology, 18*, 89-96.

Klinteberg, B. af, Schalling, D., & Magnusson, D. (1989). Hyperactive behavior in childhood and adult impulsivity: A longitudinal study of male subjects. *Personality and Individual Differences, 10*, 43-50.

Knorring, L. von, Oreland, L., Häggendal, J., Magnusson, T., Almay, B., & Johansson, F. (1986). Relationship between platelet MAO activity and concentrations of 5-HIAA and HVA in cerebrospinal fluid in chronic pain patients. *Journal of Neuronal Transmission, 66*, 37-46.

Krieger, G. (1974). The plasma level of cortisol as a predictor of suicide. *Diseases of the Nervous System, 35*, 237-240.

Lester, D., & Perdue, W. C. (1974). The detection of attempted suicides and murderers using the Rorschach. *Journal of Psychiatric Research, 10*, 101-103.

Levander, S., Mattsson, Å., Schalling, D., & Dalteg, A. (1986). Psychoendocrine patterns within a group of male juvenile delinquents as related to early psychosocial stress diagnostic classification and follow-up data. In D. Magnusson & A. Öhman (Eds.), *Psychopathology: An interactional perspective* (pp. 235-252). New York: Academic Press.

Lidberg, L., Modin, I., Oreland, L., Tuck, J. R., & Gillner, A. (1985). Platelet monoamine oxidase activity and psychopathy. *Psychiatry Research, 16*, 339-343.

Limson, R., Goldman, D., Roy, A., Lamparski, D., Ravitz, B., Adinoff, B., & Linnoila, M. (1991). Personality and cerebrospinal fluid monoamine metabolites in alcoholics and controls. *Archives of General Psychiatry, 48*, 437-441.

Lindström, L. H. (1985). Low HVA and normal 5-HIAA CSF levels in drug-free schizophrenic patients compared to healthy volunteers: Correlations to symptomatology and family history. *Psychiatry Research, 14*, 265-273.

Linnoila, M., Virkkunen, M., Scheinin, M., Nuutila, A., Rimon, R., & Goodwin, F. (1983). Low cerebrospinal fluid 5-hydroxyindoleacetic acid concentration differentiates impulsive from nonimpulsive violent behavior. *Life Sciences, 33*, 2609-2614.

Llerena, A., Edman, G., Cobaleda, J., Benitez, J., Schalling, D., & Bertilsson, L. (1991). Relationship between personality and debrisoquine hydroxylation capacity. Evidence for an endogenous neuroactive substrate or product of the cytochrome P45IID6. *Manuscript*, 1-11.

Lolas, F., Gomez, A., & Suarez, L. (1991). EPQ-R and suicide attempt: The relevance of psychoticism. *Personality and Individual Differences, 12*, 899-902.

Mason, J. W. (1968). A review of psychoendocrine research on the pituitary-adrenal cortical system. *Psychosomatic Medicine, 30*, 576-607.

Mason, J. W. (1975). Emotion as reflected in patterns of endocrine integration. In L. Levi (Ed.), *Emotions—Their parameters and measurement* (pp. 143-181). New York: Raven Press.

Mason, J. W., Kosten, T. R., Southwick, S. M., & Giller, E. L., Jr. (1990). The use of psychoendocrine strategies in post-traumatic stress disorder. *Journal of Applied Social Psychology, 20,* 1822-1846.

Mattson, Å., Gross, S., & Hall, T. W. (1971). Psychoendocrine study of adaptation in young hemophiliacs. *Psychosomatic Medicine, 33,* 215-225.

Menninger, K. (1938). *Man against himself.* New York: Harcourt, Brace & World.

Oreland, L., & Hallman, J. (1988). Monoamine oxidase activity in relation to psychiatric disorders: The state of the art. *Nordisk Psykiatrisk Tidskrift, 42,* 95-105.

Oreland, L., Knorring, L. von, & Schalling, D. (1984). Connections between MAO, temperament and disease. In W. Paton, J. Mitchell, & P. Turner (Eds.), *Proceedings of the IX International Congress of Pharmacology* (pp. 193-202). London: Macmillan.

Oreland, L., Wiberg, Å., Åsberg, M., Träskman, L., Sjöstrand, L., Thorén, P., & Bertilsson, L. (1981). Platelet MAO activity and monoamine metabolites in cerebrospinal fluid in depressed and suicidal patients and in healthy controls. *Psychiatry Research, 4,* 21-29.

Pedersen, N. L., Plomin, R. D., McClearn, G. E., & Friberg, L. (1988). Neuroticism, extraversion, and related traits in adult twins reared apart and reared together. *Journal of Personality and Social Psychology, 55,* 950-957.

Regnéll, G., Träskman-Bendz, L., Alling, C., & Öhman, R. (1991). CSF studies and long term suicidal behavior. In G. Racagni (Ed.), *Biological Psychiatry,* vol. 1 (pp. 100-102). New York: Elsevier Science.

Robinson, T. N., & Zahn, T. P. (1985). Psychoticism and arousal. Possible evidence for a linkage of P and psychopathy. *Personality and Individual Differences, 6,* 47-66.

Roy, A., Adinoff, B. L., & Linnoila, M. (1988). Acting out hostility in normal volunteers—Negative correlation with levels of 5-HIAA in cerebrospinal fluid. *Psychiatric Research, 24,* 187-194.

Rydin, E., Åsberg, M., Edman, G., & Schalling, D. (1990). Violent and non-violent suicide attempts—controlled Rorschach study. *Acta Psychiatrica Scandinavica, 82,* 30-39.

Rydin, E., Schalling, D., & Åsberg, M. (1982). Rorschach ratings in depressed and suicidal patients with low levels of 5-HIAA in CSF. *Psychiatric Research, 7,* 229-243.

Schalling, D. (1978). Psychopathy-related personality variables and the psychophysiology of socialization. In R. D. Hare & D. Schalling (Eds.), *Psychopathic behavior—Approaches to research* (pp. 85-106). Chichester, UK: John Wiley.

Schalling, D. (1986). The involvement of serotonergic mechanisms in anxiety and impulsivity in humans. *Behavioral and Brain Sciences, 9,* 343-344.

Schalling, D., & Åsberg, M. (1985). Biological and psychological correlates of impulsiveness and monotony avoidance. In J. Strelau, F. H. Farley, & A. Gale (Eds.), *The biological foundations of personality and behavior* (pp. 181-200). New York: Hemisphere.

Schalling, D., Åsberg, M., Edman, G., & Levander, S. (1984). Impulsivity, nonconformity and sensation seeking as related to biological markers for vulnerability. *Clinical Neuropharmacology, 7,* 746-747.

Schalling, D., Åsberg, M., Edman, G., & Oreland, L. (1987). Markers for vulnerability to psychopathology: Temperament traits associated with platelet MAO activity. *Acta Psychiatrica Scandinavica, 76,* 172-182.

Schalling, D., Cronholm, B., & Åsberg, M. (1975). Components of state and trait anxiety as related to personality and arousal. In L. Levi (Ed.), *Emotions—Their parameters and measurement* (pp. 603-617). New York: Raven Press.

Schalling, D., Edman, G., & Åsberg, M. (1983). Impulsive cognitive style and inability to tolerate boredom: Psychobiological studies of temperamental vulnerability. In M. Zuckerman (Ed.), *Biological bases of sensation seeking, impulsivity, and anxiety* (pp. 123-145). Hillsdale, NJ: Lawrence Erlbaum.

Schalling, D., Edman, G., Åsberg, M., & Oreland, L. (1988). Platelet MAO activity associated with impulsivity and aggressivity. *Personality and Individual Differences, 2,* 597-605.

Schooler, C., Zahn, T. P., Murphy, D. L., & Buchsbaum, M. S. (1978). Psychological correlates of monoamine oxidase activity in normals. *The Journal of Nervous and Mental Disease, 166,* 177-186.

Sedvall, G., Fyrö, B., Gullberg, B., Nybäck, H., Wiesel, F.-A., & Wode-Helgodt, B. (1980). Relationships in healthy volunteers between concentrations of monoamine metabolites in CSF and family history of psychiatric morbidity. *British Journal of Psychiatry, 136,* 366-374.

Singer, M. T., & Larsson, D. G. (1981). Borderline personality and the Rorschach test. *Archives of General Psychiatry, 38,* 693-698.

Sjöbring, H. (1913). Den individualpsykologiska frågeställningen inom psykiatrien [The problem of individual psychology within psychiatry]. Thesis, University of Uppsala, Sweden.

Sjöbring, H. (1973). Personality: Structure and development. *Acta Psychiatrica Scandinavica,* (Suppl. 244), 1-244.

Soubrié, P. (1986). Reconciling the role of central serotonin neurons in human and animal behavior. *Behavioral and Brain Sciences, 9,* 319-364.

Thorell, L. (1987). Electrodermal activity in suicidal and nonsuicidal depressive patients and in matched healthy subjects. *Acta Psychiatrica Scandinavica, 76,* 420-430.

Träskman, L., Åsberg, M., Bertilsson, L., & Sjöstrand, L. (1981). Monoamine metabolites in CSF and suicidal behavior. *Archives of General Psychiatry, 38,* 631-636.

Träskman, L., Tybring, G., Åsberg, M., Bertilsson, L., Lantto, O., & Schalling, D. (1980). Cortisol in the CSF of depressed and suicidal patients. *Archives of General Psychiatry, 37,* 761-767.

Virkkunen, M. (1985). Urinary free cortisol secretion in habitually violent offenders. *Acta Psychiatrica Scandinavica, 72,* 40-44.

Wallace, J. F., Newman, J. P., & Bachorowski, J. A. (1991). Failures of response modulation: Impulsive behavior in anxious and impulsive individuals. *Journal of Research in Personality, 25,* 23-44.

Weissman, M., Fox, K., & Klerman, G. L. (1973). Hostility and depression associated with suicidal attempts. *American Journal of Psychiatry, 130,* 450-455.

Zuckerman, M. (1979). *Sensation seeking: Beyond the optimal level of arousal.* Hillsdale, NJ: Lawrence Erlbaum.

Zuckerman, M. (Ed.). (1983). *Biological bases of sensation seeking, impulsivity, and anxiety.* Hillsdale, NJ: Lawrence Erlbaum.

Zuckerman, M. (1989). Personality in the third dimension: A psychobiological approach. *Personality and Individual Differences, 10,* 391-418.

Zuckerman, M. (1991). *The psychobiology of personality.* New York: Cambridge University Press.

12

Serotonin in Personality Disorders With Habitual Violence and Impulsivity

MATTI VIRKKUNEN
MARKKU LINNOILA

There is a body of literature that consistently links impulsive habitually aggressive behaviors in men with indices of reduced central nervous system (CNS) serotonin turnover (Coccaro, 1989). Reduced brain serotonin turnover may also be associated with other mental disorders. This is especially true for suicidal unipolar depressions (Åsberg, Nordström, & Träskman-Bendz, 1986). According to van Praag et al. (1987), serotonergic disturbances lack nosological specificity, that is, they are not linked to a particular psychiatric disorder. They are associated with psychopathological dimensions such as unregulated aggression, increased anxiety, and possible lowering of mood. Deficient impulse control is often complicated with unregulated aggression. This chapter examines the literature that has reported on impulsive violence with reduced CNS serotonin turnover.

Impulsive Violence and Mental Disorders

Mental disorders classified in DSM-III-R (American Psychiatric Association [APA], 1987) characterized relatively often by impulsive violence and behavior are the following:

(1) Antisocial personality disorder (APD);

AUTHOR'S NOTE: This chapter was prepared by a federal government employee as part of official duties, therefore the material is in the public domain.

(2) Conduct disorder (solitary aggressive type in particular), a precursor of antisocial personality disorder in adolescence;

(3) Borderline personality disorder;

(4) Intermittent explosive disorder; and

(5) Pyromania in "impulse control disorders not elsewhere classified." (APA, pp. 321-331)

Patients with organic personality syndrome or schizophrenia may exhibit aggressive and impulsive behaviors, although such traits are not very common to these patients as a group.

Type II Alcoholism and Impulsive Personality Disorders

In many countries there is a positive correlation between the prevalence of alcohol abuse and dependence, and incidence of severe violent crimes, for instance, murders (Evans, 1986). It may be the prevalence of Type II alcoholism as defined by Cloninger, Bohman, and Sigvardsson (1981) that can, to a great extent, explain such a positive correlation. According to Irwin, Schuckit, and Smith (1990), Type II alcoholics usually have an antisocial personality disorder, in which early onset of drinking is a central feature. Other groups of investigations studying alcoholics with APD have also pointed out that behavioral problems that emerge in the context of excessive consumption of alcoholic beverages are an important symptom of alcoholics with APD (Cadoret, Troughton, & Widmer, 1984; Hesselbrock, Meyer, & Keener, 1985; C. Lewis, 1990; Liskow, Powell, Nickel, & Penick, 1991; Schuckit, 1985).

Cloninger et al. (1981) have emphasized that a habitually violent and impulsive behavior under the influence of alcohol is typical of Type II alcoholism. According to our data, these problems are characteristic of men with antisocial personality or with borderline personality disorders (many of whom have explosive features but do not fulfill DSM-III-R criteria for APD). Some of them have been called violent offenders with intermittent explosive disorder in our earlier studies (see exclusion criteria for this diagnosis in APA, 1987).

The personality traits "high novelty seeking," "low harm avoidance," and "low reward dependence" in Cloninger's personality inventory, the TPQ (Cloninger, 1987; Cloninger, Sigvardsson, von Knorring, & Bohman, 1988), are characteristic of Type II alcoholics. These personality traits can be seen in the extreme among individuals fulfilling diagnostic criteria for antisocial personality disorder (Cloninger, 1987). About 3% of men in the general population of the United States fulfill the DSM-III-R criteria for APD and at least half of the inmates in prisons in the Western world carry it (APA, 1987). In adolescence most of such youngsters probably have conduct disorder (Cloninger, Sigvardsson, & Bohman, 1988). These boys commonly start to drink alcohol in their early teens and many of them grow up to have an antisocial personality (APA, 1987; Manuzza, Klein, Konig, & Giampino, 1989).

Studies by L. von Knorring et al. (1987) from Sweden have also demonstrated that the tendency to behave aggressively and impulsively under the influence of alcohol is a very characteristic feature of Type II alcoholism. They used the Karolinska Scales of Personality (KSP) and found that its Impulsive-Sensation Seeking-Psychopathy factor (Impulsiveness, Monotony Avoidance, Socialization) differentiated Type II (early onset, antisocial) from Type I (late onset, often high anxiety) alcoholism. They also suggested that alcoholism with antisocial behavior differed clinically from alcoholism without antisocial behavior. Biochemically, serotonin is thought to have a more important role in Type II than in Type I alcoholism (see Roy, Virkkunen, & Linnoila, 1987).

Serotonin and Neuroanatomy Relevant for Impulse Control

Cloninger (1987) and Cloninger, Sigvardsson, von Knorring, and Bohman (1988) postulated that the personality traits of low harm avoidance and high novelty seeking were due to low serotonin and increased dopamine turnover, respectively. In the postulated behavioral inhibition system, the serotonergic projections from raphe nuclei in the brain stem to the forebrain are thought to play a central role. Serotonergic and dopaminergic activities in certain parts of the CNS are, however, highly correlated (Agren, Mefford, Rudorfer, Linnoila, & Potter, 1986; Linnoila, Virkkunen, Roy, & Potter, 1990). Thus, either a low CSF 5-hydroxyindoleacetic (5-HIAA) or homovanillic acid (HVA) concentration can, under certain circumstances, be indicative of reduced CNS serotonergic activity.

Japanese investigators (Yamamoto, Nagai, & Nagakava, 1984, 1985) have demonstrated that rats with suprachiasmatic nucleus lesions exhibit hypoglycemia during their active period and have hyperinsulinemic and hypoglucaconemic responses to a glucose challenge. The suprachiasmatic nucleus projects to the ventromedial nucleus of the hypothalamus. This hypothalamic area, together with the lateral hypothalamus, which is connected with the suprachiasmatic nucleus, participates in the control of feeding and satiety, particularly in regard to carbohydrate intake. Interestingly, this very same nucleus is thought to be the major endogenous circadian pacemaker in the CNS (Moore & Eichler, 1972) and receives a serotonergic input from the brain stem raphe nuclei (Palkovits et al., 1977).

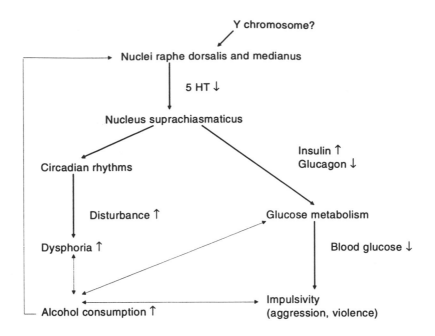

Figure 12.1. Schematic Representation of Proposed Model for Pathogenesis of Impulsivity and Type II Alcoholism

Thus this nucleus can provide an anatomical link between serotonin functions, regulation of circadian rhythms such as the sleep-wake cycle, and regulation of glucose metabolism (see Figure 12.1) (Roy, Virkkunen, & Linnoila, 1990). Diurnal rhythm and glucose metabolism disturbances are very common among patients with antisocial personality disorder and especially with very low 5-HIAA (Virkkunen, 1983; Virkkunen et al., 1992).

Brain Serotonin and Alcohol

Acute and chronic alcohol administration have a strong impact on brain serotonin metabolism in laboratory animals (Badaway, 1986; Haleem, 1990). Alcohol increases activity of the rate-limiting enzyme for serotonin synthesis, tryptophan hydroxylase, and concentrations of circulating tryptophan by inhibiting activity of hepatic tryptophan pyrrolase (Badaway, Punjani, & Evans, 1979; Kuriyama, Rauscher, & Sze, 1971). Moreover, alcohol-preferring (C57BL) mice have been found to have lower brain

TABLE 12.1 Supporting Findings for Abnormal Serotonin Metabolism in Personality Disorders With Habitual Violence and Impulsivity

---

1. Low platelet MAO (indirect evidence of abnormal serotonin metabolism)
2. Hypoglycemic tendency associated with reduced serotonin turnover (tendency for relatively slight lowering of blood glucose nadir in glucose tolerance test)
3. Low 5-HIAA concentration in cerebrospinal fluid (major metabolite of serotonin)
4. Abnormal tryptophan/large neutral amino acid ratio in plasma (evidence for abnormal precursor availability for central serotonin synthesis)
5. Abnormal prolactin and cortisol secretion in response to fenfluramine challenge (evidence of abnormal central serotonin neurotransmission)
6. Abnormal prolactin and cortisol secretion to m-CPP challenge (abnormal serotonin receptor sensitivity)
7. Abnormal peripheral serotonin functions such as elevated whole blood serotonin concentration.

---

serotonin concentrations than nonpreferring (CDA) mice. The difference has been postulated to be due to a reduction in tryptophan availability to the brain secondary to increased hepatic tryptophan pyrrolase activity in the C57BL mice (Badaway, Morgan, Lane, Dhaliwal, & Bradley, 1989).

There are no comparable clinical studies on effects of alcohol on serotonin metabolism either in healthy volunteers or in habitually violent and impulsive offenders who may have low central serotonin turnover. The latter may especially be hypothesized to exhibit robust changes in brain serotonin metabolism after alcohol intake. The situation is often complicated by eating irregularly when drinking, which is particularly characteristic of offenders with antisocial personality disorder (Virkkunen et al., 1992).

There are preliminary findings that serotonergic partial agonist, m-chlorophenylpiperazine (m-CPP) could induce a "high" and craving to drink among early onset, male alcoholics. This finding suggests that serotonin may be involved in the pathogenesis of at least certain types of alcoholism (Benkelfat et al., 1991).

Impulsive Violence and Abnormal Serotonin Metabolism

Evidence concerning abnormal serotonin metabolism in patients with personality disorders with habitual violence and impulsivity (who often also fulfill diagnostic criteria for early onset alcoholism) has been strengthened in the past few years. The following findings support the evidence (see Table 12.1).

Low Platelet Monoamine Oxidase

Brain monoamine oxidase (MAO) is the major enzyme that metabolizes biogenic monoamine neurotransmitters, including serotonin. Brain MAO activity has been found to be lower in alcoholics who have committed suicide (Gottfries, Oreland, Wiberg, & Winblad, 1975). In the early 1980s, platelet MAO was reported to be low in alcoholics, and has been found to be especially low among Type II alcoholics (A.-L. von Knorring, Bohman, von Knorring, & Oreland, 1985). Very low platelet MAO activity has also been found among criminals who have antisocial personality (Lidberg et al., 1985) or borderline personality disorder (Soloff et al., 1991). Only 1.5% of the total population belong to this very low mode of platelet MAO activity (Cloninger, von Knorring, & Oreland, 1985). Within this subgroup there is an overrepresentation of Type II or early onset alcoholism, which constitutes about 25% of all male patients with alcoholism (Cloninger et al., 1981). Personality characteristics such as impulsiveness and sensation seeking have been found to correlate with low platelet MAO activity (L. von Knorring, Oreland, & Winblad, 1984; Soloff et al., 1991).

Even though no significant correlation has been found thus far between platelet and brain MAO activities (Winblad, Gottfries, Oreland, & Wiberg, 1979; Young, Laws, Sharbrough, & Weinshilbaum, 1986), platelet MAO activity may reflect the functional capacity of the central serotonin system (Sakurai, Niwa, & Oreland, 1988). Behaviorally, low central serotonin turnover is probably associated with deficient impulse control in both animals and humans (Soubrié, 1986).

Brain Serotonin and Glucose Metabolism

In the early 1970s, Fernström and Wurtman (1971, 1972) reported that insulin secretion stimulated by glucose administration increased the availability of tryptophan to the brain and brain serotonin synthesis. Moreover, serotonin-releasing drugs, such as d-fenfluramine, can reduce appetite for carbohydrates (Wurtman et al., 1985) and impair glucose tolerance (Spring et al., 1989).

There is also preliminary evidence that brain serotonergic neurotransmission may control insulin and glucagon secretion from the pancreatic islets. Thus serotonin transmission in the brain could enhance insulin secretion and reduce glucagon excretion or alternatively, it could increase insulin sensitivity and via these mechanisms affect peripheral glucose mechanism (see Figure 12.1) (Roy et al., 1990; Virkkunen et al., 1992).

A tendency for an abnormally low blood glucose level during an oral glucose tolerance test (GTT) has been a common finding among Finnish habitually violent and impulsive offenders (Virkkunen, 1986b). It is probable that increased insulin sensitivity is the main factor to these hypoglycemic findings during GTTs (Virkkunen et al., 1992). This insulin sensitivity possibly increases with age; in younger men with conduct disorder the blood glucose nadirs are not as low (Gans et al., 1990; Virkkunen, 1983).

Earlier studies have found rapid and enhanced insulin secretion in subjects with intermittent explosive disorder during GTTs. The insulin secretion during the first 15 to 30 minutes after the oral glucose administration has especially been found to be enhanced among habitually violent offenders compared to age- and sex-matched controls (Gans et al., 1990; Roy, Virkkunen, Guthrie, & Linnoila, 1986; Virkkunen, 1983, 1986a; Virkkunen & Närvänen, 1987). These findings have been clearly shown among offenders with borderline personality disorder with explosive features who do not fulfill diagnostic criteria for antisocial personality disorder. In our studies, such subjects have been called violent offenders with intermittent explosive disorder before DSM-III-R (APA, 1987). The habitually violent offenders investigated by Gans et al. (1990) (whose findings were similar to ours) were 14 to 17 years of age, and probably fulfilled the diagnostic criteria for aggressive conduct disorder.

Excretion of a counterregulatory hormone, cortisol, during the GTT has also been found to be reduced in offenders with antisocial personality disorder (Fishbein et al., 1992).

Low CSF 5-HIAA

A majority of habitually violent, impulsive offenders (most of whom have early onset alcoholism and who often behave aggressively under the influence of alcohol) have been reported as having a low CSF 5-HIAA concentration (Brown et al., 1979; Brown et al., 1982; Linnoila et al., 1983; Virkkunen et al., 1987; see also Coccaro et al., 1989). These patients usually have antisocial personality disorder or other impulsive personality disorders such as borderline personality disorder or intermittent explosive disorder.

A prospective study of habitually violent and impulsive offenders with alcoholism showed that 13 out of 58 offenders committed new violent crimes under the influence of alcohol after an average of 3 years in the community (Virkkunen et al., 1989). Interestingly, blood glucose levels and CSF 5-HIAA levels correctly classified the offenders as recidivists or nonrecidivists in 84.2% of the cases.

When we examined the family histories of these violent offenders, we found that only the low CSF 5-HIAA was associated with a family history of alcoholism in the father (Linnoila, DeJong, & Virkkunen, 1989). Thus the relatively low CSF 5-HIAA concentration is associated with a central characteristic of Type II alcoholism, a family history positive for an alcoholic father, but the tendency for mild hypoglycemia with low CSF 5-HIAA correlates with the propensity to behave impulsively and aggressively under the influence of alcohol.

Abnormal Tryptophan/Large Neutral Amino Acid Ratio in Plasma

Tryptophan/large neutral amino acid (LNAA) ratio regulates the availability of tryptophan to the brain. This ratio is itself regulated in part by insulin (Fernström & Wurtman, 1971, 1972). Alcoholics who started to abuse alcohol very early (before 20 years of age) show an association between low tryptophan/LNAA ratio and depressive and aggressive behaviors (Buydens-Branchey, Branchey, Noumair, 1989; Buydens-Branchey, Branchey, Noumair, & Lieber, 1989). An early age of onset is a typical feature of Type II alcoholism and alcoholism with antisocial personality disorder and fits a serotonin deficit hypothesis for the common etiology of these conditions. The tryptophan/LNAA ratio was measured by Buydens-Branchey, Branchey, Noumair, and Lieber (1989) one day after cessation of drinking and it increased progressively for at least 2 to 3 weeks after detoxification. The subjects who had exhibited early onset alcohol-seeking behavior had also often committed crimes of violence and commonly had a history of paternal alcoholism.

Branchey et al. (1985) also found that memory loss under the influence of alcohol, which is a common phenomenon among subjects with personality disorders characterized by habitual violence and impulsivity, is associated with a low plasma tryptophan concentration. These measurements were done after 2 weeks of abstinence.

However, Virkkunen and Närvänen (1987) found an elevated tryptophan/LNAA ratio among impulsive, violent offenders who had an intermittent explosive disorder and enhanced insulin secretion in the glucose tolerance test. In patients with antisocial personality disorder, mean values of the ratio did not differ from normal controls.

Prolactin and Cortisol Secretion in Fenfluramine Test

Fenfluramine, an anorectic agent, acts at presynaptic sites to release serotonin and inhibit its uptake (Garattini, Buszko, Jori, & Samarin, 1975). Plasma prolactin increase following fenfluramine is believed to be mediated by serotonin (Quattrone et al., 1983). However, the fenfluramine challenge does not distinguish between presynaptic and postsynaptic functions that contribute to serotonin-mediated prolactin release. Thus both the serotonin stores available for release and altered sensitivity of postsynaptic serotonin 1 and/or 2 receptors can affect results of the fenfluramine challenge (Coccaro, 1989). Plasma corticosterone in rats and cortisol in humans can also be released following central serotonin stimulation, which releases adrenocorticotrophic hormone (ACTH) by enhancing the release of corticotropin-releasing hormone (D. Lewis & Sherman, 1984; Murphy, Mueller, Garrick, & Aulakh, 1986).

Coccaro et al. (1989) have reported blunted prolactin responses to fenfluramine in veterans who had DSM-III-R personality disorders but no alcoholism. Fishbein, Lozovsky, and Jaffe (1989), on the other hand, studied prolactin and cortisol responses in substance abusers with varying levels of aggressiveness and impulsivity. Most of their subjects had alcoholism and features of antisocial personality disorder but they did not investigate how many had early onset alcoholism. Prolactin and cortisol responses after fenfluramine were significantly elevated in subjects with increased impulsivity and aggressiveness, suggestive of altered serotonin activity associated with these behavioral traits.

The reason for apparently discordant findings on habitually violent and impulsive patients in the fenfluramine challenge and the above-mentioned tryptophan/LNAA ratios can be the difference in the subjects that have been studied. Fishbein et al. (1989) describe their subjects as violent patients who have "features of antisocial personality." These subjects may be somewhat similar to Virkkunen's intermittent explosive disorder (borderline personality with explosive features but who don't fulfil APD criteria) (Virkkunen, 1986; Virkkunen & Närvänen, 1987). Coccaro et al. (1989) described their subjects as having "DSM-III-R personality disorders," without specifying the disorder. There is preliminary evidence that excretion of hormones that have effects on serotonin metabolism (insulin, cortisol) can vary among those with antisocial personality disorder and intermittent explosive disorder (Virkkunen, 1985, 1986; Virkkunen & Närvänen, 1987). Excretion of these hormones may also vary according to age among habitually violent patients. Elucidation of these apparently contradictory findings requires further studies.

Effect of Serotonin Agonist m-CPP on Prolactin and Cortisol Response

Serotonin agonist m-CPP also increases prolactin and cortisol secretion among normal humans when given orally or intravenously (Murphy, 1990). Prolactin responses to m-CPP have been found to be low in patients with antisocial personality disorder, but cortisol responses may be increased (Moss, Yao, & Panzak, 1990). Similarly blunted prolactin responses to m-CPP have been reported among bulimic women (Brewerton,

Brandt, Lessem, Murphy, & Jimerson, 1990). In this disorder there is thought to be a blunted postsynaptic responsivity in serotonergic hypothalamo-pituitary pathways (Brewerton et al., 1990).

Other Abnormal Peripheral Serotonin Functions

Whole Blood Serotonin

Certain peripheral indices of serotonin function may also correlate positively with impulsive and aggressive behaviors. In a recent study, Pliszka et al. (1988) found a clear association between whole blood serotonin concentration and conduct disorder. Interestingly, this correlation was especially clear among patients with conduct disorder who had a tendency to behave violently according to arrest records. Thus the description is commensurate with conduct disorder, solitary, aggressive type that usually continues as violent antisocial personality disorder in adulthood.

Some investigators have reported that dominance and aggression in monkeys are associated with both low CSF 5-HIAA (Yodyingyuard et al., 1985) and high whole blood serotonin concentrations (Raleigh, Brammer, McGuire, & Yuwiler, 1984, 1985). Whether a high blood serotonin concentration is associated with high (Virkkunen & Närvänen, 1987) or low (Coccaro et al., 1989) plasma tryptophan concentration and how these values correlate with basal insulin and cortisol levels (Virkkunen, 1985; Virkkunen & Närvänen, 1987) needs to be further elucidated. These hormones can greatly influence plasma tryptophan concentrations and, therefore, serotonin metabolism by regulating the main metabolic route for tryptophan via the hepatic 2,3 dioxygenase (pyrrolase) enzyme (Salter & Pogson, 1985).

Uptake of Serotonin to Platelets

Brown et al. (1989) found uptake of serotonin to platelets to be low in male outpatients with episodic aggression. There was also a negative correlation between serotonin uptake and ratings on scales of impulsivity (Barratt Impulsivity Scale) but not of anger (Spielberger Anger Expression Scale). Therefore, it was thought that putatively disturbed serotonergic function was associated with impulsivity and disturbed "control" of aggression.

Platelet Imipramine Binding (Bmax)

One study shows that the density (Bmax) of (3H)-imipramine binding sites is significantly reduced in prepubescent children with conduct and attention deficit disorder (Stoff et al., 1987). In this study, the investigators reported a negative correlation between (3H)-imipramine Bmax and aggressive behaviors. However, in another sample of adolescents with less severe conduct disorder-related problems, they could not replicate their earlier findings of reduced density of (3H)-imipramine binding sites in platelets (Stoff et al., 1991).

A study on adults with mental retardation showed that low Bmax was connected with behavioral dyscontrol, expressed as hyperactivity and aggression (Marazziti & Conti, 1991).

Serotonin, Glucose Metabolism, and Aggressivity Among Healthy Volunteers

In healthy volunteers, Roy, Adinoff, and Linnoila (1988) found a negative correlation between verbal acting-out hostility and CSF 5-HIAA concentration. Individuals with low 5-HIAA were rated higher on a standardized scale quantifying verbal acting-out hostility than individuals with high CSF 5-HIAA.

Also, Benton, Kumari, and Brain (1982) found in 24 healthy volunteers significant correlations between the degree of hypoglycemia during the oral glucose tolerance test and scores on outward-directed aggressivity in the Rosenzweig Picture Frustration Test.

What Is the Cause of the Putative Serotonin Deficit in the Brain?

At this time the ultimate cause of the putative reduction of central serotonin turnover remains unknown. Several possible causes can, however, be directly investigated: reduced synthesis and release of serotonin, which can both be produced by reduced availability of the precursor tryptophan to the CNS; and reduced activity of tryptophan hydroxylase or abnormalities in the release or re-uptake of serotonin at the synapse. There can also be increased or decreased sensitivity of one or more serotonin receptors or abnormal interaction between receptor subtypes. Preliminary evidence suggests that there may be reduced sensitivity of 5-HT1 receptors (Coccaro, Gabriel, & Siever, 1990). Second messenger systems associated with serotonin receptors may also function abnormally. Certain clues emerge from controlled studies with antidepressant medications to reduce impulsive aggression.

Clinical Studies of Drug Treatments of Violent Behavior

In controlled studies, tryptophan and lithium have been shown to reduce violent incidents in aggressive schizophrenics (Morand, Young, & Ervin, 1983), in antisocial violent prisoners (Sheard, Marini, Bridges, & Wagner, 1976), and in children with aggressive conduct disorder (Campbell et al., 1984). Propranolol and pindolol have also reduced assaultive behavior in patients with organic brain disorders (Greendyke & Kanter, 1986; Greendyke et al., 1986). Carbamazepine has reduced aggressiveness and impulsivity in women with severe borderline personality (Cowdry & Gardner, 1988).

It has been proposed that functional serotonin agonism may be the common mechanism by which these treatments reduce unpredictable violent behavior (Linnoila, 1989). New medications have been developed to reduce impulsive violence. There are preliminary uncontrolled reports that serotonin re-uptake inhibitors, such as fluoxetine (Coccaro, Astill, Herbert, & Schut, 1990) and the partial 5-HT1A agonist buspirone (Gedye, 1991), may be clinically useful similar to their efficacy in reducing aggression in laboratory animals (Oliver et al., 1990).

Conclusions

Many different lines of evidence suggest that abnormal brain serotonin metabolism may be characteristic of habitually violent and impulsive offenders. Personality disorders diagnosed in such patients are usually connected with so-called Type II or early onset alcoholism, whose one central feature is an abnormal tendency to behave aggressively and impulsively under the influence of alcohol. Low CSF 5-HIAA has been found to be associated with paternal alcoholism. Both this and the associated tendency to a mild hypoglycemia in glucose tolerance tests prospectively predict new violent and impulsive crimes under the influence of alcohol. Peripheral measures such as platelet MAO, abnormal tryptophan/large neutral amino acid ratio in plasma, whole blood serotonin, platelet uptake of serotonin, platelet (3H)-imipramine binding (Bmax), abnormal prolactin and cortisol excretion during fenfluramine challenge test, and the serotonin agonist m-CPP challenge test (according to some investigators) correlate with impulsive aggressive behavior. Medications (lithium, carbamazepine, b-blockers, and tryptophan), which in double-blind, placebo-controlled studies have diminished impulsive aggression, all have effects on brain serotonin functions. Serotonin re-uptake inhibitors and 1A receptor agonists offer new promise for this indication.

References

Agren, H., Mefford, I. N., Rudorfer, M. V., Linnoila, M., & Potter, W. Z. (1986). Interacting neurotransmitter systems. A nonexperimental approach to the 5-HIAA-HVA correlation in human CSF. *Psychiatric Research, 20,* 175-193.

American Psychiatric Association. (1987). *Diagnostic and statistical manual of mental disorders* (3rd ed., rev.). Washington, DC: Author.

Åsberg, M., Nordström, P., & Träskman-Bendz, L. (1986). Cerebrospinal fluid studies in suicides. In J. J. Mann & M. Stanley (Eds.), *Psychobiology of suicidal behavior* (Vol. 487, pp. 243-255). New York: New York Academy of Sciences.

Badaway, A. A.-B., (1986). Alcohol as a psychopharmacological agent. In P. F. Brain (Ed.), *Alcohol and aggression* (pp. 55-83). London: Croom Helm.

Badaway, A. A.-B., Morgan, C. J., Lane, J., Dhaliwal, K., & Bradley, D. M. (1989). Liver tryptophan pyrrolase. A major determinant of the lower brain 5-hydroxytryptamine concentration in alcohol-preferring C57BL mice. *Biochemical Journal, 264,* 597-599.

Badaway, A. A.-B., Punjani, N. F., & Evans, M. (1979). Enhancement of rat brain tryptophan metabolism by chronic ethanol administration and possible involvement of decreased liver tryptophan pyrrolase. *Biochemical Journal, 178,* 575-580.

Benkelfat, C., Murphy, D. L., Hill, J. L., George, D. T., Nutt, D., & Linnoila, M. (1991). Ethanol-like properties of the serotonergic partial agonist m-chlorophenylpiperazine in chronic alcoholic patients. *Archives of General Psychiatry, 48,* 383.

Benton, D., Kumari, N., & Brain, P. F. (1982). Mild hypoglycemia and questionnaire measures of aggression. *Biological Psychology, 14,* 129-135.

Branchey, L., Branchey, M., Zucker, D., Shaw, S., & Lieber, C. S. (1985). Association between low plasma tryptophan and blackouts in male alcohol patients. *Alcohol, Clinical and Experimental Research, 9,* 393-395.

Brewerton, T. D., Brandt, H. A., Lessem, M. D., Murphy, D. L., & Jimerson, D. C. (1990). Serotonin in eating disorders. In E. F. Coccaro & D. L. Murphy (Eds.), *Serotonin in major psychiatric disorders* (pp. 153-184). Washington, DC: American Psychiatric Press.

Brown, C. S., Kent, T. A., Bryant, S. G., Gevedon, R. M., Campbell, J. L., Felthous, A. R., Barratt, E. C., & Rose, R. M. (1989). Blood platelet uptake of serotonin in episodic aggression. *Psychiatric Research, 27,* 5-12.

Brown, G. L., Ebert, M. H., Goyer, P. F., Jimerson, D. C., Klein, W. J., Bunney, W. E., & Goodwin, F. K. (1982). Aggression, suicide, and serotonin: Relationships to CSF amine metabolites. *American Journal of Psychiatry, 139,* 741-746.

Brown, G. L., Goodwin, F. K., Ballenger, J. C., Goyer, P. F., & Major, L. F. (1979). Aggression in humans correlates with cerebrospinal fluid metabolites. *Psychiatric Research, 1,* 131-139.

Buydens-Branchey, L., Branchey, M. H., & Noumair, D. (1989). Age of alcoholism onset. I. Relationship to psychopathology. *Archives of General Psychiatry, 46,* 225-230.

Buydens-Branchey, L., Branchey, M. H., Noumair, D., & Lieber, C. S. (1989). Age of alcoholism onset. II. Relation to susceptibility to serotonin precursor availability. *Archives of General Psychiatry, 46,* 231-236.

Cadoret, R., Troughton, E., & Widmer, R. (1984). Clinical differences between antisocial and primary alcoholics. *Comprehensive Psychiatry, 25,* 1-8.

Campbell, M., Anderson, L., Bennett, W. G., Green, W. H., Jennings, S. J., Perry, R., & Small, A. M. (1984). Behavioral efficacy of haloperidol and lithium carbonate. A comparison in hospitalized aggressive children with conduct disorder. *Archives of General Psychiatry, 41,* 650-656.

Cloninger, C. R. (1987). A systematic method for clinical description and classification of personality variants. *Archives of General Psychiatry, 44,* 573-588.

Cloninger, C. R., Bohman, M., & Sigvardsson, S. (1981). Inheritance of alcohol abuse: Cross-fostering analysis of adopted men. *Archives of General Psychiatry, 38,* 861-868.

Cloninger, C. R., Knorring, L. von, & Oreland, L. (1985). Pentametric distribution of platelet monoamine oxidase activity. *Psychiatric Research, 15,* 133-143.

Cloninger, C. R., Sigvardsson, S., & Bohman, M. (1989). Childhood personality predicts alcohol abuse in young adults. *Alcohol. Clinical and Experimental Research, 12,* 494-505.

Cloninger, C. R., Sigvardsson, S., Knorring, A.-L. von, & Bohman, M. (1988). The Swedish studies of the adopted children of alcoholics: A reply to Littrell. *Journal of Studies on Alcoholism, 49,* 500-509.

Coccaro, E. F. (1989). Central serotonin and impulsive aggression. *British Journal of Psychiatry Supplement 8,* 52-62.

Coccaro, E. F., Astill, J. L., Herbert, J. L., & Schut, A. G. (1990). Fluoxetine treatment of impulsive aggression in DSMIII-R personality disorder patients. *Journal of Clinical Psychopharmacology, 10,* 373-375.

Coccaro, E. F., Gabriel, S., & Siever, L. J. (1990). Buspirone challenge: Preliminary evidence for a role for central 5-HT1a receptor function in impulsive aggressive behavior in humans. *Psychopharmacological Bulletin, 26,* 244-253.

Coccaro, E. F., Siever, L. J., Klar, H. M., Maurer, G., Cochrane, K., Cooper, T. B., Mohs, R. C., Davis, K. L. (1989). Serotonergic studies in patients with affective and personality disorders. Correlates with suicidal and impulsive aggressive behavior. *Archives of General Psychiatry, 46,* 587-599.

Cowdry, R. W., & Gardner, D. L. (1988). Pharmacotherapy of borderline personality disorder. *Archives of General Psychiatry, 45,* 111-119.

Evans, C. M. (1986). Alcohol and violence: Problems relating to methodology, statistics, and causation. In D. F. Brain (Ed.), *Alcohol and aggression* (pp. 138-160). London: Croom Helm.

Fernström, J. D., & Wurtman, R. J. (1971). Brain serotonin content. Increase following ingestion of carbohydrate diet. *Science, 174,* 1023-1025.

Fernström, J. D., & Wurtman, R. J. (1972). Brain serotonin content. Physiological regulation by plasma neutral amino acids. *Science, 178,* 414-416.

Fishbein, D. H., Lozovsky, D., & Jaffe, J. H. (1989). Impulsivity, aggression and neuroendocrine responses to serotonergic stimulation in substance abusers. *Biological Psychiatry, 25,* 1049-1066.

Fishbein, D. H., Dax, E., Lozovsky, D. B., & Jaffe, J. H. (1992). Neuroendocrine responses to a glucose challenge in substance users with high and low levels of aggression, impulsivity and antisocial personality. *Neuropsychobiology, 25,* 106-114.

Gans, D. A., Harper, A. E., Bachorowski, J.-A., Newman, J. P., Shagro, E. S., & Taylor, S. L. (1990). Sucrose and delinquency: Oral sucrose tolerance test and nutritional assessment. *Pediatrics, 86,* 254-262.

Garattini, S., Buszko, W., Jori, A., & Samarin, R. (1975). The mechanism of action of fenfluramine. *Postgraduate Medical Journal, 51*(Suppl. 1), 27-35.

Gedye, A. (1991). Buspirone alone or with serotonergic diet reduced aggression in a developmentally disabled adult. *Biological Psychiatry, 30,* 88-91.

Gottfries, C. G., Oreland, L., Wiberg, A., & Winblad, B. (1975). Lowered monoamine oxidase activity in brains from alcoholic suicides. *Journal of Neurochemistry, 25,* 667-673.

Greendyke, R. M., & Kanter, D. R. (1986). Therapeutic effects on pindolol on behavioral disturbances associated with organic brain disease. A double-blind study. *Journal of Clinical Psychiatry, 47,* 423-426.

Greendyke, R. M., Kanter, D. R., Schuster, D. B., Verstreate, S., & Wooton, J. (1986). Propranolol treatment of assaultive patients with organic brain disease. *The Journal of Nervous and Mental Diseases, 174,* 290-294.

Haleem, D. J. (1990). Injected tryptophan increases brain but not plasma tryptophan levels more in ethanol treated rats. *Life Sciences, 47,* 971-979.

Hesselbrock, M. N., Meyer, R. E., & Keener, J. J. (1985). Psychopathology in hospitalized alcoholics. *Archives of General Psychiatry, 42,* 1050-1055.

Irwin, M., Schuckit, M., & Smith, T. L. (1990). Clinical importance of age of onset in type 1 and type 2 primary alcoholics. *Archives of General Psychiatry, 47,* 320-324.

Knorring, A.-L. von, Bohman, M., Knorring, L. von, & Oreland, L. (1985). Platelet MAO activity as a biological marker in subgroups of alcoholism. *Acta Psychiatrica Scandinavica, 72,* 51-58.

Knorring, L. von, Knorring, A.-L. von, Smigan, L., et al. (1987). Personality traits in subtypes of alcoholics. *Journal of Studies on Alcohol, 48,* 523-527.

Knorring, L. von, Oreland, L., & Winblad, B. (1984). Personality traits related to monoamine oxidase (MAO) in platelets. *Psychiatric Research, 12,* 11-26.

Kuriyama, K., Rauscher, G. E., & Sze, P. Y. (1971). Effect of acute and chronic administration of ethanol on the 5-hydroxytryptamine turnover and tryptophan hydroxylase activity of the mouse brain. *Brain Research, 26,* 450-454.

Lewis, C. E. (1990). Alcoholism and antisocial personality. Clinical associations and etiological implications. *Progress in Alcohol Research, 2,* 15-37.

Lewis, D. A., & Sherman, B. M. (1984). Serotonergic stimulation and adrenocorticotrophin secretion in man. *Journal of Clinical Endocrinology and Metabolism, 58,* 458-462.

Lidberg, L., Modin, I., Oreland, L., et al. (1985). Platelet MAO activity as a biological marker in subgroups of alcoholism. *Acta Psychiatrica Scandinavica, 72,* 51-58.

Linnoila, M. (1989). Monoamines and impulse control. In J. A. Swinkels & W. Blijleven (Eds.), *Depression, anxiety and aggression* (pp. 167-172). Amsterdam, The Netherlands: Medidacht.

Linnoila, M., DeJong, J., & Virkkunen, M. (1989). Family history of alcoholism in violent offenders and impulsive fire setters. *Archives of General Psychiatry, 46,* 613-616.

Linnoila, M., Virkkunen, M., Roy, A., & Potter, W. Z. (1990). Monoamines, glucose metabolism and impulse control. In H. van Praag, R. Plutchik, & A. Apter (Eds.), *Violence and suicidality. Perspectives in clinical and psychobiological research* (pp. 218-241). New York: Brunner/Mazel.

Linnoila, M., Virkkunen, M., Scheinin, M., Nuutila, A., Rimon, R., & Goodwin, F. (1983). Low cerebrospinal fluid 5-hydroxyindoleacetic acid concentration differentiates impulsive from nonimpulsive violent behavior. *Life Sciences, 33,* 2609-2614.

Liskow, B., Powell, B. J., Nickel, E., & Penick, E. (1991). Antisocial alcoholics: Are there clinically significant diagnostic subtypes? *Journal of Studies on Alcoholism, 52,* 62-69.

Manuzza, S., Klein, R. G., Konig, P. H., & Giampino, T. L. (1989). Hyperactive boys almost grown up. IV. Criminality and its relationship to psychiatric status. *Archives of General Psychiatry, 46,* 1073-1079.

Marazziti, D., & Conti, L. (1991). Aggression, hyperactivity and platelet imipramine binding. *Acta Psychiatrica Scandinavica, 84,* 209-211.

Moore, R. Y., & Eichler, V. B. (1972). Loss of a circadian adrenal corticosterone rhythm following suprachiasmatic lesions in the rat. *Brain Research, 42,* 201-206.

Morand, C., Young, S. N., & Ervin, F. R. (1983). Clinical response of aggressive schizophrenics to oral tryptophan. *Biological Psychiatry, 18,* 575-578.

Moss, H. B., Yao, J. K., & Panzak, G. L. (1990). Serotonergic responsivity and behavioral dimensions in antisocial personality disorder with substance abuse. *Biological Psychiatry, 28,* 325-338.

Murphy, D. L. (1990). Peripheral indices of central serotonin function in humans. In P. M. Whitaker-Azmitia & S. J. Peroutka (Eds.), *The neuropharmacology of serotonin* (Vol. 600, pp. 282-296). New York: New York Academy of Sciences.

Murphy, D. L., Mueller, E. A., Garrick, N. A., & Aulakh, C. S. (1986). Use of serotonergic agents in the clinical assessments of central serotonin function. *Journal of Clinical Psychiatry, 47,* 9-13.

Oliver, B., Mos, J., Tulp, M., Schipper, J., den Daas, S., & van Oortmerssen, G. (1990). Serotonergic involvement in aggressive behavior in animals. In H. M. van Praag, R. Plutchik, & A. Apter (Eds.), *Violence and suicidality. Perspectives in clinical and psychobiological research* (pp. 79-137). New York: Brunner/Mazel.

Palkovits, M., Saavedra, J. M., Jacobovits, D. M., Kizer, J. S., Zaborsky, L., & Brownstein, M. J. (1977). Serotonergic innervation of the forebrain. Effects of lesions on serotonin and tryptophan hydroxylase levels. *Brain Research, 130,* 121-124.

Pliszka, S. R., Rogeness, G. A., Renner, P., Sherman, J., & Broussard, T. (1988). Plasma neurochemistry in juvenile offenders. *American Academy of Child & Adolescent Psychiatry, 27,* 588-594.

Praag, H. M. van, Kahn, R. S., Asnis, G. M., Wetzler, S., Brown, S. L., Bleich, A., & Korn, M. L. (1987). Denosologization of biological psychiatry or the specificity of 5-HT disturbances in psychiatric disorders. *Journal of Affective Disorders, 13,* 1-8.

Quattrone, A., Tedeschi, G., Aguglia, U., Scopacasa, F., DiRenzo, G. F., & Anunziato, L. (1983). Prolactin secretion in man. A useful tool to evaluate the activity of drugs on central 5-hydroxytryptaminergic neurons. Studies with fenfluramine. *British Journal of Clinical Pharmacology, 16,* 471-475.

Raleigh, M. J., Brammer, G. L., McGuire, M. T., & Yuwiler, A. (1984). Dominant social status facilitates the behavioral effects on serotonergic agonists. *Brain Research, 348,* 274-281.

Raleigh, M. J., Brammer, G. L., McGuire, M. T., & Yuwiler, A. (1985). Social and environmental influences on blood serotonin concentrations in monkeys. *Archives of General Psychiatry, 41,* 405-410.

Roy, A., Adinoff, B. L., & Linnoila, M. (1988). Acting out hostility in normal volunteers. Negative correlation with CSF 5-HIAA levels. *Psychiatric Research, 24,* 187-194.

Roy, A., Virkkunen, M., Guthrie, S., & Linnoila, M. (1986). Indices of serotonin and glucose metabolism in violent offenders, arsonists and alcoholics. In J. J. Mann & M. Stanley (Eds.), *Psychobiology of suicidal behavior* (Vol. 487, pp. 202-220). New York: Annals of the New York Academy of Sciences.

Roy, A., Virkkunen, M., & Linnoila, M. (1990). Serotonin in suicide, violence and alcoholism. In E. F. Coccaro & D. L. Murphy (Eds.), *Serotonin in major psychiatric disorder* (pp. 187-208). Washington, DC: American Psychiatric Press.

Sakurai, E., Niwa, H., & Oreland, L. (1988). Relation between serotonin uptake rates, serotonin concentrations and monoamine oxidase activities in various regions of rat brain. *Pharmacological Research Third Amine Oxidase International Workshop* (Supplement 4), 97-99.

Salter, M., & Pogson, C. I. (1985). The role of tryptophan 2,3-dioxygenase in the hormonal control of tryptophan metabolism in isolated rat liver cells. Effects of glucocorticoids and experimental diabetes. *Biochemical Journal, 229,* 449-504.

Schuckit, M. A. (1985). The clinical implications of primary diagnostic groups among alcoholics. *Archives of General Psychiatry, 42,* 1043-1049.

Sheard, M. H., Marini, J. L., Bridges, C. I., & Wagner, E. (1976). The effect of lithium on impulsive aggressive behavior in man. *American Journal of Psychiatry, 133,* 1409-1413.

Soloff, P. H., Cornelius, J., Foglia, J., George, A., & Perel, J. M. (1991). Platelet MAO in borderline personality disorder. *Biological Psychiatry, 29,* 499-502.

Soubrié, H. P. (1986). Reconciling the role of central serotonin neurons in human and animal behavior. *Behavioral and Brain Sciences, 9,* 343-344.

Spring, B., Chiado, J., Harden, M., Bourgeois, M. J., Mason, J. D., & Lutherer, L. (1989). Psychobiological effects of carbohydrates. *Journal of Clinical Psychiatry, 50,* 27-33.

Stoff, D. M., Ieni, J., Friedman, E., Bridger, W. H., Pollock, L., & Vitiello, B. (1991). Platelet (3H)-imipramine binding, serotonin uptake, and plasma a1 acid glycoprotein in disruptive behavior disorders. *Biological Psychiatry, 29,* 494-498.

Stoff, D. M., Pollock, L., Vitiello, B., Behar, D., & Bridger, W. H. (1987). Reduction of (3H)-imipramine binding sites on platelets on conduct-disordered children. *Neuropsychopharmacology, 1,* 55-62.

Virkkunen, M. (1983). Insulin secretion during the glucose tolerance test in antisocial personality. *British Journal of Psychiatry, 142S,* 598-604.

Virkkunen, M. (1985). Urinary free cortisol secretion in habitually violent offenders. *Acta Psychiatrica Scandinavica, 229,* 449-504.

Virkkunen, M. (1986a). Insulin secretion during the glucose tolerance test among habitually violent and impulsive offenders. *Aggressive Behavior, 12,* 303-310.

Virkkunen, M. (1986b). Reactive hypoglycemic tendency among habitually violent offenders. *Nutrition Reviews, 44,* 94-103.

Virkkunen, M., DeJong, J., Goodwin, F. K., & Linnoila, M. (1987). Cerebrospinal fluid monoamine metabolite levels in male arsonists. *Archives of General Psychiatry, 11,* 241-247.

Virkkunen, M., DeJong, J., Goodwin, F. K., & Linnoila, M. (1989). Relationship of psychobiological variables to recidivism in violent offenders and impulsive fire setters. A follow-up study. *Archives of General Psychiatry, 46,* 600-603.

Virkkunen, M., & Närvänen, S. (1987). Plasma insulin, tryptophan and serotonin levels during the glucose tolerance test among habitually violent and impulsive offenders. *Neuropsychobiology, 17,* 19-23.

Virkkunen, M., Rawlings, R., Tokola, R., Kallio, E., Poland, R., Guidotti, A., Nemeroff, C., Bisette, G., Kalogeras, K., Rubinow, D., Karoner, S.-L., & Linnoila, M. (1992). *CSF biochemistries, glucose metabolism diurnal activity rhythms, personality profiles and state aggressiveness in Finnish violent offenders, impulsive fire setters, and healthy volunteers.* Manuscript submitted for publication.

Winblad, B., Gottfries, C. G., Oreland, L., & Wiberg, A. (1979). Monoamine oxidase in platelets and brains in non-psychiatric and non-neurological geriatric patients. *Medical Biology, 57,* 129-132.

Wurtman, J. J., Wurtman, R. J., Marks, S., Tsay, R., Gilbert, M., & Crowdon, J. (1985). D-fenfluramine selectively suppresses carbohydrate snacking in obese subjects. *International Journal of Eating Disorders, 4,* 89-99.

Yamamoto, H., Nagai, K., & Nagakava, H. (1984). Role of suprachiasmatic nucleus in glucose homeostasis. *Biomedical Research, 5,* 55-60.

Yamamoto, H., Nagai, K., & Nagakava, H. (1985). Lesions involving the suprachiasmatic nucleus eliminate the glucagon response to intracranial injections of 2-deoxy-D-glucose. *Endocrinology, 117,* 468-473.

Yodyingyuard, U., de LaRiva, C., Abbott, D. H., et al. (1985). Relationship between dominance hierarchy, cerebrospinal fluid levels and amine transmitter metabolites, (5-hydroxyindoleacetic acid and homovanillic acid) and plasma cortisol in monkeys. *Neuroscience, 16,* 851-858.

Young, W. R., Jr., Laws, E. R., Jr., Sharbrough, F. W., & Weinshilboum, R. M. (1986). Human monoamine oxidase. Lack of brain and platelet correlation. *Archives of General Psychiatry, 43,* 604-609.

13

Parental Psychopathology, Congenital Factors, and Violence

PATRICIA A. BRENNAN

BIRGITTE R. MEDNICK

SARNOFF A. MEDNICK

W e have used three methods of study—family, twin, and adoption— to assess the effect of genetic influences on criminal behavior. Adoption studies are best able to separate heredity and environmental influences on such behavior. For example, if the biological son of a severely criminal father is adopted at birth by a noncriminal family and that son becomes severely criminal, this may be seen as evidence (with appropriate controls) that the criminal father passed on to his son a biological characteristic that predisposed both men to criminal acts.

In our examination of the role of genetics in violent criminal behavior, we utilized an entire cohort of 14,427 nonfamilial adoptions in Denmark from 1924 to 1947 (Mednick, Gabrielli, & Hutchings, 1984). In Figure 13.1 we have plotted for this cohort the percentage of male adoptee violent and property offenders against biological parent convictions. Adoptee violent offenders may also have committed property crimes; however, no property offenders committed violent crimes.

As the figure reveals, a significant relationship exists between parents' convictions and property offending. A significant relationship does not exist for violent offending. In fact, the slight degree of relationship for violence in Figure 13.1 disappears if the property crimes of the violent offenders are partialled out.

AUTHORS' NOTE: This research was supported by National Institute of Mental Health grants No. 1-R01 MH46014-01 and No. 1-R01 MH41469-01, and by National Institute of Child Health and Development Grant No. N01-HD-62820.

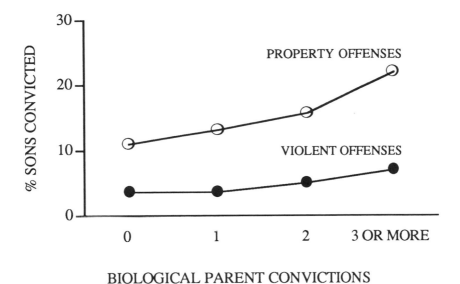

Figure 13.1. Percentage Male Adoptee Offenders and Violent Offenders by Biological Parent Convictions

Our conclusion from this study was that no direct genetic effect exists for violent criminal offending. However, later analyses of these adoption data suggested that genetics may play a role in violent criminal offending—for one particular group of criminal biological parents (Moffitt, 1984). As can be seen in the left side of Figure 13.2, the rates of violence are similarly low for the offspring of noncriminal biological parents and the offspring of recidivistically criminal biological parents (reflecting the nonsignificant finding discussed above). The right side of this figure reveals a significant increase in the rate of offspring violent offending, however, for one particular group of recidivistically criminal parents— those recidivists who had *also* been hospitalized one or more times for a psychiatric condition.

Parental Psychopathology and Violence

The findings from the above adoption studies have impelled us to take a closer look at the relationship between parental psychopathology and

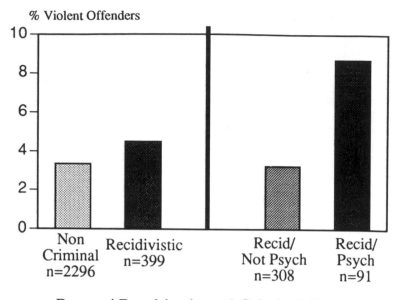

% Violent Offenders

Parents' Psychiatric and Criminal Status

Figure 13.2. Parent Recidivism and Psychopathology Predict Offspring Violent Crime in Adoption Cohort

offspring violent criminal behavior. To further assess this relationship we have utilized data drawn from a sample from a birth cohort of all 9,125 individuals born between September 1, 1959 and December 31, 1961 at Rigshospitalet in Copenhagen (Zachau-Christiansen & Ross, 1975). This sample ($n = 216$) was selected in 1972 to participate in a prospective study of children at high risk for delinquency. We will refer to this sample as the "psychopathology sample" as it consisted of 144 children with a parental history of psychopathology (hospital records of schizophrenia, psychopathy, or character disorder) and 72 matched controls. Controls were matched for sex of child, pregnancy number, sex of mentally ill parent, mother's age at delivery, father's age at delivery, social class at birth, and mother's height and weight.

Criminal records were assessed for the psychopathology sample when the subjects were between the ages of 20 and 22. Records were drawn from the Danish National Police Register, a comprehensive register of all criminal arrests and convictions in Denmark. All criminal data in this chapter reflect official arrests. Violent offenses include: domestic violence, illegal possession of a weapon, threats of violence, robbery, rape, assault, attempted murder, and murder. Following an initial examination of the very low frequency of violent offenses for females, all female subjects were dropped from the analyses. The final sample size was 108, with 72 male children of psychiatrically disturbed parents and 36 male control subjects.

A significant relationship was found between parent psychopathology and offspring criminal violence in this sample. Whereas 16.7% of the children of psychiatrically disturbed parents were arrested for at least one violent offense, only 2.8% of the control children had such an arrest on record [χ^2 (1, $N = 108$) = 4.37, $p < .05$].

The data from the psychopathology sample are consistent with the findings of the adoption studies—there does seem to be a relationship between parent psychopathology and offspring criminal violence. It is important to note, however, that only a small percentage of the children of the mentally ill are arrested for violent criminal behavior. Perhaps violent crime is influenced by some genetic characteristic that must be triggered by environmental events. Two prospective studies (Farrington, 1978; Olweus, 1979) have found that aggressive behavior is a stable characteristic from early childhood until adulthood, suggesting that these environmental triggers may occur at the very earliest stages of development—the prenatal and perinatal stages.

Perinatal Factors

In 1861, W. J. Little observed that "the act of birth does occasionally imprint upon the nervous and muscular systems of the nascent infantile organism very serious and peculiar evils." It was not until 1934 that Rosanoff and his coworkers (Rosanoff, Handy, & Plessett, 1934) suggested that adult behavioral deviance (schizophrenia) might be a consequence of perinatal events. Pasamanick, Rodgers, and Lilienfield (1956) studied the effect of obstetrical complications on behavior disorders in children. They found a significant relationship between such behavior disorders and prematurity, neonatal seizures, and pregnancy complications. Mungas (1983) noted a similar relationship between perinatal factors and violence in a sample of neuropsychiatric patients. Litt (1971) studied perinatal disturbances in a birth cohort of 1,944 individuals in Denmark born between January 1, 1936 and September 30, 1938. He discovered that perinatal trauma predicted impulsive criminal offenses that were ascertained at age 36.

The relationship between perinatal factors and criminal behavior seems to be particular to violent offending, rather than property or other less serious types of offending. In 1977, Lewis and Shanok reported nonsignificant differences between delinquents' and nondelinquents' perinatal histories. Later they compared nonincarcerated delinquents with incarcerated delinquents (who were significantly more violent), and discovered a positive relationship between more serious offending and perinatal difficulties. The combined results of these perinatal studies suggest that such factors are viable predictors of violent criminal behavior. A recent study from our laboratory suggests that these factors may also be particularly relevant for the development of criminal behavior in the offspring of the mentally ill.

In this study we found a significant relationship between delivery complications and violent criminal behavior for the members of the psychopathology sample described above (Kandel & Mednick, 1991). Delivery complications for each subject were recorded by the senior attending obstetrician at the time of the birth, and were assigned weights ranging from 0 (indicating no complication present) to 5 (indicating an extremely severe complication). Appropriate weights for the complications were established by a panel of American and Danish physicians (Mednick, Mura, Schulsinger, & Mednick, 1971). The delivery scale included such items as weak labor, forceps extraction, breech position, ruptured uterus, and umbilical cord prolapse. In calculating the scale score, the weights assigned to all relevant items were summed, yielding a cumulative weighted score for each subject. For purposes of analysis, the median delivery, complications score for the high-risk sample was used to split subjects into two groups—those with high numbers of delivery complications and those with low numbers of delivery complications. Both males and females were included in these analyses. Figure 13.3 presents the frequencies of nonoffenders, property offenders, and violent offenders in the high-risk sample with low and high numbers of delivery complications.

As can be seen from this figure, only 46.9% of the nonoffenders and 29.1% of the property offenders had high numbers of delivery complications. In contrast, 80% of the violent offenders evidenced high numbers of delivery complications. The distributional difference between nonoffenders and property offenders is not statistically significant [χ^2 (1, $N = 201$) = 2.90, p = ns], but the difference between nonoffenders and violent offenders is significant [χ^2 (1, $N = 192$) = 6.33, $p < .05$]. It is also interesting to note that all 7 (100%) of the *recidivistic* violent offenders in the cohort scored "high" on the delivery complications scale.

Upon a closer examination of the above analyses, it was revealed that the relationship between delivery complications and violent criminal

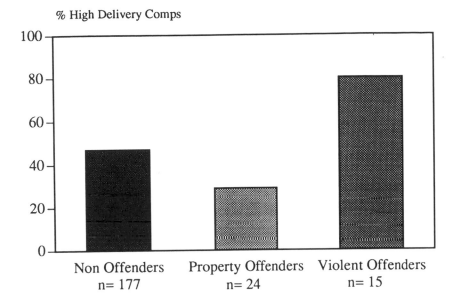

% High Delivery Comps

Figure 13.3. Percentage High Delivery Complications as a Function of Criminal Offending in the Psychopathology Sample

behavior existed only for the subjects who had psychiatrically disturbed parents, and not for the subjects in the control group.

Due to the aforementioned low rates of violence for females, and because of our sole focus on violence in this chapter, we examined the relationship between delivery complications and violent arrests for only the males in the psychopathology sample. We discovered a similar pattern of results as those noted above. Figure 13.4 compares the violent offending of male subjects with high and low delivery complications scales in two different groups: (a) those whose parents were psychiatrically disturbed, and (b) those whose parents were not psychiatrically disturbed. In the disturbed parent group, only 5.0% of the male subjects with low delivery complications were arrested for violence compared to 32.26% of the male subjects with high delivery complications [χ^2 (1, $N = 71$) = 9.24, $p < .01$]. The corresponding rates of violence for male children of psychiatrically normal parents were 4.8% for individuals with low delivery complications and 0.0% for individuals with high delivery complications. This difference is not significant [χ^2 (1, $N = 36$) = 0.74, p = ns].

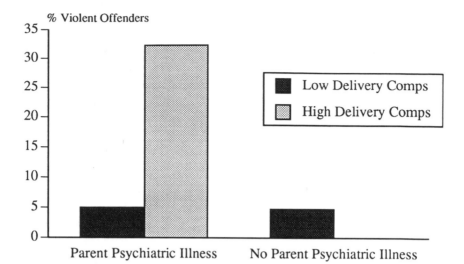

Figure 13.4. Delivery Complications and Violent Offending in Psychopathology Sample

The above findings suggest that although perinatal factors may play a triggering role in the genetic relationship between parental psychiatric status and offspring criminal violence, such factors do not seem to play a role in the development of violence in the children of psychiatrically normal individuals. This finding is consistent with studies in behavioral genetic research that have revealed a genetically determined vulnerability to teratogens. Mankes, Rosenblum, Benitz, Lefevre, and Abraham (1982) found individual differences in Long Evans rats in susceptibility to teratogens during gestation, based on their genetic background. Detrimental outcomes were dependent on *both* the genetic influence and the presence of perinatal factors.

From the above findings it seems plausible that perinatal events such as delivery complications may trigger violence in those with mental illness in their family background. However, the above analyses reveal that 67% of the male offspring of psychiatrically disturbed parents, who also evidenced high numbers of delivery complications, did *not* become criminally violent. It is possible that only some of the children of the mentally ill have the specific genetic factor that is triggered by perinatal complications. Therefore only these children would evidence an increase in the propensity for criminal violence.

Hyperactivity and Minimal Brain Damage

In those cases where perinatal factors do act as a triggering event, it may be that these factors lead to a central nervous system (CNS) malfunction, which in turn increases the likelihood of violent criminal behavior. In support of this hypothesis, several researchers have noted significantly more CNS deficits in adult violent offenders when compared to controls (Elliott, 1978; Fitzhugh, 1973; Krynicki, 1978; Yeudall, Fromm-Auch, & Davies, 1982). Moreover, perinatal complications have been found to be associated with adult brain anomalies in a variety of populations (Brann, 1985; Lewis & Murray, 1987; Pearlson, Garbacz, Moberg, Ahn, & dePaulo, 1985; Silverton, Finello, Mednick, & Schulsinger, 1985; Turner, Toone, & Brett-Jones, 1986).

We next examined whether there would be a higher level of violent arrests for those offspring of psychiatrically disturbed parents who had suffered CNS damage as a result of perinatal difficulties. We chose the behavioral syndrome of hyperactivity as an established observable indicant of CNS damage in our subjects. Hyperactive children have been found to have higher levels of neurological soft signs and more abnormal EEG readings than normal controls (Werry et al., 1972). Hyperactive children have also been found to have significantly more minor physical anomalies (MPAs) than nonhyperactive children (Fogel, Mednick, & Michelsen, 1985; Quinn & Rapoport, 1974; Waldrop, Bell, McLaughlin, & Halverson, 1978), and MPAs are considered indicators of CNS damage that has occurred prenatally (Smith, 1970). Hyperactivity in children has also been found to be genetically related to several parental psychiatric disorders including sociopathy, hysteria, and alcoholism (August & Stewart, 1983; Cadoret, Cunningham, Loftus, & Edwards, 1975; Cantwell, 1972). For all of these reasons, hyperactivity was chosen as a behavioral indicant for our analyses of the relationship among perinatal factors, apparent CNS damage, and violent criminal behavior.

In the follow-up of the psychopathology sample described above, a pediatric neurologist examined each of the subjects in 1972 when they were between 11 and 13 years of age. As a part of his examination he assessed each of the subject's behavior through the use of an extensive behavior rating scale. Five items (activity levels, concentration levels, restlessness, distractibility, and fussiness/fidgetiness) were selected from this rating scale to form a measure of childhood hyperactive behavior (Fogel et al., 1985). Reliability analysis of this rating scale resulted in an alpha coefficient of .92.

Most of the subjects obtained a score of zero on this measure of hyperactive behavior; they are considered nonhyperactive for the purposes of this study. Those subjects with scores greater than zero on this measure were classified as hyperactive.

Figure 13.5 shows the relationship among delivery complications, hyperactivity, and violent criminal behavior for the offspring of the psychiatrically disturbed parents in the psychopathology sample. The rate of violence is plotted for the following four groups of male subjects: (1) hyperactive/high delivery complications ($n = 13$), (2) hyperactive/low delivery complications ($n = 12$), (3) nonhyperactive/high delivery complications ($n = 18$), and (4) nonhyperactive/low delivery complications ($n = 28$). According to a logistic regression analysis, there is significant interaction between hyperactivity and delivery complications in the prediction of violent offending [χ^2 (1, $N = 71$) = 12.50, $p < .001$]. Whereas 3.57% of the nonhyperactive/low delivery complications group, 16.67% of the nonhyperactive/high delivery complications group, and 8.33% of the hyperactive/low delivery complications group evidenced violence, more than 53% of the subjects in the hyperactive/high delivery complications group had been arrested for a violent crime.

This finding suggests that in cases where perinatal factors have resulted in CNS damage, an increase in violent criminal behavior is found. This pattern of results is particular to the children of psychiatrically disturbed parents in this sample.

Confounding Factors

Several factors may serve as confounds in the study of the relationship among parent psychiatric status, perinatal status, childhood hyperactivity, and violent criminal outcome. For example, socioeconomic status has been found to be related to both perinatal status and violent offending (Clelland & Carter, 1980). Father's criminal status has been found to be related to mother's psychiatric status via cross-assortative mating (Kirkegaard-Sorensen & Mednick, 1977) and to rates of criminal arrests in the male offspring (Mednick et al., 1984). Both childhood conduct disorder and cognitive deficits have been found to be significantly correlated with hyperactivity and with adult criminal behavior (Hirschi & Hindelang, 1977; Olweus, 1979; Robins, 1978). At the relatively young age of follow-up (ages 20 to 22) any differences in the ages of subjects across comparison groups may also act to confound the findings.

Due to the many confounding factors that were possible, the relationship among perinatal factors, hyperactivity, and violent crime in the offspring of the mentally ill was reexamined, controlling for such factors. In the psychopathology sample, the interactive effect of childhood hyperactivity

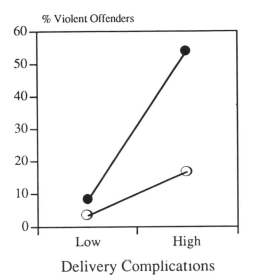

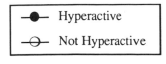

Figure 13.5. Delivery Complications and Hyperactivity Predict to Violent Criminal Offenses in the Psychopathology Sample

and delivery complications on violent crime remained significant when the possible confounds of age, socioeconomic status, childhood conduct problems, father's criminality, and childhood IQ were controlled through logistic regression [χ^2 (1, $N = 71$) = 9.39, $p < .01$]. This suggests that our findings are not a reflection of a spurious relationship between our predictors, possible confounds, and violent criminal arrest.

Overall, the findings from the psychopathology sample suggest that a genetic factor in the children of the mentally ill may act to predispose them to criminal violence. This genetic factor may be triggered by perinatal factors with the result being CNS damage that is characterized by impulsive, fast-moving behavior and a short attention span. The CNS damage triggered by perinatal factors, in turn, results in an increased propensity for criminal violence.

Replication

The psychopathology sample, upon which the previous analyses were based, is a very select sample of individuals. The subjects were chosen for the sample based on the psychiatric status of their parents. Therefore this sample does not adequately represent the birth cohort as a whole. In addition, the size of the control group was small. Due to these methodological concerns with the psychopathology sample, a second sample was examined with the overall result being a replication of the above findings.

This second sample was also drawn from the Rigshospitalet birth cohort. This sample was a randomly chosen 10% subsample of the original birth cohort ($n = 857$). Once again females were dropped from the analyses due to their low rates of violent offending. The remaining sample consisted of 420 males. Violent crime was also assessed for these subjects at the age of 20 to 22 years. Criminal data were drawn from the National Police Register, arrests were used as the unit of analysis, and violent offenses were defined in the same manner as they were in the psychopathology sample.

Parental psychiatric status, however, was defined somewhat differently in this random sample. Parents were considered to be psychiatrically disturbed if they had a recorded hospitalization for schizophrenia, affective psychoses, psychopathy, or character disorder. Mothers who were being prescribed psychopharmacological medications during the child's adolescence were also placed into the category of psychiatrically disturbed. This classification of parental psychopathology includes milder disorders and resulted in a total of 108 male subjects with psychiatrically disturbed parents, and 312 male subjects with psychiatrically normal parents.

A significant relationship was again found between parent psychopathology and offspring violent criminal behavior in this random sample. Whereas 14.8% of the parent-disturbed subjects were arrested for violence, only 6.73% of the parent-nondisturbed subjects were found to have such an arrest on their record [χ^2 (1, $N = 420$) = 6.53, $p < .05$]. These findings replicate those of the psychopathology sample and are consistent with the adoption studies that have found a genetic relationship between parental psychopathology and offspring antisocial behavior.

We next examined the effect of delivery complications on violence in the randomly drawn sample. As this sample was also drawn from the Rigshospitalet cohort, the same delivery complications scale was utilized. Once again, subjects were split on the sample's median score into high and low levels of delivery complications. Figure 13.6 presents the relationship between delivery complications and violence for the children of psychiatrically disturbed parents and the children of nonpsychiatrically disturbed parents. The pattern of results is similar to that found in the psychopathology sample—high delivery complications appear to increase the tendency for violence for the children of psychiatrically disturbed parents but not

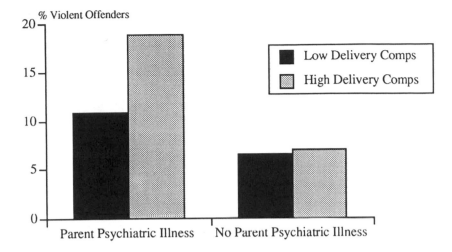

Figure 13.6. Delivery Complications and Violent Offending in the Random Sample

for the children of nonpsychiatrically disturbed parents. In the parent disturbed group, 10.9% of the subjects with low delivery complications and 18.9% of the subjects with high delivery complications evidenced violence. Although this finding is in the same direction as the results from the high-risk sample, this difference is not significant [χ^2 (1, $N = 108$) = 1.36, p = ns]. It is important to note that in the nondisturbed parent group, the rates of violence for those with high and low delivery complications were almost exactly the same—6.5% for low delivery complications and 6.9% for high delivery complications [χ^2 (1, $N = 312$) = 0.03, p = ns].

Although the pattern of results was similar in the random sample, delivery complications were not found to significantly predict to violence in the offspring of the mentally ill. This result may be explained by the more liberal definition of *parent psychopathology* in this sample. Or this result may be explained by the interaction between delivery complications and hyperactivity noted above. The interaction findings from the psychopathology sample suggested that it was only in those cases where the delivery complications led to CNS damage that an increase in violence was evident. Individuals with high numbers of delivery complications and no hyperactivity were *not* found to have an increased tendency for violent crime.

We next examined whether this interaction of hyperactivity and perinatal factors in predicting violent crime was apparent in the offspring of the psychiatrically disturbed parents in the random sample from the Rigshospitalet cohort. The follow-up of the random sample included an extensive interview of the mother administered when the subjects were between 18 and 22 years of age. Included in this interview were retrospective questions concerning the behavior of the subjects as young children. Three behavioral items from this retrospective account were found to assess for hyperactive behavior. These items were: Did you think the child was restless?, Would you say the child was good at concentrating?, and Did you think the child was passive, active, or overly active? For the purposes of classification for analysis, subjects were considered hyperactive if their mother responded to at least two of these three items in the direction that suggested hyperactivity or attentional problems. Thirty of the 108 male subjects with psychiatrically disturbed parents were classified as hyperactive according to this method.

Figure 13.7 shows the relationship between delivery complications, hyperactivity, and violent offending for the male offspring of the psychiatrically disturbed parents in this second sample. The group with high numbers of delivery complications and childhood hyperactive behavior was found to have an elevated level of arrests for violent crime. Logistic regression reveals a significant interaction between delivery complications and hyperactivity in their prediction of violent arrests [χ^2 (1, $N =$ 108) = 4.10, $p < .05$]. More than 30% of this group (group $n = 16$) had at least one arrest for violence compared to 14.3% of the hyperactive/low delivery complications group (group $n = 14$), 13.5% of the nonhyperactive/high delivery complications group (group $n = 37$), and 9.8% of the nonhyperactive/low delivery complications group (group $n = 41$). The interaction between delivery complications and hyperactivity significantly predicted to violent arrests when age, socioeconomic status, childhood conduct disorder, childhood school performance, and parents' criminality were controlled through logistic regression [χ^2 (1, $N = 108$) = 5.14, $p < .05$].

It should be noted that there was no interaction between hyperactivity and delivery complications for the children of psychiatrically normal parents in this random sample.

The interaction findings from the random sample replicate those from the psychopathology sample. Overall, these findings support the contention that perinatal damage and CNS deficits combine to increase the likelihood of criminal violence in the offspring of the mentally ill. Perhaps for some individuals the genetic predisposition to violence is triggered by perinatal damage that results in CNS damage characterized by impulsive, acting-out behavior. Those impulsive, acting-out individuals then become far more likely than other individuals to be arrested for a violent offense. It was noted that neither perinatal factors nor the combination of perinatal

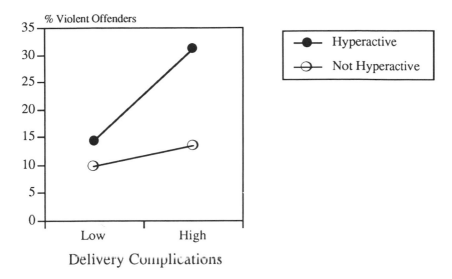

Figure 13.7. Delivery Complications and Hyperactivity Predict to Violent Criminal Offenses in the Random Sample

factors and hyperactivity predicted to violence in the offspring of psychiatrically normal parents. This suggests that parental psychopathology is a necessary component in this developmental process.

Methodological Concerns

Several possible methodological concerns with the studies are presented in this chapter. One methodological consideration particular to the random sample from the Rigshospitalet cohort is the measure that was employed for childhood hyperactive behavior. It is important to question whether the retrospective reports of psychiatrically disturbed mothers are reliable indicators of child behavior difficulties. Several factors suggest that this measure is indeed reliable. First, the results obtained with this parental report of hyperactivity are similar to those obtained with the neurologist's measure of this behavior. Second, the data reveal that the mothers discriminated between hyperactive, aggressive, and other behavior difficulties in their rating of their children. This suggests that these reports are not simply a reflection of their general attitude toward the child. Finally, the mothers in all of the comparison groups of this sample were rated as equally reliable

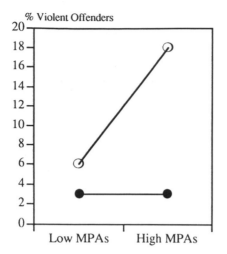

Figure 13.8. Percentage Violent Offenders as a Function of MPAs and Delivery Complications

historians by the interviewers, suggesting that this was not a confounding factor in our results.

One other methodological concern with the above studies is the assumption that our findings for hyperactive behavior are actually reflecting our theoretical stance that perinatally caused CNS damage plays a role in the development of violence in the offspring of the mentally ill. In other words, is hyperactivity a viable measure of CNS deficits in our subjects? An indirect assessment of this question can be made by reviewing a previous finding from the psychopathology sample of the Rigshospitalet cohort. As stated above, minor physical anomalies (MPAs) are thought to be a reflection of the disruption of CNS development during gestation. This particular measure of CNS damage has also been found to interact with delivery complications in the prediction of violence in our high-risk sample. As can be seen in Figure 13.8, those subjects who had both high numbers of MPAs and high numbers of delivery complications were significantly more likely than the other subjects in the sample to evidence violent crime.

Previous studies have found a relationship between hyperactivity and CNS damage (Werry et al., 1972). We have also found that this behavioral indicant of CNS deficits acts in a manner similar to MPAs (a physical indicant of CNS deficits) in its prediction of violence. Therefore we suggest that our findings concerning hyperactivity are a reflection of our theoretical stance that perinatal factors interact with CNS damage to predict to violent criminal behavior.

We have discussed the effect of parent psychopathology as a genetic influence, rather than an environmental influence on the children in the development of violent crime. While it is likely that the family environment is also quite adversely affected by the presence of mental illness in one or both parents, evidence for this genetic argument can be found in the adoption studies that have found a relationship between parent psychopathology and offspring antisocial behavior (Cadoret et al., 1975; Heston, 1966; Kety, Rosenthal, Wender, & Schulsinger, 1974; Moffitt, 1984).

There is one other very important alternative explanation for our findings that should be addressed. We have found that perinatal factors and delivery complications predict to violent offending in the offspring of the mentally ill. The data on violent criminal behavior were gathered when the subjects were between 20 and 22 years of age. Thus far there has been no further follow-up of these subjects. We do not have any knowledge about the current psychiatric status of these subjects, but we do know that those subjects with psychiatrically disturbed parents are more likely to evidence psychiatric disorders themselves. We have also found that delivery and other perinatal conditions are predictive of psychiatric disorders in high-risk children (Cannon et al., 1989). Given the possible overlap of crime and mental illness within individuals, our findings may be confounded by eventual adult psychiatric status. This possibility can be assessed in the very near future as we are in the process of obtaining follow-up psychiatric data for all members of the Rigshospitalet cohort.

In summary, our research to date suggests that the genetic influence of a psychiatrically disturbed parent may act to predispose some individuals to violent criminal behavior. When this genetic factor is triggered by environmental events in the perinatal stages, the result is a particular type of CNS damage that leads to impulsive acting-out behavior in childhood and an increased likelihood for violent criminal behavior later in life.

References

August, G. J., & Stewart, M. A. (1983). Familial subtypes of childhood hyperactivity. *The Journal of Nervous and Mental Disease, 171,* 362-368.

Brann, A. W. (1985). Factors during neonatal life that influence brain disorders. In J. M. Freeman (Ed.), *Prenatal and perinatal factors associated with brain disorders* (pp. 263-358). Washington, DC: National Institute of Health.

Cadoret, R. J., Cunningham, L., Loftus, R., & Edwards, J. (1975). Studies of adoptees from psychiatrically disturbed biologic parents II. *The Journal of Pediatrics, 87,* 301-306.

Cantwell, D. P. (1972). Psychiatric illness in the families of hyperactive children. *Archives of General Psychiatry, 27*, 414-418.

Clelland, D., & Carter, T. J. (1980). The new myth of class and crime. *Criminology, 18*, 319-336.

Elliott, F. A. (1978). Neurological aspects of antisocial behavior. In W. H. Reid (Ed), *The psychopath* (pp. 146-189). New York: Bruner/Mazel.

Farrington, D. P. (1978). The family backgrounds of aggressive youths. In L. A. Hersov, M. Berger, & D. Schaffer (Eds.), *Aggression and anti-social behavior in childhood and adolescence* (pp. 73-93). Oxford: Pergamon.

Fitzhugh, K. B. (1973). Some neuropsychological features of delinquent subjects. *Perceptual and Motor Skills, 36*, 494.

Fogel, C. A., Mednick, S. A., & Michelsen, N. (1985). Hyperactive behavior and minor physical anomalies. *Acta Psychiatrica Scandinavia, 75*, 551-556.

Heston, L. L. (1966). Psychiatric disorders in foster home reared children of schizophrenic mothers. *British Journal of Psychiatry, 112*, 819-825.

Hirschi, T., & Hindelang, M. J. (1977). Intelligence and delinquency: A revisionist review. *American Sociological Review, 42*, 571-587.

Kandel, E., & Mednick, S. A. (1991). Perinatal complications predict violent offending. *Criminology, 29*, 519-529.

Kety, S. S., Rosenthal, D., Wender, P. H., & Schulsinger, F. (1974). The types and prevalence of mental illness in the biological and adoptive families of adopted schizophrenics. In S. A. Mednick, F. Schulsinger, J. Higgins, & B. Bell (Eds.), *Genetics, environment, and psychopathology* (pp. 345-362). New York: Elsevier-North Holland.

Kirkegaard-Sorensen, L., & Mednick, S. A. (1977). A prospective study of predictors of criminality: A description of registered criminality in the high-risk and low-risk families. In S. A. Mednick & K. O. Christiansen (Eds.), *Biosocial basis of criminal behavior* (pp. 229-244). New York: Gardner.

Krynicki, V. E. (1978). Cerebral dysfunction in repetitively assaultive adolescents. *The Journal of Nervous and Mental Disease, 166*, 59-67.

Lewis, D. O., & Shanok, S. S. (1977). Medical histories of delinquent and nondelinquent children: An epidemiological study. *American Journal of Psychiatry, 134*, 1020-1025.

Lewis, S. W., & Murray, R. M. (1987). Obstetric complications, neurodevelopmental deviance, and risk for schizophrenia. *Journal of Psychiatric Research, 21*, 413-421.

Litt, S. M. (1971). *Perinatal complications and criminality.* Unpublished doctoral dissertation, University of Michigan.

Little, W. J. (1861). On the influence of abnormal parturition, difficult labours, premature birth and asphyxia nonatorum on the mental and physical condition of the child, especially in relation to deformities. *Transactions of the Obstetrical Society of London, 3*, 293-344.

Mankes, R. F., Rosenblum, I., Benitz, K., LeFevre, R., & Abraham, R. (1982). Teratogenic and reproductive effects of ethanol in Long-Evans rats. *The Journal of Toxicology and Environmental Health, 10*, 267-276.

Mednick, S. A., Gabrielli, W. F., & Hutchings, B. (1984). Genetic influences in criminal convictions: Evidence from an adoption cohort. *Science, 224*, 891-894.

Mednick, S. A., Mura, E., Schulsinger, F., & Mednick, B. (1971). Perinatal conditions and infant development in the children of schizophrenic parents. *Social Biology, 18*, 5103-5113.

Moffitt, T. E. (1984). *Genetic influences of parental psychiatric illness of violent and recidivistic criminal behavior.* Unpublished doctoral dissertation, University of Southern California.

Mungas, D. (1983). An empirical analysis of specific syndromes of violent behavior. *The Journal of Nervous and Mental Disease, 171,* 354-361.

Olweus, D. (1979). Stability of aggressive reaction patterns in males: A review. *Psychological Bulletin, 86,* 852-875.

Pasamanick, B., Rodgers, M. E., & Lilienfield, A. M. (1956). Pregnancy experience and the development of behavior disorders in children. *American Journal of Psychiatry, 112,* 613-618.

Pearlson, G. C., Garbacz, D. J., Moberg, P. J., Ahn, H. S., & dePaulo, J. R. (1985). Symptomatic, familial, perinatal, and social correlates of CAT changes in schizophrenics and bipolars. *The Journal of Nervous and Mental Disease, 173,* 42-50.

Quinn, P. O., & Rapoport, J. L. (1974). Minor physical anomalies and neurological status in hyperactive boys. *Pediatrics, 53,* 742-747.

Robins, L. (1978). Sturdy childhood predictors of adult antisocial behavior: Replications from longitudinal studies. *Psychological Medicine, 8,* 611-622.

Rosanoff, A. J., Handy, L. M., & Plessett, I. R. (1934). The etiology of manic-depressive syndrome with special reference to their occurrence in twins. *American Journal of Psychiatry, 91,* 247-286.

Silverton, L., Finello, K., Mednick, S. A., & Schulsinger, F. (1985). Low birthweight and ventricular enlargement in a high risk sample. *Journal of Abnormal Psychology, 94,* 402-407.

Smith, D. W. (1970). *Recognizable patterns of human malformation.* Philadelphia: J. B. Saunders.

Turner, S. W., Toone, B. K., & Brett-Jones, J. R. (1986). Computerized tomographic scan changes in early schizophrenia. *Psychological Medicine, 16,* 219-225.

Waldrop, M. F., Bell, R. A., McLaughlin, B., & Halverson, C. F. (1978). Newborn minor physical anomalies predict short attention span, peer aggression, and impulsivity at age 3. *Science, 199,* 563-564.

Werry, J. S., Minde, K., Guzman, A., Weiss, G., Dogan, K., & Hoy, E. (1972). Studies on the hyperactive child—VII: Neurological status compared with neurotic and normal children. *American Journal of Orthopsychiatry, 42,* 441-451.

Yeudall, L. T., Fromm-Auch, D., & Davies, P. (1982). Neuropsychological impairment of persistent delinquency. *The Journal of Nervous and Mental Disease, 170,* 257-265.

Zachau-Christiansen. B., & Ross, E. M. (1975). *Babies: Human development during the first year.* New York: Riley.

14

Alcohol/Drug Use and Aggressive Behavior

ROBERT O. PIHL

JORDAN B. PETERSON

Rates of interpersonal violence appear to be increasing in U.S. society. In the United States today, the homicide rate is roughly double what it was in 1960; violence is the leading cause of death for individuals under 45 years of age; a rape, a murder, or an assault occurs every 25 seconds; and six million individuals each year are victims of violent crime (Langan & Innes, 1985). At various times observers have attributed this apparent increase in aggression to many different factors. The breakdown of the nuclear family, the collapse of the moral community structure, and the presence of nonstop violence on television have all been implicated. Currently, however, the number one candidate is drug abuse.

Two questions must be addressed by anyone interested in considering the relationship between drug use and violence. To begin with, how is drug-related violence associated with the distribution of illegal drugs, and/or with the concomitant "war" that has evolved? Nadelmann (1989) lists four possible modes of connection. The pharmacological effect of drugs of abuse is irrelevant, with regards to three of these modes. First, illicit drug users commit crimes, sometimes violent crimes, to gain access to drugs. Second, drug use and violent behavior exist coincidentally because the factors (e.g., antisocial personality) that predispose to both may be similar. Third, those involved in the drug trade necessarily resolve issues/disputes by violent means. This chapter focuses on Nadelmann's fourth connection, the second question: How does the ingestion of certain drugs affect aggression? More specifically, this chapter will concentrate on the relationship between alcohol and aggression,

AUTHORS' NOTE: This research was supported by the Medical Research Council of Canada, by the Douglas Hospital/McGill University Alcohol Research Group, and by the Brewers Foundation of North America.

as it is in this domain that a substantial body of clinical and experimental knowledge exists. Enough information appears to exist to justify development of theories accounting for the alcohol-intoxication/aggression relationship, and one such theory is described later. This chapter additionally includes a brief discussion concerning the nature of the relationship between use of other drugs and violence.

Another, more specific, way to phrase the immediate question of concern is: How are the neurochemical processes and neurological circuits that control aggressive behavior affected by chemical intoxication? While this question is definitely germane, its utility is limited by a number of factors. First, an extensive body of literature remains conflicted as to the neurochemical and physical bases of aggression. Second, aggression is a behavioral concept, and cannot be regarded solely as a physiological process, except at a very primitive level. Any theory that attempts to account for drug-induced aggression must therefore be able to account for variance introduced by factors of personality, previous learning, and immediate context. Third, and finally, the picture is complicated by the fact that the neurochemical circuits affected by particular drugs are in many cases nonspecific in fact, or are poorly identified for methodological reasons.

Alcohol and Violence

Crime statistics and controlled experiments both demonstrate that heavy drinking and violence co-occur. Studies analyzing crime statistics are unusually unanimous. Alcohol-intoxicated individuals are involved in the majority of violent crimes, including murders, assaults, sexual assaults, and family violence (Brain, 1986; Collins, 1981; Murdoch, Pihl, & Ross, 1990; Pernanen, 1976, 1981). Murdoch et al. (1990) examined 9,304 cases reported in 26 studies from 11 countries. Overall, 62% of violent offenders were drinking at the time of the crime. Comparison between studies revealed that the range of alcohol-related violent crime was 24% to 85%, which contrasted dramatically with the range reported for alcohol-related nonviolent crimes: 12% to 38%. It might be argued additionally that these figures are underestimates as it is an irregular and relatively recent occurrence for police to record physical measures of alcohol use. Typically, in most crime reports, there is merely a statement that the perpetrator of the crime was intoxicated. Those few studies examining physical measures of inebriation have concluded that individuals involved in violence were often drinking heavily, to levels well above those of legal intoxication (Mayfield, 1976; Shupe, 1954).

Murdoch et al.'s (1990) review of 26 studies also demonstrated that 45% of victims of violence were intoxicated when victimized. One of the first studies of victim-precipitated homicide found that 60% of victims had been drinking heavily (Wolfgang & Strohan, 1956). This figure compares with that of the 47% estimated for victims drinking in offender-precipitated cases. The fact that each individual involved in a violent encounter is likely intoxicated might simply be a function of the environment in which aggression is likely to be expressed, rather than an effect of alcohol per se. In addition, crime statistics might also be affected by the fact that intoxicated individuals are perhaps both more likely to be apprehended and less likely to provide appropriate aid to their victims. Thus there are sufficient arguments to challenge any notion of causality in regard to the alcohol-aggression relationship, in the context of the real world. Nonetheless controlled laboratory studies also demonstrate that a relationship between alcohol and violence exists, and suggest that intoxication may play a direct role in increasing aggression and victimization.

Laboratory Studies and Theories of Intoxicated Behavior

A recent meta-analytic review of 30 experimental studies concluded that "alcohol does indeed cause aggression" (Bushman & Cooper, 1990, p. 341). Nonetheless the alcohol-aggression relationship is hardly direct. Numerous variables act as strong modifiers, as Bushman and Cooper (1990) and the authors of several additional alcohol-aggression reviews have noted (Evans, 1980; Pihl, 1983; Pihl & Ross, 1987; Taylor, 1983). Alcohol intoxication by no means provides the necessary and sufficient precondition for aggressive behavior. Anthropological studies (reviewed in MacAndrew & Edgerton, 1969) illustrate this fact, demonstrating large cultural variations in aggression-linked intoxicated behavior. MacAndrew and Edgerton (1969) detail the consequences of extreme drunkenness among members of numerous cultures, and note little change in social behavior when the drinking occurs in certain well-defined contexts. In addition, the behavior of intoxicated women in general is not congruent with that of intoxicated men, and there is of course marked variability in aggression among drunk males. In fact, the experimental studies on alcohol and aggression appear to demonstrate that various cognitions, social pressures, and dispositions toward aggressive behavior both increase and decrease alcohol-related aggression.

Theorists of intoxicated aggression (reviewed by Bushman & Cooper, 1990; Graham, 1980) posit that alcohol produces aggression because of disinhibition, stimulation-arousal, and/or because of social expectancies.

Theories of disinhibition postulate that normal physiological and/or cognitive processes are reduced or rendered dysfunctional during intoxication. These theories are predicated on the assumption that aggression results from an absence or dimunition of normal behavioral braking, which occurs either because relevant brain areas are reduced in function and/or because relevant cognitive processing is obviated. Arousal theorists adopt the opposite position, hypothesizing that those physical mechanisms involved in aggressive behavior are directly stimulated by the ingestion of alcohol. The accelerator is depressed, so to speak, and relevant brain areas are ignited. Finally, social-expectancy theorists posit psychological reasons for aggression and argue that alcohol simply provides a rationale for unacceptable behavior—they blame the bottle. A variation of this position is that the problem is situational: Drinking occurs in provocative environments, likely in themselves to increase aggression. These theoretical views are neither mutually exclusive nor collectively exhaustive. Recent experiments conducted in the authors' laboratory have produced results that would support or rebut each of these general theoretical positions, if considered individually.

An Interactive Process

Figure 14.1 is based upon the obvious conclusion that any explanation of the alcohol-aggression relationship cannot be predicated upon purely pharmacological, cognitive, or social considerations. Each factor modifies the other in turn and is further modified by the resultant behavior. This conclusion is not posited to negate theory-building, as the presence of each of these factors contributes to the final consequence. Indeed, the nature of each of these factors must first be assessed, and specific predictive statements generated and tested before modes of interaction can finally be identified. Prior to discussing the role of alcohol per se in producing aggression (and briefly commenting upon the contributing role of each additional factor), some basic issues of methodology and definition must be addressed.

It has proved difficult to determine precisely how the central nervous system is affected by ethanol. Alcohol flows through the body like water, and easily penetrates the blood-brain barrier. It bathes all of the body's tissues. Ethanol's effects are dependent upon dose, rate of administration, time passed postconsumption, and subject characteristics that are determined by genetic factors and by previous drinking experience. Doses below 0.5 mL 95% USP alcohol/kg of body weight produce relatively insignificant effects on the cognitive, psychophysiological, and motor functioning of experienced social drinking nonalcoholic young men (Peterson,

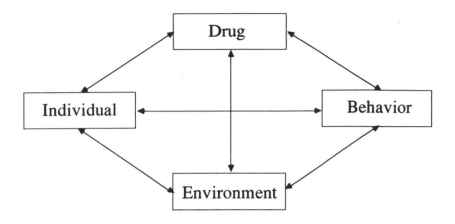

Figure 14.1. A Priori Factors Affecting the Drug-Behavior Relationship

Rothfleisch, Zelazo, & Pihl, 1990; Pihl, 1983). Extremely high doses of ethanol are capable of producing severe motor impairment and unconsciousness. Most laboratory studies of ethanol effects examine the consequences of intoxication produced by doses that are at the lower end of the range defined by these two extremes. It is the effect of alcohol, at doses high enough to have a measurable effect (but too low to produce excessive loss of coordination or unconsciousness), that provides the specific focus of this discussion.

The nature of aggression itself must also be considered. Aggressive behavior takes place in a variety of contexts, but most experimental work has been conducted within the confines of the Buss-Taylor paradigm. Within this paradigm, two subjects, one real, one confederate, participate in an experimental task. The experimental subject is required to exchange electric shocks, or an alternative punishing stimuli, with the confederate, for reasons that vary from experiment to experiment. The intensity and duration of this voluntarily administered punishment varies with subject choice, within certain confines established by the experimenter. *Aggression* is defined as intensity and duration of stimulus administered. There is evidence that aggression can be validly and reliably measured in this fashion (Bernstein, Richardson, & Hammock, 1987). Buss-Taylor procedure scores correlate positively with peer-rated aggression (Williams, Meyerson, Eron, & Semler, 1967) and self-rated oppression (Shemberg, Leventhal, & Allman, 1968), and with degree of previous antisocial behavior (Hartman, 1969).

Aggression (or active avoidance) can be reliably elicited by at least two classes of stimuli, punishment and frustrative nonreward (Gray, 1982, 1987). The Buss-Taylor task essentially punishes the experimental subject by exposure to electric shock. Most modifications of this procedure alter the context within which that shock is received, by manipulating the expectancies of the experimental subject, or by frustrating him or her, in addition to the punishment. In normal, sober human beings (and in experimental animals) the context within which any stimulus is received modifies the behavioral response that stimulus elicits. This is especially obvious in the case of *frustrative nonreward,* which is defined as the absence of a reward that the subject expects. Without expectancy, which is the context within which the experimental manipulation takes place, frustration is impossible. In addition, the consequences of a behavioral response should modify that response. Any behavior has certain benefits and certain costs, which should in turn come to alter the expression of that behavior, in an organism capable of benefiting from experience. Consideration of these methodological and theoretical issues further limits the topic of this chapter to the effects of moderate doses of alcohol on aggression elicited by punishment and frustration, presented within a variety of different experimental and ecological contexts.

Three Effects of Alcohol

Three alcohol effects appear to heighten significantly the likelihood of aggression: increased pain sensitivity, reduced response to cues of punishment and cues of frustrative nonreward, and decrease in response flexibility. Figure 14.2 illustrates how each of these putative effects independently or collectively might increase aggression.

Increased Pain Sensitivity

Pain-elicited aggressive behavior is the most consistent stimulus for aggression among most animals. Fight or flight only partially summarizes a phenomenon that occurs in response to "psychological" pain (like frustration) and that appears unconditioned, nonappetitive, and displaceable (Berkowitz, 1983; Moyer, 1976). The idea that alcohol may actually increase pain sensitivity in some individuals might seem counterintuitive, given that the pain-reducing effects of alcohol are well known and that alcohol was one of the first anesthetics ever used (Mullin & Luckhardt, 1934; Wolff, Hardy, & Goodell, 1942). However, a pharmacological agent that is anesthetic at very high doses is not necessarily analgesic at lower doses. Furthermore, it is well

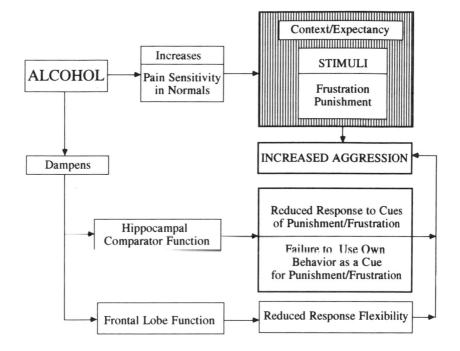

Figure 14.2. The Effect of Alcohol on Aggression

known that there is great individual variability in sober pain sensitivity and in alcohol-intoxicated pain response. Gustafson (1986) has demonstrated that subjects heightened their rating of pain-sensitivity to electric shocks experienced while participating in the Buss-Taylor task when given alcohol as opposed to placebo. In addition, Gray (1982) summarized a series of studies demonstrating that alcohol-intoxicated rats are characterized by reduced flinch and jump thresholds to electric shock.

A study recently completed by Stewart, Finn, and Pihl (1991) does not precisely replicate this phenomenon, but may help explain some of the variability in response. This study specifically demonstrated that men at heightened genetic risk for the development of alcoholism rate electric shocks as more uncomfortable and painful than low-risk control subjects at no or low doses of alcohol, but not at clearly intoxicating doses. Previous work on young men from a multigenerational family history (MGH) of high risk for alcoholism has demonstrated their susceptibility

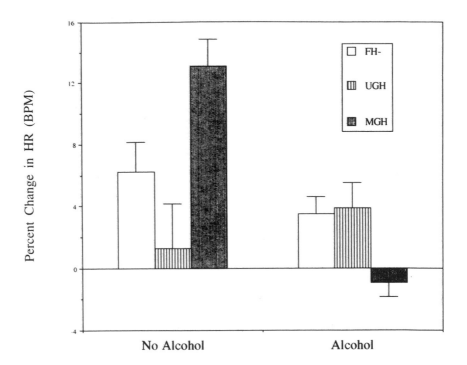

Figure 14.3. Heart Rate Reactivity to a Signaled Electric Shock Among Males With No (FH−), Unigenerational (UGH), and Multigenerational (MGH) Family History Male Alcoholism

to alcohol dampening of cardiovascular response to electric shock. Figure 14.3 presents cumulative data from four studies that illustrate this response pattern, and contrasts this pattern with that characteristic of young men with alcoholic fathers only (unigenerational family history [UGH]) and of normal controls (Pihl & Peterson, 1991). If this stress-dampening response represents an alcohol-induced decrease in pain sensitivity, like that characteristic of chronic alcoholics (Pihl, Peterson, & Finn, 1990), these MGH men should be less aggressive when intoxicated. That is in fact what appears to happen. Multigenerational family history positive individuals deliver higher-level electric shocks while competing in the Buss-Taylor task while sober, and deliver lower levels while intoxicated (with 1.32 mL 95% USP alcohol/kg of body weight), when compared to controls (Figure 14.4).

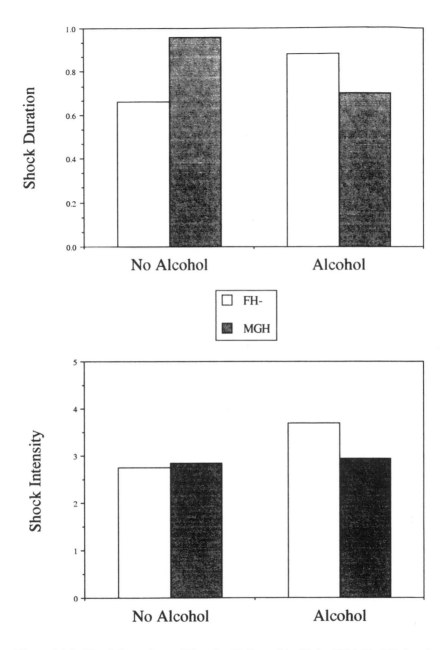

Figure 14.4. Shock Intensity and Duration Delivered by Males With No (FH–) and Multigenerational (MGH) Family Histories of Male Alcoholism, While Sober and While Alcohol-Intoxicated

Reduced Response to Cues of Punishment
and Cues of Frustrative Nonreward

Exhaustive analysis of the relevant animal and human literature led Jeffrey Gray (1982, 1987) to propose that the behavioral effects of benzo-diazepine, barbiturate, and ethanol were similar. These drugs appear to interfere with the operation of a complex limbically based neurological system responsible for governing and integrating organismal response to cues of threat, punishment, frustrative nonreward, and novelty.

This neurological circuit, the behavioral-inhibition system, is composed primarily of the septum, the hippocampus, their interconnections, and the afferent/efferent pathways connecting them with other cortical structures (Gray, 1982). In the face of threat, the behavioral inhibition system brings ongoing activity (instrumental, classically conditioned, or innate) to a halt, and initiates sensory (Sokolov, 1969) or motor/cognitive processes (Peterson & Pihl, in press) directed toward detailed analysis of current events or stimuli (Gray, 1982).

The effects of alcohol and the other antianxiety agents appear specific, within a range of moderate doses. They do not reduce (and may even enhance) response to punishment or frustration. However, they do reduce fear or anxiety generated to cues associated with these two classes of stimuli. The combination of these two facts make consideration of Gray's general neuropsychological model particularly interesting with regard to the alcohol-aggression relationship.

Aggression can be reliably elicited by punishing or frustrating an organism. The same can be said of active avoidance or escape, however. Both of these strategies, designed to reduce the probability of further punishment or frustration, have their attendant limitations. These limitations are the costs of engaging in either behavior. Active avoidance entails abandoning the search for information in a given situation. This might be considered its primary cost. Aggressive action, by contrast, has as its primary drawback high potential for structural damage. This means that the act of engaging in aggression should logically come to serve as a cue for punishment.

This line of reasoning is very fruitful when it is applied to the problem of human socialization. It might be said that the entire process of socialization revolves around attempts to teach children to regard their own participation in or initiation of certain types of behavior as a threat to their own well-being and to the well-being of the social group to which they belong, and on whose beneficence they ultimately depend. Individuals who have failed to learn such connections, for whatever reason, pose a serious threat to the safety of those around them and to the overall integrity of a given social group.

Sober, reasonable, well-socialized persons participate in aggressive acts under extremely restricted conditions. These conditions are carefully defined according to the social canon as justifiable. A justifiably aggressive act by a given individual involves threat, punishment, or frustration directed at another, who had been previously and unjustifiably threatening, punishing, or frustrating to himself or herself or others. A stable society, and the well-socialized members of that society, ensure that aggressive action outside of such extremely restricted conditions is followed by punishment or frustration. This is the threat that society ensures is attendant upon the expression of nonjustified aggression.

One of the pharmacological properties of alcohol, however, is the reduction of fear or anxiety produced to threat. This means that alcohol disinhibits all behaviors that are under the general inhibitory control of fear. Fear appropriately retards many acts of aggression, which in themselves expose the aggressor to potential damage, and which more generally might expose him or her to the revenge of society at large. The tendency for drunks to become victims can also be profitably considered in this light. Fear produced in response to threat cues helps most people avoid physical harm. If the anxiety these cues produce is reduced, then the chances for harm logically increase. This means that drunk people may continue to participate in dangerous situations, when their behavior should be inhibited by the threat of danger.

This general theory can help integrate different aspects of the literature regarding alcohol and aggression that seem surprising on first consideration. Zeichner and Pihl (1979) examined the behavior of three groups of young men administered placebo, no-alcohol, or 1.32 mL of 95% USP alcohol/kg of body weight. Subjects in these three dose groups were further subdivided into two modified Buss-Taylor paradigms: one in which they received aversive tones, whose intensity was correlated with the shocks they delivered, and one in which they received aversive tones, whose intensity was unrelated to their own behavior. Subjects who had received placebo or no-alcohol modified their behavior according to the logical contingency: They reduced the intensity of the shock they delivered in the correlated condition. Intoxicated subjects failed to modify their behavior in a similar manner (Figure 14.5).

Originally, Zeichner and Pihl (1979) hypothesized that alcohol reduced an individual's ability to "process information pertinent to the consequences of their own behaviour" (p. 159). In accordance with this hypothesis, Zeichner, Pihl, Niaura, and Zacchia (1982) tested two groups of young men, who received 1.32 mL of 95% USP alcohol/kg of body weight

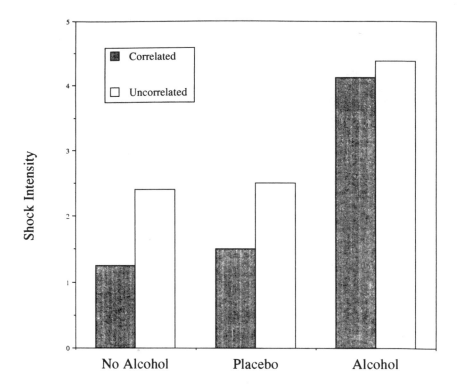

Figure 14.5. Shock Intensity Delivered by Males Who Consumed No Alcohol, Placebo, or Alcohol, When Shock Reception Was Correlated or Uncorrelated With Shock Administered

or placebo, requiring them either to complete mathematical problems or to write down the level of shock they were administering and receiving, while participating in a modified Buss-Taylor task. Distraction actually reduced the effect of alcohol on aggression, while forced attention increased it (Figure 14.6). The intoxicated subjects were aggressive not because they were unaware of their behavior and its consequences, but because that knowledge was no longer accompanied by fear. The information was still being processed, at least by the verbal system, but it no longer had an inhibitory effect on behavior.

Furthermore Zeichner and Pihl (1980) tested three groups of young men, who received placebo, no-alcohol, or 1.32 mL of 95% USP alcohol/kg of body weight, who shocked a (sham) partner, in response to that

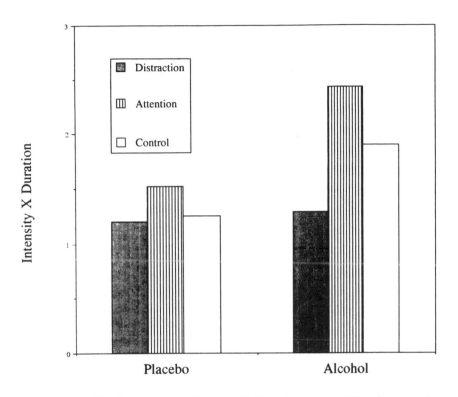

Figure 14.6. Shock Intensity × Duration Delivered by Males Who Consumed a Placebo or Alcohol, During Forced Distraction, Forced Attention, and Normal Attention (Control)

partner's administration of tones of varying aversiveness, in one of two intent conditions (Figure 14.7). In the first (neutral) condition, subjects were told that the aversiveness of the tone they were to receive from the person they were to shock was fixed according to a predetermined schedule. In the second (malicious) condition, subjects were told that they would receive whatever tone their partner freely chose to deliver. Tones in both cases were actually delivered according to an identical predetermined schedule. The intoxicated subjects were more aggressive overall than subjects in the other two groups. They chose more intense shocks, in general. In addition, they delivered the more intense shocks for a longer duration, whereas the placebo and no-alcohol subjects reduced the duration of the more intense shocks. More important, the intoxicated subjects

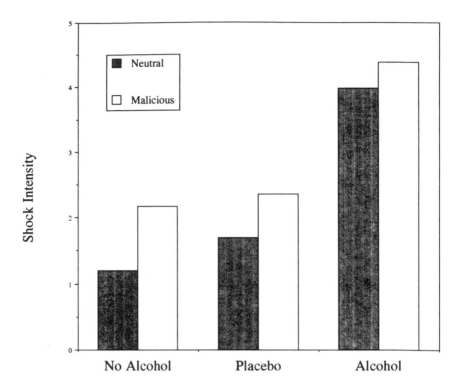

Figure 14.7. Shock Intensity Delivered by Males Who Consumed No Alcohol, Placebo, or Alcohol, Toward an Opponent of Neutral or Malicious Intent

were immune to the effects of intent on shock duration, although the placebo and no-alcohol subjects reduced their shocks in the neutral condition. Correlational analysis demonstrated that the intoxicated subjects reacted to increasing intensity of stimuli with increasing level of shock, regardless of intent, whereas the placebo and no-alcohol subjects reacted to intensity in the malicious condition only.

In Western society, aggressive behavior is restricted by considerations of intent. Acts of threat, punishment, or frustration directed toward another without consideration of that other's intent or ability are generally followed by punishment or frustration. The consideration of intent is a fundamental attribute of more sophisticated notions of justice. Intoxicated individuals in the Zeichner and Pihl (1980) study responded to the intensity of the punishing stimuli, and did not modify their behavior according to socially defined behavioral norms. The inhibitory effect of the threat inherent in breaking a social rule appears to have been essentially eliminated by alcohol intoxication.

Hull (1981) has hypothesized that alcohol interferes with encoding processes fundamental to self-control, which are separate from attentional focus. He believed that alcohol produces a temporary chemical lesion attenuating or eliminating "the encoding of information in terms of its relevance for self" (p. 589). This line of reasoning is in accordance with the general theoretical outline set forth in this chapter. Hull also states, however, that alcohol might make subjects more dependent on the superficial aspects of the situation (p. 527). This notion might be clarified by noting that alcohol intoxication does not attenuate response to punishment or frustration (Gray, 1982, 1987), classes of stimuli that could not be called superficial, but reduces the inhibitory effect of threat.

The old psychoanalytic notion that alcohol reduces superego restrictions is interesting in light of the present theory, as well. The classical superego represented the internalization of societal standards. It is within a given social context that the initiation of or participation in threatening, punishing, or frustrating behaviors are defined as justifiable or not justifiable, or are defined as a threat to self or not. If alcohol appears to reduce the inhibitory effect of threat, while leaving social and verbal knowledge intact, it could be argued, within the psychoanalytic context, that alcohol therefore performs the function of freeing the ego from the restraints of the superego. This theory holds true, however, only when the drunken ego is being punished or frustrated. There is little evidence for a general release of "innate" aggressive tendencies (Bushman & Cooper, 1990).

Decrease in Response Flexibility

The notion that alcohol has a general disinhibitory effect is further weakened by consideration of the fact that there are many forms of cognition that remain intact during intoxication, at doses that are capable of heightening aggressive response. Peterson, Rothfleisch, Zelazo, and Pihl (1990) administered a battery of neuropsychological and motor tests to six groups of young males, administered three doses of alcohol (placebo, 0.66 mL/kg 95% USP ethanol, and 1.32 mL/kg 95% USP alcohol) under two expectancy conditions: told alcohol, and told no-alcohol. The results of the test battery indicated that alcohol had particularly negative effects on delayed memory (a function of the hippocampal system [Milner, 1964]), on some tests of cognitive ability associated with the prefrontal cortex, and on motor skills that demanded self-monitoring. By contrast, alcohol had virtually no effect on standard IQ tests such as the WAIS-R

Vocabulary and Information subtests, or on functions such as simple reaction time. Alcohol does not reduce previously learned knowledge about the nature of the world; what it reduces is the ability to deal with the threatening and novel.

The fact that alcohol impairs functions associated with the prefrontal cortex further complicates the alcohol-aggression relationship. The prefrontal cortex plays a critical role in the formulation of verbal and motor strategies that are designed to gather information in the face of novelty and/or threat (Luria, 1980; Peterson & Pihl, in press). In addition, the prefrontal cortex is also involved in the organization and sequencing of memories based on the acquisition of new information (Luria, 1980). The notion that alcohol affects the operation of the threat system implies that an intoxicated individual is unlikely to respond appropriately to signals of danger. Any additional prefrontal trouble is likely to render that intoxicated individual further incapable of acting in accordance with those signals, even when they remain sufficiently powerful to inhibit his or her ongoing behavior. An intoxicated, but ambulatory, individual appears therefore characterized by inappropriate fearlessness, and by impaired ability to plan and organize behavior. The combination of these two characteristics, serious enough in itself, is likely to be heightened in severity by the addition of reduced motor coordination, a potentially fatal lack in any number of potentially dangerous and strategically complicated situations.

Summary

Increased pain sensitivity, reduced response to cues of punishment and cues of frustrative nonreward, and reduced response flexibility can all apparently occur as a result of drinking. The presence of such factors independently or collectively is likely to increase the probability of aggressive behavior. In addition, the failure to use one's own behavior as a cue for punishment or frustration may characterize intoxicated victims, as well as aggressors.

Previously, it was noted that theories of intoxicated aggression were neither mutually exclusive nor collectively exhaustive. Clearly, the theory presented in this chapter suffers from many of the same limitations. Other plausible, relatively well-documented but undiscussed interpretations of a pharmacological alcohol effect exist. Some individuals appear susceptible to states of pathological intoxication, or to hypoglycemia induced by alcohol consumption. These issues have been discussed in a previous review (Pihl & Ross, 1987). The expectancies an individual brings to the bottle should also be given due consideration. Each individual has powerful expectations regarding the effects of psychoactive substances, which are dependent on individual learning histories and cultural processes, and which may be used all too readily to justify intoxicated thought and action. The interested reader is referred to Lang and Sibrel's (1989) recent review of this literature. The personality of the individual who drinks is also relevant, as preexisting abnormalities in sensitivity to punishment, frustration, and their respective cues may well be compounded by alcohol-induced intoxication.

Other Drugs and Aggression

This chapter has focused on the alcohol-aggression relationship because there is a preponderance of evidence demonstrating its importance. Furthermore it would be reckless to discuss a "drug-aggression" relationship, with any degree of generality. Specificity of drug and dose action on aggression should be assumed automatically. There is not enough evidence available regarding most drugs of abuse and human aggression to draw even speculative conclusions. Unfortunately research in this area, difficult enough for legitimate, practical reasons, is made more complicated by bureaucratic restriction (Taylor, 1990).

Aggression is heightened or reduced by a wide variety of drugs, according to clinical reports. Cocaine, particularly in crack form (Honer, Gewertz, & Turey, 1987), THC (Nakas, 1973), phencyclidine (Fauman & Fauman, 1982), benzodiazepine (DiMascio, Shades, & Harmatz, 1969), and many other psychotropic medications, alone and in combination, have been noted to produce alterations in aggressive behavior. Unfortunately clinical reports are fraught with methodological problems (Pihl & Speirs, 1976). They are limited most severely by their inability to control for the nondrug state or trait characteristics of the patients being observed. "Chicken and egg" questions predominate, and increased violence, observed in a drug-abusing population, might as readily be attributed to unspecified premorbid characteristics of that population as to drug pharmacology per se. This is of course the reason that controlled investigations are necessary.

Laboratory studies utilizing the Buss-Taylor or similar tasks have been completed, using a wide variety of drugs. For each particular drug the literature is sparse, but some interesting findings have emerged. The ingestion of nicotine (Cherek, 1981) and caffeine or caffeinated coffee (Cherek, Steinberg, & Brauchi, 1983, 1984) decreases aggressive responding, below that obtained with placebo. In the case of nicotine, this result has been duplicated in studies of a variety of nonhuman species (Driscoll & Baettig, 1981). Although caffeine has stimulant properties, subjects typically report decreased irritability and improved mood post-ingestion (Goldstein, Kaizer,

& Whitby, 1969). THC seems to affect aggression in a similar manner, even under conditions of extreme provocation (Taylor, 1990; Taylor et al., 1976). The effects of barbiturates and benzodiazepines appear to be dose-dependent (like those of alcohol). At very low doses these drugs may decrease aggression (Cherek, 1990), while at moderate or high doses and over time they sometimes increase aggression (Taylor, 1990). Cocaine has also been demonstrated to heighten aggression (Taylor, 1990). The same thing is true of an amino acid mixture deficient in tryptophan (Pihl et al., 1991). The modes of action of most of these drugs remain unknown, and replication and extension of these basic findings is clearly necessary.

Final Comments

A final important factor clearly affecting the drug-aggression relationship is that of comorbidity. Clearly, the soup becomes a stew as co-occurring psychiatric problems are considered in addition to drug abuse and aggression. Many psychiatric problems accompany substance abuse. Antisocial and borderline personality disorders appear common among opioid addicts (Malow, West, Williams, & Sutter, 1989), for example. Antisocial personalities are characterized in part by their violent tendencies, and they are even more likely to abuse alcohol than opioids (Pihl, Peterson, & Finn, 1990). Conduct-disordered children also often become substance-abusing, antisocial adults (Pihl & Peterson, 1991). The theoretical model set forth in this chapter is not predicated on the assumption that alcohol produces aggression, only that it releases aggression, when it is provoked by frustration or by punishment, and when its expression is inhibited by fear. Abnormal levels of sober trait or state aggression (and levels of sober state or trait fear), like those characteristic of antisocial individuals, must necessarily affect the manner in which alcohol-intoxication alters behavior. Consideration of the interaction between preexistent personality characteristics and alcohol-induced aggression is, however, outside the scope of this chapter.

References

Berkowitz, L. (1983). Aversively stimulated aggression. *American Psychologist, 38,* 1135-1144.
Bernstein, S., Richardson, D., & Hammock, G. (1987). Convergent and discriminant validity of the Taylor and Buss measures of physical aggression. *Aggressive Behaviour, 13,* 15-24.
Brain, P. F. (1986). *Alcohol and aggression.* London: Croom Helm.

Bushman, B. J., & Cooper, H. M. (1990). Effects of alcohol on human aggression: An integrative research review. *Psychological Bulletin, 107,* 341-354.

Cherek, D. R. (1981). Effects of smoking different doses of nicotine on human aggressive behavior. *Psychopharmacology, 7,* 339-345.

Cherek, D. R. (1990). *Laboratory studies of aggression and drugs: Variations in behavioral effects.* Paper presented at the annual meeting of the American Psychological Association, Boston.

Cherek, D. R., Steinberg, J. L., & Brauchi, J. T. (1983). Effects of caffeine on human aggressive behavior. *Psychiatry Research, 8,* 137-145.

Cherek, D. R., Steinberg, J. L., & Brauchi, J. T. (1984). Regular or decaffeinated coffee and subsequent human aggressive behavior. *Psychiatry Research, 11,* 251-258.

Collins, J. J., Jr. (Ed). (1981). *Drinking and crime.* New York: Guilford.

DiMascio, A., Shades, R. I., & Harmatz, A. B. (1969). Psychotropic drugs and induced hostility. *Journal of Psychosomatics, 10,* 46-47.

Driscoll, P., & Baettig, K. (1981). Selective inhibition by nicotine of shock-induced fighting in the rat. *Pharmacology, Biochemistry and Behavior, 14,* 175-179.

Evans, C. M. (1980). Alcohol, violence and aggression. *British Journal on Alcohol & Alcoholism, 15,* 104-117.

Fauman, B. J., & Fauman, M. A. (1982). Phencyclidine, abuse and crime: A psychiatric perspective. *Bulletin of the AAPL, 10,* 171-176.

Goldstein, A., Kaizer, S., & Whitby, O. (1969). Psychotropic effects of caffeine in men. *Clinical Pharmacology and Therapeutics, 10,* 489.

Graham, K. (1980). Theories of intoxicated aggression. *Canadian Journal of Behavioral Science, 12,* 141-158.

Gray, J. A. (1982). *The neuropsychology of anxiety: An enquiry into the function of the septal-hippocampal system.* Oxford: Oxford University Press.

Gray, J. A. (1987). *The psychology of fear and stress.* Cambridge: Cambridge University Press.

Gustafson, R. (1986). Threat as a determinant of alcohol-related aggression. *Psychological Reports, 58,* 287-297.

Hartman, D. P. (1969). Influence of symbolically modelled instrumental aggression and pain cues on aggressive behaviour. *Journal of Personality and Social Psychology, 11,* 280-288.

Honer, W. G., Gewertz, G., & Turey, M. (1987). Psychosis and violence in cocaine smokers. *Lancet, 8556,* 451.

Hull, J. G. (1981). A self-awareness model of the causes and effects of alcohol consumption. *Journal of Abnormal Psychology, 90,* 586-600.

Lang, A. R., & Sibrel, P. (1989). Psychological perspectives on alcohol consumption and interpersonal aggression. *Criminal Justice and Behavior, 16,* 289-324.

Langan, P. A., & Innes, C. A. (1985). *The risk of violent crime* (Bureau of Justice Statistics Special Report, NCJ-97119). Washington, DC: Government Printing Office.

Luria, A. R. (1980). *Higher cortical function in man.* Moscow: Moscow University Press.

MacAndrew, C., & Edgerton, R. B. (1969). *Drunken comportment: A social explanation.* Chicago: Aldine.

Malow, R. M., West, J. A., Williams, J., & Sutter, P. (1989). Personality disorders: Classification and symptoms in cocaine and opioid addicts. *Journal of Consulting and Clinical Psychology, 57,* 765-767.

Mayfield, D. (1976). Alcoholism, alcohol intoxication, and assaultive behaviour. *Diseases of the Nervous System, 37,* 288-291.

Milner, B. (1964). Some effects of frontal lobectomy in man. In J. H. Warren & K. Akert (Eds.), *The frontal granular cortex and behavior* (pp. 313-334). New York: McGraw-Hill.

Moyer, K. W. (1976). *The psychobiology of aggression.* New York: Harper & Row.

Mullin, F., & Luckhardt, A. B. (1934). The effect of alcohol on cutaneous tactile and pain sensitivity. *American Journal of Physiology, 109,* 77-78.

Murdoch, D., Pihl, R. O., & Ross, D. (1990). Alcohol and crimes of violence: Present issues. *The International Journal of the Addictions, 25,* 1065-1081.

Nadelmann, E. A. (1989). Drug prohibition in the United States. Costs, consequences, and alternatives. *Science, 245,* 939-946.

Nakas, G. (1973). *Marihuana—Deceptive weed.* New York: Raven Press.

Pernanen, K. (1976). Alcohol and crimes of violence. In B. Kissin & H. Begleiter (Eds.), *The biology of alcoholism* (Vol. 4, pp. 351-443). New York: Plenum.

Pernanen, K. (1981). Theoretical aspects of the relationship between alcohol use and crime. In J. J. Collins (Ed.), *Drinking and crime* (pp. 1-69). New York: Guilford.

Peterson, J. B., & Pihl, R. O. (in press). Information processing, neuro-psychological function, and the inherited predisposition to alcoholism. *Neuropsychological Review.*

Peterson, J. B., Rothfleisch, J., Zelazo, P. D., & Pihl, R. O. (1990). Acute alcohol intoxication and cognitive functioning. *Journal of Studies on Alcohol, 51,* 114-122.

Pihl, R. O. (1983). Alcohol and aggression: A psychological perspective. In E. Gottheil, K. A. Druley, T. E. Skoloda, & H. M. Waxman (Eds.), *Alcohol, drug abuse, and aggression* (pp. 292-313). Springfield, IL: Charles C Thomas.

Pihl, R. O., & Peterson, J. B. (1991). A biobehavioral model for the inherited predisposition to alcoholism. In H. Kallant, J. Khanna, & Y. Israel (Eds.), *Advances in biomedical alcohol research* (pp. 151-156). Elmsford, NY: Pergamon.

Pihl, R. O., Peterson, J. B., & Finn, P. R. (1990). Characteristics of sons of male alcoholics. *Journal of Abnormal Psychology, 99,* 291-301.

Pihl, R. O., & Ross, D. (1987). Research on alcohol-related aggression: A review, and implications for understanding aggression. *Drugs and Society, 1,* 105-126.

Pihl, R. O., & Speirs, P. (1976). Individual characteristics in the etiology of drug abuse. In B. Maher (Ed.), *Progress in experimental personality research* (pp. 93-196). New York: Academic Press.

Pihl, R. O., Young, S., Harden, P., Plotnick, S., Chamberlain, B., & Ervin, F. (1991). *Alcohol, tryptophan and aggression.* Unpublished manuscript.

Shemberg, K. M., Leventhal, D. B., & Allman, L. (1968). Aggression machine performance and rated aggression. *Journal of Experimental Research in Personality, 3,* 117-119.

Shupe, L. M. (1954). Alcohol and crime: A study of the urine alcohol concentration found in 882 persons arrested during or immediately after the commission of a felony. *Journal of Criminal Law, Criminology, and Police Science, 44,* 661-664.

Sokolov, E. N. (1969). The modeling properties of the nervous system. In I. Maltzman & K. Coles (Eds.), *Handbook of contemporary Soviet psychology* (pp. 671-704). New York: Basic Books.

Stewart, S. H., Finn, P., & Pihl, R. O. (1991). *A dose response study of the effects of alcohol on the perceptions of pain and discomfort due to electric shock in men at high risk for alcoholism.* Manuscript submitted for publication.

Taylor, S. P. (1983). Alcohol and human physical aggression. In E. Gottheil, K. A. Druley, T. E. Skoloda, & H. M. Waxman (Eds.), *Alcohol, drug abuse and aggression* (pp. 280-291). Springfield, IL: Charles C Thomas.

Taylor, S. P. (1990). *Alcohol, drugs and human aggressive behavior.* Paper presented at the 98th American Psychological Association Convention, Boston.

Taylor, S. P., Vardaris, R. N., Rawtich, A. B., Gammon, C. B., Cranston, J. W., & Lubelkin, A. (1976). The effects of alcohol and A-9-tetrahydro-cannabinol on human physical aggression. *Aggressive Behavior, 2,* 153-161.

Williams, J. F., Meyerson, L. J., Eron, L. D., & Semler, I. J. (1967). Aggression and aggressive responses elicited in an experimental situation. *Child Development, 38,* 181-190.

Wolff, H. G., Hardy, J. D., & Goodell, H. (1942). Studies on pain: Measurement of the effect of ethyl alcohol on the pain threshold and on the "alarm reaction." *Journal of Pharmacology, 75,* 3849.

Wolfgang, M. E., & Strohan, R. B. (1956). The relationship between alcohol and criminal homicide. *Quarterly Journal of Studies on Alcohol, 17,* 411-425.

Zeichner, A., & Pihl, R. O. (1979). Effects of alcohol and behavior contingencies on human aggression. *Journal of Abnormal Psychology, 8,* 153-160.

Zeichner, A., & Pihl, R. O. (1980). The effects of alcohol and perceived intent on human physical aggression. *Journal of Studies on Alcohol, 41,* 265-276.

Zeichner, A., Pihl, R. O., Niaura, R., & Zacchia, C. (1982). Attentional factors in alcohol-mediated aggression. *Journal of Studies on Alcohol, 43,* 714-724.

III
Conclusions

15

Mental Disorder and Violence: Another Look

JOHN MONAHAN

In the early 1980s, Monahan and Steadman (1983a) reviewed more than 200 studies on the association between crime and mental disorder for the U.S. National Institute of Justice. This was the summary:

> The conclusion to which our review is drawn is that the relation between . . . crime and mental disorder can be accounted for largely by demographic and historical characteristics that the two groups share. When appropriate statistical controls are applied for factors such as age, gender, race, social class, and previous institutionalization, whatever relations between crime and mental disorder are reported tend to disappear. (p. 152)

I now believe that this conclusion is at least premature and may well be wrong for two reasons. First, to control statistically for factors, such as social class and previous institutionalization, that are highly related to mental disorder is problematic. For example, if in some cases mental disorder causes people to decline in social class (perhaps because they became psychotic at work) and also to become violent, then to control for low social class is, to some unknown extent, to attenuate the relationship that will be found between mental disorder and violence. "The problem," as Dohrenwend (1990) has noted, "remains what it has always been: How to unlock the riddle that low [socioeconomic status] can be either a cause or a consequence of psychopathology" (p. 45). If, in other cases, mental disorder causes people to be repeatedly violent and therefore institutionalized, then

AUTHOR'S NOTE: This chapter was supported by the Research Network on Mental Health and the Law of the John D. and Catherine T. MacArthur Foundation. It expands on themes first developed in J. Monahan (1992), Mental disorder and violent behavior: Perceptions and evidence. *American Psychologist, 47,* 511-521.

to control for previous institutionalization also masks, to some unknown degree, the relationship that will be found between mental disorder and violence.

Second, new research, by no means perfect yet by all accounts vastly superior to what had been in the literature even a few years ago, has become available. These new studies find a consistent, albeit modest, relationship between mental disorder and violent behavior. This chapter reviews this literature, both old and new, using an epidemiological framework.

Mental Disorder and Violence: Evidence for a Relationship

There are two ways to determine whether a relationship exists between mental disorder and violent behavior, and, if it does, to estimate the strength of that relationship. If being mentally disordered raises the likelihood that a person will commit a violent act—that is, if mental disorder is a "risk factor" for the occurrence of violent behavior—then the actual (or "true") prevalence rate for violence should be higher among disordered than among nondisordered populations. And to the extent that mental disorder is a contributing cause to the occurrence of violence, the true prevalence rate of mental disorder should be higher among people who commit violent acts than among people who do not. These two complementary ways of estimating relationships with epidemiological methods are presented in Table 15.1.

Within each generic category, two types of research exist. The first seeks to estimate the relationship between mental disorder and violence by studying people who are being *treated* either for mental disorder (in hospitals) or for violent behavior (in jails and prisons). The second seeks to estimate the relationship between mental disorder and violence by studying people *unselected* for treatment status in the open community. Both types of studies are valuable in themselves, but both have limitations taken in isolation, as will become clear.

Violence Among the Disordered

Three types of studies provide data from hospitalized mental patients that can be used to estimate the relationship between mental disorder and violence. One type looks at the prevalence of violent acts committed by patients *before* they entered the hospital. A second type looks at the prevalence of violent incidents committed by mental patients *during* their hospital stay. A final type of study addresses the prevalence of violent

TABLE 15.1 Methods of Estimating the Relationship Between Mental Disorder
and Violent Behavior

  I. True prevalence of violent behavior among persons with mental disorder
      A. Among identified mental patients
      B. Among random community samples
 II. True prevalence of mental disorder among persons committing violent behavior
      A. Among identified criminal offenders
      B. Among random community samples

---

behavior among mental patients *after* they have been released from the
hospital. (I restrict myself here to remarking upon findings on violent
behavior toward others, and exclude violence toward self, verbal threats
of violence, and property damage. By *mental disorder* I refer unless
otherwise noted to those "major" disorders of thought or affect that form
a subset of Axis I of the DSM-III-R.)

Three excellent recent reviews (Mullen, in press; Otto, 1992; Wessely
& Taylor, 1991) report on 11 studies published over the past 15 years that
provide data on the prevalence of violent behavior among persons who
eventually became mental patients. The time period investigated was
typically the 2 weeks prior to hospital admission. The findings across the
studies vary considerably: Between approximately 10% and 40% of the
patient samples (with a median rate of 15%) committed a physically
assaultive act against another shortly before they were hospitalized. Twelve
studies with data on the prevalence of violence by patients on mental
hospital wards are found in these reviews. The periods studied varied from
a few days to a year. The findings here also range from about 10% to 40%
(with a median rate of 25%) (see also Davis, 1991).

There is a very large body of literature, going back to the 1920s, on
violent behavior by mental patients after they have been discharged from
civil hospitals (Rabkin, 1979). The best recent studies are clearly those of
Klassen and O'Connor (1988, 1990). They find that approximately 25%
to 30% of male subjects with at least one violent incident in their past—a
very relevant but highly selective sample of patients—are violent within
a year of release from the hospital. In the ongoing MacArthur Risk
Assessment Study (Steadman et al., 1993), we are finding that 27% of
released male and female patients report at least one violent act within a
mean of 4 months after discharge.

Each of these three types of research has important policy and practice
implications. Studies of violence before hospitalization supply data on the
workings of civil commitment laws and the interaction between the mental

health and criminal justice systems (Monahan & Steadman, 1983b). Studies of violence during hospitalization have significance for the level of security required in mental health facilities and the need for staff training in managing aggressive incidents (Binder & McNiel, 1988; Roth, 1985). Studies of violence after hospitalization provide essential base-rate information for use in the risk assessments involved in release decision making and in after-care planning (Monahan, 1988).

For the purpose of determining whether there is a fundamental relationship between mental disorder and violent behavior, however, each of these three types of research is unavailing. Only rarely did the studies provide any comparative data on the prevalence of similarly defined violence among nonhospitalized groups. Steadman and Felson (1984) is one study that did. They interviewed former mental patients and a random sample of the general community in Albany County, New York. The percentage of ex-patients who reported at least one dispute involving hitting during the past year was 22.3%, compared with 15.1% for the community sample. For disputes in which a weapon had been used, the figures were 8.1% for the ex-patients and 1.6% for the community sample. When demographic factors were controlled, however, these differences were not significant. While the rates of violence by mental patients before, during, or after hospitalization reported in the other studies certainly appear much higher than would be expected by chance, the general lack of data from nonpatients makes comparison speculative. But even if such data were available, several sources of systematic bias would make their use for epidemiological purposes highly suspect. Since these studies dealt with persons who were subsequently, simultaneously, or previously institutionalized as mental patients, none of them can distinguish between the *participation* of the mentally disordered in violence—the topic of interest here—and the *selection* of that subset of the mentally disordered persons who are violent for treatment in the public sector inpatient settings in which the research was carried out. (There is virtually no research on private hospitals or on outpatients.) Further, studies of violence after hospitalization suffer from the additional selection bias that only those patients clinically predicted to be nonviolent were released. Nor can the studies of violence during and after hospitalization distinguish the effect of the *treatment* of potentially violent patients in the hospital from the existence of a prior relationship between mental disorder and violence.

For example, to use the prevalence of violence before hospitalization as an index of the fundamental relationship between mental disorder and violence would be to confound thoroughly rates of violence with the legal criteria for hospitalization. Given the rise of the "dangerousness standard" for civil commitment in the United States and throughout the world

(Monahan & Shah, 1989), it would be amazing if many patients were not violent before they were hospitalized: Violent behavior is one of the reasons that these disordered people were selected out of the total disordered population for hospitalization. Likewise, the level of violent behavior exhibited on the ward during hospitalization is determined not only by the differential selection of violent people for hospitalization (or, within the hospital, the further selection of "violence prone" patients for placement in the locked wards that were often the sites of the research), but also by the skill of ward staff in defusing potentially violent incidents and by the efficacy of treatment in mitigating disorder (or by the effect of medication in sedating patients). As Werner, Rose, and Yesavage (1983) have stated:

> To the extent that hostile, excited, suspicious, and recent assaultive behavior is viewed by ward staffing as presaging imminent violence, it is the patient manifesting such behavior who is singled out for special treatment (e.g., additional medications, more psychotherapy); such selection may reduce the likelihood of engaging in violence. Thus, paradoxically, if the patient who "looks" imminently violent in this setting is given effective treatments that forestall violent behavior, he will not in fact engage in violence as predicted. (p. 824)

Since the prevalence of violence after hospitalization may be a function of the type of patients selected for hospitalization, of the nature and duration of the treatment administered during hospitalization, and of the risk assessment cutoffs used in determining eligibility for discharge, these data, too, tell us little about whether a basic relationship between mental disorder and violence exists.

Only by augmenting studies of the prevalence of violence among *treated* (i.e., hospitalized) samples of the mentally disordered with studies of the prevalence of violence among samples of disordered people unselected for treatment status in the community can population estimates free of selection and treatment biases be offered. Fortunately a recent and seminal study by Swanson, Holzer, Ganju, and Jono (1990) provides this essential information. Swanson et al. drew their data from the National Institute of Mental Health's Epidemiological Catchment Area (ECA) study (see Robins & Regier, 1991). Representative weighted samples of adult household residents of Baltimore, Durham, and Los Angeles were pooled to form a data base of approximately 10,000 people. The Diagnostic Interview Schedule (DIS), a structured interview designed for use by trained laypersons, was used to establish mental disorder according to DSM-III criteria. Five items on the DIS[1]—four embedded among the criteria for antisocial personality disorder and one that formed part of the diagnosis of alcohol

TABLE 15.2 Percentage Violent During Past Year in ECA Sample, by Diagnosis

Diagnosis	Violence
No disorder	2.1
Schizophrenia	12.7
Major depression	11.7
Mania or bi-polar	11.0
Alcohol abuse/dependence	24.6
Drug abuse/dependence	34.7

SOURCE: From "Violence and Psychiatric Disorder in the Community" by J. Swanson, C. Holzer, V. Ganju, & R. Jono, 1990, *Hospital and Community Psychiatry, 41,* p. 765. Copyright 1990 by the American Psychiatric Association. Adapted by permission.

abuse/dependence—were used to indicate violent behavior. A respondent was counted as positive for violence if he or she endorsed at least one of these items and reported that the act occurred during the year preceding the interview. This index of violent behavior, as Swanson et al. note, is a "blunt measure": It is based on self-report without corroboration, the questions overlap considerably, and it does not differentiate in terms of the frequency or the severity of violence. Yet there is little doubt that each of target behaviors is indeed "violent," and I believe that the measure is a reasonable estimate of the prevalence of violent behavior.

Confidence in the Swanson et al. (1990) findings is increased by their conformity to the demographic correlates of violence known from the criminological literature. Violence in the ECA study was 7 times as prevalent among the young as among the old, twice as prevalent among males as among females, and 3 times as prevalent among persons of the lowest social class as among persons of the highest social class.

But it is the clinical findings that are of direct interest here. Table 15.2 presents the prevalence of violent behavior during the past year by DSM-III diagnosis. For these data, exclusion criteria were not employed: A subject who met the criteria for more than one disorder was counted as a case for each.

Three findings are immediately evident: (a) the prevalence of violence is more than 5 times higher among people who meet criteria for a DSM-III Axis I diagnosis than among people who are not diagnosable; (b) the prevalence of violence is remarkably similar among persons who meet criteria for a diagnosis of schizophrenia, major depression, or mania/bi-polar disorder; and (c) the prevalence of violence among persons who meet criteria for a diagnosis of alcoholism is 12 times that of persons who receive no diagnosis, and the prevalence of violence among persons who meet criteria for being diagnosed as abusing drugs is 16 times that of persons who receive no diagnosis. When both demographic and clinical factors were combined in a regression equation to predict the occurrence of violence, several significant predictors emerged. Violence was most likely to occur among young, lower-class males, among those with a substance abuse diagnosis, and among those with a diagnosis of major mental disorder (see Swanson & Holzer, 1991).

One source of concern about the ECA data on violent behavior might be that the rates of self-reported violence are unusually low: a mean annual violence rate for the entire sample of 3.7%. The 1985 National Family Violence Survey (Straus & Gelles, 1988), in contrast, found that 16.1% of U.S. couples reported at least one assault on a partner during the past year, and 11% of children were seriously assaulted. What can account for these seemingly large discrepancies?

An examination of the items that comprised the DIS index of violence (see Note 1) provides an explanation. Of the five items, two measured not merely the *occurrence* of violence, but its *frequency.* Item 1, regarding spousal violence, asked "Did you ever hit or throw things first *on more than one occasion?*" Item 3 asked whether the subject has "been in *more than one fight* that came to swapping blows." Also, one item measured not merely the occurrence of violence, but the *injury or disability* that followed from it. Item 2 asked whether a child was hit "hard enough so that he or she *had bruises or had to stay in bed or see a doctor?*" When it is taken into account that the ECA violence data presented by Swanson et al. (1990) are estimates not of the simple occurrence of violence, but at least to some degree of repeated violence and violence that resulted in injury or disability, the apparently low rates of self-reported violence seem less anomalous.

One final and equally notable study not only confirms the ECA data but takes them a large step further. Link, Andrews, and Cullen (1992) analyzed data from a larger study conducted by Shrout et al. (1988) using the Psychiatric Epidemiology Research Interview (PERI) to measure symptoms and life events. Link et al. compared rates of arrest and of self-reported violence (including hitting, fighting, using weapon(s), and "hurting someone badly") in a sample of approximately 400 adults from the Washington Heights area of New York City who had never been in a mental hospital or sought help from a mental health professional, with rates of arrest and self-reported violence in several samples of former mental patients from the same area. To eliminate alternative explanations for their data, the researchers controlled, in various analyses, for an extraordinary number of factors: age, gender, educational level, ethnicity (black, white, and Hispanic), socioeconomic status, family composition (e.g., married with children), homicide rate of the census tract in which a subject lived, and the subject's "need for approval." This last variable was measured by the Crowne-Marlowe social desirability scale (1960) and was included to control for the possibility that patients might be more willing to report socially undesirable behavior (such as violence) than nonpatients.

The study found that the patient groups were almost always more violent than the never-treated community sample, often 2 to 3 times as violent. As in the ECA study (Swanson et al., 1990), demographic factors clearly related to violence (e.g., males, the less educated, and those from high-crime neighborhoods were more likely to be violent). But even when all the demographic and personal factors, such as social desirability, were taken into account, significant differences between the patients and the never-treated community residents remained. The association between mental patient status and violent behavior, as the authors noted, was "remarkably robust" to attempts to explain it away as artifact.

Most important, Link et al. then controlled for "current symptomatology." They did this by using the false beliefs and perceptions scale of the PERI, which measures core psychotic symptoms via questions such as "How often have you felt that thoughts were put into your head that were not your own?" "How often have you thought you were possessed by a spirit or devil?" and "How often have you felt that your mind was dominated by forces beyond your control?" Remarkably, *not a single difference in rates of recent violent behavior between patients and never-treated community residents remained significant when current psychotic symptoms were controlled.* The psychotic symptomatology scale, on the other hand, was significantly and strongly related to most indices of recent violent behavior, even when additional factors, such as alcohol and drug use, were taken into account. Thus almost all of the difference in rates of violence between patients and nonpatients could be accounted for by the level of active psychotic symptoms that the patients were experiencing. In other words, when mental patients were actively experiencing psychotic symptoms like delusions and hallucinations, their risk of violence was significantly elevated compared to that of nonpatients, and when patients were not actively experiencing psychotic symptoms, their risk of violence was not appreciably higher than demographically similar members of their home community who had never been treated. Finally, Link et al. (1992) found that the psychotic symptomatology scale significantly predicted violent behavior *among the never-treated community residents.* Even among people who had never been formally treated for mental disorder, actively experiencing psychotic symptoms was associated with the commission of violent acts.

The data independently reported by Swanson et al. (1990) and Link et al. (1992) are remarkable and provide the crucial missing element that begins to fill out the epidemiological picture of mental disorder and violence. Together, these two studies suggest that the currently mentally disordered—those actively experiencing serious psychotic symptoms— are involved in violent behavior at rates several times those of non-disordered members of the general population, and that this difference persists even when a wide array of demographic and social factors are taken into consideration. Since the studies were conducted using representative samples of the open community, selection biases are not a plausible alternative explanation for their findings.

Disorder Among the Violent

Recall from Table 15.1 that there is a second empirical tack that might be taken to determine whether a fundamental relationship between mental disorder and violence exists and to estimate what the magnitude of that relationship might be. If mental disorder is in fact a contributing cause to the occurrence of violence, then the prevalence of mental disorder should be higher among people who commit violent acts than among people who do not. As before, there are two ways to ascertain the existence of such a relationship: by studying treated cases—in this instance, people "treated" for violence by being institutionalized in local jails and state prisons—and determining their rates of mental disorder, and by studying untreated cases—people in the open community who are violent but not institution-alized for it—and determining their rates of mental disorder.

A large number of studies exist that estimate the prevalence of mental disorder among jail and prison inmates. (In the United States, jails are usually local and house pretrial defendants and persons sentenced to less than one year of incarceration. Prisons are run by the state government and house persons sentenced to more than a year of incarceration.) Of course not all jail and prison inmates have been convicted of a violent crime. Yet 66% of state prisoners have a current or past conviction for violence (U.S. Bureau of Justice Statistics, 1991), and there is no evidence that the rates of disorder of jail inmates charged with violent offenses differ from those of jail inmates charged with nonviolent offenses. So I believe that data on the prevalence of disorder among inmates in general also apply reasonably well to violent inmates in particular.

Teplin (1990) reviewed 18 studies of mental disorder among jail sam-ples performed in the past 15 years. Most of the studies were conducted on inmates referred for a mental health evaluation, and thus present obviously inflated rates of disorder. Among those few studies that ran-domly sampled jail inmates, rates of mental disorder varied widely, from 5% to 16% psychotic. Roth (1980), in reviewing the literature on the

TABLE 15.3 Male Prison Admittees With Prior Mental Hospitalization (1978)

State	% With Prior Hospitalization
New York	9.3
California	15.2
Arizona	2.2
Texas	8.4
Iowa	16.7
Massachusetts	9.0
Mean	10.4

SOURCE: From "Impact of State Mental Hospital Deinstitutionalization on United States Prison Populations, 1968-1978" by H. Steadman, J. Monahan, B. Duffee, E. Hartstone, & P. Robbins, 1984, *Journal of Criminal Law and Criminology, 75,* p. 418. Adapted by permission.

prevalence of mental disorder among prison inmates, concluded that the rate of psychosis was "on the order of 5 percent or less of the total prison population" (p. 688), and the rate of any form of disorder was in the 15% to 20% range. More recent studies have reported somewhat higher rates of serious mental disorder. Steadman, Fabisiak, Dvoskin, and Holohean (1987), in a "level of care" survey of more than 3,000 prisoners in New York State, concluded that 8% had "severe mental disabilities" and another 16% had "significant mental disabilities" (see also Taylor & Gunn, 1984).

While the rates of mental disorder among jail and prison inmates appear very high, comparison data for similarly defined mental disorder among the general noninstitutionalized population were typically not available. As well, the methods of diagnosing mental disorder in the jail and prison studies often consisted of unstandardized clinical interviews or the use of proxy variables such as prior mental hospitalization. For example, Steadman, Monahan, Duffee, Hartstone, and Robbins (1984) reported data on the prior mental hospitalization of approximately 4,000 male prison admissions in six U.S. states. The data are presented in Table 15.3.

It can be seen that rates of prior mental hospitalization differ drastically from one state prison system to another. Arizona, with the lowest rate of prior mental hospitalization among its prisoners (2.2%) is physically adjacent to California, with one of the highest rates (15.2%). These data may say much about the management of the criminal justice and mental health systems in various states, but they say little about the relationship between mental disorder and violence. It is surely implausible to infer from these data that prisoners in Iowa are "twice as disordered" as prisoners in Texas.

TABLE 15.4 Current Prevalence of Mental Disorder (%) Among California Prisoners, Chicago Jail Detainees, and ECA Sample

Diagnosis	Jail	Prison	ECA
Schizophrenia	2.7	3.1	0.9
Major Depression	3.9	3.5	1.1
Mania/Bi-Polar	1.4	0.7	0.1
Any Severe Disorder	6.4	7.9	1.8

SOURCE: The data in columns 1 and 3 are from "The Prevalence of Severe Mental Disorder Among Male Urban Jail Detainees" by L. A. Teplin, 1990, *American Journal of Public Health, 80,* p. 665. Copyright 1990 by the *American Journal of Public Health.* Adapted by permission. The data in column 2 are from "Current Description, Evaluation, and Recommendations for Treatment of Mentally Disordered Criminal Offenders," 1982, Sacramento: California Department of Corrections.

Recently, however, four studies, one with jail inmates and three with prison inmates, have become available that use the DIS as their diagnostic instrument. This not only allows for a standardized method of assessing disorder independent of previous hospitalization, but also permits comparison across the studies and between these institutionalized populations and the random community samples of the ECA research.

In the first study, Teplin (1990) administered the DIS to a stratified random sample—half misdemeanants and half felons—of 728 males from the Cook County (Chicago) jail. In the most comparable of the prison studies, the California Department of Corrections (1989) commissioned a consortium of research organizations to administer the DIS to a stratified random sample of 362 male inmates in California prisons (see also Collins & Schlenger, 1983; Hodgins & Côté, 1990; Neighbors et al., 1987). Comparative data from the ECA study for male respondents were provided by Teplin (1990). The findings for current disorder are summarized in Table 15.4.

It can be seen that the prevalence of schizophrenia is approximately 3 times higher in the jail and prison samples than in the general population samples, the prevalence of major depression 3 to 4 times higher, the prevalence of mania or bi-polar disorder 7 to 14 times higher, and, overall, the prevalence of any severe disorder (i.e., any of the above diagnoses) 3 to 4 times higher. While there were no controls for demographic factors in the prison study, Teplin (1990) controlled for race and age in the jail study, and the difference between the jail and general population persisted. While these studies all relied on male inmates, even more dramatic data for female prisoners have been reported in one study (Daniel, Robins, Reid, & Wilfley, 1988).

These findings on the comparatively high prevalence of mental disorder among jail and prison inmates have enormous policy implications for

TABLE 15.5 Current Prevalence of Mental Disorder (%) Among Persons in ECA
Sample Who Report Violence or No Violence During Past Year

Violence	Schizophrenia	Major Affective	Substance Abuse	Any Disorder
Yes	3.9	9.4	41.6	55.5
No	1.0	3.0	4.9	19.6

SOURCE: From "Violence and Psychiatric Disorder in the Community" by J. Swanson, C. Holzer, V. Ganju, & R. Jono, 1990, *Hospital and Community Psychiatry, 41,* p. 765. Copyright 1990 by the American Psychiatric Association. Adapted by permission.

mental health screening of admissions to these facilities and for the need for mental health treatment in correctional institutions (Steadman, McCarty, & Morrissey, 1989). But given the systematic bias inherent in the use of identified criminal offenders, they cannot fully address the issue of whether there is a fundamental relationship between mental disorder and violence. Mentally disordered offenders may be more or less likely to be arrested and imprisoned than nondisordered offenders. On the one hand, Robertson (1988) found that offenders who were schizophrenic were much more likely than nondisordered offenders to be arrested at the scene of the crime or to give themselves up to the police. Teplin (1985), in the only actual field study in this area, found the police more likely to arrest disordered than nondisordered suspects. On the other hand, Klassen and O'Connor (1988) found that released mental patients whose violence in the community evoked an official response were twice as likely to be rehospitalized— and thereby to avoid going to jail—than they were to be arrested. An individual's status as a jail or prison inmate, in short, is not independent of the presence of mental disorder.

As before, complementary data on the prevalence of mental disorder among unselected samples of people in the open community who commit violent acts is necessary to address this issue fully. And as before, the analysis of the ECA data by Swanson et al. (1990) provides the required information, which is summarized in Table 15.5.

The prevalence of schizophrenia among respondents who endorsed at least one of the five questions indicating violent behavior in the past year was approximately 4 times higher than among respondents who did not report violence, the prevalence of affective disorder was 3 times higher, the prevalence of substance abuse (either alcohol or other drugs) was 8 times higher, and, overall, the prevalence of any measured DIS diagnosis—which here included anxiety disorders—was almost 3 times higher.

Implications

The data that have recently become available, fairly read, suggest the one conclusion I did not want to reach: Whether the measure is the prevalence of violence among the disordered or the prevalence of disorder among the violent, whether the sample is people who are selected for treatment as inmates or patients in institutions or people randomly chosen from the open community, and no matter how many social and demographic factors are statistically taken into account, there appears to be a relationship between mental disorder and violent behavior. Mental disorder may be a robust and significant risk factor for the occurrence of violence, as an increasing number of clinical researchers in recent years have averred (Bloom, 1989; Krakowski, Volavka, & Brizer, 1988; Mullen, in press; Wessely & Taylor, 1991).

Should further research solidify this conclusion, it does not mean that the laws restricting the freedom of mentally disordered people for long periods of time or the pervasive social rejection of former mental patients are justified, or that the media is correct in its portrayal of people with mental disorder as threats to the social order.

First, as the Link et al. (1992) study makes clear, it is only people currently experiencing psychotic symptoms who may be at increased risk of violence. Being a former patient in a mental hospital—that is, having experienced psychotic symptoms *in the past*—bears no direct relationship to violence, and bears an indirect relationship to violence only in the attenuated sense that previous disorder may raise the risk of current disorder.

Second, and more important, demonstrating the existence of a statistically significant relationship between mental disorder and violence is one thing; demonstrating the social and policy significance of the magnitude of that relationship is another. By all indications, the great majority of people who are currently disordered—approximately 90% from the ECA study—are not violent. None of the data gives any support to the sensationalized caricature of the mentally disordered served up by the media, the shunning of former patients by employers and neighbors in the community, or regressive "lock 'em all up" laws proposed by politicians pandering to public fears. The policy implications of mental disorder as a risk factor for violent behavior can be understood only in relative terms. Compared to the magnitude of risk associated with the combination of male gender, young age, and lower socioeconomic status, for example, the risk of violence presented by mental disorder is modest. Compared to the magnitude of risk associated with alcoholism and other drug abuse, the risk associated with "major" mental disorders such as schizophrenia and affective disorder is modest indeed. Clearly, mental health status makes at best a trivial contribution to the overall level of violence in society.

Note

1. The items were: (1) Did you ever hit or throw things at your wife/husband/partner? [If so] were you ever the one who threw things first, regardless of who started the argument? Did you hit or throw things first on more than one occasion? (2) Have you ever spanked or hit a child (yours or anyone else's) hard enough so that he or she had bruises or had to stay in bed or see a doctor? (3) Since age 18, have you been in more than one fight that came to swapping blows, other than fights with your husband/wife/partner? (4) Have you ever used a weapon like a stick, knife, or gun in a fight since you were 18? (5) Have you ever gotten into physical fights while drinking?

References

Binder, R., & McNiel, D. (1988). Effects of diagnosis and context on dangerousness. *American Journal of Psychiatry, 145*, 728-732.

Bloom, J. (1989). The character of danger in psychiatric practice: Are the mentally ill dangerous? *Bulletin of the American Academy of Psychiatry and the Law, 17*, 241-254.

California Department of Corrections, Office of Health Care Services. (1989). *Current description, evaluation, and recommendations for treatment of mentally disordered criminal offenders.* Sacramento: California Department of Corrections.

Collins, J., & Schlenger, W. (1983, November). *The prevalence of psychiatric disorder among admissions to prison.* Paper presented at the meeting of the American Society of Criminology, Denver, CO.

Crowne, D., & Marlowe, D. (1960). A new scale of social desirability independent of psychopathology. *Journal of Consulting Psychology, 24*, 349-354.

Daniel, A., Robins, A., Reid, J., & Wilfley, D. (1988). Lifetime and six-month prevalence of psychiatric disorders among sentenced female offenders. *Bulletin of the American Academy of Psychiatry and the Law, 16*, 333-342.

Davis, S. (1991). Violence by psychiatric inpatients: A review. *Hospital and Community Psychiatry, 42*, 585-590.

Dohrenwend, B. (1990). Socioeconomic status (SES) and psychiatric disorders: Are the issues still compelling? *Social Psychiatry and Psychiatric Epidemiology, 25*, 41-47.

Hodgins, S., & Côté, G. (1990, September). Prevalence of mental disorders among penitentiary inmates in Quebec. *Canada's Mental Health*, 1-4.

Klassen, D., & O'Connor, W. (1988). Crime, inpatient admissions, and violence among male mental patients. *International Journal of Law and Psychiatry, 11*, 305-312.

Klassen, D., & O'Connor, W. (1990). Assessing the risk of violence in released mental patients: A cross-validation study. *Psychological Assessment: A Journal of Consulting and Clinical Psychology, 1*, 75-81.

Krakowski, M., Volavka, J., & Brizer, D. (1986). Psychopathology and violence: A review of literature. *Comprehensive Psychiatry, 27*, 131-148.

Link, B., Andrews, H., & Cullen, F. (1992). The violent and illegal behavior of mental patients reconsidered. *American Sociological Review, 57,* 275-292.

Monahan, J. (1988). Risk assessment of violence among the mentally disordered: Generating useful knowledge. *International Journal of Law and Psychiatry, 11,* 249-257.

Monahan, J., & Shah, S. (1989). Dangerousness and commitment of the mentally disordered in the United States. *Schizophrenia Bulletin, 15,* 541-553.

Monahan, J., & Steadman, H. (1983a). Crime and mental disorder: An epidemiological approach. In M. Tonry & N. Morris (Eds.), *Crime and justice: An annual review of research,* (Vol. 4, pp. 145-189). Chicago: University of Chicago Press.

Monahan, J., & Steadman, H. (Eds.). (1983b). *Mentally disordered offenders: Perspectives from law and social science.* New York: Plenum.

Mullen, P. (in press). Criminality, dangerousness and schizophrenia. In D. Kavanaugh (Ed.), *Schizophrenia: An overview and practical handbook.* London: Chapman & Hall.

Neighbors, H., Williams, D., Gunnings, T., Lipscomb, W., Broman, C., & Lepkowski, J. (1987). *The prevalence of mental disorder in Michigan prisons.* Lansing, MI: Michigan Department of Corrections.

Otto, R. (1992). The prediction of dangerous behavior: A review and analysis of "second generation" research. *Forensic Reports, 5,* 103-133.

Rabkin, J. (1979). Criminal behavior of discharged mental patients: A critical appraisal of the research. *Psychological Bulletin, 86,* 1-27.

Robertson, G. (1988). Arrest patterns among mentally disordered offenders. *British Journal of Psychiatry, 153,* 313-316.

Robins, L., & Regier, D. (Eds.). (1991). *Psychiatric disorders in America: The Epidemiological Catchment Area study.* New York: Free Press.

Roth, L. (1980). Correctional psychiatry. In W. Curran, A. McGarry, & C. Petty (Eds.), *Modern legal medicine, psychiatry and forensic science.* Philadelphia: Davis.

Roth, L. (Ed.) (1985). *Clinical treatment of the violent person.* Washington, DC: Government Printing Office.

Shrout, P., Lyons, M., Dohrenwend, B., Skodol, A., Solomon, M., & Kass, F. (1988). Changing timeframes on symptom inventories. *Journal of Consulting and Clinical Psychology, 56,* 567-572.

Steadman, H., Fabisiak, S., Dvoskin, J., & Holohean, E. (1987). A survey of mental disability among state prison inmates. *Hospital and Community Psychiatry, 38,* 1086-1090.

Steadman, H., & Felson, R. (1984). Self-reports of violence: Ex-mental patients, ex-offenders, and the general population. *Criminology, 22,* 321-342.

Steadman, H., McCarty, D., & Morrissey, J. (1989). *The mentally ill in jail: Planning for essential services.* New York: Guilford.

Steadman, H., Monahan, J., Duffee, B., Hartstone, E., & Robbins, P. (1984). The impact of state mental hospital deinstitutionalization on United States prison populations, 1968-1978. *The Journal of Criminal Law & Criminology, 75,* 474-490.

Steadman, H., Monahan, J., Robbins, P., Appelbaum, P., Grisso, T., Klassen, D., Mulvey, E., & Roth, L. (1993). From dangerousness to risk assessment: Implications for appropriate research strategies. In S. Hodgins (Ed.), *Crime and mental disorder.* Newbury Park, CA: Sage.

Straus, M., & Gelles, R. (1988). How violent are American families? Estimates from the National Family Violence Resurvey and other studies. In G. Hotaling, D. Finkelhor, J. Kirkpatrick, & M. Straus (Eds.), *Family abuse and its consequences: New directions in research* (pp. 14-36). Newbury Park, CA: Sage.

Swanson, J., & Holzer, C. (1991). Violence and the ECA data. *Hospital and Community Psychiatry, 42,* 79-80.

Swanson, J., Holzer, C., Ganju, V., & Jono, R. (1990). Violence and psychiatric disorder in the community: Evidence from the Epidemiologic Catchment Area surveys. *Hospital and Community Psychiatry, 41*, 761-770.

Taylor, P., & Gunn, J. (1984). Violence and psychosis I—Risk of violence among psychotic men. *British Medical Journal, 288*, 1945-1949.

Teplin, L. (1985). The criminality of the mentally ill: A dangerous misconception. *American Journal of Psychiatry, 142*, 676-677.

Teplin, L. (1990). The prevalence of severe mental disorder among male urban jail detainees: Comparison with the Epidemiologic Catchment Area Program. *American Journal of Public Health, 80*, 663-669.

U.S. Bureau of Justice Statistics (1991). *Violent Crime in the United States* (Report No. NCJ-127855). Washington, DC: U.S. Bureau of Justice Statistics.

Werner, P., Rose, T., & Yesavage, J. (1983). Reliability, accuracy, and decision-making strategy in clinical predictions of imminent dangerousness. *Journal of Consulting and Clinical Psychology, 51*, 815-825.

Wessely, S., & Taylor, P. (1991). Madness and crime: Criminology versus psychiatry. *Criminal Behavior and Mental Health, 1*, 193-228.

16

Recent Research on Crime and Mental Disorder: Some Implications for Programs and Policies

SALEEM A. SHAH

The chapters in this book bring together a wealth of recent research on a topic that holds much theoretical, substantive, and clinical interest for scholars in the behavioral, biological, and social sciences; law; and the mental health disciplines. The subject of "crime and mental disorder" also has considerable salience for programs and policies affecting the mentally ill.

Moreover, because of longstanding, pervasive, and deeply held societal perceptions, apprehensions, and stigmatizing attitudes toward the mentally ill, the subject is also fraught with social and political sensitivity. Indeed, precisely because of the long history of such attitudes it is important that key terms and concepts be carefully defined, clarified, and used with precision. Similar care needs to be exercised in the presentation and discussion of research findings.

This chapter begins by focusing attention on some key definitional and conceptual issues; it then notes some research needs and recommendations. This is followed by a discussion of the implications of some of the research policies affecting the mentally disordered in general and offenders in particular. Finally, brief mention is made of two major types of research and the importance of "user-oriented" dissemination and related efforts to facilitate utilization of promising research findings.

AUTHOR'S NOTE: This chapter was prepared by a federal government employee as part of official duties, therefore the material is in the public domain.

Some Definitional Issues

Before discussing the relationships between "mental disorder" and "crime" it is essential to address some important definitional issues, as well as the particular characteristics and selected nature of the study samples involved in various research endeavors.

The terms *crime* and *mental disorder* encompass a very broad range of behaviors that are viewed as socially deviant. Important social, political, and public policy judgments are involved in determining what types of acts are so "harmful" to society as to require formal designation and handling as "crimes." In an analogous manner, clinical and professional judgments are made (by professional work groups and advisory committees) regarding the clusters of clinical dysfunctions and symptoms that should be duly recognized as "mental disorders" (see, e.g., American Psychiatric Association, 1987; World Health Organization, 1978). Important public policy judgments are also reflected in various laws that affect the mentally ill—for example, to authorize their involuntary hospitalization.

Mental Disorders. The definitions and classification of mental disorders in the mental health field are designed, developed, and used for a variety of clinical and research purposes. They do not have direct application in other systems and when different objectives and decisions are involved. The legal system, for example, must formulate appropriate *legal* definitions when it uses the concept of "mental disorder" for certain public and legal policy purposes—to determine "competency" for such roles and functions as entering into a contract, making a will, retaining custody of minor children, proceeding forward in the civil or criminal process, or when making judgments about exculpatory insanity. [See the important "Cautionary Statement" in the *Diagnostic and Statistical Manual of Mental Disorders*—DSM-III-R (American Psychiatric Association, 1987, p. xxix; also, Shah, 1989.]

The term *mental disorder* encompasses a very wide range of conditions and subcategories, as well as persons who may at some time during their lives meet the criteria for some disorder and be diagnosed. The term can, for example, be used to refer to all persons in the community suffering from any mental disorder—whether treated or untreated; this would constitute the *true* prevalence of mental disorders. It may be used to refer to various subcategories: for example, persons who have either sought care and treatment or who have come to the attention of health, mental health, or other social systems and/or various service providers; or, it may be applied to a smaller and more selective group of mentally ill persons who have been hospitalized. This latter category would encompass a wide range of diagnoses as well as persons who have been hospitalized for "observation" or for treatment as "voluntary" or "involuntary" patients.

The term (mental disorder) may also be used in referring to even smaller categories, such as those suffering from "severe mental disorders"—encompassing the DSM-III-R categories of schizophrenia, major mood disorders, delusional disorder, and other psychotic disorders (such as schizophreniform disorder and schizoaffective disorders) (National Institute of Mental Health [NIMH], 1991), or from "major mental disorders" (generally referring to schizophrenia and major mood disorders). Such phrases require clear specification since there do not appear to be any uniform criteria for their use.

In light of what was noted initially about long-standing stigmatizing societal attitudes toward the mentally ill, and to prevent misunderstanding and/or misreporting in the media, two points merit emphasis. First, terms such as *mental disorder* and *major mental disorder* require clear definition and specification so that readers can readily distinguish and identify the particular patient groups involved. Second, when the research findings pertain to some small and selected subcategories (e.g., persons with "major mental disorders"), the reported results should refer specifically to the *subcategory* rather than to "mental disorder" broadly.

Crime and Criminal Behavior. Although references are generally made to "crime" and "criminals," the offensive conduct and law-violators most often described in the research literature involve what are referred to as "street crimes." Much less attention has been focused on characteristics of "white-collar" offenders and "crimes in the suites." Moreover, as a criminal defendant moves through various stages of the criminal process (from arrest, to prosecution, conviction, and penal incarceration) a variety of socioeconomic status (SES) factors are typically involved. Thus, certainly in the U.S. context and more generally, persons convicted and incarcerated for various "street crimes" will quite disproportionately be from lower SES groups. Law-violators with greater skills and resources can more successfully avoid, evade, and defend against criminal prosecution and conviction; and even when convicted these offenders are less likely to receive penal confinement. [It might be noted here that among the full set of offenses measured in the National Survey of Crime Severity in 1977, as a supplement to the ongoing National Crime Survey in the United States, crimes of violence received high "seriousness" scores, especially when fatal consequences were involved. However, certain white-collar crimes resulting in fatalities (e.g., a factory knowingly polluting the water supply) also received rather high ratings (Wolfgang, Figlio, Tracy, & Singer, 1985).]

The foregoing considerations point to the selected nature of the samples of "criminals" and "mentally disordered" persons involved in many, even most, studies and the associated constraints on the interpretation and generalizability of the results. Given the numerous difficulties in gaining access to subjects and obtaining their consent, the preceding comment is *not* meant as a criticism; it is simply an observation.

Some Conceptual Issues

It is essential that some careful conceptual analysis inform and guide research endeavors looking for possible relationships between mental disorder and crime. Such analyses can also help to explain the obtained findings and provide useful information for assisting with treatment, management, and other program concerns.

What might be regarded as the "first generation" of research on the topic relied almost entirely on the clinical and diagnostic information readily available in various files and records, used poorly defined and inadequately measured variables, and had several other limitations. The methodological problems pertaining to assessments of the violence potential of the mentally ill were classified by Monahan (1988) into four areas, along with recommendations for ways of improving future research. The four problem areas were: (a) impoverished predictor variables, (b) weak criterion variables, (c) constricted validation samples, and (d) unsynchronized research efforts.

The past decade has seen the emergence of a "second generation" of research on this topic and many improvements have been made in almost all the above-listed areas. For example, a number of structured and standardized assessment instruments have been utilized, more refined and reliable diagnostic criteria have been established, larger and less selected samples have been studied, and as several of the contributions in this volume indicate (e.g., Hodgins, Chapter 1; Robins, Chapter 9; and Monahan, Chapter 15) some rather clear, consistent, and convincing evidence of relationships between criminal and violent behaviors and certain major mental disorders has been accumulated.

The heavy reliance on psychiatric diagnoses for studying these relationships continues to pose difficulties. A basic problem, of course, is that these categories and classifications were not designed for evaluating and predicting criminal and/or violent behavior. The cluster of symptoms that may be useful for purposes of clinical assessment and treatment may *not* be very helpful for research relevant to the subject of our particular concern.

Moreover, because what is classified are the *disorders* that people have—not the people—there typically are many within-category variations among individuals given the same diagnosis (e.g., with respect to the particular patterns, severity, fluctuation of symptoms, etc.). Thus one is hard-pressed to provide meaningful answers to such questions as: Was the criminal or violent act the result of and caused by the disorder?; Did it reflect some longstanding personality traits—perhaps exacerbated by the disorder?; Was the act largely influenced by the alcohol or drug-induced state at the time?; and/or Did the criminal act just happen to occur during an acute phase of a chronic condition but is better and more parsimoniously explained (as in the case of "normal" offenders) by certain demographic and criminal history variables? Stated differently, the demonstration of a statistical relationship (correlation) does not establish a *causal* link.

Trying to look for and establish some overall general relationship between crime and mental disorder has often involved, at this stage of inquiry, the posing of some conceptually crude research questions. The next challenge is to formulate and test more precisely conceptualized questions in order to relate specific symptoms and associated disabilities to particular types of offensive acts.

Leaving aside any attempt to link certain mental disorders (e.g., personality and sexual disorders) with criminality, in view of the obvious problems of circularity (since some of the same antisocial behaviors are essential defining elements for both labels), one could use a *functional* approach for hypothesizing and testing certain causal links between specific disabilities (associated with or due to some disorder, handicap, or other condition—such as acute intoxication) and subsequent criminal and/or violent behaviors. For example, when *cognitive processes* (affecting basic information processing and reality testing), *behavioral modulation and regulation,* and *social judgment* are seriously impaired (as during acute psychotic episodes), it can be hypothesized that all functionally related behaviors are likely to be affected, a variety of inappropriate and norm-violating behaviors are to be expected, and, if the person is living in the community, contacts with the criminal justice or mental health system will have markedly increased probability.

Even this type of analysis is not enough, since there are a vast array of psychotic symptoms and their associated functional impairments will vary quite markedly. The nature and severity of symptoms during acute psychotic episodes will require specification—for example, "positive" symptoms (such as hallucinations, delusions, markedly inappropriate affect, etc.) and "negative" symptoms (such as marked social withdrawal, lack of energy and initiative, etc.). While the "positive" symptoms may indeed *increase* the likelihood of deviant/criminal/violent acts and resulting contacts with the criminal justice or mental health systems, the same would not be true in regard to the "negative" symptoms (see, e.g., Taylor, Chapter 4 in this volume).

Note that the hypothesized relationships refer to specific symptoms and associated functional impairments, *not* to mental disorders. It is the functional impairments present at the particular time that would be expected to mediate, and hence to explain, the effects of the disorder on the criminal, violent, and other behaviors displayed by affected individuals. In the absence of some appreciable impairment (because the symptoms may be "mild" or the condition may be in a state of remission), why should the mental disorder necessarily have any bearing on the criminal or violent behavior?

By way of analogy, the influence of alcohol in a traffic accident must be explained in reference to the assessed level of blood-alcohol content and associated functional impairments in the driver at the time of the accident, not by the driver's diagnosis of Alcohol Dependence disorder, since he may have been completely sober at the time!

The complex relationships and mediating factors involved are not easy to identify with certainty nor to disentangle. Consider the following illustrative case.

> A mentally disordered offender, with a history of fairly extensive involvement with the criminal justice system and diagnosed as having a schizophrenic disorder, was discharged from a security hospital on Conditional Release since the disorder had been in remission and he had been functioning quite well. In keeping with the discharge plan, the patient lived and worked in the community and returned to the outpatient department of the hospital every week for monitoring and treatment sessions with his therapist. About six months after being placed on conditional release the patient was involved in an armed robbery and was arrested at the scene of the crime. The pretrial mental health evaluation found evidence of some schizophrenic symptoms, along with a long-standing personality disorder, but no major or significant deterioration since the evaluation conducted prior to the patient's conditional release. There was no evidence of any appreciable involvement of alcohol or other drugs at the time of the offense, nor was the patient judged to have been psychotic at the time. In view of the defendant's prior hospitalization, his status as a "patient on conditional release" from the hospital, and evidently also in light of his heavy caseload, the prosecutor accepted a plea of insanity—thereby ensuring the patient's return to the security hospital for an indeterminate period.

How would one classify this case in trying to determine whether the new offense was due to or can be explained by: (a) the schizophrenic disorder? (b) the personality disorder? (c) the prior and long-standing criminal history? (d) some other situational factors and stressors? or (e) some combination of all the above?

The basic point, of course, is that these are very complicated research issues and the several possible and interacting factors and explanations are immensely difficult to untangle. Relatedly, the kinds of information needed to study these questions may not often be available, even in hospital records.

Some Research Implications

As the preceding section has indicated, a major implication for future research on the topic addressed by this book is that much greater attention should be focused on a careful conceptual analysis of key issues, questions, and assumed or hypothesized relationships, in order that the research endeavors may be guided by a sound conceptual framework. In this regard, the ongoing and impressive undertaking by the MacArthur Group (Steadman et al., Chapter 3 in this volume) is a major step in that direction. Included in this study has been a focus on the identification of "risk markers" and the development, revision, and/or further refinement of various instruments to measure these markers. Not surprisingly, the Psychopathy Checklist, PCL-R (Hare, 1991) is very much in evidence.

Earlier in this chapter reference was made to the selected nature of various research samples and the related constraints on our understanding of the phenomena and relationships involved. Our knowledge of psychopathy, for example, has been greatly enriched and an excellent rating scale has resulted from the work done by Hare and his various associates over the past two decades (e.g., Hare, 1991; Hare & Hart, Chapter 6 in this volume). However, since this research has focused rather heavily on correctional and forensic mental health populations, our knowledge of psychopathy and variations in the nature and pattern of associated personality traits distributed among males and females in the general population remains quite limited. If we are to have better understanding of the phenomenon and be able to describe the phenotype in its various dimensions and manifestations, the focus of the research must be broadened.

Moreover, judges, policymakers, and others who may hold rather stereotyped notions of "psychopaths" in reference to recidivists and violent offenders, also need better understanding of persons in the business and professional worlds and various white-collar criminals. The PCL-R (Hare, 1991), suitably revised for use with a broader population, could be a valuable addition to mental health evaluations to assist courts in the sentencing of recidivistic white-collar offenders—who, it seems clear, have long been denied equal opportunity and access to prison accommodations!

Some Program Implications

Although there are many implications of the extant research for improving service programs, due to limitations of space only two major areas will be mentioned. Further discussion of these and related topics appears elsewhere (Shah, in press).

Mental Health Evaluations. In correctional and mental health settings (focusing especially on forensic programs), huge proportions of mental health resources and efforts are consumed by numerous, repeated, and often duplicative evaluations. The need for and demonstrated utility of many, perhaps even most, of these evaluations remains in question (e.g., Webster & Menzies, Chapter 2 in this volume). Another problem is that mental health professionals are not prepared adequately by their usual professional education and training to understand, evaluate, and formulate opinions and conclusions on a range of questions relevant to *legal* decision making. What compounds the problem is that all too often the law invites clinical opinions *without* explicitly clarifying the purpose of the clinical evaluation and the specific legal concerns. Not surprisingly, therefore, *psycholegal* assessments and treatment interventions (viz., services that are in specific reference to legal issues and questions) are often inadequately described and not conceptually relevant to the particular legal issue.

Such psycholegal assessments need to be improved in terms of their *legal relevance* (e.g., reflecting clear understanding of and conceptual relevance to the legal issues and related questions), *scientific integrity* (e.g., using assessment instruments that have been standardized and where information about reliability and validity is available), and *clarity of role within the legal process*—for example, the reports should provide understandable description and explanation of psychopathology, and indicate the specific areas of impaired functioning and their relevance for the legal questions of concern. However, conclusions regarding the "ultimate legal and/or normative judgments" should be left to the appropriate legal decision makers (see, e.g., Grisso, 1986).

As far as assessments of likely response to certain institutional treatments and later criminal recidivism are concerned, the usual psychiatric and psychological evaluations have limited, often unknown or undemonstrated, usefulness. Based, therefore, on the accumulated evidence of the PCL-R's excellent psychometric properties and demonstrated value in predicting response to treatment (Rice, Harris, & Cormier, 1992) and criminal recidivism among correctional inmates and mentally disordered offenders (Hare & Hart, Chapter 6 in this volume; Harris, Rice, & Cormier,

1991), serious consideration should be given to the increased utilization of this instrument in these and related mental health evaluations.

Treatment Programs for Mentally Disordered Offenders. In recent years increasing attention has been focused on the important construct of "treatability," especially with regard to mentally disordered offenders (MDOs). With the exception of the need for and effectiveness of the phenothiazines for treating psychotic disorders, for example, there appears to be very poor consensus among clinicians—even *after* a case has been discussed—as to the applicability or efficacy of specific treatments (e.g., Quinsey, 1988; Quinsey & Maguire, 1983). Referring to various programs for MDOs, Quinsey (1988) concluded that: "Today, treatment programs in secure psychiatric institutions are noteworthy primarily by their absence, poor implementation, unevaluated status, lack of conceptual sophistication, and incomplete description and documentation" (p. 444). This assessment is as accurate as it is succinct.

Focusing now on *psycholegal* or *forensic treatment programs* (viz., for mentally disordered offenders who have been committed for care and treatment by criminal courts because of incompetence or unfitness to proceed in the criminal process), the interventions need to focus more clearly on the legal questions and concerns and associated outcome criteria. For defendants who have been found incompetent or unfit to proceed, the objective is to return them to court as soon as adequate role functioning has been attained in order that the criminal charges can be resolved. These defendants are presumed to be innocent. Serious questions arise about the appropriateness of many forensic treatment programs in specific reference to the issue of fitness to proceed. More relevant and cost-effective treatment approaches have been described and should receive greater attention and wider application (see, e.g., Pendleton, 1980; Siegel & Elwork, 1990).

Finally, and for purposes of more effective utilization of scarce mental health treatment resources for MDOs, there needs to be thoughtful reconsideration of the use of certain treatments with psychopaths in view of the rather poor, even negative, results (see, e.g., Rice, Harris, & Cormier, 1992). The point, however, is not to abandon all treatment attempts. Considering the very high rates of serious and violent recidivism among psychopathic offenders, effective treatment would have obvious societal benefits. Such treatment endeavors must, however, be based on some good empirical evidence of the demonstrated effectiveness of the selected interventions (see, e.g., Andrews, Bonta, & Hoge, 1990). Thus emphasis should be given to systematic research to develop more useful and cost-effective treatments.

Some Policy Implications

This section will focus on a single fundamentally important issue—namely, laws and public policies that single out the "mentally ill" for preventive detention on the assumption that they constitute one of the most "dangerous" groups in society.

There would be little argument about the need to protect the community from conditions that pose serious threats of danger—for example, in the handling, storage, transportation, and disposal of hazardous and toxic materials. Similarly, there would be general agreement about the need to safeguard society from persons who have already demonstrated their capacity for inflicting serious harm and potentially lethal injury to others—regardless of whether they happen to be under age 18 years, seriously mentally ill, with alcohol or drug abuse problems, with numerous arrests for drunken driving, or serious and recidivistic criminals.

If one were to compare the available objective evidence, recidivistic offenders (those with 3+ convictions for serious or felonious crimes), offenders with substance abuse problems, and persons with 5+ arrests for drunken driving would clearly surpass persons with "major mental disorders" (a rather small subcategory of all "mental disorders") in terms of the danger and threat posed to the community. One might also bear in mind the long-standing and overwhelming evidence of the role of alcohol in a wide range of accidents, fatal and nonfatal automobile crashes, as well as criminal and violent behaviors (e.g., Murdoch, Pihl, & Ross, 1990; Pihl & Peterson, Chapter 14 in this volume).

In fact, the data reported in several of the chapters in this volume indicate that the rates of involvement in criminal and violent behaviors of persons with substance abuse problems consistently and markedly exceeded the rates of persons with "major mental disorders" (see, e.g., Tables 1.1, 1.2, 1.3, and 1.4 in Hodgins, Chapter 1 in this volume; Table 15.5 in Monahan, Chapter 15 in this volume; and Tables 9.5 and 9.8 in Robbins, Chapter 9 in this volume).

For purposes of enacting social defense policies the question is not whether the "mentally disordered" have higher rates of involvement in criminal and/or violent behavior than the general population, because many other groups—had they also been compared—would have had much higher rates. Rather, the key question would be whether the "mentally disordered" constitute one of *the* most "dangerous" groups in society?

Much like public intuitions and opinions, however, the legislative and political processes are not constrained by objective evidence—even when it is available and has been clearly communicated. Various subjective, stereotyped, and discriminatory public attitudes toward the mentally ill, regularly reinforced by media reports and portrayals (e.g., Monahan, Chapter 15 in this volume), appear to have greater impact on perceptions and appraisals of risk.

Perceptions of Risk. Based on studies of risk perception designed to examine the judgments people make when asked to characterize and evaluate hazardous activities and technologies, Slovic (1987) has shown that the majority of citizens rely on intuitive risk judgments. For most people, it appears that experience with hazards tends to come from the news media. In fact, Slovic points out, laboratory research on basic perceptions and cognitions has shown that

> difficulties in understanding probabilistic processes, biased media coverage, misleading personal experiences, and the anxieties generated by life's gambles cause uncertainty to be denied, risks to be misjudged (sometimes overestimated sometimes underestimated), and judgments of fact to be held with unwarranted confidence. (p. 281)

The judgment of experts appears to be prone to the same biases as affect the general public, especially when experts go beyond the limits of available data and rely on intuition.

These psychological studies also demonstrate that the concept of "risk" has different meaning for different people. For example, the judgment of experts correlates highly with technical estimates of annual fatalities, whereas "lay" judgments are related to a number of other perceived characteristics of hazard—such as familiarity, control, catastrophic potential, equity, and level of knowledge. Thus accidents or occurrences that take many lives may produce relatively little social disturbance (beyond that experienced by the victims' families and friends) *if they occur as part of a familiar and well-understood system*—such as a train wreck or automobile crash. However, a small accident in an unfamiliar system or one perceived as poorly understood, such as a nuclear reactor, may have immense social consequences.

In short, "riskiness" means more to people than "expected number of fatalities." Thus attempts to characterize, compare, and regulate risks must be sensitive to such broader conceptions of risk. As Slovic (1987) points out, "Risk concerns may provide a rationale for actions taken on other grounds or they may be a surrogate for other social or ideological concerns. When this is the case, communication about risk is simply irrelevant to the discussion. Hidden agendas need to be brought to the surface for discussion" (p. 285).

Although the "risks" and "hazards" studied by Slovic pertained to such things as nuclear power, motor vehicles, handguns, smoking, motor cycles, alcoholic beverages, police work, pesticides, skiing, and x rays, the basic psychological processes involved seem quite applicable to the issue of public perceptions of the relative "dangerousness" of the mentally ill.

This, clearly, is an important area requiring further research regarding public perceptions, risk estimates, and judgments of the dangerousness of the mentally disordered, as compared to various other "dangerous" groups, conditions, and situations. A related line of research could help to indicate how information about various risks might more effectively be communicated to the public and to policymakers (Fisher, 1991).

Types of Research and Research Utilization

Some closing remarks seem warranted about major types of research and efforts specifically designed to facilitate "user-oriented" dissemination and utilization of promising research findings.

Research endeavors are often classified as either basic or applied; a distinction that can serve a general descriptive purpose, even though at times it is used to make invidious comparisons. Drawing on Coleman (1972), I have referred to *discipline-oriented* and *program and policy-oriented* research (Shah, 1976, 1981). Stated succinctly, the former types of research are designed primarily (albeit not exclusively) to advance knowledge within a particular scientific discipline; the latter are designed primarily to provide information to guide and improve social programs and policies. Although there are overlaps and interrelationships (e.g., program and policy-oriented research often draws upon extant knowledge derived from discipline-oriented studies), there are rather fundamental philosophical differences between the two types of research endeavors.

The goal of *discipline oriented* research is the development and refinement of knowledge and the testing of discipline-related theories. Publications and reports are directed at one's scientific and research colleagues and appear in scientific and professional journals, books, scientific meetings, and other media of the disciplines. Any impact on the world of action (i.e., on programs and policies) is a possible by-product and generally not of direct interest to researchers.

The two major characteristics of program and policy-oriented research are that the research question or problem originates outside the discipline and in the world of action; and the research results are meant and destined for influencing programs and policies in the world of action (Coleman, 1972). Therefore such research endeavors often entail much consultation with program administrators and other potential "users" of the results; various developmental efforts to test the effectiveness of the interventions; and use of a variety of means to communicate and explain the findings and their most effective implementation, and to assist in evaluations of the new programs or policies in order to undertake needed improvements or refinements.

In short, program and policy-oriented research often merges the world of research with the world of action. An excellent example of such efforts is provided by Olweus's school-based intervention program to alleviate and prevent bullying/victim problems (Olweus, 1991, and Olweus, Chapter 17 in this volume).

It has very correctly been noted that governments spend significant sums of money on scientific research and development with the expectation that socially useful applications and benefits will be forthcoming. Such funds are not expended to subsidize scientists in their preferred and career-related pursuits, nor simply for the "cultural enjoyment of descriptions of discoveries" (Pitzer, 1971). It is essential, therefore, that researchers addressing various social problems bear in mind implications for programs and policies, in order not only to improve our knowledge and understanding of the phenomena, but also to help in the improvement of relevant programs and policies.

References

American Psychiatric Association. (1987). *Diagnostic and statistical manual of mental disorders* (3rd ed., rev.). Washington, DC: Author.

Andrews, D. A., Bonta, J., & Hoge, R. D. (1990). Classification for effective rehabilitation. *Criminal Justice and Behavior, 17,* 19-52.

Coleman, J. S. (1972). *Policy research in the social sciences.* Morristown, NJ: General Learning Press.

Fisher, A. (1991). Risk communication challenges. *Risk Analysis, 11,* 173-179.

Grisso, T. (1986). *Evaluating competencies: Forensic assessments and instruments.* New York: Plenum.

Hare, R. D. (1991). *The Hare Psychopathy Checklist-Revised.* Toronto: Multi-Health Systems.

Harris, G. T., Rice, M. E., & Cormier, C. A. (1991). Psychopathy and violent recidivism. *Law and Human Behavior, 15,* 625-637.

Monahan, J. (1988). Risk assessment of violence among the mentally disordered: Generating useful knowledge. *International Journal of Law and Psychiatry, 11,* 249-257.

Murdoch, D., Pihl, R. O., & Ross, D. (1990). Alcohol and crimes of violence: Present issues. *The International Journal of the Addictions, 25,* 1065-1081.

National Institute of Mental Health. (1991). *Caring for people with severe mental disorders: A national plan of research to improve services* (DHHS Publ. No. ADM-91-1762). Washington, DC: Government Printing Office.

Olweus, D. (1991). Bullying/victim problems among school children: Basic facts and effects of a school based intervention program. In K. Rubin & D. Pepler (Eds.), *The development and treatment of childhood aggression* (pp. 411-448). Hillsdale, NJ: Lawrence Erlbaum.

Pendleton, L. (1980). Treatment of persons found incompetent to stand trial. *American Journal of Psychiatry, 137,* 1098-1100.

Pitzer, K. S. (1971). Science and society: Some policy changes are needed. *Science, 172,* 223-226.

Quinsey, V. L. (1988). Assessment of the treatability of forensic patients. *Behavioral Sciences and the Law, 6*(4), 443-452.

Quinsey, V. L., & Maguire, A. (1983). Offenders remanded for a psychiatric examination: Perceived treatability and disposition. *International Journal of Law and Psychiatry, 6,* 193-205.

Rice, M. E., Harris, G. T., & Cormier, C. A. (1992). An evaluation of a maximum security therapeutic community for psychopaths and other mentally disordered offenders. *Law and Human Behavior, 16*(4), 399-412.

Shah, S. A. (1976). Some issues pertaining to the dissemination and utilization of criminological research. In *Evaluation research in criminal justice* (Publication No. 11, pp. 207-235). Rome: United Nations Social Defense Research Institute.

Shah, S. A. (1981). Legal and mental health systems interactions: Major developments and research needs. *International Journal of Law and Psychiatry, 4,* 219-270.

Shah, S. A. (1989). Mental disorder and the criminal justice system: Some overarching issues. *International Journal of Law and Psychiatry, 12,* 231-244.

Shah, S. A. (in press). A clinical approach to the mentally disordered offender: An overview and some major issues. In K. Howells & C. Hollins (Eds.), *Clinical approaches to mentally disordered offenders.* New York: John Wiley.

Siegel, A. M., & Elwork, A. (1990). Treating incompetence to stand trial. *Law and Human Behavior, 14,* 57-65.

Slovic, P. (1987). Perception of risk. *Science, 236,* 280-285.

Wolfgang, M. E., Figlio, R. M., Tracy, P. E., & Singer, S. I. (1985). *The National Survey of Crime Severity* (Bureau of Justice Statistics, Report No. NCJ-96017, U.S. Department of Justice). Washington, DC: Government Printing Office.

World Health Organization. (1978). *Mental disorders: Glossary and guide to their classification in accordance with the Ninth Revision of the International Classification of Diseases.* Geneva: Author.

17

Bully/Victim Problems Among Schoolchildren: Long-Term Consequences and an Effective Intervention Program

DAN OLWEUS

B ullying among schoolchildren is certainly a very old phenomenon. The fact that some children are frequently and systematically harassed and attacked by other children has been described in literary works, and many adults have personal experience of it from their own school days. Though many are acquainted with the bully/victim problem, it was not until fairly recently—in the early 1970s—that efforts were made to study it systematically (Olweus, 1973a, 1978). For a considerable time, these attempts were largely confined to Scandinavia. In the 1980s and early 1990s, however, bullying among schoolchildren has also received some public attention in other countries, such as Japan, England, Australia, and the United States. There are now clear indications of an increasing societal as well as research interest into bully/victim problems in several parts of the world.

In the first part of this chapter I report on a study that examines the possible long-term consequences of regular bullying or victimization by peers in school. The latter part is mainly concerned with the effects of the school-based anti-bullying intervention program that we have developed and evaluated in 42 schools in Norway. (For more details about these studies, see Olweus, in press, for the first study, and, e.g., Olweus, 1991, for the second.) Before embarking on these studies, however, I will give

AUTHOR'S NOTE: The research reported was supported by grants from the William T. Grant Foundation, the Norwegian Research Council for Social Research (NAVF), the Swedish Delegation for Social Research (DSF), and, in earlier phases, from the Norwegian Ministry of Education (KUD), for which the author is grateful.

a brief definition of what I mean by the term *bullying or victimization.* In addition, I will report some prevalence data and draw a sketchy portrait of typical victims and bullies as a general background (for more comprehensive overviews, see, e.g., Olweus, 1978, 1984, 1991, 1992).

Definition of Bullying

I define *bullying or victimization* in the following general way: *A person is being bullied or victimized when he or she is exposed, repeatedly and over time, to negative actions on the part of one or more other persons.*

The meaning of the expression *negative actions* must be specified further. It is a negative action when someone intentionally inflicts, or attempts to inflict, injury or discomfort upon another—basically what is implied in the definition of aggressive behavior (Olweus, 1973b). Negative actions can be carried out by physical contact, by words, or in other ways, such as making faces or "dirty" gestures or refusing to comply with another person's wishes.

It must be stressed that the term bullying or victimization is not (or should not be) used when two persons of approximately the same strength (physical or psychological) are fighting or quarreling. In order to use the term bullying, there should be an *imbalance in strength (an asymmetric power relationship)*: The person who is exposed to the negative actions has difficulty in defending himself or herself and is somewhat helpless against the person or persons who harass.

It is useful to distinguish between *direct bullying/victimization*—with relatively open attacks on the victim—and *indirect bullying/victimization* in the form of social isolation and exclusion from a group. It is important to pay attention also to the second, less visible form of victimization.

In this chapter the expressions *bullying, victimization,* and *bully/victim problems* are used synonymously.

Prevalence

In connection with a nationwide campaign against bully/victim problems in Norwegian comprehensive schools (all primary and junior high schools in Norway), launched by the Ministry of Education in 1983, data were collected using my Bullying Questionnaire[1] from more than 700 schools from all over Norway (Olweus, 1985, 1986, 1991, 1992).

On the basis of this survey, one can estimate that some 84,000 students, or 15% of the total in the Norwegian comprehensive schools (568,000 in

1983-1984), were involved in bully/victim problems "now and then" or more frequently—as bullies or victims (Fall 1983). This percentage represents one student out of seven. Approximately 9%, or 52,000 students, were victims, and 41,000, or 7%, bullied other students with some regularity. Approximately 9,000 students were both victims and bullies.

It can thus be stated that *bullying is a considerable problem in Norwegian comprehensive schools,* a problem that affects a very large number of students. Data from other countries such as Sweden (Olweus, 1986), Finland (Lagerspetz, Björkqvist, Berts, & King, 1982), England (Smith, 1989; Whitney & Smith, 1991), the United States (Perry, Kusel, & Perry, 1988), and Canada (Ziegler & Rosenstein-Manner, 1991) indicate that this problem also exists outside Norway and with similar or even higher prevalence rates.

Characteristics of Typical Victims and Bullies

The picture of the typical victim emerging from research is relatively unambiguous (see Olweus, 1978, 1984, 1992). Victims of bullying are more anxious and insecure than students in general. They are often cautious, sensitive, and quiet. When attacked by other students, they commonly react with crying (at least in the lower grades) and withdrawal. They have a negative view of themselves and their situation. They often look upon themselves as failures and feel stupid, ashamed, and unattractive.

Further, the victims are lonely and abandoned at school. As a rule, they don't have a single good friend in their class. They are not aggressive or teasing in their behavior; accordingly, one cannot explain the bullying as a consequence of the victims themselves being provocative to their peers. If they are boys, they are likely to be physically weaker than boys in general.

In summary, the behavior and attitude of the victims seem to signal to others that they are insecure and worthless individuals who will not retaliate if they are attacked or insulted. A slightly different way of describing typical victims is to say that they are characterized by *an anxious reaction pattern combined* (in the case of boys) *with physical weakness.*

This is a sketch of the most common type of victim, whom I have called the *passive or withdrawn victim.* There is also another, smaller group of victims, *the provocative victims,* who are characterized by a combination of both anxious and aggressive behavior patterns (see Olweus, 1978, for more information about this kind of victim).

A distinctive characteristic of *typical bullies* is their aggression toward peers; this is implied in the definition of a bully. They are, however, often also aggressive toward teachers, parents, and siblings. Generally, they have a more positive attitude to violence and use of violent means than students in general. They are often characterized by impulsivity and a strong need to dominate others. They have little empathy with victims of bullying. If they are boys, they are likely to be physically stronger than boys in general, and victims in particular.

In contrast to a fairly common assumption among psychologists and psychiatrists, we have found no indications that the aggressive bullies (boys) are anxious and insecure under a tough surface. Data based on several samples and using both direct and indirect methods such as pro-jective techniques and hormonal assays all point in the same direction: The bullies have unusually little anxiety and insecurity or are roughly average on such dimensions (Olweus, 1981, 1984). And they do not suffer from poor self-esteem.

In summary, the *typical bullies* can be described as having *an aggressive reaction pattern combined* (in the case of boys) *with physical strength.*

Bullying can also be viewed as a *component of a more general conduct-disordered, antisocial and rule-breaking behavior pattern.* From this per-spective, it is natural to predict that youngsters who are aggressive and bully others in school run a clearly increased risk of later engaging in other problem behaviors such as criminality and alcohol abuse. Several recent studies confirm this general prediction (Huesmann & Eron, 1984; Huesmann & Eron, in press; Loeber & Dishion, 1983; Magnusson, Stattin, & Dunér, 1983; Stattin & Magnusson, 1989).

In our own follow-up studies we have also found strong support for this view. Approximately 60% of boys who were characterized as bullies in Grades 6-9 had at least one conviction at the age of 24. Even more dramatically, as many as 35%-40% of the former bullies had three or more convictions at this age while this was true of only 10% of the control boys (those who were neither bullies nor victims in Grades 6-9). Thus as young adults the former school bullies had a fourfold increase in the level of relatively serious, recidivist criminality.

It should be mentioned that the former victims had an average or somewhat below average level of criminality in young adulthood.

Study 1: Long-Term Outcomes of Bullying by Peers in School

To be regularly harassed and bullied by peers in school is no doubt a very unpleasant experience that may seriously affect the mental health and well-being of the victim. It seems fairly obvious that bullying by peers should have negative effects on the victim in the short-term (see e.g., Olweus, 1992). But will the negative effects remain even several years after the bullying has ended?

Almost nothing is known about the long-term development of children who have been victimized during a sizable period of their school life. Will the reaction patterns associated with their victim status in school be found again if we study them several years later, for example, in young adulthood? Are these individuals still socially withdrawn and isolated, maybe even harassed by their working or student companions? Or, have they recovered in most respects after they have escaped the straitjacket of companionship forced upon them in comprehensive school, and they can choose more freely their own social environments? Or, does the painful experience of being victimized over long periods of time leave certain scars on their adult personality even if they seem to function well in most respects? These and related issues are explored herein, drawing from a follow-up study of young men at age 23, some of whom had been victims of bullying and harassment by peers for a period of at least 3 years, from Grade 6 through Grade 9.

A Brief Note About Methodology

The subjects of this study were 87 men who were approximately 23 years of age at follow-up in the winter of 1982-1983. All of them had participated in an assessment in Grade 9 when they were 16, and for the overwhelming majority data were also available from Grade 6.

The 87 subjects of the follow-up sample consisted of the following three groups:

(1) A largely representative sample of 64 subjects that included 6 former victims and 5 former bullies (see Olweus, 1980b, and Olweus, Mattsson, Schalling, & Löw, 1980, 1988, for additional information);

(2) A selection of 11 additional former victims. The total number of former victims in the study was thus 17. These boys can be considered to be among the most severely victimized boys in the representative cohort of 276 boys to which they belonged;

(3) A selection of 12 additional former bullies. Accordingly, the total number of former bullies was also 17. These boys were among the most pronounced bullies in the cohort (representing about 6% of the total *N* of 276).

For the purposes of the present analyses only the following two groups were used: the group of 17 former victims and the representative sample of 58 subjects (64 minus the 6 former victims). Due to missing data on some of the variables, the actual number of subjects in the present analyses were 15 and 56, respectively. To be defined as a victim in Grade 6 or 9, a subject had to fulfill the following two criteria:

(a) He had to have been nominated by at least one of the main class teachers as a victim (according to a specified definition); and

(b) He had to have received an average score of one standard deviation or more above the mean of the total distribution (for approximately 275 boys) on at least one of two peer rating variables, Aggression Target and Degree of Unpopularity. (The average of these two variables defined the peer rating variable, "degree of victimization by peers," to be used in subsequent analyses; for additional details, see Olweus, in press.)

The stability of victimization status over time was quite high. In actual fact, 16 of the total group of 17 victims in the present study qualified as victims in both Grade 6 and Grade 9. Assuming continuity over the interval covered, they had thus been exposed to fairly severe bullying and harassment for a very long period of time. In addition to having the typical characteristics described above, the habitual victims were also found to have elevated levels of the stress hormone adrenaline at age 16 in comparison with the control boys. At follow-up, the subjects of this study completed a number of questionnaires designed to tap various dimensions of assumed relevance: scales for being directly harassed (e.g., "Others are fairly often mean and nasty to me"); being indirectly harassed (social isolation, loneliness); social anxiety (shyness, social-evaluative concerns); emotionality-worrying in achievement-related situations; involvement in antisocial activities; several dimensions of aggression (assertiveness) and aggression inhibition; frustration tolerance; neuroticism and extraversion (slightly abbreviated versions of the Eysenck scales; Eysenck & Eysenck, 1975); global self-esteem (7 items from Rosenberg's scale; Rosenberg, 1979); and depression (9 items from Beck's scale; Beck, Ward, Mendelsohn, Mock, & Erbaugh, 1961). Most of the items had a 6-point Likert format. The internal-consistency (alpha) reliabilities of the scales were generally quite satisfactory, in most cases lying in the .80-.95 range.

In one of the questionnaires, the subjects were asked to look back to the year they were in Grade 9 and to assess (retrospectively), among other things, the degree to which they had been exposed to direct and indirect bullying and harassment by peers. The five items covering these domains were combined into one scale.

Several samples of blood and urine were also collected from the subjects at two different points in time separated by an interval of about 8 weeks.

These samples were used for the assessment of several hormones, including adrenaline, noradrenaline, testosterone, and cortisol.

It was considered appropriate to focus the present analyses not only on significance testing but also on effect sizes (in this context I used the standardized mean difference measure d defined as the difference between the means of the two groups divided by the standard deviation of the nonvictim or control group; Cohen, 1977). One reason for this strategy is that we are here mainly concerned with exploring possible causal relationships and mechanisms, and from this perspective effect size measures give better information about the relationships of interest than tests of significance. Correlation (Pearson) and regression analyses were also used.

Results and Discussion

Lack of Continuity in Victimization

The first important result to report is an absence of relationship between indicators of victimization in school and data on both direct and indirect harassment in young adulthood. The point-biserial correlation between "being directly harassed" in young adulthood (alpha = .91) and victim/nonvictim status in Grades 6-9 (group membership) was only .06 (n.s.). The corresponding correlation for "being indirectly harassed" (alpha = .84) was .15 (n.s.). Similarly, the product-moment correlations of these two adult harassment variables with the peer rating variable "degree of victimization by peers," averaged across Grades 6 and 9, were .07 and .18 (both n.s.). The fact that a boy had been regularly victimized by his peers in school for a long period of time was thus basically unrelated to (self-reported) later harassment and social isolation. Obviously, the experience of victimization in school did not seem to increase the boy's probability of being victimized in young adulthood.

Considering this finding, one might wonder if the experience of being bullied and victimized in school had been so painful to many former victims that they had simply come to deny or repress any indications that they were being victimized as young adults. This hypothesis, however, could be safely ruled out by means of the retrospective data. Here we found substantial correlations between the retrospective estimates of degree of direct/indirect harassment in Grade 9 and victim/nonvictim status ($r = .42$), as well as degree of victimization in Grade 9 as measured by the peer ratings ($r = .58$). These findings show that a considerable proportion of the subjects had a fairly realistic view of their peer relationships in school 7 years earlier. *The "denial/repression hypotheses" was thus not a viable explanation* of the lack of association between degree of harassment in school and in young adulthood.

One might also wonder if the lack of association was a consequence of different methods of assessment being used at the two time points: The categorization of the subjects as victims and nonvictims in school was based on a combination of teacher nominations and peer ratings, whereas the adult measure of harassment was derived from self-reports. Accordingly, one could argue that use of "noncongruent" assessment techniques, which sample partly different aspects of the phenomenon under consideration, might lead to a substantial underestimate of the "true relationship."

Fortunately, this possibility could be checked within the present study because self-report data on degree of victimization/harassment in school were also available. Four 6-point questionnaire items (such as "Other boys are nasty to me" and "I feel lonely and abandoned at school") that were part of the assessment battery in both Grade 6 and Grade 9, were combined into a composite averaged across grades (alpha = .84). This composite correlated .42 with concurrent victim/nonvictim status and .61 with the peer rating variable degree of victimization by peers (the correlation within the victim group was even higher, .73). Accordingly, the composite must be considered a valid and meaningful self-report indicator of victimization/harassment in school.

When this scale of self-reported victimization in school was correlated with the adult measures of harassment, the results were very much the same as those obtained with the "other-based" measure of victimization in school: The correlation with being directly harassed in young adulthood was .05 (the corresponding value for victim/nonvictim status in school was .06, above), whereas the correlation with being indirectly harassed was .16 (and the corresponding value for victim/nonvictim status was .15, above). Obviously, use of "congruent" methods of assessment would not lead to a different conclusion.

Summing up, the lack of association between victim/nonvictim status in school and degree of harassment in young adulthood could not be explained as a consequence of denial/repression or of "noncongruence" of methods of assessment. In all probability, then, the lack of a relation was a reflection of reality (I am also basing this judgment on the substantial correlation of degree of adult harassment with concurrent levels of depression and self-esteem, reported below).

Long-Term Effects of Victimization

In spite of the fact that the former victims were no more harassed or socially isolated than the control boys as young adults, they had clearly

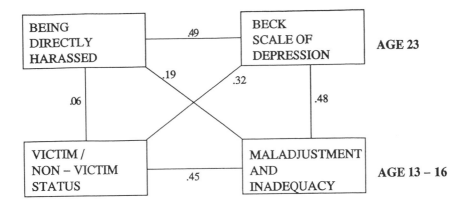

Figure 17.1. Overview of Relations (Pearson correlations) Among Key Variables at Age 13-16 and Age 23 ($n = 71$)

higher levels of depression, or maybe depressive tendencies, and a more negative view of themselves (poorer self-esteem) at age 23. On the somewhat abbreviated but highly reliable Beck scale of depression (alpha = .87), the *t* value for the mean difference between the victim and nonvictim groups was 2.77 ($p < .01$ on a two-tailed test) and the effect size *d* a substantial .87 (a "large" effect size according to Cohen, 1977). The point-biserial correlation between group membership and the depression scale was .32. For the equally reliable Rosenberg scale of global self-esteem (also somewhat abbreviated; alpha = .89) the *t* value was 2.28 ($p = .03$ on a two-tailed test) and the value of *d* was .70. The corresponding point-biserial correlation amounted to .26.

To get a better understanding of how to interpret these results, a more elaborate analysis of the data is required. The key variables and relationships in terms of correlation coefficients are shown in Figure 17.1 with the Beck scale of depression as the "ultimate" dependent variable.

Three of the variables in the figure have already been discussed and we note the approximately zero correlation between victim/nonvictim status during the school period and later degree of direct harassment. The fourth variable in the graph is a scale that was derived through factor analysis of a Q-sort inventory used in both Grade 6 and Grade 9. The factorially derived scale consists of 12 items and was interpreted to reflect feelings of maladjustment, anxiety, and personal inadequacy (Olweus, 1978). The reaction patterns covered by this dimension can be assumed to be precursors of later depressive tendencies and this assumption was supported by the fairly substantial correlation of .48 between this scale (averaged over Grade 6 and Grade 9) and the Beck scale 7-10 years later. The reliability of the scale can be estimated at .92.

The basic starting point for interpretation of the results is the finding that the former victims had higher levels of depressive tendencies than nonvictims in young adulthood (alternatively, the correlation of .32 in Figure 17.1 of victim/nonvictim status with later depressive tendencies). This difference or correlation clearly cannot be a consequence of different levels of concurrent harassment, since the former victims and nonvictims did not differ in that respect at age 23, as discussed above under Lack of Continuity in Victimization (and as evidenced in the .06 correlation in Figure 17.1). So, even though there is a substantial correlation between level of contemporaneous harassment and depressive tendencies ($r = .49$), this relation is not linked to former victim/nonvictim status.

Accordingly one has to look more closely at the relation with the variables in the right-hand part of the figure. Generally it seems reasonable to assume that there should be *no direct effect* (in a causal-analytic sense) of former victim/nonvictim status on depressive tendencies that were measured at a much later point in time (7-10 years later). If there were an effect, it would much more likely be *an indirect one,* with marked, relatively immediate (direct) effects that were in some way "internalized" and manifested (also) later in life as a predisposition to react with depressive tendencies.

Applying this reasoning to the data in Figure 17.1, one would expect that most of the effect of victim/nonvictim status on depressive tendencies was mediated via the concurrent variable "maladjustment and inadequacy." Such a mechanism would also largely account for the cross-lagged correlation of .32, making it close to zero in a path-analytic framework. This is actually what happens if the Beck scale is regressed on maladjustment and inadequacy and victim/nonvictim status: The cross-lagged standardized path coefficient becomes almost zero ($\beta = .13$, n.s.) whereas the path from maladjustment and inadequacy is .42 (and highly significant).

The pattern of relations discussed thus far is certainly consistent with an assumption of an indirect causal effect of victimization in school on later depressive tendencies. Before drawing conclusions along these lines, however, one should also consider the possibility of a causal relationship in the opposite direction, from feelings of maladjustment and depression to victimization/harassment.

Although there are indications (as discussed above) that early psychological characteristics of a boy (in addition to physical weakness and child-rearing variables) affect his probability of being victimized, the present data covering somewhat later periods and more anxiety/depression-related characteristics do not seem to support the idea of a causal relationship in this direction. In particular, since the maladjustment and inadequacy variable (a proxy for depressive tendencies) shows considerable continuity with later depressive tendencies, it would seem intuitively reasonable to expect some degree of continuity also for the victimization/harassment variable (rather than the obtained zero-correlation), *if* there were a causal relation as postulated.

In contrast, the substantial continuity of the depression-related variables can be partly accounted for by an "indirect-effect" mechanism as discussed above, if we assume that victimization/harassment exerts a causal influence on the depression-related variables. It should be added that part of the continuity of the depression-related variables is probably explained by the continuing influence of other factors not included in the model.

All in all, the above results support the view that *the major causal influence is from victimization to depression-related variables, and not the other way around.* This interpretation is strengthened by a consideration of the nature of the peer relationships concerned. As mentioned, the victims tend to be physically weaker than their peers and are typically nonaggressive and nonprovocative. Accordingly it is very reasonable to assume that they simply fall prey to harassment and dominance on the part of other, more aggressive students (bullies, in particular). And naturally, the humiliating and hostile treatment they are exposed to is likely to affect their self-evaluations and levels of anxiety/depression.

Further support of this reasoning is gained through examination of the relation between degree of victimization in Grades 6-9 and level of depressive tendencies at age 23 *within the victim group.* In this group, there was a substantial .54 ($p < .02$) correlation of degree of victimization with later depressive tendencies. Although it is possible that chance has played some role in producing the amazingly high correlation in the relatively homogenous victim group, it should be emphasized that the result was not due to one or two extreme outliers; the scatterplot displayed an essentially linear and fairly regular pattern. This within-group correlation becomes even more impressive when one considers the fact that the two variables involved were derived from completely different sources of data—peer ratings and self-reports, respectively—thereby precluding the possibility that the correlation was inflated due to potentially shared method variance.

Taken together, all of this evidence indicates a pattern of causal relationships among the variables as portrayed in Figure 17.2. Victimization in school (victim status) leads concurrently to heightened depression-related tendencies that continue to be elevated 7-10 years later, even though the former victims are no more harassed than their controls at that

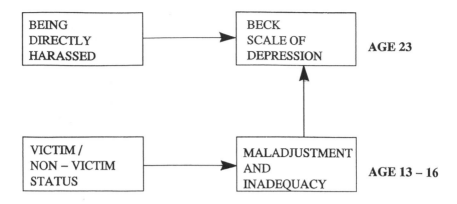

Figure 17.2. Major Causal Relations Among Key Variables at Age 13-16 and Age 23

point in time. Depressive tendencies at age 23 are also affected by concurrent (adult) harassment but the degree of such harassment is not related to earlier victim status. It is worth nothing that the correlation between the two adult measures may be somewhat inflated due to shared method variance, because they were both derived from self-reports.

It should be added that an analysis parallel to that presented above was conducted with Beck's depression scale replaced by Rosenberg's scale of global self-esteem and the maladjustment and inadequacy scale exchanged with a scale of poor self-esteem in Grades 6-9. The latter a priori defined scale consisted of nine items, five of which were included in the factorially derived maladjustment and inadequacy scale (see Appendix in Olweus, 1978). The correlation of this scale with scores on the Rosenberg scale collected 7-10 years later was .56, whereas its correlation with concurrent victim/nonvictim status was .36 (and the cross-lagged correlation of victim/nonvictim status with the Rosenberg scale was .26, as previously reported). The relations among these variables were thus very similar to those displayed in Figure 17.1 and were given a very similar interpretation.

Nondeviant Development on Several Dimensions

On several adult dimensions on which it would be natural to expect differences between former victims and nonvictims, considering their situation and characteristics in Grades 6-9, there were basically no differences. These dimensions included social anxiety (shyness, social-evaluative concerns), emotionality-worrying, different forms of aggression/assertiveness and aggression inhibition, and neuroticism (several of these dimensions correlated .40-.50 with similar dimensions assessed in Grades 6-9). In contrast to the findings from Grade 9, the victims also did not have elevated levels of the stress hormone adrenaline (in spite of a correlation around .70 for the group as a whole between adrenaline levels at ages 16 and 23, respectively), nor were they more introverted than the controls at 23. In agreement with expectations, however, the former victims had been somewhat less involved in criminal activities, both according to self-reports and official records.

Summary of Study 1 and Major Implications

Methodological Adequacy

Before summarizing the findings of this study and pointing out major implications, I would like to emphasize that the results were based on a relatively limited number of subjects. This fact should make us regard the conclusions to be drawn as somewhat tentative and in need of replication. At the same time, it should be emphasized that the findings obtained presented a conceptually very meaningful and coherent pattern, in addition to being quite consistent across two distinct but theoretically and empirically related "ultimate" dependent variables, depressive tendencies and global self-esteem. Also, the victim group was well delineated and its members had no doubt been exposed to fairly severe bullying and harassment for several years. Finally, the quality of the data was quite good according to standard psychometric criteria. These aspects of the study should lead to an increased confidence in the conclusions made.

Lack of Continuity in Victimization

A major finding was the absence of a relation between victim/nonvictim status in Grades 6-9 and the highly reliable measure of harassment at age 23. The retrospective data showed the lack of correlation not to be an effect of denial/repression. In all probability, this *lack of continuity is an indication that the subjects,* after having left school, *had considerably greater freedom to choose their own social and physical environments.* In this way, the former victims had succeeded in escaping later harassment and victimization to approximately the same degree as their peers. This finding is, of course, encouraging though our reactions should be mitigated by the lasting negative effects of earlier victimization, to be discussed below.

It should be added that the lack of continuity with victimization as measured at age 23 does not preclude the possibility that a former school victim could have an increased probability of being victimized under more circumscribed conditions, for example, in a marital relationship.

Situation-Related Strain Rather Than Personality Disturbance

Another finding was that the former victims had "recovered" or scored in the normal range (like the controls) on several "internalizing" dimensions at age 23: They were no longer particularly anxious, inhibited, introverted, or nonassertive in interactions with others, nor were there indications that they had elevated stress levels. This pattern of results implies that *a good deal of the anxiety-related/internalizing characteristics of the victims* as measured during the school years *were situationally determined,* that is, relatively transient effects of the harsh treatment they were exposed to from aggressive peers.

A related implication is that a considerable proportion of the school victims cannot be characterized as having a "disturbed" or pathological personality. As already discussed, boys who get victimized are likely to have certain previctim characteristics, but many of them would probably function reasonably well if they were not exposed to repeated bullying and harassment over long periods of time. The elevated levels of anxiety and stress that we could register in the school years were thus more a reflection of situation-related strain than of a relatively permanent personality disturbance.

In a similar vein, the "normal" adult outcome with regard to peer relationships and social interaction (according to self-reports) would seem to suggest that *the victims were not lacking in "social skills"* (e.g., Asher & Coie, 1900; Ladd, 1985). Or, if they were deficient in such skills in the school period, these problems were not serious enough to prevent normal development in the area of social interaction in young adulthood.

Implications for Intervention

All of this evidence supports the view that *intervention efforts* in this domain should not be primarily focused on *changing* the reactions and characteristics of the victims but rather *the behavior and attitudes of the social environment,* in particular the aggressive bullies (see below). Such a view does not preclude installment of intervention measures specifically designed for the victims: Such measures may help the victims make the harassment stop more quickly and may have positive effects on their self-perceptions.

A further implication of the preceding analyses is that the *high stability of individual differences in victimization over the junior high school years* is largely *a reflection of the stability of the social environment* (Olweus,

1977, 1979, 1980a), in particular the continuing influence of aggressive bullies and their followers. Although it has been shown (and will be shown, below) that it is possible to achieve dramatic reductions in bully/victim problems with a suitable intervention program, and it is my conviction that such problems should largely be solved through a "restructuring of the social environment" (Olweus, 1991, 1992), the results obtained suggest that *a well-planned change of environment may sometimes be helpful to victims.* Among other things, victims might benefit from interacting with peer groups other than that of his or her own class, for example, in connection with sports or musical activities. Also, if an identified bully/victim problem in a class does not seem to be solvable, in spite of serious efforts, it may be useful as a last resort to move the victim to a different class or even school. It must be stressed, however, that such changes of environment should be carefully planned to be successful (Olweus, 1986, 1992).

The Negative Long-Term Effects

Even though the former victims seemed to function well in a number of respects as young adults, there were two dimensions on which they clearly differed from their peers: depressive tendencies and poor self-esteem. The elevated levels on these dimensions can be interpreted as a consequence of earlier persistent victimization that had marked effects on the self-system or personality of some proportion of the young victims; in all probability, they had gradually come to *take over the social environment's* (the dominant peers') *negative evaluations* of themselves as worthless and inadequate individuals (cf. Olweus, 1991, p. 423). These negative self-perceptions which also imply an *increased vulnerability to depressive reactions,* tended to become internalized and "cemented" within the individuals. From a different perspective, one can say that these perceptions and reaction tendencies had gradually become "functionally autonomous" (Allport, 1937), "living a life of their own" independent of their original, immediate causes.

We don't have data available to accurately assess how serious the depression-related problems of the victim group were from a clinical point of view. It is reasonable to believe, however, that they were serious enough to deprive some proportion of the victims of considerable joy and satisfaction with their lives and generally to worsen the quality of their existence. In addition, it is quite possible that the full consequences of the increased vulnerability of the victims will become evident only at a somewhat higher age. These results make it *urgent* for school authorities and parents *to intervene* against bully/victim problems, not only to stop current suffering of the victims (Olweus, 1991, 1992) but *also because of the long-term sequelae* for these individuals (as well as for the bullies; see above).

Peer Rejection as a Predictor of Later Outcomes

It is also natural to connect the findings of the present study with some of the results and research issues from the peer relationships literature. In this area, much attention has been directed to the phenomenon of peer rejection, in part on the assumption that peer rejection may have a causal effect on later adjustment, for example, by making rejected-aggressive children more delinquent or criminal than peers who are aggressive but not rejected (Asher & Coie, 1990; Parker & Asher, 1987).

Very few longitudinal studies have been conducted in which it has been possible to test this assumption adequately (see Kupersmidt, Coie, & Dodge, 1990; Olweus, 1989a). The empirical evidence obtained so far, however, has produced mixed or negative results (Kupersmidt et al., 1990). My own study (Olweus, 1989a), for example, failed to show that aggressive-rejected (unpopular) Grade 6-9 boys had a worse long-term outcome than their nonrejected aggressive peers. In one of the two samples analyzed (n_1 = 276 and n_2 = 195), there were even indications that aggressive-rejected boys were better off than their nonrejected counterparts. In this study, the long-term outcome was indexed by number of officially registered criminal offenses up to age 23.

Whereas much attention has been directed at the connection between rejection and aggression, recent peer relationships research has shown very little interest in the combination of rejection and social withdrawal. In part, this may stem from the fact that it is only quite recently that the heterogeneity of the rejected group has been documented within this research tradition (e.g., French, 1988). Considering the present data from this perspective, our results clearly indicate that rejection, in the form of victimization combined with social withdrawal and passivity, has negative long-term effects on depressive tendencies and self-esteem.

The Causal Role of Victimization in Depression/Suicide

It can be added that victimization/harassment by peers in school appears to be a factor whose causal role in the development of depressive reaction patterns in adolescents and young adults has been much neglected. Because it is known that a considerable proportion of young people who actually commit or attempt to commit suicide are depressed (e.g., Sudak, Ford, & Roshforth, 1984), it is by extension likely that *victimization/harassment may also be an important causal factor in suicidal behavior.*

Incidentally, it is worth noting that the nationwide campaign against bully/victim problems in Norwegian schools, launched by the Ministry of Education, was initiated after it had been discovered that three 10- to 14-year-old boys had committed suicide as a consequence of severe bullying and harassment by peers (Olweus, 1991, 1992).

Study 2: Effects of a School-Based Intervention Program Against Bullying

Against this background, it is now appropriate to describe briefly the effects of the intervention program that we developed in connection with the campaign against bully/victim problems in Norwegian schools.

The *major goals of the program* were to reduce as much as possible existing bully/victim problems and to prevent the development of new problems.

The *main components* of the program, which was aimed at teachers and parents as well as students, were the following:

(1) A 32-page booklet for school personnel describing what is known about bully/victim problems (or rather, what was known in 1983) and giving detailed suggestions about what teachers and the school can do to counteract and prevent the problems (Olweus & Roland, 1983). Efforts were also made to dispel common myths about the nature and causes of bully/victim problems that might interfere with an adequate handling of them. This booklet was distributed free of charge to all primary and junior high schools in Norway.

(2) A 4-page folder with information and advice to parents of victims and bullies as well as "ordinary" children. This folder was distributed by the schools to all families in Norway with school-age children (also free of charge).

(3) A 20-minute videocassette showing episodes from the everyday lives of two bullied children, a 10-year-old boy and a 14-year-old girl. This cassette could be bought or rented at a highly subsidized price.

(4) A short questionnaire designed to obtain information about different aspects of bully/victim problems in the school, including frequency and the readiness of teachers and students to interfere with the problems. The questionnaire was completed by the students individually (in class) and anonymously. Registration of the level and nature of bully/victim problems in the school was thought to serve as a basis and starting point for active interventions on the part of the school and the parents. The results on prevalence of bully/victim problems presented earlier in this chapter were based on information collected with this questionnaire.[2]

Another "component" was added to the program as used in Bergen, the city in which the evaluation of the effects of the intervention program took place. Approximately 15 months after the program was first offered to the schools (in early October 1983) we gave, in a 2-hour meeting with the staff, individual feedback information to each of the 42 schools participating in the study (Manger & Olweus, 1985). This information, derived from the students' responses to the questionnaire in 1983, focused on the level of problems and the social environment's reactions to the problems in the particular school as related to data from comparable schools obtained in the nationwide survey (October 1983). At the same time, the main principles of the program and the major procedures suggested for intervention were presented and discussed with the staff. Because we know from experience that many (Norwegian) teachers have somewhat distorted views of the characteristics of bullying students, particular emphasis was placed on a discussion of this topic and on appropriate ways of handling bullying behavior. Finally, the teachers rated different aspects of the program, in particular its feasibility and potential efficacy. Generally this addition to the program as well as the program itself were quite favorably received by the teachers, as expressed in their ratings.

Subjects and Design

Space limitations prevent detailed presentation of methodological information including sampling scheme, definition of measuring instruments and variables, and significance tests. Only summary descriptions and main results will be provided in this context (for more details, see Olweus, 1991, and Olweus & Alsaker, 1991).

Evaluation of the effects of the intervention program is based on data from approximately 2,500 students originally belonging to 112 Grade 4-7 classes in 42 primary and junior high schools in Bergen (modal ages at Time 1 were 11, 12, 13, and 14 years respectively). Each of the four grade/age cohorts consisted of 600-700 subjects with a roughly equal distribution of boys and girls. The first time of data collection (Time 1) was in late May (and early June) 1983, approximately 4 months before the initiation of the campaign. New measurements were taken in May 1984 (Time 2) and May 1985 (Time 3).

Statistical Analyses

Because classes rather than students were the basic sampling units (with students nested within classes), it was considered important to choose a data analytic strategy that reflected the basic features of the design. Accordingly, data were analyzed with ANOVA (analysis of variance) with students nested within classes nested within schools nested within times/occasions (Time 1 vs. Time 2, Time 1 vs. Time 3). Sex of the subjects was crossed with times, schools (within times), and classes (within schools). Since several of the cohorts figured in two comparisons, the analyses had to be conducted separately for each combination of cohorts (for further information, see Olweus, 1991, and Olweus & Alsaker, 1991).

For several of the variables (or derivatives of them such as percentages), less refined analyses with *t* tests and chi-square were also carried out. The findings from these analyses were in general agreement with those obtained in the ANOVAs.

Properties of the outcome variables analyzed are discussed elsewhere in some detail (Olweus, 1991). Generally, it was concluded that the evidence available attests to the adequacy and validity of the data employed.

Results

Results for the self-report variables "Being exposed to direct bullying" and "Bullying other students" are presented separately for boys and girls in Figure 17.3 through Figure 17.6. (Due to space limitations, only the results for these two variables are shown graphically; see Olweus, 1991, for a more complete presentation.) Because the design of the study is relatively complex, a few words about how to read the figures are in order.

The panel to the left shows the effects after 8 months of intervention, while the one to the right displays the results after 20 months. The upper curves (designated Before) show the baseline data (Time 1) for the relevant cohorts (the Grade 5, Grade 6, and Grade 7 cohorts in the left panel and the Grade 6 and Grade 7 cohorts in the right). The lower curves (designated After) display data collected at Time 2 (after 8 months of intervention) in the panel to the left and at Time 3 (after 20 months of intervention) in the right-hand panel for the age-equivalent cohorts (the Grade 4, Grade 5, and Grade 6 cohorts at Time 2 and the Grade 4 and Grade 5 cohorts at Time 3).

The main findings of the analyses can be summarized as follows:

- There were marked reductions in the levels of bully/victim problems for the periods studied, 8 and 20 months of intervention respectively. By and large, reductions were obtained for both boys and girls and across all cohorts compared. For the longer time period the effects persisted in the case of "Being exposed to direct bullying" and "Being exposed to indirect bullying" and were strengthened for the variable "Bullying other students."

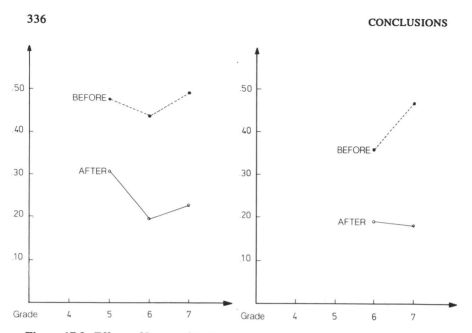

Figure 17.3. Effects of Intervention Program on "Being Exposed to Direct Bullying" for Boys

NOTE: Panel to the left shows effects after 8 months of intervention, and panel to the right displays results after 20 months of intervention. Upper curves (designated Before) show baseline data (Time 1), and the lower curves (designated After) display data collected at Time 2 in the left panel and at Time 3 in the panel to the right.

- Similar reductions were obtained for the aggregated peer rating variables "Number of students being bullied in the class" and "Number of students in the class bullying other students." There was thus consensual agreement in the classes that bully/victim problems had decreased during the periods studied.

- In terms of percentages of students reporting being bullied or bullying others "now and then" or more frequently, the reductions amounted to approximately 50% or more in most comparisons.

- There was no displacement of bullying from the school to the way to and from school. There were reductions or no changes with regard to bully/victim problems on the way to and from school.

- There was also a reduction in general antisocial behavior such as vandalism, theft, and truancy. (For the Grade 6 comparisons the effects were marginal for both time periods.)

- In addition, marked improvement in other aspects of the "social climate" of the class was observed: improved order and discipline, more positive social relationships, and a more positive attitude toward schoolwork and the school.

- At the same time, there was an increase in student satisfaction with school life as reflected in "liking recess time."

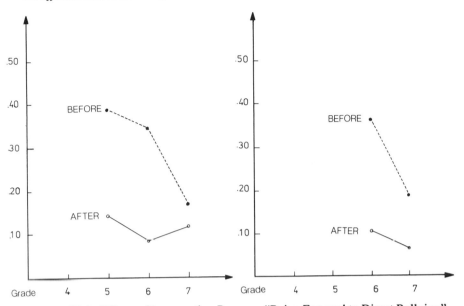

Figure 17.4. Effects of Intervention Program "Being Exposed to Direct Bullying" for Girls

NOTE: Panel to the left shows effects after 8 months of intervention, and panel to the right displays results after 20 months of intervention. Upper curves (designated Before) show baseline data (Time 1), and the lower curves (designated After) display data collected at Time 2 in the left panel and at Time 3 in the panel to the right.

- The intervention program not only affected already existing victimization problems; it also reduced considerably the number (and percentage) of *new* victims (Cowen, 1984; Olweus, 1989b); the program had thus both primary and secondary prevention effects.

In the majority of comparisons for which reductions were reported above, the differences between baseline and intervention groups were highly significant or significant.

Quality of Data and Possible Alternative Interpretations

It is beyond the scope of this chapter to discuss in detail the quality of the data collected and the possibility of alternative interpretations of the findings. An extensive discussion of these matters can be found elsewhere (Olweus, 1991). Here I limit myself to summarizing the conclusions in the following "point statements":

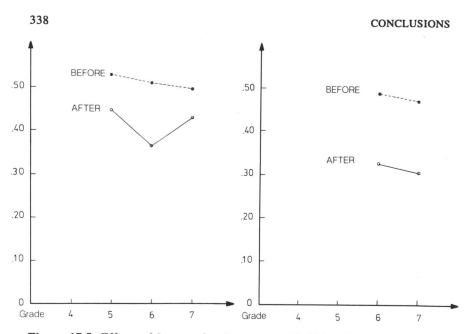

Figure 17.5. Effects of Intervention Program on "Bullying Other Students" for Boys

NOTE: Panel to the left shows effects after 8 months of intervention, and panel to the right displays results after 20 months of intervention. Upper curves (designated Before) show baseline data (Time 1), and the lower curves (designated After) display data collected at Time 2 in the left panel and at Time 3 in the panel to the right.

- Self-reports, which were implicated in most of the analyses conducted so far, are probably the best data source for the purposes of this study.
- It is very difficult to explain the results obtained as a consequence of (a) underreporting by the students; (b) gradual changes in the students' attitudes to bully/victim problems; (c) repeated measurement; and (d) concomitant changes in other factors. All in all, it is concluded that *the reductions in bully/victim and associated problems described above are likely to be mainly a consequence of the intervention program and not of some other "irrelevant" factor.*

In addition, a clear "dosage-response" relationship ($r = .51$, $n = 80$) has been established in preliminary analyses at the class level (which is the natural unit of analysis in this case): Those classes that showed larger reductions in bully/victim problems had implemented three presumably essential components of the intervention program (including establishment of class rules against bullying and use of class meetings) to a greater extent than those with smaller changes (additional information on these analyses can be found in Olweus & Alsaker, 1991). This finding certainly provides corroborating

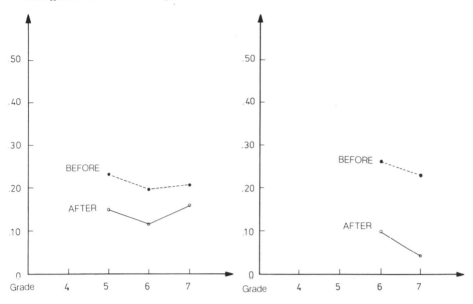

Figure 17.6. Effects of Intervention Program on "Bullying Other Students" for Girls

NOTE: Panel to the left shows effects after 8 months of intervention, and panel to the right displays results after 20 months of intervention. Upper curves (designated Before) show baseline data (Time 1), and the lower curves (designated After) display data collected at Time 2 in the left panel and at Time 3 in the panel to the right.

evidence for the effects of the intervention program. It will be followed up with more systematic and comprehensive analyses.

Brief Comments

The reported effects of the intervention program must be considered quite positive in particular since most previous attempts to systematically reduce aggressive and antisocial behavior in preadolescents/adolescents have been relatively unsuccessful (e.g., Dumas, 1989; Gottfredson, 1987; Kazdin, 1987). The importance of the results is also accentuated by the fact that there has been a highly disturbing increase in the prevalence of violence and other antisocial behavior in most industrialized societies in the past decades. In the Scandinavian countries, for instance, various forms of registered criminality have typically increased by 400%-500% since the 1950s (and these increases cannot, or only to a very small degree, be explained as a consequence of changes in risk of detection).

As mentioned above, we can estimate that approximately 80,000 students in Norwegian comprehensive schools were involved in bully/victim problems in 1983. On the basis of the reported results the following conclusion can be drawn: *If all comprehensive schools in Norway used the intervention program in the way it was used in Bergen, the number of students involved in bully/victim problems would be reduced to 40,000 or less in a relatively short period.* Effective use of the intervention program would also result in lower levels of theft, vandalism, and other antisocial behavior, which would save society large amounts of money. In all probability, it would also improve classroom discipline and other aspects of the social climate of the class and the school.

Basic Principles

Having reported the main goals and components of the intervention program, as well as some of its effects, it is now natural to present its underlying principles and major subgoals.

The intervention program is built around *a limited set of key principles* derived chiefly from research on the development and modification of the implicated problem behaviors, in particular aggressive behavior. It is considered important to try to create a school (and ideally, also home) environment characterized by *warmth, positive interest, and involvement from adults* on one hand and *firm limits to unacceptable behavior* on the other. Third, in cases of violations of limits and rules, *nonhostile, nonphysical sanctions* should be consistently applied. Implied in the latter two principles is also a certain degree of monitoring and surveillance of the students' activities in and out of school (Patterson, 1986). Finally, *adults* are supposed to *act as authorities, at least in some respects.*

The first three of these principles largely represent the opposite of the child-rearing dimensions that have been found in our research to be important in the development of an aggressive personality pattern (Olweus, 1980b; see also Eron, Walder, & Lefkowitz, 1971): negativism on the part of the primary caretaker, permissiveness and lack of clear limits, and use of power-assertive methods. In a sense, the present intervention program is based on an *authoritative adult-child interaction, or child-rearing, model* (cf., e.g., Baumrind, 1967) *applied to the school setting.*

The principles listed above can be translated into a number of specific measures to be used at the *school, class,* and *individual levels.* It is considered important to work on all of these levels, if possible. Space limitations prevent a description of the various measures suggested but such an account can be found in a small book designed for teachers and

General Prerequisites

\+ + Awareness and involvement on the part of adults

Measures at the School Level

\+ + Questionnaire survey

\+ + School conference day

\+ + Better supervision during recess

  + Meeting staff-parents (PTA meeting)

Measures at the Class Level

\+ + Class rules against bullying

\+ + Class meetings

Measures at the Individual Level

\+ + Serious talks with bullies and victims

\+ + Serious talks with parents of involved students

  + Teacher and parent use of imagination

Figure 17.7. Overview of Core Components of the Olweus Anti-Bullying Intervention Program at the School, Class, and Individual Levels

parents (Olweus, 1986; an English version of this book will soon be available, Olweus, 1992). Figure 17.7 lists a set of core components that are considered, on the basis of statistical analyses and our experience with the program, to be particularly important in any implementation of the program (see Olweus, 1992).

With regard to implementation and execution, the program is mainly based on a *utilization of the existing social environment:* teachers and other school personnel, students, and parents. Non-mental health professionals thus play a major role in the desired *"restructuring of the social environment."* Experts such as school psychologists and social workers also serve important functions such as planning and coordinating, counseling teacher and parent groups, and handling more serious cases.

It may be added that the intervention program has been evaluated by more than 1,000 Norwegian and Swedish teachers. In short, their reactions have generally been quite favorable, indicating among other things that the teachers see the proposed principles and measures as useful and realistic.

Some Possible Reasons for Program Effectiveness

In this concluding section, I would like to discuss briefly some of my personal views about why the intervention program has been effective. I will present my comments in six main points:

(1) First, I think it is important to emphasize generally that the intervention program rests on a *decent knowledge base* (cf. Cowen, 1984). Over the years, we have devoted a considerable amount of time to testing in empirical research a number of more or less popular conceptions or hypotheses about the causes and mechanisms behind bully/victim problems. As shown elsewhere (e.g., Olweus, 1978, 1991), several of these conceptions have proven to be "myths" with no or little empirical support. In this way, it has been possible to avoid at least some "false leads" about how to reduce or prevent bully/victim problems in school (by avoiding the focusing of intervention efforts, for example, on external deviations in the victims, anxiety and poor self-esteem in the bullies, or on reducing class or school size).

At the same time, research-based knowledge has been accumulating about the causes and mechanisms involved in bully/victim problems as well as in the two broader categories of "adjustment reactions" of which these problems form a part: aggressive, conduct-disordered, externalizing reaction patterns and anxious, withdrawn, internalizing reaction patterns. We have tried to build a good deal of this knowledge into the program. As stated above, several of the principles underlying the program are directly derived from research on the development and modification of the implicated problem behaviors.

(2) An additional reason for the relative efficacy of the program probably lies in its *direct focus on the relevant behaviors and associated norms* (e.g., "we don't accept bullying in our school and will see to it that it comes to an end") rather than on some assumed underlying or mediating mechanism.

Implied in the above is also a view of aggressive behavior that differs in important respects from several contemporary approaches. Many present-day researchers and clinicians seem to have the understanding that aggressive children usually share society's and the school's values and norms about appropriate behavior and are basically interested in conforming to them. However, due to such personal characteristics as lack of conflict-management capacities, cognitive or behavior (social) deficits, or a poor self-image, they are believed to be unable to do so.

Though I recognize that a certain proportion of aggressive children may have skills deficits or poor self-esteem (which may or may not show up as statistically significant differences in group comparisons), I do not think there is much evidence to support the hypothesis that these factors actually cause aggressive behavior (or at least are major causal factors; cf. Dumas, 1989). In my own approach, I stress the view that a good deal of *aggressive behavior,* and in particular bullying, can be seen *as "self-initiated behavior"* with the deliberate aim of inflicting pain and discomfort, of dominating and oppressing others, and of obtaining tangible and prestigious rewards through coercion. In this view, bullying behavior is not primarily seen as a consequence of lack of skills or abilities but rather as *a function of "deviant" motivations and habits.* It is more a question of what the aggressors want to do and are used to doing than what they are able to do. In line with this view, major foci of the present intervention program are the bullying behavior itself and its "opportunity structure" (opportunities to bully others with associated expected positive or negative consequences), to borrow a term from criminology.

(3) Related to the above formulations is the fact that program participants are encouraged via the program to *take a clear stance against bullying behavior:* "Bullying is not tolerated in our class/school." The program also makes clear the power relationships in that regard: The adults are in charge and have the authority (and responsibility) to stop such behavior.

It is also important, however, to make the students take a clear stance. This can be done, for example, in the context of the development of class rules (norms) against bullying as well as in follow-up discussions at class meetings.

While the program stresses the importance of repudiating bullying behavior, it also makes it clear that such repudiation should not be made in a harsh, hostile, or punitive way. Consistent use of nonhostile, noncorporal sanctions in cases of rule violations is an important part of the intervention program. At the same time, it is considered essential to develop a class/school climate characterized by warmth and involvement.

(4) Another presumably important aspect of the program is that it is *directed toward the school as "system" and works* simultaneously *at several levels:* the school, the class, and the individual levels. In addition, it is highly desirable to get the students' parents involved, although less control over this is possible. In this way, measures used at different levels and in different settings can support each other and will result, under favorable conditions, in *consistent "messages"* from most of the students' social environment. This approach also makes it possible to achieve a

certain degree of *collective commitment* to the program, in particular on the part of the adults at school. If these possibilities are adequately realized, the program is likely to have powerful effects that may also generalize from one setting to another.

From a somewhat different perspective it may be said that the program is *both environment- or systems-oriented and person-oriented.* Although its main focus is on the environment or the system ("a restructuring of the social environment"), it also contains person-oriented components (e.g., serious talks with the students involved in an identified bully/victim problem and their parents). It is likely that the combination of these two approaches is better than either alone.

(5) The positive effects of the intervention, and in particular their maintenance, are likely to be related to the fact that the program is built to achieve not only relatively immediate, more or less short-lived effects on already existing bully/victim problems. It is also designed to prevent the development of new problems and the reemergence of earlier problems. It is reasonable to assume that bully/victim problems may occur whenever several children are together without adequate adult "supervision." Accordingly, it is of great importance for the school to have a *constant readiness* to detect such problems and to counteract them effectively. For example, by use of class rules against bullying in combination with regular class meetings, problems can be discovered at an early stage before they have become ingrained or have taken a dramatic turn. In this way, these and similar mechanisms built into the program are likely to prevent the emergence of new problems and the reemergence of problems from earlier periods. They may also have preventive effects, for example, through change of the class or school norms and the nature of the interactions among students.

(6) Finally, there are several *advantages to formulating the problems* to be targeted in the intervention as *bully/victim problems* and not in some other way such as problems with aggressive and antisocial behavior or conduct disorder problems.

In the first place, by conceptualizing it as a bully/victim problem, the aggressive behavior is placed or anchored in a social context: The recipient of the aggression, the victim, comes into focus in addition to the aggressor. In this way, the repeated humiliation and suffering of the victim are brought into the foreground. This serves an important function in justifying use of the program.

To a considerable degree, *installment of the program is in fact legitimized by the suffering of the victims,* that is, by reference to the immediate, current situation and not to possible long-term effects on the aggressive, antisocial students. Future beneficial effects for the bullies will hopefully occur, but in trying to use such effects as an argument for an intervention program, one is usually met (at least in more sophisticated quarters) with the problem of "false positives" (individuals who are predicted to have a "deviant" outcome but who in fact become "nondeviant" over time). As is well known from research, a sizable proportion of aggressive antisocial children and youths will "normalize" when they grow older and will not turn delinquent or criminal (or whatever outcome is expected) in the absence of any systematic intervention. Because there is usually no way of knowing with suitable accuracy which students will become "false positives" (or "true positives"), this may make it difficult to argue for the necessity of installing an intervention program, at least if it is person-oriented.

These problems are nicely avoided when the main justification of the program lies in the current suffering of the victims as in the present anti-bullying program. Here the possible long-term changes of the bullies, though highly desirable, are not the key argument for use of the program; they only serve as accessory justification.

By focusing on bully/victim problems, it is usually also relatively *easy to reach consensual agreement* among teachers, parents, and (the majority of) students that such problems should not be tolerated in the class or the school: Psychologically and physically stronger students must not be allowed to harass and humiliate weaker and more anxious students. For several reasons, it may be much more difficult to come to consensus about the desirability of counteracting aggressive or antisocial behavior in general.

Though it is certainly important to address bully/victim problems for their own sake, it should be noted that the program had beneficial effects also with regard to other forms of antisocial or conduct-disordered behavior such as vandalism and truancy. In addition, it increased the students' satisfaction with school life and was conducive to improved classroom discipline. In this way, bully/victim problems can be regarded as *a nice entry point* for dealing with several other major problems that plague present-day schools.

Related to the last point is the fact that many components and activities of the program (e.g., class rules against bullying, regular class meetings, role playing, better recess supervision, PTA meetings) are aimed at the total population of students, not only at particularly targeted, "deviant," or at-risk children. Due to this *"universal" orientation,* the necessity of deciding which students will and will not be involved or focused on in the program—and possible stigmatization problems—are (partly) avoided. The program may not only reduce and prevent undesirable behaviors and attitudes; it is also likely to improve social relationships generally (as evidenced, e.g., in a better social climate of the class) and to enhance prosocial behavior. In this way, the present program shares some of the features of what has been called "mental health promoting" programs (Peters, 1990).

All in all, the above characteristics of the program may make it not only acceptable but often even attractive to the school staff (and to many parents). Formulating the problems in this way is likely *to make schools more willing to "take ownership of the problems"* and to recognize that it is primarily their responsibility to do something about them. Again, if the problems were conceptualized in a different way, for instance, in terms of the level of conduct disordered behavior, the schools would be more inclined to disengage themselves from responsibility for the problems and to regard their solution as a task for the child psychiatrist or school psychologist. In sum, the way in which a problem is conceptualized, formulated, and presented to the school has important implications for the school's readiness to do something about it.

Concluding Words

Although what has been presented in this chapter about the effects of the intervention program represents only the first stages of analysis, the basic message of our findings is quite clear: *It is definitely possible to reduce substantially bully/victim problems in school and related problem behaviors with a suitable intervention program.* And such a program need not entail large costs in terms of money or time. Whether these problems will be tackled or not no longer depends on whether we have the knowledge necessary to achieve desirable changes. It is much more a matter of our willingness to involve ourselves and to use the existing knowledge to counteract the problems.

Notes

1. There is an (expanded) English version of the Bullying Questionnaire (one version for Grades 1-4, and another for Grades 5-9 and higher grades). For more information, see Note 2 (below) and write to Dan Olweus, University of Bergen, Öysteinsgate 3, N-5007 Bergen, Norway.

2. The updated package related to the intervention program against bully/victim problems consists of the Bullying Questionnaire for the measurement of bully/victim problems (above and Note 1); a copy of a small book, *Bullying at School—What We Know and What We Can Do* (Olweus, 1992), which describes in detail the program and its implementation; and a 20-minute videocassette (with English subtitles; for European 220v or North American

110v). These materials are copyrighted, which implies certain restrictions on their use. For more information, please write to the author at the address given in Note 1.

References

Allport, G. W. (1937). The functional autonomy of motives. *American Journal of Psychology, 50,* 141-156.

Asher, S. R., & Coie, J. D. (Eds.). (1990). *Peer rejection in childhood.* New York: Cambridge University Press.

Baumrind, D. (1967). Child care practices anteceding three patterns of preschool behavior. *Genetic Psychology Monographs, 75,* 43-88.

Beck, A. T., Ward, C. H., Mendelsohn, M., Mock, J., & Erbaugh, J. (1961). An inventory for measuring depression. *Archives of General Psychiatry, 4,* 561-571.

Cohen, J. (1977). *Statistical power analysis for the behavioral sciences* (rev. ed.). New York: Academic Press.

Cowen, E. L. (1984). A general structural model for primary program development in mental health. *Personnel and Guidance Journal, 62,* 485-490.

Dumas, J. E. (1989). Treating antisocial behavior in children: Child and family approaches. *Clinical Psychology Review, 9,* 197-222.

Eron, L. D., Walder, L. O., & Lefkowitz, M. M. (1971). *Learning of aggression in children.* Boston: Little, Brown.

Eysenck, S. B. G., & Eysenck, H. J. (1975). *Manual of the Eysenck Personality Questionnaire.* London: University of London.

French, D. C. (1988). Heterogeneity of peer-rejected boys: Aggressive and nonaggressive subtypes. *Child Development, 59,* 976-985.

Gottfredson, G. D. (1987). Peer group interventions to reduce the risk of delinquent behavior: A selective review and a new evaluation. *Criminology, 25,* 187-203.

Huesmann, L. R., & Eron, L. D. (1984). Cognitive processes and the persistence of aggressive behavior. *Aggressive Behavior, 10,* 243-251.

Huesmann, L. R., & Eron, L. D. (in press). Childhood aggression and adult criminality. In J. McCord (Ed.), *Advances in criminological theory: Crime facts, fictions, and theory.* New Brunswick, NJ: Transaction Books.

Kazdin, A. E. (1987). Treatment of antisocial behavior in children: Current status and future directions. *Psychological Bulletin, 102,* 187-203.

Kupersmidt, J. B., Coie, J. D., & Dodge, K. A. (1990). The role of poor peer relationships in the development of disorder. In S. R. Asher & J. D. Coie (Eds.), *Peer rejection in childhood* (pp. 217-249). New York: Cambridge University Press.

Ladd, G. W. (1985). Documenting the effect of social skill training with children: Process and outcome assessment. In B. H. Schneider, K. H. Rubin, & J. E. Ledigham (Eds.), *Children's peer relations: Issues in assessment and intervention* (pp. 243-269). New York: Springer.

Lagerspetz, K. M., Björkqvist, K., Berts, M., & King, E. (1982). Group aggression among school children in three schools. *Scandinavian Journal of Psychology, 23,* 45-52.

Loeber, R., & Dishion, T. (1983). Early predictors of male delinquency: A review. *Psychological Bulletin, 94,* 69-99.

Magnusson, D., Stattin, H., & Dunér, A. (1983). Aggression and criminality in a longitudinal perspective. In K. T. Van Dusen & S. A. Mednick (Eds.), *Prospective studies of crime and delinquency* (pp. 277-302). Boston: Kluwer-Nijhoff.

Manger, T., & Olweus, D. (1985). Tilbakemelding til skulane. *Norsk Skoleblad* (Oslo, Norway), *35*, 20-22.

Olweus, D. (1973a). *Hackkycklingar och översittare: Forskning om skolmobbning.* Stockholm: Almqvist & Wiksell.

Olweus, D. (1973b). Personality and aggression. In J. K. Cole & D. D. Jensen (Eds.), *Nebraska Symposium on Motivation, 1972* (Vol. 20) (pp. 261-321). Lincoln: University of Nebraska Press.

Olweus, D. (1977). Aggression and peer acceptance in adolescent boys: Two short-term longitudinal studies of ratings. *Child Development, 48,* 1301-1313.

Olweus, D. (1978). *Aggression in the schools: Bullies and whipping boys.* Washington, DC: Hemisphere (Wiley).

Olweus, D. (1979). Stability of aggressive reaction patterns in males: A review. *Psychological Bulletin, 86,* 852-875.

Olweus, D. (1980a). The consistency issue in personality psychology revisited—With special reference to aggression. *British Journal of Social and Clinical Psychology, 19,* 377-390.

Olweus, D. (1980b). Familial and temperamental determinants of aggressive behavior in adolescent boys: A causal analysis. *Developmental Psychology, 16,* 644-660.

Olweus, D. (1985). 80 000 barn er innblandet i mobbing. *Norsk Skoleblad* (Oslo, Norway), *35,* 18-23.

Olweus, D. (1986). *Mobbning—Vad vi vet och vad vi kan göra.* Stockholm: Liber.

Olweus, D. (1989a, April). *Peer relationship problems: Conceptual issues and a successful intervention program against bully/victim problems.* Paper presented at the biannual meeting of the Society for Research in Child Development, Kansas City, MO.

Olweus, D. (1989b). Prevalence and incidence in the study of antisocial behavior: Definitions and measurement. In M. Klein (Ed.), *Cross-national research in self-reported crime and delinquency* (pp. 187-201). Dordrecht, The Netherlands: Kluwer.

Olweus, D. (1991). Bully/victim problems among schoolchildren: Basic facts and effects of a school based intervention program. In D. Pepler & K. H. Rubin (Eds.), *The development and treatment of childhood aggression* (pp. 411-448). Hillsdale, NJ: Lawrence Erlbaum.

Olweus, D. (1992). *Bullying at school—What we know and what we can do.* Book manuscript.

Olweus, D. (in press). Victimization by peers: Antecedents and long-term outcomes. In K. H. Rubin & J. B. Asendorf (Eds.), *Social withdrawal, inhibition, and shyness in childhood.* Chicago: University of Chicago Press.

Olweus, D., & Alsaker, F. D. (1991). Assessing change in a cohort longitudinal study with hierarchical data. In D. Magnusson, L. Bergman, G. Rudinger, & B. Törestad (Eds.), *Problems and methods in longitudinal research* (pp. 107-137). New York: Cambridge University Press.

Olweus, D., Mattsson, Å., Schalling, D., & Löw, H. (1980). Testosterone, aggression, physical, and personality dimensions in normal adolescent males. *Psychosomatic Medicine, 42,* 253-269.

Olweus, D., Mattsson, Å., Schalling, D., & Löw, H. (1988). Circulating testosterone levels and aggression in adolescent males: A causal analysis. *Psychosomatic Medicine, 50,* 261-272.

Olweus, D., & Roland, E. (1983). *Mobbing—Bakgrunn og tiltak.* Oslo, Norway: Kirke- og undervisningsdepartementet.

Parker, J. G., & Asher, S. R. (1987). Peer relations and later personal adjustment: Are low-accepted children at risk? *Psychological Bulletin, 102,* 357-389.

Patterson, G. R. (1986). Performance models for antisocial boys. *American Psychologist, 41,* 432-444.

Perry, D. G., Kusel, S. J., & Perry, L. C. (1988). Victims of peer aggression. *Developmental Psychology, 24,* 807-814.

Peters, R. DeV. (1990). Adolescent mental health promotion: Policy and practice. In R.J. McMahon & R. DeV. Peters (Eds.), *Behavior disorders of adolescence*. New York: Plenum.

Rosenberg, M. (1979). *Conceiving the self*. New York: Basic Books.

Smith, P. (1989). *The silent nightmare: Bullying and victimization in school peer groups*. Paper presented at the meeting of the British Psychological Society, London.

Stattin, H., & Magnusson, D. (1989). The role of early aggressive behavior in the frequency, seriousness, and types of later crime. *Journal of Consulting and Clinical Psychology, 57*, 710-718.

Sudak, H. S., Ford, A. B., & Roshforth, N. B. (1984). *Suicide in the young*. Littleton, MA: PSG Publishing.

Whitney, I., & Smith, P. K. (1991). *A survey of the nature and extent of bullying in junior/middle and secondary schools*. Unpublished manuscript, University of Sheffield, England.

Ziegler, S., & Rosenstein-Manner, M. (1991). *Bullying at school: Toronto in an international context* (Report No. 196). Toronto: Toronto Board of Education, Research Services.

Author Index

Subject Index

Affective disorders, major:
  children with, 173
  people with, 10
  violence and, ix, 298
Aggression, instrumental, 23
Aggressive behavior, x
  alcohol abuse and, xv, 123
  alcohol/drug use and, 263-280
  in childhood, xvi
  pathological models of, 200-201
  stability of, xvi
Aggressive offending, childhood precursors
  in personality-disordered adults, 119-
  134
Agoraphobia, 179
  in women, 181
Albany County, New York, 290
Alcohol, effects of, 268-278
Alcohol abuse:
  among Cook County jail detainees/ex-
    detainees, 92, 94, 95
  impulsivity and, xiv
  violent behavior and, xv
  See also Substance abuse
Alcohol abusers, 10
  as criminal offenders, 81
Alcohol/drug use, aggressive behavior and,
  263-280
Alcoholism:
  early onset of and violent offenses, 123,
    228, 229, 235
  paternal, 238

type II and impulsive personality disorders, 228-229, 234, 238
violence and, 292
Alcohol use disorders, 98
  psychopathy and, 111-112
American Psychiatric Association, 191
Anger, as risk marker for violence, 42, 43
Anticonvulsant drugs, controlling violent
  behavior with, 195-196
Antisocial personality disorder, 105, 134, 176,
  181, 192, 227, 228, 234, 235
  alcohol use and, 280
  and aggressive crime, 121-122, 173
  and psychopathy, 123
  as predictor of crime, 181, 186, 188, 191
  as type of psychopathology, 191
  drug treatments for, 238
  in violent offender populations, 119, 121
  psychopathy and, 111
Anxiety disorders, 179
  as type of psychopathology, 191
  in Gray's personality theory, 209
  in prison inmates, 173
  violence and, 298
Arizona, prison admittees with prior mental
  hospitalization in, 296
Arrest age, long-term outcomes of, 140
Asperger's syndrome, 120
  and aggressive offending, 120-121, 134
  traits of children with, 120
Australia, bully/victim problems in schools
  in, 317

About the Authors

Karen M. Abram, Ph.D., is Assistant Professor of Psychiatry and Behavioral Science at Northwestern University Medical School, where she also received her doctorate in clinical psychology. She is a research coordinator at the Psycho-Legal Studies Program Program at Northwestern University Medical School. Her research focus is on the mental health needs of offenders.

Paul Appelbaum, M.D., is A. F. Zelenik Distinguished Professor of Psychiatry; Chairman of Psychiatry; and Director of the Law and Psychiatry Program at the University of Massachusetts Medical School. He is the author of many articles and several books on law in clinical practice, including (with Thomas G. Gutheil, M.D.) *The Clinical Handbook of Psychiatry and the Law* (2nd ed., 1991) and (with Charles Lidz and Alan Meisel) *Informed Consent: Legal Theory and Clinical Practice.* He is President of the Massachusetts Psychiatric Society, Chair of the Council on Psychiatry and the Law for the American Psychiatric Association, and a member of the MacArthur Foundation Research Network on Mental Health and the Law. In 1990, he was the recipient of the Isaac Ray Award of the American Psychiatric Association for "outstanding contributions to forensic psychiatry and the psychiatric aspects of jurisprudence."

Patricia A. Brennan, Ph.D., is Research Associate at the Social Science Research Institute, University of Southern California. Her research interests include the relationship between violence and mental illness, and the development of aggression in children.

Burr Eichelman, M.D., Ph.D., is Professor and Chairman, Department of Psychiatry, School of Medicine, Temple University. He is a clinician-researcher bridging the preclinical and clinical areas of research regarding aggressive behavior and the treatment of the violent patient. His research areas are the neurochemistry and psychopharmacology of aggressive behavior.

Thomas Grisso, Ph.D. (clinical psychology), is Professor of Psychiatry and Director of Forensic Training and Research at the University of Massachusetts Medical School. He is the author of numerous articles and three books on psychology related to legal issues, including *Evaluating Competencies: Forensic Assessments and Instruments* (1986) and *Juveniles' Waiver of Rights: Legal and Psychological Competence* (1981). He is past president of the American Psychology-Law Society, editor of the *Perspectives in Law and Psychology* book series, and a member of the MacArthur Foundation Research Network on Mental Health and the Law. In 1988 he recieved the American Academy of Forensic Psychology's award for "outstanding contributions to forensic psychology."

Robert D. Hare, Ph.D., is Professor of Psychology at the University of British Columbia. He has been studying psychopathy for the past 30 years, and is acknowledged as one of the world's leading experts in the area. The first half of his career focused on laboratory research, identifying the psychophysiological, cognitive, and affective correlates of psychopathy. More recently, he has focused on assessment and diagnostic issues, culminating in the publication of the *Psychopathy Checklist.*

Stephen D. Hart, Ph.D., is Assistant Professor at the Mental Health, Law, and Policy Institute, Simon Fraser University in Burnaby, British Columbia, and a researcher with the British Columbia Forensic Psychiatric Services Commission. He completed his doctoral research in clinical forensic psychology under Robert D. Hare, Ph.D., at the University of British Columbia. His major research interests are the assessment of psychopathy and the association between psychopathy and other mental disorders (particularly other personality disorders); he also works in the areas of wife assault and mentally disordered offenders. He is coauthor (with Robert D. Hare and David Cox) of the *Psychopathy Checklist: Screening Version,* a clinical rating scale for the assessment of psychopathy in civil and forensic populations, and coeditor (with Robert D. Hare) of a forthcoming volume on the assessment and management of criminal psychopaths.

Sheilagh Hodgins, Ph.D., is Professor of Psychology at the Université de Montréal. She has spent her career conducting research in psychiatric hospitals and correctional facilities in an effort to contribute knowledge that can be used to prevent violence among the mentally disordered. She is the author of a number of journal articles and book chapters describing this research. She has also served as a consultant to national and provincial governments and has authored numerous government reports.

Deidre Klassen, Ph.D., is Director of Research at the Greater Kansas City Mental Health Foundation and Assistant Clinical Professor in the Department of Psychiatry, School of Medicine, University of Missouri–Kansas City. She is principal investigator of an NIMH-funded grant on violence risk assessment in mental patients, and has received previous grants from NIMH in this area. In addition, she is Site Director for the Kansas City site of the MacArthur Risk Assessment project. Her recent publications are in the area of violence and mental disorder.

Markku Linnoila, M.D., Ph.D., is Director of the Laboratory of Clinical Studies, Division of Intramural Biological and Clinical Research, National Institute of Alcohol Abuse and Alcoholism.

Gary M. McClelland, Ph.D., is Instructor of Clinical Psychiatry and Behavioral Sciences at Northwestern University Medical School. He has research interests in government, policing, and social change. In addition to working with the Psycho-Legal Studies Program at Northwestern University, his book, *Statebuilders and the States They Have Built: Capitalist Agriculture in a Federal System, 1877-1950,* is being published by the University of North Carolina Press.

Barbara Maughan is Senior Lecturer at the Institute of Psychiatry, University of London, and Senior Scientific Officer in the Medical Research Council Child Psychiatry Unit, London, Great Britain. From a background in social work, she has pursued research in child psychiatry for many years. She has contributed to a range of studies of school effects on children's development, and more recently undertaken follow-up investigations of a series of high-risk childhood groups into adulthood. Her interests center on environmental effects on development; links between learning and behavioral problems; and continuities between childhood difficulties and disorder and psychosocial functioning in adult life.

Birgitte R. Mednick, Ph.D., is Associate Professor in the Department of Educational Psychology, University of Southern California. Her research interests include the neurological functioning of children and she is currently engaged in a project examining two generations of small-for-date (premature) females.

Sarnoff A. Mednick, M.D., Ph.D, is Professor of Psychology at the University of Southern California, and Chairman, Institut for Sygdomsforebyggelse [Institute of Preventive Medicine] in Copenhagen, Denmark. He is world renowned for his research on the etiology of schizophrenia. He was one of the first scientists to note the association between major mental disorder and violence. His research areas include schizophrenia, violence and schizophrenia, biosocial bases of antisocial behavior, and fetal neural development and schizophrenia. He has published hundreds of journal articles, book chapters, and books.

Robert J. Menzies, Ph.D., is Associate Professor of Criminology at Simon Fraser University in Burnaby, British Columbia. He has published widely on the relationship between mental illness and criminal justice, on the social construction of violence and dangerousness, and on theories and practices of social control. He is the author of *Survival of the Sanest,* coauthor (with Christopher D. Webster and Margaret A. Jackson) of *Clinical Assessment Before Trial* (1982), and coeditor (with John Lowman and Ted Palys) of *Transcarceration* (1987). Among his current projects are a historical study of psychiatric institutionalization in British Columbia, a survey of ideological perspectives among Canadian criminologists, and an investigation of media portrayals of political criminality in Canada.

John Monahan, Ph.D., holds the Doherty Chair in Law at the University of Virginia, Charlottesville, where he is also Professor of Psychology and of Legal Medicine. He was the founding President of the American Psychological Association's Division of Psychology and Law, and received the APA's Distinguished Contribution to Research in Public Policy Award in 1990. His 1981 book, *The Clinical Prediction of Violent Behavior,* won the Manfred Guttmacher Award of the American Psychiatric Association. He currently directs the Research Network on Mental Health and the Law of the John D. and Catherine T. MacArthur Foundation.

Edward P. Mulvey, Ph.D., is Associate Professor of Child Psychiatry in the Law and Psychiatric Program at Western Psychiatric Institute and Clinic at the University of Pittsburgh School of Medicine. He received his B.A. in psychology from Yale University in 1973, and his Ph.D. in community/clinical psychology from the University of Virginia in 1982. He also spent a year as a postdoctoral fellow at the Urban Systems Institute at Carnegie-Mellon University. He has been at the University of Pittsburgh since 1983. He is a recipient of a Faculty Scholar's Award from the W. T. Grant Foundation, and a member of the MacArthur Network on Mental Health and the Law. His research has been primarily focused on determining how clinicians make judgments regarding the type of risk posed by adult mental patients and juvenile offenders, and how clinicians decide what treatment might be appropriate for these types of cases.

Dan Olweus, Ph.D., is Professor of Psychology at the University of Bergen, Norway. He is known around the world for his now classic work on the stability over time of aggressive behavior. He has authored numerous books, articles, and book chapters on his longitudinal studies of children designed to identify the determinants of aggressive behavior. His successful school-based programs for aggressive boys are now in place in a number of different countries. His research areas include human aggressive behavior, bullying, and school-based intervention programs to eliminate aggressive behavior.

Gerald R. Patterson, Ph.D., is Director of the Oregon Social Learning Center, Eugene. He is the foremost clinical researcher in the area of families of antisocial children. His career spans 30 years, in which he has published extensively for both the scientific and clinical communities, as well as for parents. His research centers on families with antisocial children, and the effective treatment of these families. In recent years he has begun a longitudinal study of children growing up in Oregon in an effort to identify the determinants of their antisocial behavior.

Jordan B. Peterson, Ph.D., was born and raised in Alberta, Canada. He acquired his bachelor of arts degree (political science and psychology) at Grande Prairie Regional College and the University of Alberta, and his doctorate in clinical psychology at McGill University, Montreal. He is interested in drug use, drug abuse, and aggression, and is presently completing a 2-year postdoctorate with the Douglas Hospital–McGill University Alcohol Research Group.

Robert O. Pihl, Ph.D., is Professor of Psychology and of Psychiatry at McGill University in Montreal. He has extensively studied the relationship between violence and drug abuse, and since 1979 has had an active experimental program looking at alcohol intoxication and violence. He has published more than 150 journal articles.

Lee N. Robins, Ph.D., is University Professor of Social Science at Washington University, St. Louis, MO. She is the author of 14 monographs and

227 papers. Her major research contributions include a follow-up of 500 child guidance clinic patients and 100 normal controls into their forties; a study of outcomes of 900 Vietnam War veterans and 300 matched controls, 1 and 3 years after leaving Vietnam; and the design of the Diagnostic Interview Schedule and its utilization in the Epidemiologic Catchment Area study.

Pamela Clark Robbins, B.A., is Vice President of Policy Research Associates, Inc., in Delmar, NY. Currently she is the Project Coordinator for the John D. and Catherine T. MacArthur Foundation Violence Risk Assessment Study, a 3-year prospective study of 1,000 mentally ill persons after their release to the community. In addition, she has recently been involved in several research projects, including a 6-year, NIMH-funded study investigating the impact of insanity defense reforms in eight states and a survey under contract to the U.S. Secret Service of mental health therapists' reporting practices of threats against the U.S. President. Her primary research interests continue to focus on issues of mental illness and law, specifically on violence among mental patients.

Loren Roth, M.D., M.P.H., is Professor of Psychiatry at the University of Pittsburgh, Chief of Clinical Services at Western Psychiatric Institute and Clinic, and Director of the Law and Psychiatry Program at the Institute. A graduate of the Harvard Medical School and the Harvard School of Public Health, he has conducted seminal research in law and psychiatry over the last 15 years. He has chaired important American Psychiatric Association committees and is a past winner of the Association's Isaac Ray Award, given for outstanding career contributions to law and psychiatry.

Daisy Schalling, Ph.D., is Professor of Psychiatry and Psychology, University of Stockholm, and Karolinska Hospital, Stockholm. Her career includes important contributions in the development of several measures of personality traits, and discoveries of the biological variables associated with various traits. Her work is widely known to scientists studying personality and individual differences, to biological scientists, and to those studying the relation of mental disorders to crime.

Saleem A. Shah, Ph.D., is Senior Research Scholar, Division of Applied and Services Research, National Institute of Mental Health, Rockville, MD. His main areas of research and scholarly work have been various aspects of law and mental health, biological factors in criminal and violent behaviors, and program and policy issues pertaining to the treatment and handling of mentally disordered offenders. He has worked in the field of law and mental health for almost 35 years; he headed the NIMH Center for Studies of Antisocial and Violent Behaviors for 20 years; has published extensively in the areas mentioned above; and has been the recipient of several awards, including Distinguished Contribution to Psychology and Law (Division of Psychology and Law, American Psychological Association) and the Isaac Ray Award (for outstanding contributions to forensic psychiatry) from the American Psychiatric Association.

Henry J. Steadman, Ph.D., is President of Policy Research Associates, Inc. Prior to 1987 when he assumed this position, he ran a nationally known research bureau for 17 years for the New York State Office of Mental Health. His work has resulted in numerous reports, more than 80 journal articles, 18 book chapters, and 5 books. He is also Director of the John D. and Catherine T. MacArthur Foundation Violence Risk Assessment Study. His other current projects include directing the National Resource Center on Homelessness and Mental Illness under contract to the National Institute of Mental Health and a 3-year national study of programs to divert mentally ill persons from local jails. He has received the Amicus Award from the American Academy of Psychiatry and the Law in 1987 for his "numerous contributions over many years," and the Philippe Pinel Award from the International Academy of Law and Mental Health in 1988 for his exceptional contribution to research on aggression among the mentally ill.

Pamela J. Taylor, M.D., is Head of Medical Services for the Special Hospitals Service Authority, London, and Honorary Senior Lecturer at the Institute of Psychiatry, University of London, Great Britain. She collaborated with John Monahan and his team for the John D. and Catherine T. MacArthur Foundation in developing schedules for the measure of risk (specifically, the Maudsley Assessment of Delusions Schedule—the MADS). She is coeditor (with John Gunn) of the forthcoming textbook, *Forensic Psychiatry: Clinical, Legal, and Ethical Issues,* and coeditor (with John Gunn and David Farrington) of *Criminal Behaviour and Mental Health,* and Editor, Forensic Psychiatry Section, of *Current Opinion in Psychiatry.*

Linda A. Teplin, Ph.D., is Professor of Psychiatry and Behavioral Sciences and Director of the Psycho-Legal Studies Program at Northwestern University Medical School, Chicago. She is well known in the United States for her ground-breaking work on the criminalization of the mentally disordered. Her honors include a MERIT award by NIMH, the Young Scientist Award by the National Alliance for the Mentally Ill, and the 1992

American Psychological Association Award for Distinguished Contributions to Research in Public Policy.

Matti Virkkunen, M.D., is Associate Professor of Psychiatry and Chief of the Forensic Psychiatric Department, Helsinki University Central Hospital, in Helsinki, Finland. He has studied violent offenders for 20 years. During the 1980s and early 1990s he conducted investigations of the biological basis of habitual violence and impulsivity with the National Institute of Alcohol Abuse and Alcoholism (NIAAA) in Bethesda, MD. He and Markku Linnoila of NIAAA were the first to find that habitually violent prisoners and impulsive arsonists have abnormal brain serotonin and peripheral glucose metabolism and that these variables can predict further violence; their publications have focused on the relationship among these variables and impulsivity and/or poor control of aggression and Type II alcoholism.

Christopher D. Webster, Ph.D., is Head of the Impulsivity Program at the Clarke Institute of Psychiatry, Toronto. He has served as consultant to national and provincial governments and held a variety of research grants and contracts. He has written approximately 100 articles, about half of which are on forensic subjects, and has published or edited a half dozen books or monographs on topics within forensic psychiatry including (with Robert J. Menzies and Margaret A. Jackson) *Clinical Assessment Before Trial* (1981) and (coedited with S. J. Hucker and M. A. Ben-Aron) *Dangerousness: Probability and Prediction: Psychiatry and Public Policy* (1985).

Karen Yoerger is a Senior Data Analyst at the Oregon Social Learning Center, Eugene. Her project contributions draw on experience with structural equation modeling, latent growth modeling, event history analysis, and generalized estimating equations.